REVISITING THE ARAB UPRISINGS

COMPARATIVE POLITICS
AND INTERNATIONAL STUDIES SERIES

Series editors, Christophe Jaffrelot and Alain Dieckhoff
Series managing editor, Miriam Perier

The series consists of original manuscripts and translations of noteworthy manuscripts and publications in the social sciences emanating from the foremost French researchers.

The focus of the series is the transformation of politics and society by transnational and domestic factors—globalisation, migration and religion. States are more permeable to external influence than ever before and this phenomenon is accelerating processes of social and political change the world over. In seeking to understand and interpret these transformations, this series gives priority to social trends from below as much as to the interventions of state and non-state actors.

EDITED BY STÉPHANE LACROIX
AND JEAN-PIERRE FILIU

Revisiting the Arab Uprisings

*The Politics of a
Revolutionary Moment*

OXFORD
UNIVERSITY PRESS

OXFORD
UNIVERSITY PRESS

Oxford University Press is a department of the
University of Oxford. It furthers the University's objective
of excellence in research, scholarship, and education
by publishing worldwide.

Oxford   New York

Auckland   Cape Town   Dar es Salaam   Hong Kong   Karachi
Kuala Lumpur   Madrid   Melbourne   Mexico City   Nairobi
New Delhi   Shanghai   Taipei   Toronto

With offices in

Argentina   Austria   Brazil   Chile   Czech Republic   France   Greece
Guatemala   Hungary   Italy   Japan   Poland   Portugal   Singapore
South Korea   Switzerland   Thailand   Turkey   Ukraine   Vietnam

Oxford is a registered trade mark of Oxford University Press
in the UK and certain other countries.

Published in the United States of America by
Oxford University Press
198 Madison Avenue, New York, NY 10016

Library of Congress Cataloging-in-Publication Data is available
Stéphane Lacroix and Jean-Pierre Filiu.
Revisiting the Arab Uprisings: The Politics of a Revolutionary Moment.
ISBN: 9780190876081

Printed in Great Britain by Bell and Bain Ltd, Glasgow

We would like to dedicate this volume to Alfred Stepan (1936–2017), one of its distinguished contributors, whose work and scholarship have always been a source of inspiration.

CONTENTS

About the Contributors   ix

Introduction: Taking the Arab Transitions Seriously
                                    Stéphane Lacroix and *Jean-Pierre Filiu*   1

1. Toward a 'Democracy with Democrats' in Tunisia: Mutual
   Accommodation Between Islamic and Secular Activists
                                           Alfred Stepan   9

2. Constituting Constitutionalism: Lessons from the Arab World
                                         Nathan Brown   29

3. Bullets Beat Ballots: The Arab Uprisings and Civil-Military
   Relations in Egypt   *Omar Ashour*   45

4. Militaries and Democracies in the Middle East: Too Much and
   Too Little   *Steven Cook*   61

5. Modern Mamlouks and Arab Counter-Revolution
                                   Jean-Pierre Filiu   77

6. Trashing Transitions: The Role of Arab Media After the Uprisings
                                     Marc Lynch   93

7. Not Ready for Democracy: Modernisation, Pluralism and the
   Arab Spring   *Tarek Masoud*   111

8. International Assistance to Arab Spring Transitions   *Zaid al-Ali*   141

9. Confronting the Dictatorial Past in Tunisia: Towards a Political
   Understanding of Transitional justice   *Kora Andrieu*   165

CONTENTS

10. With or Without You? Transitional Justice and Political Transitions
    in Morocco and Tunisia   *Frédéric Vairel*   199

11. Transitional Justice in Post-Revolutionary Egypt
                                 Nathalie Bernard-Maugiron   219

Notes   235
Bibliography   285
Index   309

ABOUT THE CONTRIBUTORS

Editors

Jean-Pierre Filiu is Professor of Middle East Studies at Sciences Po, Paris School of International Affairs (PSIA) and Centre for International Studies (CERI), France.

Stéphane Lacroix is Associate Professor of Political Science at Sciences Po, Paris School of International Affairs (PSIA) and Centre for International Studies (CERI), France.

Contributors

Kora Andrieu is Political Affairs Officer with the United Nations Support Mission in Libya (2016–2018). Previously Human Rights Officer at the Office of the High Commissioner for Human Rights in Tunisia (2012–2015) and with the United Nations Multidimensional Support Mission in Mali (2015–2016).

Omar Ashour is Associate Professor of Security and Strategic Studies at the Doha Institute for Graduate Studies.

Zaid Al Ali is a senior programme officer on constitution building in the Africa and West Asia region at International IDEA and was a Law and Public Affairs Fellow at Princeton University in 2015–2016.

Nathalie Bernard-Maugrion is Senior Researcher at the French Institut de recherche pour le développement (IRD).

Nathan Brown is Professor of Political Science and International Affairs; Director, Institute for Middle East Studies, Elliott School of International Affairs, George Washington University.

ABOUT THE CONTRIBUTORS

Steven A. Cook is Eni Enrico Mattei senior fellow for Middle East and Africa studies at the Council on Foreign Relations (CFR).

Marc Lynch is a Professor of Political Science and International Affairs at George Washington University, where he is also director of the Project on Middle East Political Science (POMEPS).

Tarek Masoud is the Sultan of Oman Professor of International Relations at Harvard University's John F. Kennedy School of Government.

Frédéric Vairel is Associate Professor of Political Science, School of Political Studies, University of Ottawa.

Alfred C. Stepan (1936–2017) was a comparative political scientist and Wallace S. Sayre Professor of Government at Columbia University, where he was also director of the Center for the Study of Democracy, Toleration and Religion.

INTRODUCTION

TAKING THE ARAB TRANSITIONS SERIOUSLY

Stéphane Lacroix and *Jean-Pierre Filiu*

The uprisings that swept the Arab world in 2011 were driven by calls for 'bread, liberty and social justice', as the slogan popular on Cairo's Tahrir square put it. They brought together millions of people, many of them young adults, in an outburst that surprised observers and regimes alike. During a short 'moment of enthusiasm' ideological differences were set aside, and people began to dream together of a better future. The scene appeared to be set for dramatic change across the Arab region where, after decades of authoritarian dominance, democracy was finally expected to take hold. There are still many reasons to keep faith in the long-term evolution of the region, because the forces of change unleashed in 2011 have not disappeared. But the short-term aftermath of the uprisings has fallen far short of the expectations held by those who risked their lives to take to the streets in 2011.

Since 2013, the Middle East has moved in two diverging directions— toward chaos and civil war on the one hand, and a resurgence of authoritarian- ism on the other. In Syria, the brutal repression of political protests led to a protracted military confrontation between the regime and its opponents, fracturing the country and paving the way for the renewed rise of jihadism. An organization known as the 'Islamic State' (IS), whose original stronghold had been in the disenfranchised Sunni regions of Iraq, seized the moment and expanded into Syrian territory, while control over the rest of the country was divided between pro-regime and anti-regime factions. In Yemen and Libya, groups that had first taken part in the uprisings now favoured a rapprochement with supporters of the former regime in order to challenge—politically and militarily—a fragile and unstable transitional order. The result in both cases was political partition and an ongoing civil war. In Egypt, in contrast, the army's intervention on 3 July 2013 to overthrow the country's first democratically elected president, Muslim Brotherhood senior official Mohamed Morsi, in the wake of major protests against his rule, led to the establishment of a new authoritarian regime centered around the army under the leadership of General (later Field Marshall) Abdel Fattah al-Sisi. The brutality of the repression directed against Morsi's supporters has fuelled a low-key insurgency, centered in but not limited to the troubled Sinai region. In all of these conflicts, the role played by regional and international actors—particularly Iran and the Gulf monarchies, but also Russia and the Western countries—cannot be overstated.

Only Tunisia appears to have escaped the fate of the other 'Arab Spring' countries: a democratic constitution supported by all sides of the political spectrum, including the Islamist party Ennahda, was adopted in January 2014. The country has, moreover, passed the 'two-election' test, widely recognized as evidence of successful democratic transitions. Yet, even there, the same worrying dynamics that have swept the rest of the region are far from absent. Tunisia has provided IS with more fighters in proportion to its population than any other country in the world—a recruitment fuelled by the persistence and even aggravation of socio-economic inequalities in the country. And in the face of the jihadi threat, politicians have expressed authoritarian tendencies, adopting laws that have opened the way for a restriction of public liberties.

This two-fold path toward civil war and authoritarian resurgence, which now dominates scholarly attention, has eclipsed the transitions that occurred in the countries whose leaders were toppled in 2011, as if those transitions were merely footnotes in a narrative that progresses naturally from an Arab 'spring' to an Arab 'winter'. This volume aims to bring the focus back to those transitions, by considering them as expressions of a 'revolutionary moment' whose outcome was never pre-determined but depended on the choices and actions of a large range of actors, old and new. Our contributors thus do not address the causes of the uprisings, which are the subject already of many

INTRODUCTION

excellent books and edited volumes,[1] but they focus instead on their aftermath.

By considering the transitions as the expression of a 'revolutionary moment', we certainly do not intend to say that the actors' choices and actions were not influenced or conditioned by structural or historical elements that pre-existed the Arab uprisings. They obviously were, as is emphasised by some of the contributors to this volume. But, as French political sociologist Michel Dobry argues, what makes political crises (and what are transitions if not protracted political crises?) so unique is that they are moments of 'political fluidity' in which the course of politics as usual is disrupted and where agency matters more than ever.[2] This is why reflecting on what actually happened during those transitions is so crucial. Beside factual histories, this needs also to be done in a more systematic way.

The use of the term 'transition' here is in no way meant to reopen the debate on the vices and virtues of the 'transitology' paradigm that was so prevalent in the 1980s and 1990s. One of the main criticisms directed at this paradigm targeted the underlying teleological assumptions it contained, as if the paradigm had been designed with the necessity of a democratic outcome in mind. Yet, if there is one lesson from the Arab uprisings, it is that no such necessity exists. A transition, as we define it, is thus simply the period that follows the breakdown of an authoritarian regime—a 'transition from authoritarian rule' (as O'Donnell, Schmitter and Whitehead put it in their seminal 1986 volume), the outcome of which remains entirely open.[3] A transition is most visibly characterised by institutional events, such as elections and constitution drafting, major foci of transitology. But it is no way limited to such events. Extra-institutional dynamics—civil society mobilisation and (re)organisation, street politics, youth culture, etc.—matter just as much, if only because of the huge impact they have on the institutional process.

A better understanding of these transitions is crucial for several reasons. The moments of authoritarian breakdown have a lot to tell us about the societies where they occur. Authoritarian regimes tend to engineer an institutional façade of political normality that conceals or distorts the reality of social forces. Authoritarian breakdowns liberate those social forces and allow us—if only for a limited period of time—to get a fuller grasp of social complexities. Very few had for instance imagined that in Egypt, Salafism was such a grassroots force that a Salafi party, Hizb al-Nour, would be able to come second in the country's first democratic elections. In Syria, local coordination committees (*tansiqiyyat*) showed an unprecedented vitality and resilience that enabled them to stand as formidable alternatives to the traditional power struggles centered in Damascus.

Most importantly, studying the transitions is key not just to explaining their current outcomes (a valuable yet ultimately inconclusive endeavour given how volatile those outcomes may be), but also to understanding the political equations that continue to shape Arab politics. This is true even in countries that have experienced an authoritarian backlash, because the transitions have reshaped—and in some way continue to reshape—the local scene, making of the new authoritarianism something quite different from the old one. In this sense, and despite the efforts of the new authoritarians who would love to close what they see as a dangerous parenthesis, the transitional moment that started in 2011 is far from over.

Scope of the book

This book focuses on the few countries where actual transitions have happened: Tunisia and Egypt, primarily, but also Libya and Yemen. Syria, where the authoritarian breakdown was only partial, will also be considered. Most of the book's contributors adopt a comparative approach, either comparing those different countries among themselves, or comparing them with other Arab and non-Arab countries with similar features (i.e., Morocco, Algeria, and even Turkey). The choice was made to focus on a limited number of themes which have not received systematic comparative attention, and which offer crucial insights into the dynamics of the Arab transitions as they took place. A first draft of each of the papers included here was presented at an international conference held in Sciences Po in November 2014. Entitled 'Revisiting Democratic Transition Theory: Whither the Arab World?', it was chaired by the then dean of Sciences Po's Paris School of International Affairs (PSIA), Ghassan Salamé, himself a contributor and editor, in 1994, of a seminal work on democratic transitions (or, rather, at that time, on the lack thereof) in the Arab world: *Democracy without Democrats*.[4]

The first part of this book deals with the dynamics of accommodation and polarisation generated by the institutional process during transitions. Alfred Stepan's paper (Chapter 1), which opens this volume, is the contribution most explicitly anchored in democratic transition theory (of which Stepan was a pioneer), while introducing a dimension that democratic transition theory had never much considered: religion. By contrasting Tunisia with Egypt, Stepan seeks to explain why a democratic transition happened in the former.

His argument is two-fold: one pre-condition, he believes, was the rapprochement between the leading Islamist party Ennahda and secular forces on a democratic platform in the years leading to the 2011 revolution, which created the ground for a sustainable cross-ideological coalition. But this outcome was above all made possible, at a moment in 2013 when the institutional process was on the verge of collapse, by the personal commitment and leadership of the heads of the Islamist and secular blocks, leading to what Stepan calls a 'two sheikhs' compromise. Nathan Brown (Chapter 2) looks at the constitutions that were drafted in Arab countries after 2011 through the prism of the 'new constitutionalism', which emphasises the need for democratic and participatory processes and has recently gained traction among constitutionalists. Instead of focusing on the actual texts that were produced, Brown looks at the peculiar circumstances in which those constitutions were written and explains how, in the chaotic context of 'passionate reality' which characterises transitions, certain procedural choices were made (or imposed) that greatly affected the outcome.

The second part of the volume looks at the role of militaries in the different transitions. After classifying the military's involvement in politics in the Arab region according to four historical models, Omar Ashour (Chapter 3) focuses on Egypt, an example of what he calls the 'dominant institution' model. There, he aims at explaining the series of political stances the army took in the wake of the 25 January 2011 uprising. The Egyptian military's decision to oust elected Muslim Brotherhood president Mohamed Morsi on 3 July 2013 presents a major puzzle, given the fact that the army's interests were not being directly threatened under Morsi's rule. Ashour shows that this move can only be properly understood by taking into consideration organisational and psychological factors. Steven Cook's contribution (Chapter 4) adopts a more comparative approach by putting the Egyptian case in perspective with Turkey and Libya. The Turkish case shows that while a civilian government has the ability to domesticate an army, this does not guarantee a democratic outcome. And the Libyan case demonstrates that, contrary to some of the optimistic assumptions prevalent in 2011, having "not enough" military poses other challenges in terms of national cohesion and security. Finally, Jean-Pierre Filiu (Chapter 5) adopts a broader historical view by drawing a comparison between today's military regimes in Egypt, Syria, Algeria and Yemen, and the 'Mamluks' who ruled Egypt and Syria from 1250 to 1516. According to Filiu, the brutal way in which the 'neo-Mamluk' regime in Algeria derailed the political transition in Algeria from 1992 onwards set the 'counter-revolutionary' pattern which similarly configured regimes in Egypt, Syria and Yemen followed in dealing with the 2011 uprisings and their aftermath. This goes a long way in explaining why the only country where the bases of a democratic political order were successfully established is non-Mamluk Tunisia.

The third part of the book looks at several non-state actors that have impacted the transitions. Marc Lynch (Chapter 6) examines the paradoxes of Arab media—in which he includes TV channels, radios and newspapers, both national and transnational, as well as websites and social media outlets, all of which form a single 'media ecosystem'—which both proved crucial to the uprisings and contributed to the failure of democratic transitions. While discussing the significant differences that exist among Arab countries, he shows that the media's susceptibility to political capture (by regional actors or domestic forces) and its tendency to magnify fear and uncertainty helped fuel the political polarisation that would eventually tear the democratic transitions apart. Comparing Egypt and Tunisia, Tarek Masoud (Chapter 7) argues that the distinctive make-ups and strengths of civil society in those two countries explain why their transitions took different paths. He dismisses previous arguments about the role of the army or the democratic commitment of politicians, arguing instead that Tunisian civil society was stronger and had a less pronounced religious coloration than Egypt's, with the result that its secular politicians could easily acquire a substantial political base, leading to more balanced electoral results. As no single party or camp had hegemony, leading politicians were forced to make the necessary political compromises. Masoud then builds on this conclusion to suggest a more structural argument: that the greater economic development, industrialisation and urbanisation of Tunisia explains why its civil society had those specific features that Egypt's lacked. Finally, Zaid al-Ali (Chapter 8) examines the action of international actors— especially those with ties to the United Nations—during the transitions in Libya and Yemen. He paints a rather depressing picture of international organisations with no genuine roadmaps and no sound analyses of the countries where they operated. Individuals who happened to be in charge of UN missions (sometimes more or less by chance) were left to act according to their own preferences and biases. Though the international community was not responsible for the collapse of the democratic process in Yemen and Libya, it was not capable of preventing it.

The last part of the volume addresses the often overlooked issue of transitional justice, or the lack thereof. Kora Andrieu (Chapter 9) examines how the concepts and procedures of transitional justice, as developed through transitology and adopted by international organisations, were uncritically embraced by Tunisian politicians in the wake of the uprising. She then shows how her case study challenges the common understanding of transitional justice as being a neutral and strictly judicial tool. In Tunisia, it quickly became politicised, reawakening polarising debates about the fundamental issues of memory and identity. Frédéric Vairel (Chapter 10) offers a comparison between transitional justice processes in Tunisia and Morocco. He shows how the Moroccan Equity and Reconciliation Commission established in 2004, the first in an Arab country, inspired and partly informed Tunisia's Truth and Justice Commission. He discusses the similarities and differences between the two entities and their actions. While in authoritarian Morocco, the top-down process through which the commission was created allowed it to work reasonably well, though with quite limited results, its Tunisian counterpart followed a much more ambitious roadmap but was not able to function efficiently due to the politicisation of transitional justice in Tunisia's new democratising context. Finally, Nathalie Bernard-Maugiron (Chapter 11) offers a contrasting perspective on Egypt, where a highly biased version of transitional justice—or, in other words, no transitional justice at all—was implemented. Since February 2011, criminal cases against state officials have been dropped and fact-finding committees investigating massacres perpetrated by state officials either delivered conclusions favorable to the perpetrators or were silenced. In contrast, since the summer 2013, Muslim Brotherhood leaders and members, as well as secular revolutionaries, have been heavily prosecuted and subjected to harsh sentences.

A Defining Moment

As this brief presentation suggests, this book seeks to address, and hopefully cover, quite a broad chunk of largely unchartered ground, from political accommodation to transitional justice, through the various military entanglements and the paradoxes of non-state dynamics. It offers alternative angles and original interpretations as part of a collective contribution to the general analysis of post-2011 Arab reality. There is no doubt that the academic community faces a significant intellectual challenge in undertaking such an analysis, and this volume, through its multidisciplinary approach, aims at proposing some ideas, tools and concepts to enable a firmer grasp on the complexity of these unprecedented processes.

The revolutionary moment which began in 2011 is indeed a defining one. This is obvious in Tunisia, where a Second Republic was established, and in

Libya, where Gaddafi's system effectively collapsed. Yet nowhere in the countries affected by the 2011 uprisings has the status quo been restored: the Assad regime is relying heavily on foreign forces to control only a portion of the Syrian territory, while the late Ali Abdallah Saleh chose to strike a deal with the Houthi guerrillas he had so bitterly fought in order to regain some power in Sanaa. Even al-Sisi's Egypt is struggling hard to design new ways to avoid a potential wave of popular protest and to curb the jihadi insurgency, especially in the Sinai peninsula.

This is why it is so crucial to revisit those Arab uprisings whose intensity and density have led to a certain degree of conceptual fatigue, with the attached risk of confusion and repetition. A frequent focus on Islamist movements and jihadi militancy has obscured the central actors of state repression and their own dynamics. This is also true of a 'civil society' that was sometimes perceived in very narrow terms, without the proper inclusion of workers' mobilisation and trade unions, or the media. The numerous hurdles and pitfalls any constitutional transition would have to face were more than once overlooked.

The politics of this Arab revolutionary moment is a fascinating topic that will justify and motivate further academic endeavour in the coming years. We hope that this book, through the diversity of its perspectives and the expertise of its contributors, will help to shape and structure that intellectual field. We would like to thank the Kuwait Foundation for the Advancement of Science (KFAS) at Sciences Po which funded the conference and provided financial and material support for this publication. Finally, we would like to thank Xavier Guignard, Jon de Peyer and Eva Jaunzems for helping us edit the contributions gathered in this volume, as well as Marie-Zénaïde Jolys and Miriam Périer for their precious logistical support.

1

TOWARDS A 'DEMOCRACY WITH DEMOCRATS' IN TUNISIA

MUTUAL ACCOMMODATION BETWEEN ISLAMIC AND SECULAR ACTIVISTS

Alfred Stepan

What does classic democratic theory say, and not say, about religion and secularism? First, the modern political analysis of democracy, while it requires the use of concepts such as voting, and relative freedom to organise, does not necessarily need the concept of secularism. Robert Dahl, Arend Lijphart, and Juan L. Linz (the first three winners of the Johan Skytte Prize, often called the Nobel Prize of Political Science) did not feel the need to include any discussion of secularism in their definitions of modern democracies, much less to include secularism as a necessary condition for a democracy. Dahl, in his elaboration of the 'institutional guarantees' that must be created for the functioning of a democracy, nowhere mentions secularism. Neither does Lijphart in his analysis of long-standing democracies in the modern world. Linz and I, in our analysis of what we considered the five major regime types in the modern world in our book, *Problems of Democratic*

Transition and Consolidation, also decided not to use the concept of secularism in characterising any of our regime types, because each type includes some countries that call themselves secular.[1]

But democratic institutions do need sufficient political space from religion to function, just as citizens need to be given sufficient space by democratic institutions to exercise their religious freedom. I call this mutual giving of space the 'twin tolerations'.[2] Religious institutions should not have constitutionally privileged prerogatives that give them the authority to mandate public policy to democratically elected officials or to deny critical freedoms to any citizens. The minimal degree of toleration that religion needs to receive from democracy, if a democracy respects Dahl's eight institutional guarantees, is not only the complete right to worship, but also the freedom of religious individuals and groups to advance their values in civil society publicly and to sponsor organisations and movements in political society, as long as their public advancement of these beliefs does not impinge negatively on the liberties of other citizens or violate democracy and the law by violence or other means. After a period of 'self-secularization', the Christian Democratic political parties of Europe, as Stathis N. Kalyvas has shown, became autonomous democratic parties in contexts where neither of the twin tolerations was violated.[3]

The historical influence of the American and the French revolutions, and the fact that both France and the United States are close to the 'separatist' pole in democratic patterns of religion-state relations, make many commentators assume that separatism is the normatively preferable and empirically predominant form of modern democracies. But, for comparative purposes, particularly for readers in the United States and France, it is important to be aware that many of the existing members of the European Union are strong democracies despite violating both the US norm of a 'wall of separation between the state and religion' and the spirit of French *laïcité* in its 1905 version, as found in the 'Law Concerning the Separation of Churches and the State'.

For example, in 2009, of the twenty-seven European Union democracies, all of them funded religious education in some way. Some 89 per cent had religious education in state schools as a standard offering (in many, but not all, with the option not to attend); 44 per cent funded some of the clergy; and 19 per cent had established religions. Indeed, all of the Scandinavian states— Norway, Sweden, Denmark, Finland, and Iceland—had at the time constitutionally embedded Evangelical Lutheranism as their established religion, with Evangelical Lutheranism having a series of specified prerogatives for almost all of the countries' democratic histories. Thus when speaking of secularism, I prefer to use the concept of 'multiple secularisms', so as to draw attention to the varieties of possible democratic secularisms, and to forgo limiting my use of the word 'secularism' to French or American models.[4]

Certainly one of the greatest intellectual tasks facing the rethinking of such multiple democratic secularisms is to examine how, despite many obstacles, 'democracy with democrats' might be constructed in countries with large Muslim populations. 'Democracy with democrats' alludes to, but also reverses the meaning, of the title of the classic book around which the discussions in this volume have been organised, namely Ghassan Salamé's edited volume, *Democracy Without Democrats? The Renewal of Politics in the Muslim World*.[5] This volume appeared in 1994, and explored the persistence of authoritarian regimes in the Middle East, the fragility of democracy and the absence, in many countries in the region, of democrats to support democracy. Thus there was among some the goal of democracy, but without democrats to give it substance. Here, twenty years later, we return to an examination of democracy in Muslim countries. This task is particularly important in any revision of democratisation theory, given that neither of the two most cited comparative democratisation books deal with any Muslim countries.[6]

My goal in this chapter is to explore the challenges and successes of an ongoing effort to achieve such a democratic transition, namely in Tunisia.[7] In many ways Tunisia has made a successful transition to democracy and created a 'democracy with democrats'. The *Economist* in December 2014 named Tunisia its 'Country of the Year'.[8] Freedom House in 2015 gave Tunisia its highest possible score for political rights, the first time any Arab country has ever received this ranking.[9]

How did Tunisia make such progress in political rights? What, if any, are the implications of this achievement for standard democratisation theory? In my effort to address these questions I will build upon my previous study on how democracy was actually constructed in Indonesia, the world's most populous Muslim country. For the last ten years in a row, Indonesia has received a higher democracy rating than any of the other nine countries in the Association of South East Asian Nations (ASEAN).[10] I will also be building on my research into how democracy was crafted and sustained in Muslim-majority Senegal, the longest-standing democracy in West Africa.[11] I believe it is also useful for such a rethinking to include some observations about India, since before Independence the country had the world's largest Muslim population. Mahatma Gandhi, Jawaharlal Nehru, and the Congress Party had to think hard about how to create a democratic political culture and democratic political practices that accommodated their large Muslim minority. Finally, there is the experience of transitions to democracy in non-Muslim countries, such as those in Latin America. Here the example of Chile is particularly relevant because of the importance of religion in the political process.

The central point of my argument so far is that 'democracy with democrats' can be, and has been, crafted in many important democracies without French *laïcité* or America's 'wall of separation'. Indeed, some of the world's 'multiple democratic secularisms' allow substantial participation of religious Muslims in the public space, as in India, Indonesia, Senegal, and as I shall document recently in Tunisia, without violating the 'twin tolerations'.[12]

Democratisation Theory: Creating an Anti-Regime Coalition from One–Time Enemies

A key lesson in democratisation theory is that successful democratic transitions often involve the formation of a coalition, within the opposition, of one-time enemies. Some might call this kind of transition a 'pacted transition', except that a pacted transition is a four-player game involving a coalition of regime soft-liners and opposition soft-liners, against regime hard-liners and opposition hard-liners.[13] What we are examining in this section is a three-player game: namely, how to get two opposition groups who do not trust each other to somehow work together against a hardline authoritarian regime, and better still, craft some mutually supportive alliances, even a potential governing coalition, before any eventual effort at a democratic transition. I look briefly at how this task was accomplished in two important cases in which religion figured prominently: Chile and Indonesia.

In 1973, the Christian Democratic Party in Chile, with the tacit support of the US government, in essence asked General Pinochet to overthrow the legally elected socialist government of Salvador Allende. After this, from 1973 until the early 1980s, any possibility of joint cooperation against Pinochet by the Christian Democrats and Socialists was impossible. However, with the support of the German Christian Democratic 'Konrad Adenauer Stiftung', and the German Social Democratic 'Friedrich Ebert Stiftung', in the early 1980s the Chilean Christian Democrats and the Chilean Socialists began to discuss whether they hated each other less than they hated Pinochet. Eventually, by the mid-1980s, the two parties mobilised joint anti-Pinochet protest demonstrations. These shared activities slowly turned into shared political programs. They formed an electoral coalition with a joint platform in 1988 which defeated Pinochet in a plebiscite based on Pinochet's own 1980 constitution. In 1989, this coalition won the presidency and ruled together as a successful, reformist coalition from 1990–2010, with the presidency rotating from Socialist to Christian Democratic presidents.[14]

In Indonesia, in the decade leading up to the fall of the thirty-six year military dictatorship of General Suharto, the leader of the largest Muslim civil society group, Abdurrahman Wahid, created the 'Democratic Forum', in which all the potentially conflicting religious groups met regularly and increasingly released joint documents in favor of human rights, greater political freedoms and democratic values.[15] These years of cooperation turned out to be very helpful in the surprisingly successful constitution-building process after the fall of Suharto in May, 1998, a process that Donald L. Horowitz, a major comparative constitutional scholar, recently called 'meticulously consensual'.[16]

In Tunisia, one of the biggest obstacles to achieving a 'democracy with democrats' was the hostility between secularists and Islamists which inhibited their joint cooperation against the non-democratic regime of Ben Ali. One of the reasons for this was that, unlike in Indonesia, India, or even Senegal, by the time Tunisia became independent from France in 1956, the country formed a part of what I call the 'iron triangle' of aggressive *laïcité* secularism; the three points in the triangle were made up of France, from 1905 to 1958 (before De Gaulle allowed the state to subsidise Catholic schools); Atatürk's Turkey; and Tunisia under Habib Bourguiba and Zine el-Abidine Ben Ali (1956–2011).[17]

Islam in Tunisia had been relatively progressive in the mid-nineteenth century. The country abolished slavery in 1846, two years before France. In 1861 Tunisia created the first constitution in the Arab world. This constitution, in Jean-Pierre Filiu's judgement, 'enshrined a political power distinct from religion' and built upon the previous Covenant of Social Peace emphasizing 'freedom of religion'.[18] The doyen of Arabists, Albert Hourani, highlights the progressive role of Zeitouna Mosque University in this period, and the disruptive role of the French: '[This Tunisian] experiment in constitutional government ... left its mark: it helped to form a new political consciousness in Tunis, and to bring to the front a group of reforming statesman, officials, and writers ... until they were scattered by the French occupation in 1881. This group had two origins: one of them was the Zaytuna Mosque [University].'[19]

After independence in 1956, Habib Bourguiba, in the name of modernism and *laïcité*, attempted to remove religion from the public square, from most programs of higher education, and, in essence, closed the progressive Zeitouna

Mosque University (which had been founded in Tunis in 737 more than two centuries before Cairo's Al-Azhar University).[20]

From independence until 2011, Tunisia was ruled by only two presidents, Habib Bourguiba and then Ben Ali. In this entire period they never allowed a single fully free and fair election. However, Bourguiba saw himself, and was seen by many, as a one-party state modernising leader. He passed the most progressive family code concerning women's rights in the Muslim world, and at the time, one of the most advanced in the world. Polygamy was banned and polygamists subject to imprisonment, men's right to divorce their wives unilaterally was abolished, and women's rights to initiate divorce, receive alimony, and have greater child custody entered into law. Abortion was legalised under some conditions as early as 1965. Women's access to higher education soon rivaled men's.[21]

Bourguiba and Ben Ali skillfully used the progressive family code and women-friendly educational policies to help build what I call a 'constituency for coercion.' They crafted this constituency by regularly implying that if there were free elections, Muslim extremists would win and curtail freedoms, so it was better not to push too hard for them. Parties with religious affiliations were forbidden, and many Islamist leaders were accused of being terrorists, and were imprisoned and tortured. The autocratic state's discourse about Muslim terrorism strengthened the constituency of coercion and was intensified after the events in Algeria. After the Islamist party had won the first round of elections in 1991 in Algeria, the second round was cancelled in January 1992 by the military; the outcome was a civil war between Islamists and the military that ravaged the country from 1992 to 1997, in which as many as 100,000 people died.[22]

In these circumstances, it was highly unlikely that potential democratic secularist opponents of the regime in Tunisia would be trusted by Islamic activists, who viewed *laïcité* secularists as deeply anti-religious and complicit in the repression of Islamic parties. Likewise, secularists who opposed the authoritarian regime of Ben Ali and wanted democracy did not see Islamists as desirable or even possible allies, given what they assumed were their anti-democratic ideologies and jihadist tendencies.

But, from 2003 to 2011, something similar to what happened in Chile and Indonesia began to take place—an accommodation among enemies. In the Tunisian case, this accommodation was helped greatly by the internal changes in a democratic direction that occurred within the major Islamic activist group starting many years earlier, in the early 1980s.

So I turn now to the largest Islamist Party and movement in Tunisia, Ennahda ['Renaissance'], and its most important thinker and political leader,

Rached Ghannouchi, in order to analyse how and why Ennahda was able to create, with two center-left secular parties, the ruling coalition in the Constituent National Assembly in 2011, and indeed why it wanted to. In my judgement the following ideological and political processes that occurred in Tunisia are worth special attention.

Gradual Ideological and Political Moderation: Ghannouchi and Ennahda

One of Ghannouchi's key thoughts about democracy that eased Ennahda's entry into electoral politics, first briefly in 1989, and then as the largest party in the Constituent Assembly from 2011–2014 was that, while democracy has universal principles, each democratic country has some historic 'specificities' that new political parties, such as Ennahda, should respect. One such 'specificity' for Ghannouchi was Tunisia's women-friendly educational and legal system. During a brief thaw in the transition from Bourguiba to Ben Ali, Ennahda participated in the 1989 elections, and articulated the reasons why good Muslims should treat men and women as equals. Ennahda polled very well in the capital city, Tunis, before the party was outlawed by Ben Ali on terrorism charges that have never been properly documented. In the two decades of exile in the United Kingdom that followed for Ghannouchi, from 1991 to 2011, he wrote hundreds of articles in English, French and Arabic, in which he increasingly advanced arguments against violence and against the imposition of Sharia on people (whether Muslims or not). He also insisted, along with the key Islamic democratic leaders in Indonesia and Senegal, that, as stated in one of the shortest and most explicit injunctions in the Koran (Sura 256), 'in matters of religion there can be no compulsion'. Ghannouchi further stressed that in the modern conditions of cities, with their populations in millions, the traditional Islamic virtue of *shûrâ* (consultation) is best achieved by consulting the citizens of a polity, both Muslim and non-Muslim, in open competitive elections. Ghannouchi often noted also that the Islamic juridical virtue of *ijmâ'* (consensus), when combined with the Koranic injunction against compulsion in matters of religion, creates a space in Islam for a version of democracy that respects individual rights and pluralism. To some extent, Ghannouchi, while often sharply critical of the policies of specific democracies, by the mid-1990s had endorsed the view of Winston Churchill that: 'Democracy is the worst form of government, except for all those other forms that have been tried from time to time.'[23]

Notwithstanding the evidence that Ghannouchi and Ennahda were becoming increasingly supportive of democracy as a set of valuable procedures and norms, these changes in outlook would not have become politically important in Tunisian politics had Ennahda not been able to cooperate with some of the secularists, many of whom, as I have noted already, deeply distrusted any Islamist party. But, starting in 2003, a process of mutual accommodation between democratically friendly secularists and democratically friendly Islamists began that weakened, but did not entirely erode, Ben Ali's 'constituency of coercion'.

Growing Exchanges and Accommodations Between Anti-Ben Ali Moderate Secularists and Moderate Islamists: 2003–2010

In June 2003 representatives from approximately twenty opposition organisations met in France in order to see if they could overcome secular-Islamist differences and become more unified and powerful. Participants at the meeting included Islamist Ennahda, and two secular, center-left parties, CPR (Congress for the Republic) and Ettakatol. Together, these three parties would eventually between 2011 and 2014 constitute the ruling coalition in Tunisia's Constituent National Assembly (CNA). The largest party in the coalition would be Ennahda; the President of the Constituent Assembly, Mustapha Ben Jaafar, would come from Ettakatol; and the president of Tunisia, Moncef Marzouki, would be from CPR.

The first meeting of the twenty political groups from Tunisia resulted in an only recently widely known or available document, 'Call from Tunis'.[24] This document in essence endorsed the two fundamental principles of the 'twin tolerations'. First, any future elected government would have to be 'founded on the sovereignty of the people as the sole source of legitimacy.' Second, the state, while showing 'respect for the people's identity and its Arab-Muslim values', would provide 'the guarantee of liberty of beliefs to all and the political neutralisation of places of worship.' Ennahda accepted both these fundamental agreements. The 'Call' also went on to demand 'the full equality of women and men.'[25]

The three main opposition political parties at the meeting, together with representatives of smaller parties and some civil society leaders, met nearly every year after 2003 to reaffirm, and even deepen, their commitment to the 'Call from Tunis' principles. Their key 2005 manifesto, 'Collectif du 18 Octobre pour les Droits et les Libertés', stated that, after a 'three-month dialogue among party leaders', they had reached consensus on a number of crucial issues. All of the parties, including Ennahda, supported in great detail the existing liberal family code. Moreover, the manifesto added that any future democratic state would have to be a 'civic state ... drawing its sole legitimacy from the will of the people', for 'political practice is a human discipline [without] any form of sanctity.' Finally, the manifesto re-asserted that 'there can be no compulsion in religion. This includes the right to adopt a religion or doctrine or not.'[26]

Agreement on a 'civic state' in which citizens were to be the sole source of legitimacy helped weaken any anti-democratic claim against elections along the lines that 'only God makes laws, not men'. As we have discussed, Ennahda could easily accept that 'there can be no compulsion in religion' because the phrase is found in a Koranic verse that Ghannouchi in Tunisia, Abdurrahman Wahid in Indonesia, and Sufi leaders in Senegal like Bashir Souleymane Diagne, have constantly employed in their arguments against their own fundamentalists and to reassure classic secularists.

Ghannouchi could not participate directly in these meetings because he was forbidden from entering France. Unlike the British government, the French government insisted on designating Ghannouchi a terrorist. However, the extraordinary exchanges between some secular leaders and Ghannouchi were made possible by human agency and will. One of the leading secular leaders of the democratic opposition, Moncef Marzouki, made over twenty trips from France to London to meet with Ghannouchi.[27] Trust and cooperation between the secular and Islamist democratic opposition was deepened by the fact that Marzouki had taken the risk of a major confrontation with Ben Ali by using the Tunisian League of Human Rights, an organisation he had once headed, to defend the basic human and political rights of Ennahda. Democracy in Tunisia was beginning to be built with many secular and Islamic democrats.

However, while I consider these accommodations and agreements of great importance, it would be a mistake to leave the impression that all secularists and feminists were in agreement with these conversations.[28] A militant core of secularists never joined these dialogues, indeed they denounced them in their own documents.[29] Nonetheless, in comparison to Egypt, the existence of secular-Islamic dialogues in Tunisia were of critical importance.

Egyptian Democracy without Democrats: Brumaireanism and Eradicationism

In order to drive home my theoretical and political point that it is crucial in efforts at democratisation to broaden agreement among most of the potential opposition groups to the authoritarian regime, I will show briefly how, unlike in Tunisia, nothing like this occurred in Egypt, and this was a major cause of the failure of the democratic transition in that country.

Nothing comparable to Ennahda's internal reforms and external outreach to secularists was aimed for by the Muslim Brotherhood in Egypt. The leading US scholar of the Muslim Brotherhood, Carrie Rosefsky Wickham, concludes her recent book with the flat charge that 'leaders affiliated with the reformist trend have never gained more than a marginal presence in the Guidance Bureau, the group's highest decision-making body.'[30]

Given this doctrinal opposition within the Muslim Brotherhood to internal reform, intensive negotiations among leading secularists and leading Islamists to overcome mutual fears of the sort we have documented for Tunisia never really occurred in Egypt. This may account for the fact that in Egypt, after the fall of Mubarak, the attitudes and behavior of many citizens were, at best, those of a 'hybrid democracy'. In December 2011, 68 per cent of Egyptian respondents agreed that: 'democracy in which multiple parties compete for power through free elections is the best system for governing Egypt.' However, in the same poll, six months before the Muslim Brotherhood's Mohamed Morsi became president, 62 per cent of respondents hedged their democratic bets by also agreeing that the military 'should continue to intervene when it [i.e. the military] thinks necessary.'[31] This explains why a columnist in a widely read Cairo publication, Ahram Online, asserted that: 'In general, liberal parties would like the constitution to be written before the elections take place, fearing that a post-election constitution-making process will be dominated by Islamists.'[32]

Thus, in a classic Eighteenth Brumairean fashion, many Egyptian citizens were willing to abdicate their right to rule to a non-democratic force such as the military, in return for protection from a potential and unwanted, but democratically elected, government.[33]

The responses to the assertion that 'democracy is preferable to any other form of government' were slightly more positive in Egypt (68 per cent) than in Tunisia (63 per cent). But more significant politically is the fact that in 2013 (the year of the Tunisian crisis I examine shortly), Tunisia had a relatively low percentage of respondents who gave a Brumairean type of answer to the assertion that 'in some circumstances an authoritarian government can be preferable to a democratic government.' Approving answers to this non-democratic option were 27 per cent in South Korea, 21 per cent in Brazil, 18 per cent in Chile, 17 per cent in Tunisia, 9 per cent in Spain and 8 per cent in

Uruguay.[34] Compare this with the 62 per cent of Egyptians polled who were willing to abdicate power to the military to act 'when it [i.e. the military] thinks necessary'.

The Growth of Political Society (as well as Civil Society) in Tunisia

At the beginning of the so-called Arab Spring, both Egypt and Tunisia had creative civil societies. If anything, Egypt's civil society was deeper and more diverse. However, while civil society can break a dictatorship, civil society by itself cannot construct a democracy, because this latter requires actions by political society, such as intensive and widely collaborative discussions about procedures for elections, the organisation of political parties, and negotiations and bargaining until at least a working agreement is achieved on how the incipient polity will organise itself to rule democratically.

In the first four months after the fall of Ben Ali in Tunisia in 2011, 155 members of a diverse group were tasked with forming a commission, usually referred to as the Ben Achour Commision (named after its president, Yadh Ben Achour); its purpose was not to write the new constitution, but to deliberate on what political choices had to be made before elections could even be held, i.e. to create an even stronger political society.[35]

One of the key provisions the Ben Achour Commission agreed on was that the first polity-wide election should be to elect a Constituent Assembly, but not a President, because it was decided that the decision as to whether the political system should be presidential, parliamentary or semi-presidential should be made by an elected Constituent Assembly, and not an unelected working group such as the Ben Achour Commission.

The commission also agreed that there could not be an election without an electoral law, without agreed-on procedures on how to run the elections, and that transparency should be enhanced by a large network of national and international election observers. They decided to use an electoral system of proportional representation (PR), rather than a 'first-past-the-post' single-member district system (as is used in the UK), because the general agreement, shared by Ennahda, was that the British system would produce an overwhelming Ennahda majority. In an interview in Tunis in early March 2011, Ghannouchi told me that should Ennahda win 90 per cent of the seats under a first-past-the-post system, it could well produce an anti-democratic, Algerian-style backlash. Ghannouchi went on to estimate that with a PR system, Ennahda would not get more than 40 per cent of the seats, and would thus need to govern with one or two secular parties, an outcome which he said would help democracy get started in Tunisia. There was also a decision, backed strongly by Ennahda, to have what is called a 'closed list' PR system, with every other name, on each electoral list, being that of a woman.

The final 11 April 2011 vote on all the proposals saw only two abstentions and two walk-outs; all the other members of the Commission voted yes. This exceptionally creative and consensual political society work helped contribute to the success of the October 2011 election for the Constituent National Assembly, an election that was widely considered by national and international observers alike to be free and fair. The results were roughly as predicted, with Ennahda receiving just under 40 per cent of the vote, and therefore forming a coalition government with the two secular parties. Once again, nothing remotely like this consensual, political society-building process occurred in Egypt.

The Constituent Assembly: Innovative Consensus Building in the Midst of Crisis

Some commentators on the democratic transition literature argue that the word 'transition' is teleological, in that it implies achievement of its goal. This is wrong. As Juan Linz and I have stated categorically: 'As comparativists we are painfully aware that most political transformations away from a once stable non-democratic regime do not end in a completed democratic transition.'[36]

Indeed, most transitions encounter numerous setbacks and crises which are overcome only by skilled political leadership, individual or collective. I have in mind the leadership in Spain from 1976–1982 that allowed the transition to survive the near-successful 23 February 1981 military coup attempt; or in Brazil in 1994–1995, when a democracy-threatening, annualised inflation rate of over 2000 per cent was overcome, largely owing to future president Fernando Henrique Cardoso's convincing leadership, which resulted in an enduring, union-based constituency against inflation. Indonesia provides another example; from 1999–2004, the country managed to reverse threatening ethnic and religious conflicts and remilitarisation, by consensual constitution-making.[37]

In this regard, Tunisia is no exception. Despite its auspicious beginning in free and fair elections in 2011, for a six-month period, starting in July 2013, Tunisia experienced an intense crisis that threatened the transition process. But by December of that year it had managed to re-equilibrate, and consensually pass an inclusionary, if at times excessively unclear, constitution in January 2014. In this section I want to explore how innovative consensus-building, in the midst of crisis, enabled this democratic re-equilibration in Tunisia.[38]

The roots of the crisis lay in the constitution-making process and expectations about its speed. As I have noted, most of the decisions made by the Ben Achour Commission about Tunisia's future system of governance were democratically sound. However, one very unsound political commitment was made after the election to the Constituent Assembly. The vast majority of the members of the Constituent Assembly publicly committed themselves (some say 'solemnly pledged') to completing the new constitution within one year of starting their deliberations. This was unnecessary and dangerous. In comparison, India's post-independence Constituent Assembly took three years (1947–1950) to publish its new constitution. The Spanish constitution-writing process took two years (from 'The Law for Political Reform' in November 1976 to the acceptance of the final constitution in December 1978).

In Tunisia, the then President of the country, Moncef Marzouki, actually (and wisely) refused to make a one-year commitment for constitution-writing, saying the process might take three years. Nonetheless, some of the major actors in Tunisia, such as Tunisia's (and indeed North Africa's) most politically prominent trade union, UGTT, and Beji Caid Essebsi, who had once been the interior minister under Bourguiba and had founded a new opposition party, Nidaa Tounes, in the summer of 2012, began to declare that the Constituent National Assembly in Tunisia would become illegitimate on the first year anniversary of its opening session (namely, on 24 October, 2012).[39] Essebsi suggested that some other groups (of unclear origin) should draft a new constitution, and then send it to the reactivated CNA for its ratification. It is not clear to this day whether Essebsi was serious about closing the CNA (and thereby getting the elected 'Troika' interim government made up of Ennahda, the CPR and Ekkataol parties to resign almost immediately); but what is clear is that his actions were at best what Juan J. Linz would call 'semi-loyal' to democracy.

In the middle of this real but still rather vague crisis over the constitution-writing process, two leading leftist Ennahda critics were assassinated in February and July of 2013. The killings, and the fact that they were not solved, led to charges of Ennahda incompetence, or worse, complicity. Events in Egypt colored the interpretations of those in Tunisia. The massive petition movement called Tamarod ('Rebellion'), directed against the Muslim Brotherhood President, Mohamed Morsi, facilitated the Egyptian military's coup against Morsi on 3 July 2013. This in turn appeared to have strengthened the copy-cat Tamarod movement in Tunisia. Demands for the closure of the CNA, on the grounds that it had not yet completed the new constitution, and for the resignation of the Ennahda-led government, intensified, with large demonstrations being held outside the parliament.

In this highly charged context, on 6 August 2013, the President of the Constituent Assembly, Mustapha Ben Jaafar, temporally suspended the work of the CNA in order to gain time for the democratic groups inside and outside of the CNA, to create new ways to transcend the crisis.[40] Ben Jaafar achieved something that is virtually unprecedented in the history of democratic constitution-making within an already elected constituent assembly. He managed to convince every party with seats in the CNA, no matter how large or small, to agree to only have one 'voice' in the decisions about every contested article in what came to be called the Consensus Committee. This was a major sacrifice in terms of power for Ennahda, because with 41 per cent of the seats in the CNA, their representation in the Consensus Committee was no more than that of a number of parties with less than 5 per cent of the seats. It was also agreed that there would be no formal votes in the Consensus Committee. Rather, an article would be considered consensually agreed-upon when it was approved as the 'sense of the meeting' by two-thirds of the participants. Progress in overcoming deadlocks in this fashion commenced rapidly once Ben Jaafar reopened the CNA.

Ben Jaafar used the period when the CNA was suspended to reach out to as many key actors in civil society outside the Constituent Assembly as possible, to widen the dialogue and explore possible compromises. He told us: 'I spent the whole month of August bringing people together, talking to all the political parties, and even with political leaders who had nothing to do with the CNA. The UGTT was also bringing people together. So when I had these signals—sparks of light that people are indeed coming together to discuss— then step by step we started to bring people back to the Constituent Assembly.'[41] Once it was apparent that the Consensus Committee could work well, and that constructive dialogues were beginning with the opposition, Ben Jaafar slowly reopened the CNA in early September 2013. In this new atmosphere the copy-cat Tamarod campaign to close the CNA and to sack the electorally based Troika government rapidly lost momentum.[42]

An external secular group initiated by the trade union UGTT was rapidly supported by the Tunisian League of Human Rights and the Tunisian Bar Association, and was eventually joined by the leading employers' association, UTICA.[43] These four groups intensified a process increasingly referred to as 'The Dialogue'. This external group was never a formal part of the Consensus Committee, but its leaders told us that, with the agreement of the Consensus Committee, they regularly sent two people to listen to key meetings of the Consensus Committee, and to give the Committee the Dialogue group's suggestions.

The Dialogue leaders eventually brought other weighty political and social actors into discussions about a 'roadmap' to transcend the crisis. This road map, which approximately twenty groups and parties supported, entailed dates for signing the constitution, the voluntary resignation of the Ennahda-led Troika coalition, the appointment of an interim technocratic prime minister and government, the final appointment of an electoral commission, and the holding of parliamentary and then presidential elections.

Ennahda agreed to everything in this road map but they refused to resign until the day the final constitution was signed. In my judgment, they were correct to insist on this latter point. Once the constitution was approved on 27 January 2014, Ennahda duly stepped down, the interim government of technocrats took over, with the interim prime minister, Mehdi Jomaa, receiving a very high approval rating of 81 per cent in a public opinion poll before the Parliamentary elections. The crisis had been consensually resolved. What was in the final constitution?

An Inclusionary, Consensual, and Democratic Constitution

The Tunisian Constitution, after four drafts, was voted on and approved on 27 January 2014. The final vote of the 216 deputies to the Constituent Assembly was quite consensual: 200 voted Yes, 12 No, with 4 abstentions. Some of the articles in the final constitution are the most progressive ever passed in an Arab country, indeed in any Muslim country, or even in many long-standing democracies. For example, a sub-committee draft on human rights had stirred the intense opposition of feminists and human rights activists, because in the French and English translations it appeared to describe women as only being 'complementary' to men.[44] However, in the final, approved constitution, this offending phrase was removed, and the Preamble states flatly that the Tunisian polity is based upon 'equality of rights and duties between all citizens, male and female'. Article 46 also affirms that 'the state works to attain parity between women and men in elected Assemblies.'

To accuse a person in many Muslim countries of being an 'apostate' often puts that person at great risk, possibly even death. In Article 6 of the Tunisian constitution, probably for the first time ever in the constitution of a Muslim majority country, making such a charge has been criminalised.

Other improvements are a Constitutional Court, which is particularly necessary in Tunisia, given that the semi-presidential executive type of system selected by the CNA often generates conflicts of jurisdiction over the correct prerogatives of the president and the prime minister. The CNA also passed a 'limitations clause' that may help prevent legislators and presidents from eroding constitutionally-embedded human rights provisions by introducing new intrusive laws or decrees.

Although many members of Ennahda's base might have wanted Sharia law, Ghannouchi gave a major speech arguing against Sharia being in the constitution. This was followed by the chief executive body of Ennahda, the Shura Council, voting against including any reference to Sharia in the Constitution. Like Indonesia, and unlike Egypt, there is no reference to Sharia in the 2014 Tunisian constitution.[45]

To be sure, the constitution has many 'creative ambiguities' that enabled its overwhelming approval but may create problems later. For example, there is Article 1, which in its entirety stipulates that 'Tunisia is a free, independent, sovereign state; its religion is Islam, its language Arabic, and its system is republican. This article may not be amended.'

Some analysts maintain that Article 1 creates an Islamic state. Others, myself included, note that it is identical to the article inserted into the 1959 constitution by the first president of Tunisia, Habib Bourguiba, who along with Kemal Atatürk of Turkey, and the French 1905 law on *laïcité*, constituted the 'iron triangle' of aggressive secularist forces. They thus defend the language as 'sociologically descriptive' rather than 'legally prescriptive'. At some point, however, the language of Article 1 could possibly be revised to become less creatively ambiguous, removing a source of conflict.

An article even more laden with dangerous creative compromises is Article 6. On the one hand it criminalises calling someone an apostate, but on the other hand it stipulates that the state commits itself 'to the protection of the sacred and the prohibition of any offenses thereto.' The head of Human Rights Watch for Tunisia, Amna Guellali, argues that this clause is too vague and allows for 'the most repressive of interpretations in the name of offense against the sacred. Citing the constitution, lawyers, judges, and politicians could interpret Article 6 however they see fit. This ambivalence could hold grave consequences for the country.'[46]

Democratic Alternation of Power in 2015

In 2014, during the lead-up to the first free parliamentary and presidential elections in Tunisia's history, Ennahda mistakenly assumed they would win the first plurality in the parliament and thus again play a leading role in any government-ruling coalition. They were worried that if they ran a presidential candidate there was a danger that they would be seen as having too much power. They thus decided, after many internal discussions and debates in the Shura Council, not to run a candidate for the presidency. As the elections approached, and there were some indications that a Nidaa Tounes coalition, led by Beji Caid Essebsi, with anti-Ennahda secularists and many former activists of Ben Ali's RCD party, was gaining strength, they debated again whether they should nominate a presidential candidate before the deadline for getting on the ballot. Ghannouchi and other key Ennahda leaders played a major role in deciding not to, because they did not want, as the Muslim Brotherhood had done in Egypt, to undo promises made—to first claim they would not run a candidate, and then do so, thus proving to many that as a party, the Islamists were not to be trusted.

As it turned out, in the parliamentary elections, Essebsi's party, Nidaa Tounes, won the first plurality and the right to nominate the prime minister; three weeks later, Essebsi won the presidency in a tight, second-round run-off election.

Many commentators have argued that once an Islamist party wins power in elections, they will never relinquish such power. I talked to Ghannouchi after Ennahda's parliamentary defeat. He was philosophical and his main reflections concerned the future of democracy in Tunisia, to which he was convinced Ennahda had contributed. He said: 'In a period of transition it was useful we did not push religion too hard. We are very keen to make a success of the transition. We have a very heavy responsibility for the success of democracy. Even if we lose in elections, democracy gains. The main goal is to make a success of democracy. Tunisia has got rid of despotism. There is chaos in Syria, Yemen, Egypt, and Iraq. We saved our country. We lost power but we saved Tunisia. We will try to oblige Nidaa Tounes to accept the game of democracy. Moving from government to opposition, and preserving the right to come back, this is the point of democracy.'[47]

On the night of the presidential elections, Ghannouchi quickly phoned Essebsi to congratulate him on his victory and to accept the results of the free and fair election.[48]

Conclusion

President Essebsi's party, Nidaa Tounes, won a plurality in the parliamentary elections with eighty-six seats, but this was twenty-three seats short of the absolute majority needed to form a government by itself. After first attempting, and failing, to form a minority government with one minor party, Nidaa Tounes put together a more inclusive coalition of four parties, including Ennahda, that gave them a comfortable majority of 179 seats.[49] The formation of this coalition was very unpopular with those members of Nidaa Tounes' base, and allies, who had fought an especially anti-Islamist campaign.[50] The idea of the coalition was also initially quite unpopular with many of Ennahda's base who feared a return to anti-Islamist repression and did not want to share the inevitable costs of government with opponents. There thus was wide support within the Ennahda base for the Shura Council's opposition to the first Nidaa Tounes proposed government.

So why did the coalition that included Ennahda come about even though Nidaa Tounes and Essebsi could have put together a majority without Ennadha, and though Ennadha, despite its sixty-nine seats in Parliament was only given one ministry, while a party with only eight seats in Parliament, was given three?

No one knows for sure. But let me offer one tentative contending proposition. Even before the Presidential election I heard talk of the possibility of a 'two Sheikh' compromise. The two Sheikh metaphor refers to the founder presidents of their parties, Nidaa Tounes' Beji Caid Essebsi, and Ennahda's Rached Ghannouchi.

For Essebsi, and the majority of the realist members of his still fragile party, the coalition offered the promise of majority support for many of their difficult economic reforms. They knew that if one drew a series of circles representing the economic policies of the biggest parties in parliament the only two large parties with significant overlaps—despite great ideological differences on Islam—are Nidaa Tounes and Ennahda. Furthermore, Essebsi was 88 years old and on dialysis. If he wanted to leave a legacy of statesman-led growth and party-building, Ennahda, rather than an alliance with the Marxist-secularist Popular Front, could help him and his new party more.

For their part, Ghannouchi and the leaders of Ennahda may have calculated that they were in a better position to 'oblige Nidaa Tounes to accept the game of democracy' within, rather than outside, the ruling coalition. The Shura Council thus voted, without great opposition from their base, to join the now more inclusive coalition. There is some party and historical logic to their experiment. As a member of the coalition Ennahda can more effectively pressure Essebsi and his allies to accept Ennahda as a normal part of democratic participation in Tunisia. Also, within the logic of parliamentary ruling coalitions, Ennahda retains the capacity to possibly cause the fall of the government if for example, the government ever attempted Ben Ali type un-democratic repression against their party. For Ghannouchi and many of Ennahda's leaders, the achievement of the 'normalcy' of Ennahda, within a successful democratic transition in Tunisia, would be their great legacy.

For something like this 'two sheikhs' metaphorical policy to work, both the sheikhs must value 'democracy with democrats' for the present and the future of Tunisia.

2

CONSTITUTING CONSTITUTIONALISM

LESSONS FROM THE ARAB WORLD

Nathan J. Brown

Academic study of constitution drafting has shifted from focusing almost exclusively on questions of what constitutions say, to give primary attention to how they are written: how is a society best to craft a document that will guide its political system in the desired direction? Such writings are often infused with the spirit of American political philosopher John Rawls and his 'veil of ignorance', in which the fairness of arrangements are judged as if we do not know what our particular position might be after their adoption. A good process is one in which the interests of particular groups are accommodated, but the healthiest outcomes stem from those documents that are written with a view towards the long-term benefit of the society as a whole, and broad consensus, rather than short term particular interests. Writings by practitioners have taken a similar procedural turn, though perhaps a more realistic one friendlier to particular interests: sound constitutions are products of inclusive and public processes in which all interests are represented in a participatory and transparent bargaining.

What both strands oddly overlook is the political reality that the choice of process is itself a deeply fraught political outcome and not merely a philosophical abstraction: whom to include; how to draft; how to solicit expertise; and how to ratify a constitution are not products of academic and disinterested wisdom but contested or manipulated political processes. In the Arab world since 2011, there has been much political upheaval, and that has been reflected by a sharp disruption in the constitutional stasis that had set in for decades in many societies. Each attempt at constitutional change—in Bahrain, Jordan, Morocco, Egypt, Libya and Tunisia—illustrates that those who ask 'How should a constitution be written?' may be missing the truly important questions: 'How is it decided how a constitution is written?' and 'Who makes the decision?'

This chapter will proceed in five steps: first, it will provide a historical introduction and briefly consider how Arab constitutions have been written in the past, and why those processes have been criticised; second, it will probe the 'new constitutionalism' that focuses on democratic and participatory mechanisms to supplant the older, often more closed processes; third, it will examine what processes were actually employed in the wake of the Arab uprisings of 2011; fourth, it will examine how constitutions were written after regime change; and finally it will consider those processes that took place without regime change. The goal throughout will be to understand how the Arab experience can help us understand how constitutions actually are written, as opposed to the current focus on how they should be written.

Historical Background: Laying New Constitutionalism on Top of Old

The Arab experience with constitutional texts betrays surprising similarity to European constitutions. Some of this formal similarity occurs in the detailed clauses of constitutional documents in the two quite different regions. Arab and European constitutional documents often resemble each other in structure and detailed wording, though the former tend to be richer in escape hatches and weaker on implementing structures.

But the similarity in form goes deeper than structure and language: Arab and European constitutional documents both tend to present themselves in similarly august terms as an expression of sovereign will. The source of sovereignty has similarly evolved: in the nineteenth century in both regions, the sovereign tended to be the monarch, and the constitutional text was therefore issued in the name of a sovereign sultan, king, emperor, or bey. Occasionally, a European constitution nodded in the direction of popular sovereignty, in theory if not in practice. But in the twentieth century, the people have become sovereign virtually everywhere in both Europe and the Arab world (only in some Arab states in the Arabian peninsula has this trend been resisted). When sovereignty was relocated from the ruler to the entire people, a constitution came to have a very different meaning—it became the expression of the will of a sovereign people that imposed genuine limits on a ruler. A constitution became not a concession by a ruler to his people but a binding document that established boundaries and procedures for determining who held authority and how it could be used.

But how could the will of an abstract entity be expressed? In the nineteenth century, the people were generally held to act through parliaments or occasionally constitutional conventions; in the twentieth century a variety of more plebiscitary methods was devised. But in the Arab world (as in central and eastern Europe before 1989) existing rulers so mastered the techniques used to express the popular will that constitutional texts reliably ratified in popular referenda, simply expressed the rulers' wills in their peoples' name. This pattern continued, and even intensified, after popular sovereignty became formally endorsed in all but the most royalist texts. In other words, constitutions spoke in the name of the people but really reflected the will of the existing regime.

Perhaps it is the cynicism engendered by such ventriloquism (in which rulers spoke their wills by pretending to use the voice of the nation) that led to widespread dissatisfaction with limiting popular participation to plebiscitary forms. There have been other motivations as well behind the new constitutionalism. In many cases the state—or even the nation itself—had not been fully constituted, and no consensus existed among members of the polity to be formed about its fundamental nature. In such cases, a minimal agreement among leaders of various parties and communities has been seen as necessary before constitution drafting can proceed; while such elite bargaining is not necessarily democratic, it can become so if the leaderships feel the need to mobilise their constituencies. In other cases, the new constitutionalism has been motivated by a desire to move even farther beyond elite bargaining as a means to avoid complete delegation of a nation's fate to a small and unaccountable group. And in still more cases—especially those that involved a transition from authoritarian or communist rule—key members of the opposition have been democratic in approach or ideology and have insisted on participatory constitution-making as a matter of principle (aided, perhaps, by a perception that their positions are popular and likely to be reinforced in a democratic process).

The New Constitutionalism in Scholarship and Practice

The desire to move beyond merely formal popular involvement to truly participatory constitution-making has given birth to what is sometimes termed a 'new constitutionalism': a set of approaches that barely made an appearance in the Arab world until 2011, even as they gained traction elsewhere.

There are two different sources for approaching the new constitutionalism. One is based very much in recent political practice and developed by practitioners, consultants, and advisors attempting to work inductively from their own expertise and experience. Another is more scholarly in approach, attempting to situate the new constitutionalism in terms of broader theoretical debates about the nature of democracy and legitimacy.[1]

More practical approaches tend to focus on the new constitutionalism as a set of practices that is emerging as far more common, sometimes even standardised, in political systems where there is a concerted attempt to move beyond authoritarianism, ethnic conflict, or civil strife. The emphasis is often enormously practical, connected with the need to develop a political system that is viewed as legitimate by all members of the society. In order to achieve such an outcome, elite agreement is unlikely to be sufficient. Nor is it enough to insist that a constitution is what makes democratic politics possible and therefore cannot be fully subject to democratic mechanisms.[2]

The process is thus not simply more participatory, but also more political and protracted; it is also more likely to avoid a firm delineation between constitutional politics—concerning the rules by which politics operates—and normal daily politics. And it is precisely such a delineation that has been central to some very influential approaches to constitutionalism (such as that of Bruce Ackerman).[3] According to Vivien Hart, 'We used to think of a constitution as a contract, negotiated by appropriate representatives, concluded, signed, and observed. The constitution of new constitutionalism is, in contrast, a conversation, conducted by all concerned, open to new entrants and issues, seeking a workable formula that will be sustainable rather than assuredly stable."[4]

Yet—as most practitioners realise—devising practices for implementing the new constitutionalism is far more difficult than accepting the principle. While it is possible to point to some model cases (such as South Africa), it is far more difficult to describe how democratic politics can operate in a political system in which the basic rules of politics are neither established nor accepted. It is sometimes possible to point to specific devices (town meetings, interim constitutions) that are designed to facilitate the new constitutionalism. But the fundamental difficulties stem from the circular logic behind the new constitutionalism: democracy must be practiced in writing the rules by which it must be practiced.

It is not surprising that scholars with a more theoretical bent have been attracted to addressing this problem (rather than simply pointing to successful cases). Such scholars have contributed the second source of thought about the new constitutionalism. Perhaps the most sophisticated and well-grounded effort is Andrew Arato's *Civil Society, Constitution, and Legitimacy*, a theoretical reflection on the problem of democratic constitutionalism, based partly on the experience of central European states after 1989.[5] Arato's argument, while often highly abstract, also contains some immensely practical suggestions for assessing the democratic legitimacy of constitutional processes.

As do the practitioners, Arato embraces the political nature of constitution making: 'There are still those who think that constitution making is simply the hour of the lawyers. Indeed, all constitutional texts in modern times have been drafted by lawyers. But behind them are the most important political actors and forces of a given society.'[6] However this leads him directly to confront the problem of circularity:

> From the point of view of democratic theories that recognise the importance of written constitutions, it is of course even more important that constitution making be itself democratic. Most democratic theories do not and cannot recognise any source of legitimacy other than direct or electoral participation by all full members of the political community. If it is important that the rules of the game provide for democratic participation, it is equally or even more important that these rules themselves emerge in a democratic process ... It is nevertheless true that any democracy is conceivable only according to some rules. Thus one easily runs into the problem of circularity when one demands that constitutions be made democratically.[7]

Wishing to reject attempts to base constitutions on a moment of revolutionary violence or a lawgiver, Arato seeks to explore more practical ways of ensuring that a constitution still attains democratic legitimacy. He suggests six principles that focus on constitutional process rather than content, noting that 'while one would not expect to institutionalise all of these principles in current designs of the procedures of constitutional politics, without paying attention to a sufficient combination of them, constitutional construction cannot become democratically legitimate.'[8] The principles are:

- Publicity, allowing for extensive public discussion;
- Consensus, moving beyond simple majority rule;
- Legal continuity, suggesting that the new constitution will be made through procedures sanctioned in the old order, thus signalling that political leaders will observe legal limitations;
- Plurality of democracies, meaning that multiple democratic forms (direct, representative, parliamentary, constituent assembly, national, and federal) be used at different points in the drafting process;
- Veil of ignorance, requiring not a total Rawlsian mechanism but merely favoring those techniques that introduce some uncertainty in how constitutional mechanisms will operate and therefore tend to break the link between partisan interest and institutional design; and
- Reflexivity, meaning ability to learn past constitutional experiences, sometimes by using interim texts and extended processes that allow for reflection on constitution making as it is occurring.[9]

Arato's ideas combine principled and normative guidance with hardened experience and realism. In the years since he developed them, he has widened his geographical focus, developing particular interest in constitutional processes in Turkey and Iraq.[10] In doing so, he has used these ideas to develop harsh critiques of actual practice; he has also used actual practice to flesh out some of his ideas. Consensus, for instance, has become particularly critical in some of his writings; it is an idea that does not lend itself to generalisation because there are no standardised procedures for generating consensus, the nature of the actors involved varies considerably from one setting to another, and there is an increasing resort to disingenuous devices to produce the illusion of consensus. Arato has also explored specific mechanisms, such as the device of a temporary or 'mini' constitution. The demands he places on a proper process are sufficiently difficult that an appropriate path generally requires extended drafting.

Other authors have similarly refined some of the ideas emerging in the new constitutionalism. Donald Horowitz, for instance, frames his writing as being at some critical distance from the emerging scholarly and non-scholarly consensus. But in so doing he forces students of constitutional processes to develop further what is useful about ideas like 'consensus' and 'publicity'.

Linking process to outcome is not an easy task, despite the increasing sophistication of the methodological tools brought to bear and the impressive refinement of concepts and categories beyond the very general ones that pre-dominated even a decade or two ago. In one very useful overview of the litera-ture, Jennifer Widner notes:

> Our instincts tell us that process makes a difference. Constitution writing has sometimes inflamed passions and sparked violence, as it did in the Solomon Islands, Iraq, Chad, and the Republic of the Congo, for example. It has pro-duced better than expected results in some other countries, including South Africa. It is devilishly difficult to show, empirically, that procedures made the difference in these cases, however.[11]

Even more bluntly, Tom Ginsburg, Zachary Elkins, and Justin Blount note: 'In general, scholars have been far better at generating hypotheses relating process to outcomes than at testing them.'[12] To be sure, that situation is slowly beginning to change.[13] But the search for empirical support for the connection between process and outcome—a search predicated on strong normative con-cerns for constitutions that are durable, just, protective of human rights, and democratic—has distracted us from trying to understand how processes are actually designed. We have spent so much time focused on how drafters should draft that we are left to throw up our hands when we see how they actually do so. The recent experience of the Arab world initially only deepens our exasperation. After a consideration of this experience, however, we will work to supplement this exasperation by understanding—and understanding that can build in part on the path-breaking empirical analysis by Zachary Elkins, Tom Ginsburg, and James Melton that proclaims that 'the overall thrust of our argument is to emphasise the similarities between constitutional politics and ordinary politics.'[14]

These ideas are attractive and have been buttressed by much normative writing and empirical analysis. But precious little of that empirical work has been done in the Arab world. Does it have any purchase there? The question does not seem relevant for most pre-2011 experiences. But in the wake of the 2011 uprisings, the question of how to write a democratic constitution in a democratic fashion arose with unexpected force.

Arab Constitution Writing after 2011—and Interesting Analytic Constructs

In the wake of the 2011 uprisings, Arab societies from Morocco to Bahrain found themselves thrust into constitutional controversies—with 'constitu-tional' here meaning not simply disputes about the fundamental structures of governance but also, and sometimes particularly, arguments about texts: the fine print, the pompous preambles, and everything in between. Beyond the consistency of various political actors in rendering their positions in constitutional form, something else stands out: how badly most of these struggles turned (or are turning) out. State collapse, rejiggered authoritarianism, and unreformed authoritarianism seem to be the three most common outcomes.

The marriage of normative concerns with empirical analysis presented in the previous section should leave us disappointed but utterly unsurprised. Virtually nobody did what wise scholars and international consultants advised them to do. Worse, they often pretended to follow the advice, setting up websites and holding public hearings, circulating drafts and inviting ordinary citizens to write their own, inviting everybody to have a seat at the table. Then they rammed through the texts they wanted, ripped up texts they did not like, and used political techniques that resembled a boxing match more than a Habermasian public sphere. At the heart of this cynicism was a set of procedural decisions that seemed to overlook (or turn into Potemkin pledges) the collective wisdom of several decades: 'consensus' was a word deployed by the majoritarians; 'inclusiveness' was a slogan deployed by minorities to demand a disproportionate voice and by majorities to insist that minorities simply show up to give legitimacy to the process; 'publicity' was used to parade; 'legal continuity' was used by existing regimes to avoid change rather than facilitate it. Victors imposed their will and then declared 'the door is open' as a means of signalling to the opposition less a willingness to adjust and more a demand for surrender.

Why did people behave so badly? One possible explanation is that they did not understand what they were doing. Long ago, when trying to understand why policy makers did not behave in a manner as supportive of free trade as economists told them they should, Stephen Krasner offered an insight that may be helpful here: 'Historical experience suggests that policy makers are dense, or that the assumptions of the conventional argument are wrong. Free trade has hardly been the norm. Stupidity is not a very interesting analytic category.'[15]

The 'stupidity' was structural and not personal, but it was profound. Individuals and political actors often behaved cagily and carefully and even self-defeating actions were carefully considered. Two different sets of processes were at work in the constitutional struggles in the Arab world that occurred after 2011. In one set, the problem was that nobody was in control. In the second set, the problem was that there was somebody in control.

Societies in a Hurry with Nobody in Control

In Egypt, Tunisia, Libya, and Yemen, constitutional processes were initiated as old regimes partially or completely crumbled. In none of these cases was there a clear political actor that could manage every step of the process. Even a fairly dominant actor, like the Egyptian military, seemed uncertain both as to how to proceed and what precise outcome it wanted. In such cases, normative concerns about just and democratic outcomes took a back seat to hard-headed calculations about how various actors and their interests would fare. Or rather, the absence of a normative consensus in the society (on fundamental questions of democracy, rights, and religion, for instance) made it unlikely that any actor would view the process as a consensual one in which actors moved toward a common goal. Politics was not suspended nor did it move to a higher plane where partisan and institutional interests were shelved for the moment; instead, the constitutional processes were hastily designed but continuously contested even as they operated. They were products not of a master sorcerer but of a collection of sorcerer's apprentices, each with a different agenda.

In attempting to understand politics in such chaotic times, I have written elsewhere about the role of passion and rationality.[16] In many of the dramatic moments of political transition that have occurred in the past quarter-century, the sensation most frequently mentioned in the recollections of leading participants has been extreme and exhilarating uncertainty. In Spain in 1976 and 1977, the far left did not know whether daring language or audacious action would provoke a reversal of liberalisation; in Poland in the mid- and late-1980s, the likely reaction of the Soviet Union to events was both critical for calculating likely outcomes and completely unclear. In many South American transitions, the positions of the military were discovered only by probing. In many cases in which a founding election has not been held, the relative electoral strength of various actors is a matter of much uncertainty. Aristide Zolberg referred to periods in which everything seems possible as 'moments of madness'. Writing in 1972, he describes such moments using what seems now to be an uncannily prescient allusion to the revolutions of 1989: 'the wall between the instrumental and the expressive collapses.'[17] And it is precisely such a phenomenon that makes rational calculation extremely difficult: one knows neither one's own strength nor the strength of other potential allies and opponents; one does not even know where others stand with any certainty.[18] In some countries, not only is the relative strength of various actors unknown, but the identity of the actors themselves and the context in which they act may radically shift. As one survey of the 1989 transitions noted: 'The question of the moment was not "What is to be done?" but "Is there anyone who might be able to do anything—including defining what needs to be done?"[19]

To be sure, many of these features of such moments have been noted before. Jon Elster, who has likened constitutions to Peter sober binding Peter drunk admitted that the metaphor may be less than apt because 'it is not obvious that the framers will be particularly sober.'[20] Or, less metaphorically, there is:

> an inherent paradox in the constitution-making process. On the one hand, because they are written for the indefinite future, constitutions ought to be adopted in maximally calm and undisturbed conditions. On the other hand, the call for a new constitution usually arises in turbulent circumstances. The task of constitution making demands procedures based on rational argument, but the external circumstances of constitution making generate passion and invite resorts to force.[21]

But Peter's problem is not of drunkenness but of thick fog: he will not be able to make out where he stands or who else is nearby; his guesses about his options and the effects of his actions will be unreliable and are likely to shift rapidly with events. Adam Przeworski has argued that such uncertain situations are likely to lead conflicting political forces to 'seek institutions that provide guarantees against temporary political adversity, against unfavorable tides of opinion, against contrary shifts of alliances.'[22] But this reasoning recognises only some of the uncertainty in such moments of madness—it still assumes that the identities of the actors and their preferences are fairly constant.

The problem is not that actors lose their rationality but that rationality becomes a less certain tool. In a 'moment of madness', whatever calculations are made are likely to be tentative and shift rapidly along with the situation. Perhaps most importantly, short-term rationality will have no advantage over long-term. In normal times, short-term calculations are usually easier because one can hold much constant. That is no longer the case when rapid and radical change seems possible. When yesterday's impossible dream becomes today's imaginable, even imminent goal, many political actors may be tempted to think in terms of long-term changes; those who feel no such temptation will still likely feel forced by the pressure of events to stake out positions. And as actors shift in their goals and identities, they may dissolve and recombine in dizzying ways as yesterday's partner turns into today's mortal adversary (or vice versa).

Thus actors will likely be infused with what might be termed 'passionate rationality'. They will act rationally in that they will seek to use efficient means to pursue given ends—but they are likely to be uncertain as to which means are most efficient and the ends may be less than given (and indeed evolve rapidly as the impossible and unthinkable are possible and thinkable and perhaps even realised). They may become less certain who is on their side, who or what they are struggling against, and even who they themselves are. The metaphor of 'rebuilding the ship at sea'—used to describe how framers after 1989 had to use whatever tools they had at their disposal in order to reconstruct their societies—is more fortunate than its authors realise.[23] It implies that framers must focus on long-term issues of design at a time when it is virtually impossible to overlook short-term considerations. Ignoring the immediate effects of one's actions and concentrating only on ultimate design could easily lead to sinking or scuttling the ship; ignoring the ultimate design will mean missing an opportunity that may never be repeated. It may not even be possible to tell the difference between the short-term and long-term issues.

Passionate rationality does not imply acting without regard to consequences. In that sense, it is perfectly rational, but it may have all the predictability of quirky passionate impulses—it means acting amidst tremendous uncertainty about the consequences of one's actions, radical shifts in the consequences desired, and even fundamental debates about who one is (and who the adversaries are). When consequences, preferences, and identities are both unsettled and difficult to predict, rational actors will behave in surprising and shifting ways. However, the resulting uncertainty is hardly Rawlsian in nature. Actors are likely to purse their own interests—even as their interests change and calculations prove to give little guidance. The emphasis on the long-term is not disinterested; participants view the future through a gauzy veil of confusion rather than a totally opaque veil of ignorance.

Arab societies undergoing uncontrolled constitutional processes after 2011 may help us understand that even in such confusing situations there are clear patterns. One of the most obvious ones would vindicate Arato's gritty insistence on inclusiveness: as long as there is a powerful actor sitting outside the room or capable of overturning the outcome, there is little likelihood of a stable outcome. What Arato and the other normatively-inspired authors do not help us understand is what might make such an actor behave in a manner that is supportive of the process and not merely bullying (that is, when powerful players, like Tunisia's Ennahda, Egypt's military, or Egypt's Muslim Brotherhood, decide to persuade rather than defeat their adversaries).

Yet there are some indications from the Arab experience even on this difficult question—and one of the main ones is that history matters. This is not a mere vacuous slogan; history plays a powerful role in three ways.

First, past patterns of interaction among political actors condition their expectations of future behavior. It was not unusual to hear Egyptian leaders speculate on the military's intentions by referring to events in the period between 1952 and 1954. But it is not simply past behavior that is at issue here; it is the nature of interactions among various actors. Countries that had long periods in which opposition groups came to understand each other and coalesce around common platforms proceed into periods of rapid change with at least some residue of trust; this was the case for some of the post-1989 transitions in Eastern Europe and may have been a positive influence in both Yemen and Tunisia. In Egypt, by contrast, such efforts had only progressed to a superficial extent when the uprising suddenly seemed to triumph. Michaelle Browers has explored how political discussions among various ideological camps developed in the recent past (focusing largely though not exclusively on Egypt). While difficult issues were discussed—in settings that seemed to encourage deliberation—the failure to overcome differences over issues involving gender and non-Muslims ultimately meant that when protest movements arose to public prominence, the participants could at most only bargain with each other to hammer out a thin opposition consensus.[24] That consensus, of course, came apart quite quickly in Egypt—limited deliberation may take place in the quiet of a workshop, but it is hardly likely to be helpful in the middle of street protests and the pressure of elections (as happened in Egypt in 2011 and 2012).

Second, history matters in that it often offers certain default options, especially when it comes to process. In a visit to Tunisia in the summer of 2011, I was struck by how often those involved explained procedural choices made by reference to what steps had been taken when the country received independence. In a country where nobody knew what was to be done, past practices at least offered a starting point for discussion. And indeed, that is generally what the Tunisians did; even as debates grew increasingly angry and contentious, actors could always agree, however crankily, on a fallback position of going back to independence and following the process of constituting the political system all over again. Egypt, bereft of anything other than a formally plebiscitary history in which constitutions were drafted by appointed committees and then presented to the people for a 'yes' vote had to make up new processes on the spot—and failed to find any one that did not make some important actors feel excluded.

Finally, history offers texts. The best predictor of what a country includes in a constitution was what it inserted in its previous one. As with processes, past texts offer a starting point for parties who, like generals fighting the last war, begin with what happened in the past and seek to make corrections rather than start from scratch.

Rulers' Constitutions

It is possible to write a constitution that is devoid of the influence of passion and bargaining among self-interested and confused parties in a chaotic setting. Indeed, many of the world's constitutions are written precisely in such a manner. Such documents are often derided as 'façade' constitutions that are routinely violated.

But the term façade is misleading—the problem is not so much that the constitutions are violated (they sometimes are, but much less often than is supposed) but that they express only the will of an existing regime.[25] So-called façade constitutional documents often present the political system with as much candour and comprehensiveness as their supposedly authentic counterparts. Perhaps the most cited example of a country with a façade constitution was the Soviet Union. But Soviet constitutions were far too honest and clear to be simply disingenuous façades. They included a clause on the leading role of the Communist Party that one observer described as abolishing 'not only the rest of its text, but the rest of legislation also.'[26] Nineteenth-century Latin American constitutions similarly established the basis for non-constitutionalist government with essentially unchecked executive authority and extensive and poorly supervised provisions for emergency rule.[27]

The flaw of such documents is not that they have fallen under the sway of passionate and partisan drafters but that they are robbed of all passion and do not reflect any plurality of interests. They are written by existing regimes entrenching themselves.

And indeed, that was precisely the other pattern followed in the Arab world. In 2011, watching their colleagues forced from office, rulers in Morocco and Jordan initiated constitutional revision processes that offered genuine concessions. The opposition had demanded greater powers for the parliament and stronger protections for judicial independence for years; they had formulated specific demands for translating the vague guarantees of the constitution into political practice. Armed with a set of clear constitutional issues to focus on, regimes could signal some serious commitment to change by acceding to some of the opposition's requests. In Jordan, for instance, the ability of the executive to issues laws in the absence of parliament could be limited; this was a tool that had been used in the past to decree significant changes in the electoral system and in basic rights and freedoms. A new constitutional court was also to be created, a step that had been promised two decades earlier but never fulfilled. In Morocco, cabinet responsibility to parliament was enhanced and powers were transferred from the king to the cabinet, essentially making electoral outcomes far more significant.

These changes went beyond past merely symbolic changes in two ways: first, they were very specific institutional steps rather than merely vague promises; and second, they answered very specific opposition demands. But while they were significant steps, they were clearly steps that rulers felt they could take in the direction of a fuller constitutional democracy without actually nearing the line at which real regime change was possible. In other words, Przeworski's definition of authoritarianism—a political system in which there exists 'some power apparatus capable of overturning the outcomes of the institutionalised political process'—still applied to the regimes in question.[28] Parties could run, people could vote, parliaments could pass laws, and prime ministers could govern but only within a framework in which a set of security institutions and royal prerogatives sat outside constitutional channels, able to overturn the outcome, suspend the process, and reverse any changes.

In such cases, the passage of time revealed what should have been very clear from the start: what was offered was a set of constitutional changes that liberalised the rules of the political game only insofar as those rules did not threaten to overturn the game. The constitutional moment in these societies was one in which the ultimate source of authority and even sovereignty was not open to question. There was always an ultimate power in the country that could dictate but not be dictated to.

Conclusion

The new constitutionalism asks drafters—and even more those who design drafting processes—to make sincere efforts to engage in a participatory, public, and consensual process. The Arab experience reminds us of several lessons. First, there may not be a single designer. Second, every procedural decision generates winners and losers and is hardly politically neutral. Third, parties are likely to be most insistent—but also least able to reason—in the confused situations that surround the reality or threat of rapid political change.

And that may be the main lesson. It should be remembered that constitutions are rarely written except at moments of political crisis; the new constitutionalism itself was an outcome of reflections on some extraordinary crises, including state collapse, civil war, and revolutionary transformation. An attempt to construct participatory and consensual process in a deeply (and even violently) divided society may sometimes entrench existing divisions rather than heal them. At a minimum, the techniques of the new constitutionalism are likely to make it difficult indeed to induce parties to separate partisan interest from design; if the final product does not operate in order to guarantee the interests of the constitutional architects, it is likely to be because of the miscalculation inevitable in such tumultuous times.

None of this suggests that the new constitutionalism should be abandoned. But enthusiasm for the new constitutionalism should not obscure how difficult—and perhaps contradictory—its demands may become. And it may illustrate as well that those countries most likely to follow its prescriptions are those that least need to do so.

3

BULLETS BEAT BALLOTS

THE ARAB UPRISINGS AND CIVIL–MILITARY RELATIONS IN EGYPT

Omar Ashour

Armed Politics in the Arab-Majority World

'We haven't seen the end of this yet ... there is a coming parliament, it may ask questions, and I wonder what will we do about that ... we have to prepare to confront this without negatively affecting us.' So said General Abdel Fattah al-Sisi to a group of military officers during a 2013 meeting.[1] The statement summarised the military's weariness of elected institutional oversight. It reflected an environment in which the supremacy of armed institutions over other state institutions has been a legacy in the last six decades. This legacy was briefly challenged in the aftermath of the January 2011 uprising. But a military coup on 3 July 2013 has reasserted the supremacy in an unprecedentedly violent fashion.[2]

Steps to reassert continuity in civil–military relations, and to abort change, were visible to observers and activists on the ground as early as March 2011.

In September 2011, a diverse group of Egyptian activists, including secular liberals, socialist revolutionaries and Islamist youth was set up for a single purpose: to persuade all candidates running in the presidential elections to commit to keeping the military out of politics.[3] The then presidential candidates sent a petition to the Supreme Council of the Armed Forces (SCAF), the military junta that took over after Mubarak. It asked them to make the same pledge: to end military rule and give a date for handing over power to civilians. The SCAF did not reply to seven presidential candidates who, put together, had more than 90 per cent of the potential votes at the time. The incident had clear implications. It re-highlighted the crisis of civil–military relations in Egypt as well as the lack of regard military commanders have had for civilian politicians.

The saga of politicised, armed institutions in the Arab-majority world is not new. It manifested itself in a trend that started with Bakr Sidqi's coup in Iraq in 1936. It now directly impacts national reconciliations, the functioning of state institutions, civil societies, citizens' security, democratisation, and human rights. In the 'Arab Spring' countries, prospects for social stability, and thereby economic recovery, will remain bleak if the relationship between civilian and armed institutions is not redefined and gradually brought under the control of democratic rules of political competition.

This chapter attempts to understand how the military decides when to deal with domestic opposition, especially with forces that have significant support on the ground. It argues that these decisions are largely dependent on the nature of the militaries in question and can be partly understood by four decision-making models. It applies the hypothesis to the case of the military in Egypt and its decision to stage the 2013 coup, after staging two other coups on 11 February 2011 against Mubarak and on 7 June 2012 against Egypt's first freely elected parliament. The first part addresses the nature of the militaries in the Middle East and North Africa. It situates the Egyptian military within a typology. The second part is a brief overview of the legacies of military rule in Egypt since the July 1952 coup. The chapter then turns to domestic decision-making processes within the Egyptian military establishment. It analyses how the military has made its most critical decisions by considering four models: a rational actor model, an organisational model, a factionalism model, and a psychological model. And finally it presents a conclusion based on the analysis. So far, a comparative decision-making analysis of Islamist organisations and the military in Egypt has not been made. This chapter represents an original attempt at addressing such a critical research agenda.

This chapter does not focus on regional and foreign patronage and its impact on a military's decision-making. This is mainly due to space limitations, but is also an attempt to isolate the domestic environment and its factors. Nonetheless, it must be mentioned that regional and foreign patronage is a crucial factor in the process. The Egyptian military is by far the largest and the most consistent recipient of foreign funding, equipping, and training in Egypt, outpacing any and all other institutions and non-governmental organisations (NGOs) put together. Between 1948 and 2014, the United States alone has provided Egypt's military with $74.65 billion in aid, with more than half of that coming since 1979.[4]

Militaries in Arab-Majority States: Natures and Behavioural Impacts

Militaries' involvements in the politics of the Middle East and North Africa have yielded at least four models: a 'guardian' model, a 'dominant institution' model, a 'sectarian-tribal' model, and a 'less-politicised' model. Turkey's military establishment prior to the reforms of the Justice and Development Party (AKP) represented the first model: an armed institution that believes it created the modern Turkish state. It also believed that it gave Turkey its modern identity and that its mission should be to protect that identity in a supra-constitutional fashion.[5] The second, dominant institution model, is represented by the Egyptian and Algerian militaries. In this case, the army neither created the state, nor gave it its identity. However, it is an intact, independent institution that believes in its superiority compared to any other state institution or non-state entity, including elected bodies, civilian judicial ones, and political parties/groups. That superior armed institution has specific privileges, which usually include a package of economic benefits and at least a veto in high politics.[6] A third model is a tribal-sectarian one. Here, the armed institution has the same benefits of the 'dominant institutional' model, but a specific faction/subgroup within a religious sect or a tribal coalition controls it. The model is exemplified by the Assad's regime in Syria and the Gaddafi regime in Libya. A relatively less-politicised model exists in Tunisia; almost a unique case in the region. Here, the armed institution does not fit any of the above. But guarantees to sustain a relatively apolitical army still need further developments. Coup-proofing measures, building a de-politicised professional identity, fostering loyalty to the constitution as opposed to the direct commanders, transparency and oversight by elected bodies, and legal reform measures are all critical to maintain and enhance such a model.

Major disruptions to the aforementioned models developed in the last few decades. Such developments challenged the dominance of the armed establishment. Sudan (1985–1989) and Algeria (1989–1992) initiated the developments in the second half of the twentieth century. This was followed by major shifts in civil–military and in the nature of the Iraqi military after the American-led occupation in 2003. More critical developments occurred during the Arab-majority uprisings, optimistically termed the 'Arab Spring', in which military dominance in various forms was challenged by pro-change forces, both reformists and revolutionaries. During the uprisings, the different natures of the militaries affected their political behaviour quite significantly. In Egypt and Tunisia, the military has a strong institutional identity and *esprit de corps*. Due to their less-tribal and less-sectarian nature—compared to the militaries of Libya, Yemen and Syria—their leadership was able to keep the institution intact in times of uprisings and upheavals. By 2013, the military in Egypt, belonging to the dominant institution category, needed nonetheless to reassert its supremacy over politics. The Tunisian military did not. In Syria, Libya and Yemen, military institutions fractured in times of crisis over mainly, but not exclusively, ethnic, tribal and regional lines.

By Way of Background: The Egyptian Case

In the past hundred years, Egypt has witnessed three major transitional periods that significantly affected its contemporary politics. The first occurred between 1919 and 1923, when Egypt reclaimed partial independence from Great Britain and established a constitutional monarchy through the promulgation of the 1923 constitution. This transitional period yielded a relatively liberal constitution, a system of institutionalised party politics, and a parliament, though its powers were much inferior to those held by the ruling monarch and the British consul-general. However, social injustices, corruption, and the co-optation of the political elite by the palace and the former colonial power, as well as the humiliating 1948 defeat against Israel, all contributed to the popularity of the Free Officers' military coup, staged on 23 July 1952. This was the first major coordination between army officers and the Muslim Brothers, a rising non-state Islamist actor with a significant popular base, to oust a ruling regime. This coup sparked another transitional period, which lasted until November 1954. By then, the victorious faction within the army had put an end to Egypt's limited democratic experience. That transition yielded a military-dominated system, a state-controlled economy, and a ban on political parties. From this point onward, the military establishment became the most powerful political actor in Egypt, wiping out or co-opting every rival and creating a new set of political rules.

Within this phase of military dominance, two small transitions occurred as a result of intra-military elite struggles for power. The first was between 1970 and 1971, when a dispute between army officers following the death of Gamal Abdel Nasser (1954–1970) triggered the rise to power of Anwar Sadat (1970–1981). Sadat eventually reoriented Egypt's international alliances (towards the United States) and domestic economic policies (towards a relatively market-friendly economy), and, most importantly, initiated a limited process of political liberalisation. A crackdown in September 1981, however, led to Sadat's assassination on 6 October by a group of Islamist army officers protesting the arrest of more than 300 major political and religious figures, and condemning the peace treaty with Israel. That event led to the second minor transition within the era of military dominance: the rise of Hosni Mubarak, Sadat's deputy. For three decades Mubarak ruled Egypt with a mix of crony co-optation and brutal repression. In his last decade, especially after the 9/11 terrorist attacks on the United States, repression dominated his policies as many Western governments turned a blind eye to human rights violations in the context of the 'war on terror'. But Mubarak's most significant contribution in the security sector was the massive empowerment of the State Security Investigations or *Mabahith Amn al-Dawla* (MAD), the domestic intelligence apparatus that technically operates under the Ministry of Interior. Indeed, under Mubarak, Egypt transformed from a military-dominated state to one run by the MAD. This transformation partly explains the supportive attitude toward the 2011 uprising from many mid- and low-ranking officers, as they felt less empowered compared to their supposed subordinates in the MAD.

During these three decades Mubarak continued what Sadat had started: controlled political liberalisation, an electoral façade with consistently rigged elections and increasing reliance on two specific security institutions—the MAD and the Central Security Forces or *Quwat al-Amn al-Markazi* (QAM)—to co-opt, control, or eliminate political rivals. Mubarak was the head of the Supreme Council of the Police, the highest commanding body in the force, which he used to buttress his regime. In many ways the revolution of 2011 was a revolt against police brutality and the Ministry of Interior, represented by Supreme Commander Mubarak and his Minister of Interior, General Habib el-Adly. But in addition to police brutality, three other issues contributed to the revolution's outbreak. The first was the 'inheritance' issue (*Al-tawrith*), which meant the succession of Mubarak by his son Gamal as the new president. That was unacceptable to the majority of Egypt's opposition forces. 'Egypt is not a fiefdom to be inherited like that, and Egyptians are not serfs anymore', an Egyptian senior diplomat serving under Mubarak said.[7] The second issue was the rigged parliamentary elections of 2010. Mubarak's National Democratic Party (NDP) had a notorious reputation of corruption, yet it apparently won over 88 per cent of the vote. The rest of the vote was spilt between 'independents' associated with the NDP, and a much lesser portion went to loyalist parties, effectively controlled by the MAD. This signalled to many Egyptians that the electoral process was hopeless, even for very limited change. The third factor was the nepotism and corruption of the main figures of Mubarak's regime, most notably his sons Alaa and Gamal, their in-laws and their cronies, such as NDP politician Ahmed Ezz.

Before 2011, none of the aforementioned transition periods since 1954 yielded any serious disruption of the military's political supremacy. In that sense, Egypt has never witnessed a consolidated democratisation process at any point in its history. But the January 2011 uprising changed the intra-regime power dynamics quite significantly. Traditionally, since Nasser's reign, the military officer who occupied the presidential establishment was more powerful than the military officer who was at the helm of the army. And whenever they clashed, the former would defeat the latter. When Nasser clashed with 'Field-Marshal' Amer, the latter allegedly killed himself or was killed. When Sadat clashed with General Mohamed Fawzy and other generals, it was the generals who ended up in jail. And even when mere rumours about the potential political rise of Field-Marshal Mohamed Abd el-Halim Abu Ghazala circulated, Mubarak suddenly sacked, and later humiliated, him.

Since February 2011, that pattern has changed. The officer at the helm of the high command of the army—the Supreme Council of the Armed Forces (SCAF)—became the most powerful political actor, even compared to the officers dominating the presidential institution, the intelligence establishment, and the security apparatuses (including the MAD). When interests clashed, the SCAF removed Hosni Mubarak in February 2011, and then Mohamed Morsi in July 2013. The SCAF then appointed a third figure as an 'interim president' after the July 2013 coup. In January 2014, the SCAF 'endorsed' one of its members as a presidential candidate;[8] not that different from any local political party, except that the endorsement was communicated to a regional sponsor before it actually took place, according to a recent leak.[9] The endorsed candidate, Abdel Fattah al-Sisi, became president in May 2014 by 96.9 per cent of the votes. But contrary to Saddam, Gaddafi, Assad, and the rest of Arab leaders 'voted' in with over 90 per cent majorities, al-Sisi has fewer powers. He cannot, for example, sack the defence minister except after the approval of the SCAF, according to the post-coup 2014 constitution.

What do the Generals Want? The Not-So-Unique Case of Egypt

The January 2011 uprising was a product of the struggle of several socio-political forces that challenged the Mubarak status quo, but these pro-change forces had different motivations. The pro-revolution forces, whether Islamist or non-Islamist, were motivated by the regime's corruption and repression. In contrast, the military establishment, led by the SCAF, believed that some of Mubarak's policies, mainly those influenced by his son Gamal and his wife Susan, were undermining the interests of the establishment's leaders. They nevertheless believed that the principal elements of the status quo should be maintained, especially the military establishment's veto power over political decision-making. This difference in perceptions and objectives caused tensions and clashes throughout the SCAF's rule, as well as Morsi's. For example, to the SCAF, comprehensive security sector reform—bringing the armed forces under the control and oversight of democratically elected civilians—and budgetary transparency are at best radical concepts and at worst threatening taboos that should be eliminated or rendered meaningless.[10]

Between February 2011 and July 2013, the SCAF would have liked to combine a parliament with limited powers, a presidency that was subordinate to the military, and constitutional prerogatives that legitimised the military's autonomy and potential control over high politics. The minimum the SCAF insisted on was a veto on foreign and security policy, independence for the army's budget and economic complexes, legal immunity from prosecution on charges stemming from corruption or repression, and constitutional prerogatives to guarantee these arrangements. The veto power over political decision-making would include any issues that touch on national security or sensitive foreign policy, most importantly the relationship with Israel. To control high politics, the SCAF decreed a constitutional addendum in July 2012 that gave it the prerogatives of the dissolved parliament, including dominant legislative authority, and the rights to form a constitutional assembly and veto constitutional articles.[11] The addendum also ordered the formation of a national defense council dominated by the military and granted military intelligence and military police the power to arrest civilians on charges as minor as traffic disruption and 'insulting' the army.

The independent military–economic complexes, which benefit from preferential customs and exchange rates, tax exemption, land ownership and confiscation rights (without paying the treasury), and an army of almost-free labourers (conscripted soldiers) is the source of much military influence and thus another thorny issue for any elected civilian. With the Egyptian economy suffering, elected politicians might well seek to improve conditions by moving against the military's civilian assets—by imposing a form of taxation and revising the preferential rates and land confiscation policies. Corruption and immunity from prosecution are no less salient. Despite its power, the SCAF was quite sensitive to certain factors. Pressure from the United States is one of them, due to its provision of arms, training, and funds. Street mobilisation is another factor. Most of the SCAF's pro-democracy decisions came as a result of massive pressure from Tahrir Square protests. These included the removal of Mubarak, his trial (and that of other regime figures), and bringing the date of the presidential election forward from June 2013 to June 2012. Another factor that influenced the SCAF's decision-making was the army's internal cohesion. It is no secret that internal reports about potential mutiny within the middle and lower ranks were among the factors that caused the SCAF to abandon Mubarak and disobey his orders to crack down on protesters.[12] 'The sight of officers in uniform protesting in Tahrir Square and speaking on Al-Jazeera really worries the Field Marshal,' said a former officer.[13]

If those were the minimum objectives and the visible constraints, then what explains the decision to stage the July 2013 coup and the repressive follow-up? Coups, in general, are high-risk, illegal endeavours. The risks are even higher when the coups are staged against an elected institution, which has been recently in power. This is due to the presence of significant numbers of supporters and therefore a higher possibility of resistance. This all complicates the decision-making to stage them, especially if the military leadership was not a loser in the transition process.

How Do the Generals Decide? Also, the Not-So-Unique Case of Egypt

There are several explanatory models to consider how the military generals decide. Rational explanations for state and non-state political violence exist. Morality aside, the benefits of repression simply outweighed the costs of accommodation or inclusion in the calculations of the generals. If the generals perceived the elected bodies as potential future threats, and they could suspend a publicly approved constitution, dissolve an elected parliament, arrest an elected president, and kill, injure, or detain thousands who oppose these measures without accountability, why would they risk a future change in the balance of power?

Yet the military was by no means a loser in the 2011–2013 transition process. Not only did it enjoy multiple domains of power under President Morsi, but these domains were constitutionally legal. In the 2012 constitution, supported by the Muslim Brotherhood's Freedom and Justice Party (FJP) and approved by 63.83 per cent of voters, the defence minister had to be a military officer (Article 195), and the National Defense Council would have a majority of military commanders (Article 197). This effectively gave the military a veto over any national security or sensitive foreign policy issue. Article 198 allowed military tribunals for civilians 'when a crime harms the armed forces.' Legal immunity from civilian courts was granted and there were no public indicators showing that civilian politicians were capable or willing to move against the military's industrial complex, a black hole in the Egyptian economy. '[Morsi] did not really harm us. ... I mean the stuff [officers] care about like the salaries, the benefits, the pensions were all fine,' said a mid-ranking army officer three months before the July 2013 coup.[14] Given the costs, benefits, and high probability of a bloody aftermath, the rational actor model alone does not explain the July coup, unless there was a miscalculation of the likely scale, scope, and intensity of popular anti-coup reactions.

Another explanation for the military's decisions and behaviour lies in its organisational routines. Every institution has a set of 'standard operating procedures' or SOPs: formal and informal rules according to which actions and reactions are determined.[15] In the case of confronting anti-government protests, the use of intimidation and repression has been SOP for both the army and police forces over the last six decades of Egyptian politics.[16] The January 2011 uprising posed a serious challenge to that model by directly challenging the power of coercive institutions, such as the Central Security Forces or the Military Police, while also demanding greater accountability from security services of all stripes. The military clearly felt uncomfortable with this new state of affairs. 'What police officers have been faced with in the last two years has created a new environment. ... In that new environment, the police officer will stand up to you up to a certain point. [But he] won't be prepared to use tear gas, grenades or shotguns. If someone dies, if something happens to somebody, [the officer] might get tried... [The officer] is not going to do it. And I want to tell you all the protestors have realised this,' General Abdel Fattah al-Sisi was compelled to explain to several officers in a widely-disseminated video.[17] He stresses that the police would be of less help to the military in the event of a crackdown given fears of being held liable for any abuse or killing. Despite these concerns, continuity rather than change seemed the order of the day. This was certainly true for Egypt's security services. One police officer, speaking in the wake of an October 2013 crackdown that killed fifty protestors, said, 'Look, this is how we used to work for two decades. We played by the book in October ... it is a bad book but there is no chance of replacing it now.'[18] Even before Mohamed Morsi took office, the military was only too willing to play by the same book. Military forces condoned or participated in harsh responses to demonstrations and sit-ins throughout 2011, most notably against Coptic Christian demonstrators in front of the Maspero government television building in October 2011.

A third potential explanation for how the military makes decisions relates to factionalism within the security establishment and its political allies. Coup perpetrators and supporters often divide into two coalitions after a coup: one advocates the eradication of the ousted party while the other calls for limited inclusion and controlled repression. The *erradicadors* versus *diálogistas* ('eradicators' versus 'dialogists') saga is common in the history of South American juntas. O'Donnell and Schmitter refer to them as 'hard-liners' (*duros*) and 'soft-liners' (*blandos*). In addition to their stance on eradication and limited inclusion, the first group believes 'that the perpetuation of authoritarian rule is possible and desirable, if not by rejecting outright all democratic forms, then by erecting some façade behind which they can maintain the hierarchical and authoritarian nature of their power.' The second group agrees with the first on using repression in the initial phases, but believes it is necessary to reintroduce certain freedoms and some degree of electoral legitimation to maintain the system.[19] Such divides have played out elsewhere away from South America, including in Greece in 1967, Algeria in 1992, and, as described above, in Egypt following its 1952 coup.[20] By August 2013, major parts of the pro-coup factional map were clear for analysts and observers. Speaking about General Mohamed Farid el-Tohamy, the head of the General Intelligence apparatus, one Western diplomat told the *New York Times*: 'He was the most hardline, the most absolutely unreformed.'[21] Tohamy was a strong advocate of the August 2013 crackdown on Rabaa Square that yielded more than 1200 fatalities.[22] Within that faction, there is a strong belief that Field Marshal Tantawy was lenient in dealing with protestors. Therefore, the lesson learned from

Mubarak and Tantawy's days was to crack down harder. The SCAF understood that if it used Gaddafi- or Assad-like tactics following the coup, the likelihood of a NATO intervention to save the revolution (as in Libya) or any significant armed resistance (as in Syria) would be almost null. If parts of the latter scenario did materialise, however, the army and the police would have a superior capacity to utilise violence and win any armed conflict, as it did in Upper Egypt in the 1990s. It would also have the legitimacy to do so, due to the armed dimension of the conflict.

In August 2013, European Union envoy Bernardino León and Deputy U.S. Secretary of State William Burns led a mediation process aimed at containing and potentially resolving the post-coup crisis.[23] 'They told us that there are moderates in the government ... they meant Dr Mohamed El-Baradei,' said Dr Amr Darrag, the former minister of planning and international cooperation and an FJP politician.[24] The core of the plan was to release the heads of two political parties, FJP leader and former parliament speaker Saad El-Ketatny and Al-Wasat Party leader Abu al-Ila Mady, to negotiate a resolution with international guarantees in exchange for calling off the sit-ins in Rabaa and Al-Nahda Squares. On 6 August León phoned Darrag to tell him that the crisis was about to be resolved peacefully, but over the following week, the dialogist side, a weak minority within the military-appointed government, was successfully marginalised.[25] On 14 August, hours after the Rabaa crackdown, León said: 'We had a political plan that was on the table, that had been accepted by the [Muslim Brothers] [...] The SCAF could have taken this option. So all that has happened today was unnecessary.'[26] El-Baradei, the Nobel laureate who plotted the coup with the junta and served as a vice president in the post-coup government, but was marginalised after calling for limiting the repression after a third major crackdown against anti-coup activists on 27 July 2013, resigned the same day as the Rabaa massacre.[27]

It is important to note that the 'eradicator' and 'dialogist' categories—referred to above—by no means correspond to a military–civilian divide. In almost all of the aforementioned cases, including in Egypt, civilian figures have strongly supported and lobbied for 'eradication' policies, including journalists, politicians, clerics and other religious figures, businessmen, youth activists, and even 'human rights' activists.[28] One former human rights activist and academic called for turning mosques and schools into concentration camps for 750,000 alleged members of the ousted party.[29] In a conversation with a pro-dialogue brigadier-general who focuses on negotiations within the Egyptian armed forces, the author asked if he or other specialists within the military were consulted on how to resolve the crisis without further bloodshed. 'Our [pro-dialogue] opinions were not welcomed at that moment,' he replied.[30]

There is also a psychological explanation for the military's decision to perpetrate a coup and the subsequent repression of its opponents. This aspect of the military's decision-making is perhaps the least studied and is certainly harder to research. Since the 1952 coup, a superiority complex has steadily developed within the military. General Gamal Hammad, a member of the Free Officers and author of the first communiqué of the 1952 coup, mentioned that newly ruling officers had become 'crazy with power' once they gradually realised that their 'words have become laws ... and that they became the new masters of Egypt.'[31] Sixty years later, having a civilian declare himself the 'supreme commander of the armed forces' was unacceptable for many military commanders, not only because 'civilian' is believed to be an inferior category, but also because an *ikhwan* (Muslim Brother) is believed to have low status within that inferior category, and is usually associated with lower-middle class, rural migrants. 'Every time he [Morsi] says "I am the supreme commander of the armed forces," I want to hit him with something,' said an army officer in April 2013, three months before the coup.[32]

The effect of this superiority complex on behaviour and decision-making was reinforced by interactions between the SCAF and various civilian politicians and activists during the transition period. 'The SCAF would weigh them, analyse them, dissect them, understand what they want, what they crave [...] the [SCAF] member in charge of this was Abdel Fattah al-Sisi, the head of the military intelligence,' said a retired army major general.[33] 'They [civilian politicians] certainly did not earn their [SCAF] respect. By March 2011, the question became: how can we [military] handover the country to these people [civilian politicians]? [...] Ideas such as a "safe exit" for the SCAF were laughable. We [military] should give them a safe exit if we were generous, not the other way around [...] that was the thinking,' said the general. Far from 'handing over the country,' the issue of civilian oversight, even within a weak institutional arrangement, was psychologically problematic. This was reflected in General al-Sisi's comments while meeting with military officers: 'We haven't seen the end of this yet [...]. There is a coming parliament, it may ask questions, and I wonder what will we do about that [...]. We have to prepare to confront this without negatively affecting us.'[34] This pre-coup, forthcoming parliament would have probably had a significant percentage, if not a majority, of Islamist MPs.

The military's superiority complex is not limited to civilian politicians and civilian institutions. It is also directed at other armed institutions, such as the police force. Despite a dominant military dimension in the police force hierarchy, rankings, laws, organisational structures, training and curricula, the force is described in its bylaws and constitutions as a 'civilian entity' hence—in terms of prestige—it is seen as inferior to the military, especially after the January uprising. 'Military officers believe that they saved the Ministry of Interior from protesters, and protected police stations and prisons[...]. And without them the Ministry [of Interior] would have collapsed,' said a police officer attempting to explain the military's superiority complex over the police force following the January 2011 uprising.[35]

Arab Civil–Military Relations and Future of Democratisation in the Region

What happens in Egypt usually never stays in Egypt. The coup of 2013 was certainly a setback for balanced civil–military relations. Regionally, the message sent to the rest of the Arab-majority world, including Libya, Syria, Yemen and beyond, is that only arms guarantee political survival, not the constitution, not democratic institutions and certainly not votes. The supremacy of the armed over the elected created a political context where bullets are much more significant than ballots and laws as a method for attaining and remaining in power. Such a context, where political violence is legitimated in various forms and consistently proves effective, is less likely to lead to democratisation in any form. This may have significant implications on political behaviour and social attitudes towards political violence, thus affecting security matters, national reconciliations, and human rights.

No democratic transition is complete without targeting abuse and ending the impunity with which the armed forces can act. Effective and meaningful elected civilian control of both the armed forces and the security establishments is required. So, in addition to reconfiguring civil–military relations, a thorough process of reforming the security sector is essential. The reform process should entail changing the SOPs, training and education curricula, leadership and promotions criteria, as well as oversight and accountability by elected and judicial institutions. The violations of the security sector, and a lack of accountability in addressing such violations, have been major contributors to sparking and sustaining armed radicalisation. Jihadism and Takfirism were both born in Egyptian political prisons in the 1960s, where torture ranged from a systematic daily practice in some periods to a selective-but-widespread practice in others—not that different from today's Egypt.[36]

Regarding civil–military relations, the aforementioned decision-making frames are not mutually exclusive and can sometimes be applied in combination. Overall, within a domestic framework, they help explain why the military leadership decided to pursue the risky course of carrying out a coup followed by a crackdown in its aftermath. But there were other facilitating factors that assisted the decision-making processes. Extreme political polarisation between pro-change forces (whether reformists or revolutionaries) has led to an increased reliance on the military as an 'arbiter' and a 'saviour'. Political polarisation *per se* should not lead directly to military dominance. The diversity in the political spectrum, the heated debates, the intense arguments and the general difference of opinion should be celebrated as gains of the pro-democracy uprisings. This freedom of opinion and expression should be the goal for other Arab-majority countries. However, some of the ramifications of such polarisation have negatively affected civil–military relations. One of the consequences of the extreme polarisation is the politicisation of the military and the security services by rival politicians. On talk-shows, political figures would call for security sector reform and civilian control to be implemented and for police/military brutality to end. At the same time, the very same political figures would praise generals known for their support of brutal tactics, when they crackdown on their political rivals. As shown in other comparative cases, the unity of political forces on the very particular demands of de-politicising the military and civilian control of the armed forces is key for the success of a democratic transition. And the polarisation works directly against such unity of demands.

Weak democratic institutions that failed to contain the political polarisation and limit the political conflict to the institutional realm has been another factor that helped the military to stage the coup. In addition to the weak mandate of these institutions, limited knowledge and experience of civil–military relations and security sector reform requirements among stakeholders has been an additional source of weakness. The lower house of the parliament (Egypt's People's Assembly), elected following the January 2011 uprising, was dissolved by the SCAF following a Constitutional Court verdict that deemed parts of the electoral law unconstitutional in June 2012. The Upper House (Consultative Council) was dissolved following the military coup of July 2013. What was clear in the dissolved lower-house and upper-house is the big gap between the revolutionary demands of eradicating torture, ending impunity and reflecting transparency and the limited knowledge of how to translate such demands into policies and procedures of security sector reform.[37] A general understanding of such limitations in Tunisia, for example, led the government and the Ministry of Interior to collaborate with an international organisation and several security sector reform experts as early as July 2011.[38] In Egypt, similar attempts were foiled; most notably an attempt by the presidential establishment in the fall of 2013, that sought international assistance.

A final point: the impact of regional and international sponsors on the military's decision-making is significant. Although the chapter did not analyse and assess such an impact, the limited support for democratic control of the armed forces among democracies was negligible compared to the regional support for authoritarianism. This had some similarities with the eighteenth-century European monarchies rallying to put an end to the French Revolution, which challenged a dominant regional status quo. In an attempt to defend the regional status quo, whose main feature is authoritarianism, several regional actors did not perceive a balance in civil–military relations and security sector reform processes, as well as any meaningful democratisation process, as beneficial to their interests; more as threats to their regimes' security and stability. As a result, most of the pro-status quo forces in Egypt and other Arab-majority uprising countries had strong, wealthy and aggressive regional backers. This result has bolstered their stances, morally, logistically, financially as well as by intensive propaganda campaigns of deception and misinformation. On the other hand, most western and regional democracies were hesitant to commit or to assist in a time-consuming, resource-draining, no-holds-barred conflict for civilian control of armed forces. This stance differed from the support granted to Eastern European transitions during the 'third wave' of democratisation, and thus weakened most of pro-change and pro-reform Arab forces.

4

MILITARIES AND DEMOCRACY
IN THE MIDDLE EAST

TOO MUCH AND TOO LITTLE

Steven A. Cook

Contrary to expectations at the time, the spontaneous displays of people power that brought down long-standing autocrats around the Middle East in 2010 and 2011 did not necessarily create more advantageous environments for the emergence of democratic polities. In retrospect, the uprisings in the Arab world were a triumph of democratic ideas at the expense of democrats and democracy. This chapter uses an historical institutionalist approach to identify why transitions were thwarted in Egypt and Turkey and to rethink the conditions, modalities, and political processes of democratic change. It also briefly explores the Libyan experience, which is quite different from the other two cases.

At different times in the last three decades, observers have posited that each of Egypt, Turkey, and Libya was well positioned to make transitions to democracy. In the late 1980s and early 1990s, a number of analysts argued that Egypt's democratisation was manifest in judicial decisions that declared electoral laws unconstitutional, broader (though still circumscribed) press freedoms, and the growth of civil society. Turkey's October 2004 invitation to begin European Union membership talks was believed to be both an indication and driver of the consolidation of Turkish democracy. After Libyan leader Muammar Gaddafi's fall, some within the policy community speculated that because Gaddafi left few meaningful national, political, and social institutions, Libya's transition to democracy might be easier than Egypt's, for example, where the institutions of the old order remained. To varying degrees, democratisation in all three cases proved to be more apparent than real. Egypt remained, and continues to be stuck in, an authoritarian political system; Turkey has become a case study in the reversal of democratic reforms; and Libya is disintegrating. Across these three different settings, structural realities and institutional legacies conspired to impede democratic political development. In each of them the military, or legacies of military domination, played an important role to thwart democratic transitions.

Egypt: To Rule But Not Govern

Egypt is, of course, the easy case. Even before former president Hosni Mubarak fell there was ample reason to believe that a military intervention would not lead to a democratic transition.[1] Lost in much of the early exhilaration surrounding the 25 January uprising is the fact that Egypt's senior commanders were among the primary beneficiaries of the political order against which Egyptians were protesting.[2] They are the direct descendants of the Free Officers who, through trial and error, 'discovered' a set of authoritarian institutions—rules, laws, decrees, and regulations—that resolved myriad internal and external political problems in the armed forces' favour.

For these reasons alone it should have been clear that the military would likely be spoilers of a democratic transition. The officers' alignment with what they called the 'legitimate demands of the people' served a number of purposes, none of which were in the service of democracy. First, it shielded the Ministry of Defence from the ire and the demands of the people packing Egypt's streets. This proved to be spectacularly successful as most Egyptians seemed to accept without reservation the idea that the military was prepared to forge a more open, just, and democratic society. Second, when the military obliged protestors demanding that Mubarak leave, they resolved a political and economic problem represented by the former president's second son, Gamal. Although Mubarak never indicated that his son would succeed him, pushing the president from office rendered the possibility of Gamal's succession moot. Having never served in the armed forces, Gamal's succession would have severed a critical informal institutional link between the military command and the presidency that was a channel for the officer corps' influence and prestige. Third, it gave the military the opportunity to dramatically reduce the standing of the business–political class that had extended its influence in the late Mubarak period. These crony capitalists had profited from their proximity to Gamal and, importantly, the neoliberal economic reforms with which this class had become associated and so posed a potential threat to the officers' statist worldview and thus the military's own economic interests. As a result, it seemed clear from the time the military deployed its forces to Tahrir Square on 28 January 2011, that the officer corps was most interested in preserving the special status with which it had endowed itself in the aftermath of the June 1967 war—ruling Egypt without the burden of governing it.

Other scholars have argued that the uprising also provided an opportunity for the military to alter the balance of power in the political system that they claim had tipped in favour of the Ministry of Interior and the police in the late Mubarak period.[3] Mubarak's unhappy coexistence with the charismatic Field Marshal Abdel Halim Abu Ghazala, whom he retired (along with seventy other officers) in April 1989, created a certain amount of distrust of the officer corps, prompting Mubarak to build up the police. Consequently, by the time the 25 January uprising erupted, the Ministry of Interior commanded various forces from the police to the paramilitary Central Security Forces and State Security Investigations Service, all of which were about 2 million strong.

There are compelling aspects to this narrative, especially the size of Egypt's internal security forces during the late Mubarak period, which were reportedly significantly larger than the manpower of the armed forces.[4] Yet the analysis overlooks a number of factors that significantly weaken the idea that the military was leveraging the uprising to reestablish itself as the premier power centre in the Egyptian system. First, although budgets and manpower offer insight into the way the system worked in the later Mubarak period, they do not provide as clear a picture of the relative positions of the military and the Ministry of Interior as analysts might suggest. It is important to recognise that securing Egypt's streets is a significant task in a country of approximately 91 million, and one that the officer corps regards as beneath it—especially in comparison to the far more noble mission of defending the nation. Against this backdrop, it is not at all clear that the senior command was concerned about the size of the Ministry of Interior, though it no doubt coveted the financial resources devoted to the police. Second, the military had reminded all the relevant political actors that it was the regime's centre of power on a number of occasions in the past when the police faltered, specifically during the 1977 bread riots and when the military was deployed to put down rioting troopers from the Ministry of Interior's own Central Security Forces in 1986. These were, of course, spectacular events that happened decades ago, but they reinforce the often cited (and somewhat clichéd) idea that the military is the 'backbone of the regime'. In a more routine way, although the military removed itself from the day-to-day governance of the country after the 1967 defeat, its personnel remained important to the staffing and operations of important agencies like the General Intelligence Service and the presidency.[5] Third, although no one is quite sure of the extent of the military's stake in the economy—estimates range from 5 to 65 per cent—it is clear that the Ministry of Defence is an important economic actor.[6] With interests in real estate, security, aviation services, light manufacturing, weapons productions, processed foods, consumer goods, and infrastructure development, the military's economic activities render the officers significant political actors. Fourth, despite the authoritarian nature of the Egyptian political system, public opinion has always mattered in important, though generally limited, ways. Egypt's authoritarian order, like many others, featured a circumscribed pluralism and relatively autonomous institutions within the overall contours of a nondemocratic system.[7] The presence of oppositions, including anti-regime groups, produced a kind of politics that could never occur in totalitarian orders, but was limited in comparison to democracies. Thus, the nationalist mythology surrounding the Egyptian Armed Forces and the officer corps' insistence that it be kept at a distance from maintaining the security of Egypt's streets contributed to the military's high public esteem in comparison to the Ministry of Interior, which was (and remains) widely despised. Under these circumstances, even in Egypt's highly circumscribed political environment, the police generals may have possessed robust means of coercion and the political authority to employ it, but they nevertheless did not wield the kind of prestige and ultimate authority of the military. Finally, if the buildup of the Ministry of Interior was intended to 'coup proof' Mubarak's rule, it did not work.[8] By stepping into politics at a moment of crisis and removing Mubarak in what was essentially a coup, the military underscored that it was what it had been all along—the locus of power in Egypt's political system.

In the abstract, the objectives of the Supreme Council of the Armed Forces (SCAF) on 12 February 2011—the day after the officers pushed

Mubarak from power—were strikingly similar to those they had on 24 January 2011, the day before the uprising: ensuring stability, maintaining the Ministry of Defence's economic prerogatives, and most importantly, preserving the military's position as the source of power, authority, and prestige in the political system.

In the eighteen months between Mubarak's fall and Mohamed Morsi's inauguration, the officer corps was forced to take responsibility for the day-to-day administration of the country in order to ensure these interests. This violated the military's four-decades-long guiding principle of ruling Egypt without governing it, which underscored for the officers the great risk the military's participation in the governance of the country posed to themselves, the armed forces, as a coherent organisation, and to the regime. The SCAF thus accepted the burdens and risks of governance with the intention of quickly negotiating political and economic guarantees that would allow the commanders to return to the barracks and shield themselves from the vicissitudes of politics. After pushing out Mubarak's last prime minister, Ahmed Shafiq, and stacking interim governments with largely secondary figures from the discredited National Democratic Party, the officers began talks with various groups and individuals in search of an accommodation that would serve their interests. These interlocutors included those commonly known as 'the revolution'; politically acceptable elder statesmen, such as the former secretary-general of the Arab League and Mubarak's long-standing foreign minister, Amr Moussa; the former director of the International Atomic Energy Agency, Mohamed El-Baradei, who had been a vocal and active opponent of Mubarak; a variety of intellectuals; and, of course, the Muslim Brotherhood.

These negotiations proved to be extraordinarily difficult given the pressures, demands, and often contradictory signals that Egyptian society brought to bear on both the military and its interlocutors. The officers of the SCAF were also confronted with the fact that none of the groups with whom it was talking were willing to accept the military's terms for the handover of power. In time, the officers determined that an accommodation with elites was unlikely and focused its attention on what they believed to be Egypt's 'silent majority', reinforcing among average Egyptians the military's post-Mubarak narrative about being 'one hand with the people' and 'preparing the country for democracy.' Critical to this effort was holding parliamentary elections, even though a variety of activist and revolutionary groups were demanding a delay. When those elections took place between November 2011 and January 2012, the silent majority produced a parliamentary plurality for the Muslim

Brotherhood's Freedom and Justice Party. The subsequent presidential election brought the Brotherhood's Mohamed Morsi to power.

Despite the SCAF's previous efforts to find some type of accommodation with the organisation, the Brotherhood's domination of the executive and legislature were outcomes that the SCAF looked upon unfavourably. On the eve of Morsi's election, the SCAF announced that all decisions related to defence and national security were solely the province of the Ministry of Defence. Egypt's military had long been autonomous, but prior to the post-Mubarak period it never had to act to assert its interests, which Mubarak secured. The announcement gutting the formal prerogatives of the Egyptian presidency was not the first time the SCAF, unsure about Egypt's political trajectory and the durability of the informal institutions that contributed to the military's position, sought to clarify its privileges and rights. In November 2011, the so-called Selmi Document, which among other powers included the authority to veto aspects of the proposed constitution and dismiss the constituent assembly charged with drafting it, required that the constitution give the Ministry of Defence sole responsibility for the military budget, making it exempt from parliamentary oversight. The military's control over a budget that was to be shielded from public view was not an innovation. This was the prevailing practice in Egypt, despite the legislature's formal oversight powers over all of the state's institutions, including the military. Yet because no one ever questioned the military, there was no real oversight in practice. The Selmi Document proposed institutionalising the military's autonomy formally in a constitution that was supposed to be the founding document of a new democracy. This proved to be politically untenable, contributing to major street demonstrations in late 2011 that turned violent. Upon Morsi's election, however, the high command sought to reinforce its predominance on these issues by fiat with the clear expectation that the military's autonomy would be enshrined in a new constitution.

The most dramatic event of the early post-Mubarak era was, of course, the 3 July 2013 coup d'état that brought Morsi's tenure to a premature end. The military intervention, made possible by widespread public opposition to Morsi, represented an effort that included not just the officers but also the General Intelligence Service, the Ministry of Interior, and the judiciary to restore what these groups believe to be the 'natural order' in Egypt. Consequently, in the aftermath of the intervention, Major General Abdel Fattah al-Sisi—now president—and his civilian collaborators have sought to reengineer Egypt's political institutions to ensure that the 25 January uprising, its ensuing crises, and the accumulation of power by anti-system parties cannot happen again. Since al-Sisi came to power, the Egyptian government has passed, proposed, or amended laws that restrict demonstrations; increase surveillance on non-governmental organisations; ban university students, faculty, and staff from engaging in political activity; expand the penalties for receiving funding from a foreign government; broaden the definition of what it means to destabilise the country and undermine its national interests; expand the jurisdiction of military courts; render reporting on the military a crime; and limit due process. In addition, the Brotherhood's political party was dissolved and affiliated groups along with secular opposition movements and individual activists were banned or jailed under the provisions of an overly broad antiterrorism law. Finally, although Egypt's 2014 constitution endows Egyptians with important political and civil rights, these rights are restricted through other regulations, rules, laws, and decrees. Overall, the path dependencies that these changes produce will have a profound impact on Egypt's political trajectory, presaging an authoritarian future.

The Turkish Model?

The return of Egypt's military to politics in 2011 and its ouster of two presidents in eighteen months have renewed comparisions to the Turkish military, which brought four governments to an end through coups d'état in 1960, 1971, 1980, and 1997. For all of the analytic attention paid to the Turkish military—including comparisons with its Egyptian counterpart—observers have consistently confused the officer corps' interventions with power.[9] In fact, the military's four coups and countless other non-coup intrusions into politics indicates not strength, but rather the relative weakness and fragility of Turkey's military-dominated political system.[10] Had Kemalism—a worldview associated with the Turkish republic's founder, Mustafa Kemal, or Atatürk as he is commonly known—which is hostile to pluralism and inclusivity, become embedded in Turkish society in a way that made it common sense, there would have been little need for military surveillance and intervention in the political arena. The fact that Turks refused to accept the drab political conformity that Kemalism required forced the military to leverage democratic and non-democratic political institutions to establish political control.

With each coup beginning in 1971, Turkey's officers oversaw the reengineering and renovation of political institutions in ways that they believed would make future interventions unnecessary. Thus, the so-called 'coup by memorandum' of 12 March 1971, demanded that the Grand National Assembly amend the more liberal aspects of the 1961 constitution that were deemed to be a threat to social cohesion. After the violence between leftist and rightist political groups in the second half of the 1970s, that killed between 4,500 and 5,000 people, forced the military to step into the political system, the ruling National Security Council supervised the writing of a constitution that was geared more toward protecting the Kemalist system and the Turkish state than ensuring individual liberties. Then, during Turkey's first experiment with Islamist political power, the military issued National Security Decision 406, which is referred to as the 28 February Process (for the date of the decision). In it the military demanded that the coalition government, under the leadership of the Islamist Welfare Party's Necmettin Erbakan, modify laws to ensure Turkey's secular system; establish greater state control over religious education; prohibit the use of religious facilities for political purposes; control media groups critical of the military; prohibit military officers that had been purged for anti-secular activities from employment in the bureaucracy; prevent 'extremist infiltration' into the armed forces, universities, judiciary, and bureaucracy; ensure that individuals found to be in violation of the Law on Political Parties, the penal code, and the Law on Municipalities be punished; and prevent communal as opposed to governmental solutions to Turkey's political problems.[11] Erbakan's failure to implement the military's demands resulted in what is known as the 'Blank Coup'—because no tanks or troops were deployed into Turkey's streets—that pushed Erbakan from office in June 1997. The 28 February Process, previous coups, and the routine military interventions in a broad range of areas beyond the military's professional competence exemplified how Turkey's national security state was a spoiler. The Welfare Party–led government of the mid-1990s was not particularly competent, but it came to power legally. The military's effort to undermine Turkey's democratic practices (again) was based on the General Staff's calculations that even if voters turned Erbakan and the Welfare Party from power in the elections scheduled for April 1999, the party would have had enough time to seed the bureaucracy with party activists who could alter the Kemalist system from within.

Despite the coup and pressure on subsequent governments to implement the 28 February Process, the Welfare Party's demise did not end Islamist political activity in Turkey. In August 2001, a younger generation of Islamists founded the Justice and Development Party (AKP). A little more than a year later, the party came to power with 34.3 per cent of the popular vote, which, due to the particularities of the Turkish electoral law, gave the new party an absolute majority in the 550-seat parliament. The party's decidely non-Kemalist vision of Turkey's future, which included a commitment to European Union membership, hastened the demise of the military-dominated state. The simultaneous political reforms to harmonise the Turkish political system with the European Union's Copenhagen criteria led analysts to conclude that the Turkish officer corps had been forced to remain in the barracks and, more importantly, their channels of political influence had been closed, and that Turkey was making a transition to democracy. The former proved accurate, but the latter is far more problematic given the illiberal trajectory in Turkish politics today.

Although the military has largely been an observer of Turkish politics for the better part of the last decade, the legacies of the military's domination have created a set of practices and norms that have helped make the rollback of liberal political reforms possible. The four coups between 1960 and 1997 were, of course, the most dramatic examples of the military's expansive role in politics, but the analytic focus on them obscures how the military sought to ensure the survival of the Kemalist regime through the routine manipulation of institutions.[12] The AKP's ongoing effort to subordinate the General Staff and intimidate traditional elites in the service of a new political order has required a similar kind of instrumentalisation or disregard for the institutions of the Turkish state.

That story begins with the AKP's first term, which lasted from 2002 through 2007. In those days pragmatism and consensus marked Turkish politics. There were controversies, of course, but then Prime Minister Recep Tayyip Erdoğan seemed determined not to do anything that would unnecessarily aggravate opponents and jeopardise his ambitious agenda. The first outward signs that something was amiss—that the AKP and others sought to use the institutions of the state as well as circumvent them—came with the Ergenekon conspiracy, an alleged plot between military officers, intelligence operatives, and organised crime figures to overthrow the government. After Ergenekon came the Sledgehammer investigation in 2010, which led to the arrest and trial of large numbers of senior military commanders suspected of trying to bring down the government. In time it came to light that significant portions of the evidence in both cases were flimsy or even fabricated. Ergenekon, in particular, became a conspiracy within a conspiracy, used to prosecute people who could very well have been plotting to overthrow the elected government as well as outspoken but otherwise peaceful critics of the

AKP. Also a target were those who criticised the party's allies at the time, the followers of Fethullah Gülen—a Turkish cleric in self-imposed exile in the United States—who were heavily represented in the Turkish bureaucracy, particularly among the police and prosecutors. The armed forces had previously screened out officers with Islamist sympathies, but during the AKP era they—including Gülenists—were permitted to advance through the ranks.

The Ergenekon and Sledgehammer cases may have reduced the role of the Turkish armed forces in politics, but it hardly resolved the problem of authoritarian politics in Turkey. In the prosecutors' apparent zeal to raze Turkey's national security state, they took license with the rule of law. Their case failed to meet even minimum legal standards and became little more than a witch hunt. Turkey is not unique in this regard, of course, but the Ergenekon and Sledgehammer episodes were clearly as much about using the institutions of the state for retribution and political intimidation as they were about seeking justice for wrongdoing. The September 2010 referendum on constitutional amendments similarly highlighted the way in which the AKP has sought to leverage the country's legal institutions in the service of the party's political ends. The vote, which was trumpeted as another step in the AKP's drive to forge a more democratic Turkey, included a little more than two dozen changes, among which were innocuous provisions for the protection of children's rights; freedom of residence and movement; and the right to petition, acquire information, and appeal. At the heart of the referendum, though, was an effort to alter the political complexion of a judiciary that had proved hostile to the AKP, finding in 2008 that the party was a 'center of anti-secular activity', though the Constitutional Court fell one vote shy of ordering the closure of the AKP. At an abstract level, the party sought to engineer or 'update' the rules, regulations, and decrees concerning the judiciary in a manner similar to the way senior commanders had long sought to protect the Kemalist system and themselves from political challenges.

Few objective observers of Turkish politics would argue that Turkey's judicial system is not in need of reform. The courts do not meet international standards and the judiciary has been a bastion of Kemalism. The AKP's proposed constitutional amendments to revamp the judicial system did little to resolve either problem, however. Rather, they gave the government greater ability to appoint new judges and fill vacancies with justices whose views align with those of the AKP. Critics may argue that court packing is hardly unique to Turkey. In the United States, President Franklin D. Roosevelt attempted to pack the Supreme Court in order to ensure the integrity of the

New Deal. Yet the Turkish and American cases are hardly comparable. Erdoğan's thinly veiled effort to use the courts to empower the AKP is hardly the equivalent of Roosevelt's effort to confront the massive social dislocation of the Great Depression.

Beyond altering the ideological complexion of the courts, the Turkish leadership has sought to leverage Turkey's need for a new constitution to its own political ends. The 1982 constitution, which was written at the behest of the military junta that took over the country in 1980, is not democratic, despite the many amendments to it. Turks have long acknowledged that the country should have a civil constitution geared toward safeguarding citizens' rights rather than protecting the state from citizens. In October 2011, Erdoğan announced with much fanfare that Turkey would get that new constitution within a year. But, unsurprisingly, the twelve-month timeline proved to be too ambitious. Constitution drafting is never easy; although the final document ultimately reflects the interests of those who hold power, they are also the product of heated political struggle and compromise. As a result of what was turning out to be a long delay, in the spring of 2013, Erdoğan floated the idea of going around the commission charged with drafting the constitution and taking the AKP's own version directly to the people in a referendum.

Although Erdoğan has never offered details of the changes he seeks in the powers of the presidency, he and other Turkish leaders clearly envision a greatly expanded and powerful role for the Turkish president under a new constitution. After the Gezi Park protests in the spring and summer of 2013, it became clear that what Turks have come to refer to as an 'executive presidency' was too much weight for the Turkish political system to bear. The AKP let the entire constitutional enterprise die for the moment. Since becoming president in August 2014, however, Erdoğan has once again taken up the issue. Given the fact that Turkey's opposition parties remain steadfastly opposed to the executive presidency, Erdoğan employed both his political skills and the political institutions of the state to undermine government coalition talks after the AKP lost its parliamentary majority in June 2015. In a new round of elections the following November, the AKP won almost 50 per cent of the vote and the right to rule without other parties. Still, the party remained thirteen seats short of the 330 needed in Turkey's 550-seat parliament to bring a draft constitution directly to the Turkish people through a referendum. Erdoğan was in the process of using Turkey's anti-terrorism measures to weaken the Kurdish-based People's Democratic Party and employing a variety of political maneuvers to destabilise the Nationalist

Movement Party in order to push the AKP's total above the 330-seat threshold when elements of the Turkish armed forces sought to overthrow the government in mid-July 2016. The coup failed and, in its aftermath, Erdoğan undertook a wide-ranging purge of the officer corps and other parts of the bureaucracy. Then, in April 2017, instead of writing a new constitution the government held a referendum on eighteen proposed constitutional changes that greatly enhanced the power of the presidency. The 'Yes' vote won narrowly and controversially, but those who put forth credible claims of fraud had no redress once Turkey's Supreme Election Council certified that 51.3 per cent of voters approved of the amendments.

If the Ergenekon and Sledgehammer cases, as well as the September 2010 and April 2017 referenda, showcase how Turkey's political leaders have sought to use democratic political institutions for their own non-democratic ends, the spectacular corruption scandal that shook the country in the winter and spring of 2014 highlights the willingness of the AKP to go beyond the bounds of democratic institutions to achieve its goals. Confronted with mounting corruption charges, Erdoğan and his party openly interfered with the investigation. Within a week of the initial police raids on high-profile, AKP-affiliated businessmen, politicians, and their kin, Erdoğan sacked more than fifty police commanders and investigators. He politicised the investigation, undermined the constitutional prerogatives of the police and prosecutors, and ensured that his core constituency would never accept the outcome of the inquiry because of their wariness of foreign meddling. In addition, by floating the idea of freeing military officers under the pretence of prosecutorial misconduct, at the time Erdoğan raised the prospect that the Turkish military could once again play a role in politics, this time in collaboration with the AKP. This would violate both a set of norms and formal institutions concerned with the proper place of the military in a democracy that Erdoğan and his colleagues within the party have worked hard to embed in the Turkish political system during the past decade. None of this mattered to Erdoğan and to party leaders, whose fealty to democratic change extends only insofar as it advances their interests. Confronted with the most serious political threat of the AKP era until 2016's failed coup, the party's leaders have demonstrated a total disregard for the rule of law and Turkey's existing democratic institutions.

The Ergenekon and Sledgehammer cases and the constitutional changes tailored specifically to the needs of the AKP and Erdoğan are contemporary analogues of the Turkish armed forces' various constitutional innovations;

bans on politicians; closure of political parties; and overly broad interpretation of rules, regulations, and decrees, which sometimes means just ignoring
them to ensure the integrity of the Kemalist system. Clearly, the pattern of
politics that the military established through its interventions and surveillance of the political system since the 1960s has provided even Turkey's for-
merly anti-system elites with a model to ensure their dominance of the
political arena.

Libya's Militias

If Egypt and Turkey are struggling with the return of military domination or
the powerful legacies of the officers' influence, Libya lacks military structures
that, in a counterintuitive way, might have arrested the country's plunge into
militia warfare and disintegration. Muammar Gaddafi left Libya with little in
the way of formal institutions, which, at one time, some analysts posited to be
a potential advantage in a transition to democracy, but has turned out to be
rather devastating for Libyan society.[13] Instead of the blank slate on which to
build a new society, the lack of formal institutions combined with informal
ones that had long been far more important to shaping the behavior and
expectations of Libyans had a devastating impact on post-Gaddafi Libya.
Tribal and regional affiliations have long been important to Libyans as sources
of support and security. In the chaos and violence that engulfed Libya beginning in February 2011, they became even more critical in these spheres. And
when Gaddafi's Jamahiriyya finally collapsed the following summer, when the
longtime leader was chased from Tripoli, various tribal and regional militias
pursued their own interests, regardless of whatever political process transitional authorities and subsequent governments sought to follow. As such,
Misratan and Zintani militias, as well as the army that General Khalifa Haftar
raised without the Tripoli government's knowledge, became central actors in
Libya's fragmentation. Throughout the period immediately following
Gaddafi's fall, efforts to reestablish national military structures and absorb
militias within them failed because transitional governments lacked the coercive capacity to impose their will on competing groups. Militiamen accepted
payments from the government but pursued their own interests, which did
not align with those of leaders in Tripoli. A similar fate has befallen the
Government of National Accord (GNA), which the United Nations helped
establish in late 2015. There are forces that are loyal to the GNA, but Haftar
controls what he and his supporters call the Libyan National Army. Haftar has

little chance of establishing himself as Libya's new leader, but as long as he and his military exist it will be difficult for any one government in Tripoli to assert its control over the country.

Libya's fragmentation raises a number of important questions about militaries in the transition process. There is an analytic bias in the literature concerning the obtacles that militaries pose to democratic change, but there is good reason for this. The impact of the military and the institutions derived from military domination in Egypt and Turkey have had profound impacts on the durability of authoritarianism in those countries. Yet if the Egyptians and Turks have had too much military, the Libyans have not had enough. With no institutions and no military in any meaningful sense of the term, there was no well-developed officer corps to provide coherence and security in the post-Gaddafi period. Having come to power via a coup d'état in 1969, Gaddafi spent the next four decades ensuring that he would not fall victim to the same fate. As a result, the officer corps was weakened and divided in favour of a combination of separate intelligence organisations whose chiefs reported directly to Gaddafi, a military that was split along regional and tribal lines with no means of independent coordination, and praetorian guard-like mercenaries. It was thus not surprising that the Libyan military—a force of anywhere between 50,000 and 100,000—experienced a wave of defections and proved to be an ineffective fighting force. The defence of Gaddafi, his family, and the political order he created was left to hired soldiers from sub-Saharan countries. Libya's fragmentation reflects the problems of the tribal-sectarian model of armed forces (see Omar Ashour's contribution to this volume).

Conclusion

For good reason, the analytic community is wary of a military role in transitional politics. The subordination of officers to civilians provides a more favourable environment for the development of democracy, though this is hardly a sufficient condition. Turkey is, of course, a prime example of civilian control of the military in a non-democracy. Still, observers risk overemphasising the Egyptian case, which is at one end of a spectrum, in their concerns about the role of the officer corps after uprisings and revolutions. For all of the problems associated with a given military's intervention in politics, the officer corps can play an important role in providing a sense of security, coherence, and organisation in uncertain and unstable political environments. The challenge is less about getting the officers back into the barracks—the place they would most like to be—after the immediate crisis has passed, and more to do with ensuring that they do not interfere in the political process from there. The ideal type is the professional officer corps that Samuel Huntington theorised in his study of civil–military relations in the United States—a military establishment in which the commanders remain in the barracks and respect the institutions of the state, but also an officer corps that is institutionalised and autonomous unto itself.[14] Huntington's work has been a point of departure and criticism for civil–military relations specialists interested in Middle Eastern militaries.

The Arab military that likely comes closest to Huntington's ideal type is Tunisia, whose military officers rescued the country from chaos in January 2011 and subsequently demonstrated a desire to remain apolitical. In Filiu's framework, Tunisia's "non-Mamluk" status has made its post-uprising success possible, especially in comparison to those countries in which modern Mamluks have appropriated the state, notably Egypt, Syria, Algeria, and Yemen. Yet analysts should be cautious. Very little is actually known about the Tunisian military other than the fact that its officers were not particularly privileged during Habib Bourguiba's presidency or under Zine el-Abidine Ben Ali, that it is small by regional standards, and that Tunisia's civilian leaders have demonstrated little interest in the armed forces. It may very well be that the Tunisian military, like the country it defends, is an outlier in the region as a provider of security that is also not a democratic spoiler.

Given the institutional legacies and vested interests in Egypt and Turkey as well as other cases including Syria and Algeria, it is difficult to discern how the Tunisian experience can be replicated. That the Egyptian and Turkish cases clearly indicate that the military capacity to spoil democratic transitions is well developed, even after there is a return to the barracks, is not especially new or even interesting. The solution in these cases is not merely the subordination of the officers to civilians or the institutions of the state, but the far more difficult challenge of altering the military's worldview according to which it is a vanguard of modernisation and the officer corps is endowed with unique responsibilities beyond defending the country. This is a long-term process that begins with a fundamental alteration to the way in which military officers are educated and socialised, which is why, for example, despite the Turkish officer corps' recent quiescence, civil–military relations there remain problematic. Despite the abolition of aspects of the military's internal service codes, which gave the officers a responsibility to intervene in politics when they saw fit, the military remains committed to Kemalist principles.

Recognising that they have no current option, the officers have chosen to wait out Erdoğan and have at times subtly resisted the government on matters important to the ruling party. In Egypt, the military's return to politics has, at least for now, reinforced both the Ministry of Defence's autonomy and the commanders' narrative about the centrality of the military in Egypt. The ideational aspect of the military's approach is an issue with which a variety of analysts have grappled given the manner in which it encourages militaries to be democratic spoilers, but there is less analytic traction on how a shift can take place. Of course, in Chile, a pacted transition was successful in altering the officer corps' views over the long term, which helped facilitate the country's return to democracy. Yet the officer corps needs to be willing to allow this change to take place, an element that is missing in the Middle East. For these reasons, militaries in the region are likely to continue to be spoilers of democratic transitions.

5

MODERN MAMLUKS
AND ARAB COUNTER-REVOLUTION

Jean-Pierre Filiu

The democratic uprising that shook the Arab world in the winter of 2011 should not be caricatured as a seasonal 'spring', to be followed by an inevitable 'autumn', whether Islamist or authoritarian. It should rather be studied against the backdrop of a two-centuries long history, the history of the Arab Renaissance, or Nahda, which according to Arab historians began with the French expedition into Egypt in 1798–99.

What Albert Hourani described as the 'liberal age' of the Arab world (1798–1939) ended with the gradual accession of the former Arab colonies to sovereign independence.[1] The collective emancipation of the Arab people was then frustrated by various cliques that quite literally 'hijacked' those national independences. This is why I have elsewhere proposed that we should describe the 2011 protest wave as an 'Arab revolution' aimed at bringing the popular struggle for self-determination at last to a successful conclusion.[2]

Seven years into this 'revolution', it appears that only Tunisia's political transition has lived up to such expectations. This has been discussed by my colleagues in fascinating and compelling ways, most notably in comparisons between the parallel evolutions of post–Ben Ali Tunisia and post-Mubarak Egypt. They have advanced detailed arguments as to why the democratic process engineered in Tunisia derailed in Egypt, despite the ousting of the dictators in the two countries in January and February of 2011.

I will attempt in this chapter to add a comparative historical dimension to this perspective by positing the notion of 'modern Mamluks'. I will try to explain how these modern Mamluks emerged after the Arab independences and how they have progressively taken control of Egypt, Syria, Algeria and Yemen. The fact that Egypt is 'Mamluk-run' will prove to play a major role in the failure of the democratic experience, compared to its success in 'non-Mamluk' Tunisia. My approach is therefore distinct from both the focus on Egypt in Omar Ashour's chapter in this volume and the comparative studies of the Egyptian, Turkish and Libyan cases in Steven Cook's contribution.

Three Historical Cycles

My hypothesis is based on the coexistence of three historical cycles, whose dynamics and counter-dynamics impact the current crisis. The long-term Nahda cycle began in 1798 and is still open-ended, as the goals set by the Arab Renaissance's main contributors—the emancipation of the nation or of the individual in the Arab world—are far from accomplished.

The Nahda was a movement encompassing the entire Arab world, with the notable exception of central Arabia, where Wahhabism developed upon the 1744 'pact' between the Saud family and Ibn Abd al-Wahhab, first as a state-building ideology, and then later as a political tool directed against the Nahda and legitimizing jihad against fellow Arabs and fellow Muslims. The Nahda was never a structured and coherent movement, since deeply different trends coexisted in this collective endeavor to assert Arab identity against both Ottoman rule and Western imperialism. (This ambivalent nature stems from the initial shock of the 1798 French expedition, which was both a military aggression on an Arab country and a civilisational challenge to the Istanbul-led order).

Two main political currents can be identified within the Nahda mainstream. There was, however, no clear-cut boundary between the two, which might conveniently be labeled 'Islamist' and 'Nationalist', though these terms were not relevant in the nineteenth-century political lexicon. The 'Islamist' blamed the 'Turkish' caliphate for most of the decadence in the Muslim world, and vowed that only a rejuvenated and Arab-led community could uphold the values of Islam and live up to its message. The 'Nationalist' turned against the European invaders the very tools of nationalism they were using for their own advancement: one people, with one language, on one land. This promotion of Arab culture as a vehicle for a collective affirmation relied heavily on the contribution of Middle East Christians, especially in 'Greater Syria'.

Modernising dynasties that had achieved autonomy from the Ottoman Empire led the top–down Nahda in Tunisia and Egypt. In both cases, an emphasis on land and tax reform substantiated the emerging notion of public interest (*maslaha*). And, in both cases, these Renaissance dynamics were crushed by the Western invasion: by the French protectorate over Tunisia in 1881, and by the British occupation of Egypt in 1882. During the First World War, Sharif Hussein ibn Ali, the Hashemite governor of Mecca and Medina, became a champion of Arab rights. The 'Nationalist' longed for the 'Arab kingdom' that the British had in 1916 promised Hussein they would establish after the Ottoman defeat. And the 'Islamist' considered that this scion of the Prophet Muhammad had a far more legitimate title to the caliphate than the ruling Turkish sultan. The demise of the Ottoman Empire, instead of bringing emancipation to the Arabs, saw only a short-lived 'Arab kingdom' in Damascus (1918–20) before its dismantlement by the French Empire. The caliphate envisioned in Mecca in 1924, after Mustafa Kemal, later known as Ataturk, had abolished the Ottoman caliphate, was even more short-lived, for it was destroyed six months later by the Saud-led Wahhabis. The Arab world, divided between colonised Arabs and Ottoman Arabs before the First World War, was now utterly dominated by the Western powers, with the sole exception, as during the nineteenth century Nahda, of central Arabia which stood in sharp contrast. The Saud-led Wahhabi-state accessed full sovereignty in 1932, when the 'Kingdom of Nejd and Hijaz' became Saudi Arabia.

It took half a century for the Arabs to progressively win their independence from their British, French and Italian occupiers. The Egyptian *thawra* (revolution) of 1919 challenged Britain's denial of sovereignty through a popular campaign of civil disobedience whose major mobilisation tactics were echoed in the 2011 Tahrir revolution. It forced London to recognize, in 1922, a formal independence of Egypt that would remain incomplete for the next three decades. From 1922 to 1971, the fifty-year cycle of Arab independences went on, with the foundation of the League of Arab States in 1945 (Syria and Lebanon, despite being founding members, had to wait one more year for the departure of the French occupying forces, while the British troops left Egyptian soil only a decade later). The Algerian struggle against French colonization was by far the longest and the bloodiest, with an eight-year 'war of liberation' (1954–62). The admission of the UK-protected Gulf Emirates to the United Nations in 1971 ended this cycle. But the creation of the state of Israel in 1948 through the first Israeli–Arab war has left the question of Palestinian independence suspended to the present today. And the shockwaves the Zionist victory generated across the whole Arab world triggered a cycle of military coups, beginning in Syria in 1949 and ending in Libya in 1969.

Monarchies that had achieved at least formal independences were toppled in Egypt (1952), Iraq (1958) and Libya (1969). In Syria and Algeria, the nationalist elite who had liberated the country from French colonialism was eliminated by military cliques whose 'resistance' credentials were at best debatable. In Tunisia, Habib Bourguiba eliminated his rival Salah Ben Youssef in 1955–57, along with his nationalist supporters, at the same time as he was abolishing the constitutional monarchy in favor of an authoritarian republic. Yemen was a very special case, divided until 1967 between an Egyptian Republican protectorate in the north (under heavy opposition from a pro-Saudi monarchical insurgency) and a fragmented southern territory under British rule. In 1969, Marxist activists eliminated the southern nationalist elite in what would become in Aden the People's Democratic Republic of Yemen (PDRY), the only Soviet satellite in the Arab world. This Marxist takeover in the south triggered in the north a historic compromise between conservative Republicans (now emancipated from Egyptian tutelage) and pro-Saudi monarchists, which led to the formation of a Yemen Arab Republic (YAR). A complex sequence of coups and conflicts led Ali Abdallah Saleh to become president of the YAR in 1978, and then to unify North and South Yemen under his leadership in 1990.

This radical summary has aimed at highlighting the three cycles involved in the current crisis: the open-ended Nahda cycle, which began in 1798; the independence cycle from 1922 to 1971; and the cycle of hijackings between 1949 and 1969, which saw military rulers seizing power in the newly sovereign states. The most ruthless rulers who emerged from this process I would describe as the modern Mamluks.

The Mamluks of Our Time

In Arabic Mamluk means literally 'slave', and Abbasid caliphs sometimes chose to recruit emancipated slaves, mostly Turkish, into their personal guard, because their loyalty as absolute outsiders would be less questionable in times of local power struggles.

This scheme became an institution in the last part of the twelfth century, when Saladin's heirs established their dynasty of Ayyubid sultans in Egypt and Syria. In 1249, the French king Louis IX led the Seventh Crusade into Egypt. He was defeated at Mansoura, but the Mamluks considered this victory theirs, and they toppled the sultan. With the Crusaders' threat out of the way, the Mamluks could face the far greater menace of the Mongols, who devastated Bagdad and killed its Abbasid caliph in 1258. Two years later, the Muslim victory at Ayn Jalut, near the Palestinian city of Nablus, brought a dramatic halt to the Mongols' invasion.

Baybars, a hero of the battles of Mansoura and Ayn Jalut, had killed the last Ayyubid sultan and he then had the Mamluk sultan Qutuz assassinated so that he could occupy his throne. Baybars's stroke of genius was to take under his protection in Cairo, and proclaim as 'caliph', a survivor of the Mongol massacre of the Abbasid family. This powerless caliph transferred his legitimacy as a descendant of the Prophet to the non-Arab rulers of Cairo and Damascus, who often spoke very poor Arabic. Thus emasculated, the caliphate continued along dynastic lines, a path that ran contrary to the very dynamics of the Mamluk ethos, which followed a Darwinian logic that awarded power to the most ruthless competitors. Mamluk rule lasted two centuries and a half. The Ottomans, who conquered the Middle East in 1516–17, drove the Mamluks out of Syria, but allowed the survivors among them to serve them in Egypt.

French historian André Clot insisted on the strategic importance of the 'intelligence service', monitored by the sultan himself in the Mamluk system, and he described in vivid terms its Darwinian dynamics: 'Mamluks who form the sultan's inner circle have no more scruples than he does himself. Impressive warriors with unmatched talents, they are adamant in their will to climb up the ladder of prestige and fortune, to become richer and more powerful, and they are ready to use all the means already chosen by their master to consolidate his own domination.'[3] I must emphasise here that the Mamluk paradigm I use refers to this 1260–1516 period of Egyptian–Syrian rule. I therefore differ from the approach Amira El-Azhary Sonbol followed in her 'New Mamluks', where she chose to concentrate on the Ottomanised Mamluks, and then only in the context of Egypt.[4] I consider the modern Mamluks a contemporary projection of my Middle-Age precedent, ruling today in Egypt, Syria, Algeria and Yemen. The validity of this classification rests on the following common traits, shared by the modern Mamluks and their medieval predecessors:

1. Modern Mamluks are certainly not emancipated slaves, but they originate from the humbler classes in society, and they found, first through military

careers and then by political intrigue, shortcuts by which to access the political elite (this is the main argument of Hanna Batatu's seminal book about Syria and its 'lesser rural notables'.)[5]

2. Historical Mamluks, initially loyal to the ruling sultans, eventually toppled the Ayyubid dynasty in the context of the Seventh Crusade and settled their scores among themselves in the wake of the Mongol invasion. Their 'modern' counterparts seized power in Egypt and Syria in the context of the Israeli–Arab conflict, while using its various rounds to eliminate their Mamluk rivals (Nasser against Amer in Egypt, al-Assad against Jadid in Syria); the same pattern came to be seen in Algeria during the 1963 war with Morocco, and in the then North-Yemen in the context of its recurrent conflict with the South.

3. Once entrenched in power, modern Mamluks, like their medieval predecessors, constituted a counter-society with its privileges, rites and hierarchy, in what Steven Cook has aptly described as 'military enclaves'; the security mantra, preaching that secrecy should prevail in matters of military spending, also provided a convenient cover for a ruling clique engaged in the plundering of national resources.[6]

4. Darwinian logic prevailed among both historical and contemporary Mamluks, with power eventually passing not to the most patriotic or the most talented, but to those who had survived coups and other forms of political intrigue; Houari Boumediene in 1965 Algeria, Hafez al-Assad in 1970 Syria, Anwar Sadat in 1971 Egypt, all referred to their power grabs as 'corrective' movements in order to diminish their predecessors' legacies. (Ibrahim Hamdi's own 'corrective movement' lasted only from 1974 to 1977, but his assassination and the turmoil that followed paved the way for Saleh's rule in Yemen).

5. Last but not least, the modern Mamluks have found their own caliph-in-a-golden-cage from whom they extract legitimacy, without conceding to him any field of action: namely, the people, or its abstraction—the 'masses', which are regularly summoned to staged plebiscites where they renew their pact of submission to the country's master.

A main difference between historical Mamluks and their contemporary counterparts lies in their respective combat capabilities. Baybars and his successors were war heroes, whose victories echo through the centuries from Mansoura (1250) and Aïn Jalout (1260) to Kayseri (1418) and the conquest of Cyprus (1426), climaxing in the takeover of Acre in 1291, that closed the two-century long chapter of the Eastern crusades. By contrast, the modern top brass are far more efficient at waging war against their own people than against a foreign enemy (even though the local opposition is regularly branded 'a bunch of foreign agents'); most of the generals have only fought their own compatriots in the civil wars of 1979–82 in Syria, 1994 in Yemen, and during the 'black decade' of the nineties in Algeria. Since the 1979 peace with Israel, the main achievement of the Egyptian army has been crushing the Cairo police riot in 1986.

Despots are not always Mamluks

Monarchies could have fallen to the Palestinian insurgency (in Jordan in 1970) or to a military coup (in Morocco in 1971 and in 1972). Their resilience in both instances testifies to the solidness of their legitimacy, rooted in Rabat as well as in Amman in the Prophet Muhammad's lineage. The ruling dynasty is also intimately associated: in Jordan with nation-building itself, and in Morocco with the struggle for independence. We have seen how the Saud family eventually grounded its own nation-state on a vigorously anti-Nahda Wahhabi ideology. From Kuwait to Oman, no Persian Gulf monarchy could be alienated from its ruling dynasty, especially when the nationals became a minority among a mass of immigrants. The Mamluk paradigm is therefore irrelevant to the Arab monarchies and applies only to Arab republics, and then only to a certain number of them, as we will see.

As a result of the 1975 civil war, Lebanon fell into the clutches of political warlords, who in 1990, concluded a 'peace deal' under Syrian tutelage.[7] During nearly three decades of Syrian occupation (from 1976 to 2005), Lebanon has not only lost its sovereignty to a significant degree, but it too has repeatedly been plundered by Mamluks deployed from the neighboring country. The Lebanese routinely describe them as 'locusts'. In Tunisia, as mentioned earlier, Habib Bourguiba and his supporters eliminated Salah Ben Youssef and the rival nationalist faction in the course of the independence process (Ben Youssef was eventually killed by a Tunisian hit squad in Frankfurt in August 1961). But Bourguiba had miscalculated the French response when, in July of 1961, he issued an ultimatum to Charles De Gaulle to force him to evacuate the French military base in the northern port of Bizerte in anticipation of its transfer to Tunisia two years later.

De Gaulle refused adamantly, not so much because of Tunisia, but to avoid jeopardising through any display of (relative) weakness the negotiations between France and the Algerian insurgency. The showdown in Bizerte proved a disaster for the Tunisian army. There were hundreds of casualties, and the French base was evacuated according to schedule, not one day earlier. This humiliation nurtured an anti-Bourguiba conspiracy inside the armed forces that aimed at taking revenge against the president for the Bizerte bloodbath. The plot was uncovered in December 1962, and the ten ringleaders were swiftly tried and executed. Bourguiba decided after the crisis to gradually downgrade the army, promoting instead the political police that would back the one-party system in controlling the Tunisian population. In 1975, Bourguiba was officially proclaimed 'president for life', a title no Mamluk autocrat had dared to adopt, though the lifelong presidency was a core reality of their despotic rule.[8] The police dimension of the Tunisian dictatorship stands in sharp contrast to Mamluk dynamics. In November 1987, it was a police general, Zine el-Abidine Ben Ali, then prime minister, who toppled the senile Bourguiba for 'health reasons'. What has since been called a 'medical coup' was therefore non-military and bloodless, in contrast to the violent power struggles that kept the Mamluk spheres in constant turmoil.

Two other Arab regimes, Muammar Gaddafi's Libya and Saddam Hussein's Iraq, do not fit into the Mamluk category, first and foremost because of their totalitarian tendencies. Gaddafi engineered a coup against King Idris of Libya in September 1969. A self-proclaimed admirer and disciple of Nasser, he initially ruled, like his Mamluk mentor, through a Revolutionary Command Council (RCC) staffed by his fellow plotters, the so-called 'Free Officers'. But an aborted conspiracy originating from within the RCC in 1975 led Gaddafi to establish two years later a *jamahiriyya*, literally a 'massocracy'. This unique system banned any form of elections, parties or even associations. It was a smokescreen for the despotic rule of the 'Revolutionary Committees', the euphemistic designation of the pro-Gaddafi armed militias which spread all over the country. The promotion of Gaddafi's *Green Book* contributed to the totalitarian flavor of these institutions. Iraq had fallen under the rule of the Baath party in 1968, five years after neighboring Syria. This political proximity, far from uniting Damascus and Baghdad under the same flag, only fuelled a deadly rivalry between the two competing branches of the Baath party, each one branding the other as 'deviant'. Ahmad Hassan al-Bakr, who acceded to supreme power in Iraq in 1968, had a military background, but his deputy (and distant kin), Saddam Hussein, had risen steadily through the civilian structure of the Baath party. In 1979, Saddam Hussein toppled Bakr, citing 'health reasons', before conducting bloody purges of the political hierarchy. This triumph of the civilian wing of the Baath against the military apparatus of the party was never to be echoed among modern Mamluks. One might also add that Saddam Hussein had no interest in staging bogus plebiscites. He waited until 1995 to organise a first referendum to legitimise his presidency (a second would take place in 2002). In both instances, the Iraqi despot was much more concerned to challenge the outside world (his country has been under strict UN sanctions from 1991 to 2003) than to indulge in Mamluk-style electoral rites.

The paradigm of the modern Mamluks therefore applies to only four Arab regimes: Algeria, Egypt, Syria and Yemen. Here presidencies for life were the rule—Algeria between the years 1992 and 1999 being an exception, to which we will turn shortly. Syria invented the hereditary republic (ironically described in Arabic as *jamlaka*, literally 'repumonarchy') when in 2000 Bashar al-Assad inherited the presidency that his deceased father had occupied since 1970. Hosni Mubarak in Egypt and Ali Abdallah Saleh in Yemen also were ostensibly grooming their sons as heirs-apparent.

The Algerian Precedent

One generation before the Arab democratic uprising of 2011, the years 1988–91 had seen a cycle of popular protests that shook some Arab regimes. The May 1989 riots in Jordan forced King Hussein to organise, the following November, the first general elections in a quarter of century (Islamists won a relative majority in these polls, entering the government). A disastrous invasion and annexation of Kuwait prompted the 'Desert Storm' operation, which saw a US-led coalition force Saddam Hussein's army back to Iraq, where, in reaction, a revolutionary insurgency spread through most of the provinces in March 1991. But Washington, obsessed with the Iranian threat, chose to allow Saddam Hussein to crush the rebellion, even at the cost of severe violations of the recently concluded US–Iraqi ceasefire.

The Mamluk regime of Algeria, where Chadli Bendjedid had succeeded Houari Boumediene after his death in 1978, trembled on its foundations during the October 1988 riots, when the armed forces killed hundreds of protesters. Bendjedid was compelled to abolish the one-party system, and the National Liberation Front (FLN in its French acronym) was soon challenged by the Islamic Salvation Front (FIS).[9] In December 1991, the FIS came out clearly ahead in the first round of parliamentary elections and was bound to form the next government. President Bendjedid had agreed to the principle of an executive cohabitation, with him as head of state, and an Islamist-backed prime minister. But his fellow Mamluks, designated in Algeria as the 'decision-makers', moved in to prevent any devolution of their power.[10] In January 1992, Bendjedid was deposed and the electoral process was officially 'suspended'. Interestingly, the plotters never made themselves known. Their public face was a powerless collective leadership, the Higher State Committee (HCE), whose president was supposed to be the supreme leader of the country.[11] In fact, the first HCE president, Mohamed Boudiaf, one of the few surviving founders of the FLN, was killed in June 1992 by one of his bodyguards, perhaps because he had tried to exercise a modicum of authority over the 'decision-makers'.

The innocuous Ali Kafi, the secretary general of the veterans' organisation (a bastion of FLN patronage), was HCE president from June 1992 to January 1994. But the real strong man of the Committee was General Khaled Nezzar, one of the 'decision-makers' and minister of defence. He bequeathed his defence portfolio to his fellow general Liamine Zeroual in July 1993, but retained most of its real power inside the armed forces. Zeroual succeeded Kafi in January 1994 with a conciliatory discourse designed to appease the outside world. The 'suspension' of the electoral process and the ruthless repression of the FIS had contributed to the rise of the jihadi insurgency of the Islamic Armed Group (GIA).[12] The plural would have been more appropriate for this 'group' as it represented a confusing galaxy of jihadi guerrillas each fighting under the guidance of its local *emir* or commander. An unprecedented escalation of violence led in 1993 and 1994 to a weekly death toll of 500, most of them civilians.

The composition of the January 1992 nucleus of Mamluk generals who deposed Bendjedid was never made public, but the 'decision-makers' whose names were most often heard were generals Nezzar, Larbi Belkheir (minister of the interior), Abdelmalek Guenaizia (the chief of staff), Mohammed Mediene (aka Tewfik, chief of military intelligence), Mohammed Lamari (chief of the land forces) and Ben Abbès Ghezaiel (chief of the gendarmerie). This covert leadership was never without its tensions, but it closed ranks when it came to the supreme interests of the Mamluk clique, meaning an overwhelming military force and a monopoly on the national rent (basically the oil and gas exports and their derived benefits). Interestingly, the 'decision-makers' pushed to the forefront General Zeroual, who had no constituency of his own inside the military institution. Zeroual was elected president in November of 1995, with 61 per cent of the vote, a historic low by Mamluk standards. The 71 per cent turnout proclaimed officially was much higher than the actual participation even though war fatigue had probably driven a significant proportion of the electorate to the polls. A Mamluk-compatible Islamic party, the Movement of Society for Peace (MSP or 'Hamas' in its Arab acronym) was constituted to occupy the space left vacant by the banned FIS. However, this political reconfiguration did not adequate to de-escalate what had become a full-fledged civil war. In 1997, and to a lesser extent in 1998, horrendous massacres were committed against whole populations. The GIA was accused of most of those crimes, often targeted at FIS-supportive localities. But human rights defenders claimed that the military was at least a passive accomplice in the slaughters. This wave of carnage dealt a fatal blow to the Mamluk dream of 'eradicating' the Islamist opposition.

Zeroual was the first casualty of this reality check: he resigned from the presidency and set the date for anticipated elections in April 1999. The 'decision-makers', in their quest for a civilian front capable of running the new phase, chose Abdelaziz Bouteflika, who had been Boumediene's minister of foreign affairs and had lived mostly in exile since 1980. Bouteflika was voted in as the sole candidate, since his six challengers decided collectively to with-draw their candidacies in protest against blatant electoral manipulation. Bouteflika has been repeatedly returned to office—in 2004, 2009 and 2014—even though he voted in the last of these elections in a wheelchair and left his prime minister to campaign on his behalf. His pleas for 'national reconcilia-tion' and 'concord' have never been sufficient to end the jihadi insurgency, falling short most notably in 2007, when Al-Qaeda in the Islamic Maghreb (AQIM) twice struck Algiers in a string of coordinated terror attacks. But Bouteflika was popularly associated with the end of the 'black decade' of the nineties, with its 100–200,000 deaths, and its millions of displaced persons. This national tragedy mattered less for the 'decision-makers' than the fact that their collective power and privileges had emerged unscathed from this trial by fire. This Algerian lesson would be remembered by the other ruling Mamluks when the popular protests of the winter 2011 erupted all over the Arab world.

The Arab Counter-Revolution of 2011–14

The democratic uprising of 2011 could be interpreted as a collective attempt to at last fulfill the promises of the Nahda, thereby closing the cycle of eman-cipation struggles that began in 1798. But the Arab Mamluks were adamant in confronting, and eventually crushing, these popular movements, and they did not shy away from emulating the Algerian 'decision-makers' by subverting any genuine democratic process, even at the cost of civil war. The trauma of the 'black decade' was still vivid in Algeria when Ben Ali was expelled from power (and from Tunisia) in January 2011, after three weeks of unabated riots.

But the Algerian Mamluks soon understood that they would have to redistribute a significant proportion of the rent to their fellow citizens if they were to prevent social unrest. Record highs in gas and oil prices undergirded the state's generosity and prevented the spread of protests from neighboring Tunisia.

In Egypt, by contrast, the Tunisian breakthrough gave impetus to a popular wave of mass protests, forcing the local Mamluks to move in and to depose Hosni Mubarak. Far from being a 'revolution', Mubarak's fall in February 2011 was technically a coup, strongly reminiscent of Bendjedid's deposition by the Algerian Mamluks: the ruling clique were ridding themselves of an appointed leader who had jeopardised their collective interests by endorsing the electoral process in Algeria in 1992 and by fuelling the protests through his denial syndrome in Egypt in 2011.

In non-Mamluk Tunisia, the armed forces had refused Ben Ali's orders to shoot at protesters, thereby contributing to the dictator's demise. But the Tunisian military had soon withdrawn from the political frontlines, pledging their sincere intentions to defend the democratic transition. By contrast, the Egyptian Mamluks had seized power after they had deposed Mubarak through their Supreme Council of the Armed Forces (SCAF), led by Field-Marshal Mohammed Hussein Tantawi. While Tunisia had convened elections for a Constituent Assembly in October 2011, paving the way for the establishment of a Second Republic, Egypt's Mamluks had rallied the Muslim Brotherhood to support the draft of a slightly amended constitution, approved in a March 2011 referendum by 77 per cent of the voters (a sharp defeat for the revolutionary coalition). The SCAF could then count on the approval of the Muslim Brothers as they repressed popular protests throughout the summer and autumn of 2011, actions that culminated in the massacre of dozens of anti-SCAF soccer fans (designated by the generic term 'Ultras') in the Port Said stadium in February of 2012. Now that the Egyptian Mamluks had eliminated the revolutionary threat, they could turn against the Muslim Brotherhood, the main beneficiary of the legislative elections that took place from November 2011 to January 2012. The SCAF remained the supreme executive power, as the government rested solely on the military leadership, and not on the parliamentary majority.

Post-Saddam Iraq, under US occupation, had proved that more frequent elections did not equate to more vibrant democracy. On the contrary, post-

Ben Ali Tunisia had voted only once in October 2011, and its constitution would be drafted and approved by the assembly chosen in this election, and not through referendum. Meanwhile Egypt went on voting twice a year after Mubarak's fall, with a constitutional watchdog designated by the former dictator still in place (the Supreme Constitutional Council, SCC). The SCC played the SCAF game by invalidating the parliamentary elections that the Islamists had won. The Egyptian Mamluks bet on the victory of their *protégé*, former general Ahmed Shafiq, Mubarak's last prime minister, in a highly polarised presidential contest held in May and June of 2012. But the Muslim Brotherhood's candidate, Mohamed Morsi, reaped 51.7 percent of the votes in the second and final round against Shafiq.

The Egyptian Mamluks were stunned by the Islamist victory, and they wavered before eventually endorsing it. Their shock largely explains why the military clique accepted Morsi's removal of Tantawi and his replacement by the SCAF most junior member, General Abdul Fatah al-Sisi. Now minister of defence, al-Sisi took pains to avoid being associated with Morsi's increasingly divisive policy. Future historians will, it is hoped, be able to retrace the details of the Egyptian Mamluks conspiracy against the first democratically elected president of the country's history. What is certain is that the destabilisation campaign swung into full gear in the spring of 2013, with the military supporting the Tamarrod (Rebellion) movement. The mass demonstrations of the last day of June 2013 led to al-Sisi's ultimatum to Morsi, followed by Morsi's deposition and incarceration. The interim president, Adly Mansour, worked hand in hand with the vengeful SCC, but real power laid in the hands of al-Sisi, nominally only minister of defence. It was he who pushed for the showdown against Islamist rallies that in August of 2013 left hundreds dead in the streets of Cairo. After those massacres, the Muslim Brotherhood was banned as a 'terrorist organisation'. The rabid repression did not spare the revolutionary militants either, no matter how critical of Morsi they had been.

While the Mamluk-led counter-revolution was running full speed in Egypt, Tunisia was evolving in the opposite direction. The grave crisis induced by the killing of two prominent leftist leaders by a jihadi hit-squad, in February and July of 2013, had prompted the powerful trade union UGTT (the General Union of Tunisian Labour) to sponsor a 'national dialogue' between the Islamist Ennahda party, which controlled the government, and the nationalist opposition.[13] This dialogue paved the way for the Islamists abandoning the prime-ministership in January 2014, leaving a technocratic cabinet to run the country until the October 2014 elections, won by the main opposition party, Nidaa Tounes (the Call for Tunis). Meanwhile, in Egypt, general al-Sisi had been promoted to field-marshal, before running for president in a Mubarak-style plebiscite (he won 97 per cent of the votes) in May of 2014.

The authoritarian restoration in Egypt, far from returning the country to peace after the massacres of August 2013, had only increased the jihadi threat: Ansar Beit Maqdis (ABM, the Champions of Jerusalem) and other extremist groups, originally active in the Sinai Peninsula, were now striking in downtown Cairo and the Nile Delta. By contrast, although Tunisia had suffered a string of jihadi attacks and lived with a terrorist sanctuary in the Chambi mountain range at its Algerian border, the country had managed to contain this menace without jeopardising the democratic transition. Syrian and Yemeni Mamluks had reacted with unbridled brutality to the peaceful protests against their regimes in the spring of 2011. Bashar al-Assad released scores of jihadi detainees, while abducting and torturing thousands of non-violent activists. Ali Abdallah Saleh ordered his own army to abandon whole cities to Al-Qaeda in the Arabian Peninsula (AQAP). Both dictators were motivated by a desire to blackmail the West into keeping them in power as the only rampart against the jihadi threat, while associating their opposition with the most extremist groups.

This playing with jihadi fire echoed the cold-blooded escalation Algerian Mamluks had fuelled to crush any hope of a democratic process in the nineties. It did not save Saleh from having to leave power in February 2012, but he did so with full immunity for him and his family, despite all their crimes. The former dictator soon began a covert campaign against the new authorities, subverting their 'national dialogue', eventually supporting the Houthi guerrillas in the north, while backing their AQAP nemesis in a balance of terror that proved lethal for the Yemeni transition. Bashar al-Assad carried manipulation of the jihadi boogeyman even further by means of a 'divide and rule' tactic that proved devastating for the Syrian civilian opposition and the armed insurgency. In April 2013, an 'Islamic State in Iraq and Syria' (ISIS) was proclaimed in the Syrian city of Raqqa, in the Euphrates Valley. ISIS grew even stronger after its takeover of Mosul, the second largest city in Iraq, in June of 2014, when ISIS leader Abu Bakr al-Baghdadi proclaimed himself 'caliph' (the Egyptian ABM later pledged allegiance to him).

Conclusion

Arab democrats and liberals have consistently been caught between the rock of the ruling Mamluks and the hard place of jihadi extremism. In Syria and in

Yemen, and also to a lesser extent in Egypt, military cliques have consistently preferred to deal with radical insurgencies than with popular protests. The scenario of the 'black decade' of nineties Algeria is being repeated again and again, but this time with the risk that the jihadi Frankenstein the Mamluks helped to create might escape their control entirely. The Mamluk paradigm that was used to interpret this historical sequence cannot provide all the answers to such intellectual and political challenges. But it may shed light on the dynamics at work in the Arab counter-revolution, which is far better equipped for the current confrontation than its democrat opponents. A popular slogan among al-Assad's supporters in Syria was 'Assad or we burn the country'. It seems now that this sinister warning is being echoed also in Yemen, and possibly in Egypt. The Algerian precedent of the nineties, which has led to a presidential mummy now sitting at the head of the state in Algiers, is further proof that a Mamluk system is not able to reform itself. The future of the Arab world depends therefore largely on the resilience of its civil societies, despite the horrors that Mamluk violence has unleashed upon them. This popular steadfastness, along with the relative success of the Tunisian transition, is the main reason why among the ruins left by the current Arab counter-revolution there is hope for reconstruction.

6

TRASHING TRANSITIONS

THE ROLE OF ARAB MEDIA AFTER THE UPRISINGS

Marc Lynch

The 2000s was a decade of structural transformation in the Arab media, rooted in satellite television, local radio, semi-independent press, and the radical new vistas of the internet and social media.[1] Those new media brought critical news and opinion before a broad public, empowered previously silenced voices, facilitated connections between activists and ordinary citizens, and linked together local protests into a powerful master narrative of regional uprising. This new political information environment created the conditions under which the 2010–11 Arab uprisings erupted and profoundly shaped the course of the transitions which followed.[2] Conventional arguments for and against the role of Facebook or Twitter in sparking the revolutions have largely missed the point: these new media platforms shaped the political environment within which the protests erupted and the subsequent transitions and wars unfolded.

The uprisings in turn created dramatic new opportunities for the emergence of new independent media. In cases from Egypt and Tunisia to Libya and Syria, the overthrow of the leader was followed by the rapid launch of dozens of new independent television stations, newspapers and websites which together constituted a hyperactive new national public sphere. Within a few short years, however, most of those attempted democratic transitions had failed, multiple states had collapsed into civil war, and much of the Arab media had degenerated into highly partisan platforms at the service of political movements or states. The same media which proved so crucial to the uprisings contributed manifestly to their failure. Why did this media contribute both to the wave of mobilisation which rocked the Arab world in 2011 and to the failure of those Arab uprisings to consolidate democratic institutions?[3]

The failings of the Arab media after the uprisings offer a cautionary tale about generally hopeful expectations for a plural public sphere following transitions from authoritarian rule. Its lessons are both specific to the Arab world and general to transitions. Many of the same qualities which facilitated the sudden emergence and spread of mass protest movements proved detrimental to the consolidation of democratic transitions after the overthrow of the targeted regime. The failure to reform state media at the outset of transitional periods, the intense fear triggered by radical institutional uncertainty and deep conflicts over the identity and power structures of transitional states, and the prevalence of highly partisan and deeply polarised media, together helped drive social division, political disenchantment, state failure or authoritarian resurgence.[4] These effects were exacerbated by the Arab world's distinctive combination of an influential shared transnational media, state-dominated national media, and highly politicised nascent social media. It is most useful to conceptualise these different platforms as a singular media ecology: broadcast media content was frequently circulated on social media, while social media became an important source of images, video and information for the mass media (particularly from conflict zones such as Syria where few journalists dared tread).

Arab media played a destructive role in the transitions for three major reasons: political capture, the marketing of fear, and polarisation. First, the media proved susceptible to political capture by states, political movements, or by old elites.[5] Transnational satellite television stations such as Al-Jazeera, which had served as a virtual Arab public sphere as recently as early 2011, increasingly morphed into transparently partisan actors supporting the interests of their state patrons and local proxies. State media sectors largely resisted meaningful reforms in the aftermath of the uprisings, leaving widely-viewed state television as a potent weapon in the hands of the security state and the old regime.

Most new television stations and other mass media were owned by wealthy, politically ambitious businessmen or by political movements, and tailored their coverage accordingly.

Second, the media magnified the fear and uncertainty which inevitably accompany transitions, particularly when those transitions involve profound institutional uncertainty and potentially incipient anarchy.[6] Where the media tended to support revolutionary enthusiasm by demonstrating success in the early Arab Spring, by the middle of 2011 it frightened viewers with terrifying accounts of violence and mayhem from Libya, Syria, Iraq and Yemen. The types of media which characterised the period of the uprisings were particularly prone to exacerbating the fear of violence or political subjugation by publicising worrisome information, ideas and rumors and by encouraging the self-segregation of sectors of the public into echo chambers where only such polarising information tended to circulate. The Arab transitions were shaped by intense uncertainty about the rules of the game, especially in Egypt with its politicised judicial interventions, poorly designed and endlessly delayed constitutional talks, and spiralling existential divides between Islamists and their enemies.

Finally, political capture and institutional uncertainty created the ideal conditions for intense polarisation. Media outlets typically sought out a distinctive political niche and catered to that constituency to the exclusion of others. Islamists watched one set of television stations and Twitter feeds, while anti-Islamists watched an entirely different set. Those that attempted to remain even-handed often struggled to find an audience. This process unfolded at all levels, from the transnational to the national to the individual level of social media. Transnationally, Al-Jazeera went from the primary source for news and political discourse across ideological lines to an outlet catering to Islamists and shunned by their enemies. Nationally, the media in transitional states like Egypt and Tunisia rapidly polarised as the moment of revolutionary enthusiasm gave way to hard political combat over the extent of reforms, the distribution of power and the identity of the state. In failing states like Libya and Yemen, media aligned with local or ideological political trends. Iraqi Shi'ites and Sunnis watched entirely different media presenting almost irreconcilable realities. On social media, self-segregation into ideological or sectarian clusters drove politics towards the extremes, undermined the common ground of politics, and intensified and accelerated conflicts and divisions.

In short, then, at least part of the explanation for the failure of the Arab transitions can be found in the intersection of the destructive effects of the new media environment with the effects of institutional failure and the strategic mobilisation of fear.[7] Challenged or even overturned regimes saw manipulation of fear, anger and disgust through the media as a way to destroy hope for change and to rebuild support for the old order. The media contributed to the failure of Egypt's transition and almost sabotaged Tunisia's. In cases of failed states and civil wars such as Libya, Syria and Yemen, fragmented and polarised media contributed to the breakdown of institutions, provided a key vehicle for proxy warfare by regional powers, and helped to shape the logic of violence by insurgent and regime forces alike. Even states which successfully deflected popular mobilisation through political and constitutional reforms, such as Morocco and Jordan, leaned on national and transnational media to build support for the process and to undermine support for protestors. Independent media and online activist networks, which proved so effective in the mobilisational phases, were far less able to command the field in these conflicted transitional and post-transitional stages.

The Arab Media After the Uprisings

The role of the Arab media after the uprisings can only be understood in light of its history over the previous decades. In the 1970s and 1980s, most Arab countries developed intensely repressive forms of censorship and state domination of the media. While the specificities of national systems of control differed, mass media generally served as a tool for control over information and mobilisation in service of power.[8] Highly sophisticated citizens were able to seek out independent sources of information, such as VOA or BBC radio broadcasts, but most continued to rely primarily on national media.

This changed in the 1990s and 2000s, when Al-Jazeera's free-to-view satellite television station shattered these state monopolies over information, ushering in an era of proliferating, competitive transnational Arab television stations. The competition from abroad forced most national television stations to modernise and adapt in order to maintain market share.[9] Some countries, such as Egypt, developed a diverse and cantankerous political press, as well as some intriguing experiments in radio broadcasting and private television stations. These changes, along with the rapid spread of internet access and social media use, transformed most of the Arab world from an informational black hole into a media-saturated society. By the late 2000s, most Arabs had hundreds of free to view satellite channels from which to choose, while internet access spread widely from initially low levels to near ubiquity in key urban centers.

The Arab information environment therefore differed from most other regions experiencing democratic transitions in three ways. First, each individual Arab country was embedded within a transnational Arabic language media ecosystem of satellite television, pan-Arab newspapers and websites, and social media. Few of the transitions outside the Arab world have a comparable level of regular, intense transnational media involvement in national political spheres. Second, Arab national media sectors had a comparatively high degree of direct and indirect state control. Finally, the rapidly evolving social media introduced very new dynamics into the familiar democratic transitions of decades past.

These different media platforms interacted in a singular media ecology shaping the distribution of information and ideas circulating through Arab politics. Independent Egyptian media and social media formed symbiotic relationships, with newspapers reporting on stories and publishing images appearing on blogs. Syrian social media provided much of the sources, information and images for the international media.[10] Many Tunisian internet activists who had been based in France before the revolution returned to set up important experiments with online news and opinion portals. In Saudi Arabia and much of the Gulf, Twitter is the most important location of the public sphere, which in turn attracted disproportionate state repression—long prison terms for satirical tweets have become common in recent years. Overall, the Arab transitions were a hyper-mediated environment in which states retained considerable structural power and in which all political actors saw the media as a potential weapon.

This section examines each of these three dimensions in depth, showing how the distinctive combination of transnational broadcasting, national media systems, and social media shaped both the revolutionary contributions of 2011 and the trashing of the transitions which followed.

Transnational Broadcasting

The new media environment played a key role in the Arab uprisings of late 2010 and early 2011. Al-Jazeera played a key role in publicising the Tunisian and Egyptian protests, and framing them as part of a broader Arab story of popular uprising which inspired Arabs in every corner of the world. These broadcasts facilitated 'scale shift', the linking together of local struggles into a common narrative frame which helped to spread protest from one country to another.[11] The diffusion of protest from Tunisia to Egypt and then to virtually the entire region is difficult to imagine without the unifying media environment.

The very power of this Gulf-owned media made its corruption inevitable. By March 2011, satellite television stations such as Al-Jazeera and Al-Arabiya became ever more transparent weapons for their state sponsors within severely divided arenas rather than a neutral public sphere open to all factions. Arab stations either did not cover Bahrain's uprising, or slanted their coverage in sectarian terms to justify the Saudi-led intervention. In Syria and Libya, most pan-Arab stations openly campaigned for chosen rebel groups, and then for particular factions within those insurgencies. Al-Jazeera came to be viewed as a publicity machine for Islamists such as Egypt's Muslim Brotherhood and Tunisia's Ennahda, while other Gulf-based stations peddled wild, sensational stories which fed anti-Islamist anger and suspicion.

The transnational media soon degenerated into an arena for regional power struggles and proxy wars, with Al-Jazeera serving the interests of the Qatari regime and Saudi-owned media closely aligned with Riyadh's regional policies. This partisan turn, along with the images of horrific violence and state collapse in Libya and Syria, likely contributed to the diminishing enthusiasm for popular uprisings. It also removed the possibility that transnational media could provide a neutral forum to help bridge the political divides between intensely contested national media. Transnational broadcasting, so essential to galvanising and spreading the uprisings, thus proved far less conducive to democratic consolidation. Transnational Arab media mattered most in cases such as Syria, where it filled the void left by the absence of any significant domestic broadcast or print media.

National Media

A democratic transition from authoritarian rule should in principle entail the emergence of a more open national public sphere able to monitor domestic politics and hold politicians to account, devote sustained attention to local issues, and become the site for national opinion formation. The early post-uprisings period in some Arab states did see the flourishing of a wide variety of new national media, from television to radio and newspapers. It did not last, however, due to the limited extent of institutional and legal reforms and the rapid polarisation of politics. National media contributed to undermining transitions by breaking down political consensus on national identity and the necessary institutional rules.

Egypt and Tunisia, the two cases where leaders actually fell in the face of popular protest, share a surprisingly similar trajectory in terms of national media. While Egypt's media had always been far more contentious and rambunctious than Tunisia's rigorously controlled public sphere, both countries had witnessed a limited media liberalisation in the decade before the uprisings. New media platforms blossomed following the fall of long-entrenched dictators, but resource constraints and lack of professional experience left these new media initiatives vulnerable to capture by wealthy interests, political movements, or the state. Failure to reform state media sectors left intact a powerful weapon for old elites to mobilise in defense of their threatened status.

It is worth briefly explaining why reforms to the media sector proved so difficult.[12] Given a lack of settled rules and intense polarisation, all sides feared that these new institutions could quickly come to be dominated by their political rivals. Where there is a broad political consensus, there could be the chance to establish independent, non-partisan institutional reforms. But where politics quickly becomes zero-sum and highly polarised, then every move towards institutional reform will be interpreted as a political purge aimed at institutional capture. Egypt's newly elected President Morsi, for instance, had every reason to seek fundamental change in the institutions at the heart of the old regime, from the Ministry of Interior to state broadcasting, and most revolutionaries would agree that such change was essential. But every effort to bring about that change frightened political opponents who feared that Muslim Brothers would simply take over those institutions to impose their rule. Similarly, in Tunisia Ennahda hoped to 'cleanse the media and prevent them from becoming opposition platforms,' but the new government was never able to implement such plans.[13] The attempt led civil society and journalists to rally against what they viewed as an attempt by Ennahda to capture the media and the state in the service of an Islamist agenda. The failure to reform broadcast media and major newspapers left the commanding heights of the media in the hands of elites who benefited from the old order and feared its change.

Social Media

Social media, which many had hoped would provide an antidote to the toxic legacy of official Arab media, has significantly changed the nature of Arab media but could not escape its pathologies during the transitions—and often exacerbated them.[14] While internet penetration in the region had been relatively low, young urban activists were early and enthusiastic users of all platforms. By the time of the uprisings, the Arab world had one of the highest growth rates in the world for internet and social media.

This dramatic increase in social media usage did not in and of itself cause revolutions. Social media rarely causes political instability in the absence of prior grievances or structural conditions, but it does act as an accelerant and intensifier of many forms of political mobilisation and can facilitate the very sudden eruption of intense political disagreement.[15] Social media platforms created new opportunities for protestors to organise movements, disseminate information, and evade state control over information. Social media may also help to build 'warm ties' across distance in ways which facilitate costly forms of political action, and also link together protest movements from Tunisia to Yemen. Social media, with its immediacy and mediated intimacy, may create a greater willingness to sacrifice for a shared cause, whether by sending money or—at the extreme—deciding to travel to a conflict zone to join the battle.

Two common features of socially mediated environments are particularly destructive in transitional situations: the tendency towards homophilia, in which individuals select themselves into communities of the like-minded; and the accelerating and intensifying effects of the extremely rapid spread of information and dissemination of visceral imagery. Individuals embedded within informational clusters tend to be exposed only to confirming information, and when discordant information does appear it is usually only to be mocked or challenged. Debates within like-minded clusters tend to favour the more extreme voices over the voices of caution or moderation. This has very disturbing implications for socially, ethnically or politically divided countries, where social media homophilia may tend to exacerbate such cleavages and fuel the potential for violent conflict. Social media is very good at cultivating a sense of aggrieved identity among an in-group and mobilising resentment and fury against out-groups. The enthusiastic online embrace of Egypt's military coup in the summer of 2013, the sectarianism which ran rampant through Gulf social media, and regional online support for violent jihadist factions in Syria show very powerfully how illiberal forces can be empowered by social media.

Social media, then, served to reinforce rather than to counteract the negative effects of transnational and national broadcast media during the post-uprisings period. The propensity towards social clustering and the intensification of conflict trends empowered extreme voices, facilitated the spread of alarming rumours, and undermined the moderate center. Those dynamics made meaningful reform more difficult, intensified social polarisation, and accelerated the failure of transitions. The type of media, whether broadcast or social, which aids activism does not necessarily help with consolidating democracy. Enthusiastic media coverage or social media engagement with street battles and the politics of moral outrage can prove far more attractive than normal politics to mobilised youth. In highly un-institutionalised contexts such as Libya's, Facebook and Twitter have been used to spread highly destructive rumors and falsehoods which have contributed to undermining confidence in transitional orders.

The Arab Media as a Socially-Mediated Ecosystem

Transnational, national, and social media should not be understood as discrete sources of information or opinion. They interact with each other closely. Broadcast media has relied heavily on social media videos and images, especially from war zones such as Syria and Libya, while social media users frequently retweet and discuss stories disseminated by broadcast and print media. Broadcast and print media enjoy a strong presence on social media, often driving the agenda of online discussions. Information travels across platforms, and most individuals follow multiple channels and accounts across many different types of media.

To demonstrate the different configurations of these three media types, I draw on a unique Twitter dataset constructed with Deen Freelon, which includes every public tweet including the words Egypt or Syria in Arabic or English between January 2011 and August 2013.[16] Focusing only on the top 200 most retweeted tweets for each month in the two datasets produced a sample of 4,881,079 tweets for Egypt and 4,298,358 for Syria, for a total of more than 9 million tweets. I then identified every unique tweet from a broadcast or print media outlet, coding each of those media outlets as either 'national' (i.e. an Egyptian newspaper or television station), 'regional' (i.e. a pan-Arab television station such as Al-Jazeera), or 'international' (i.e. a Western media source such as CNN or the *New York Times*). Finally, I calculated the number of retweets for all these tweets from media accounts.

Figure 6.1 shows the monthly percentage of retweets in the top 200 from any media platform in the Egypt and the Syria dataset. This gives a sense of the extent to which the mainstream media was an organic part of social media discourse. Some 19 per cent of all the top 200 retweets about Egypt and 17.5 per cent about Syria were from media accounts. There is a very pronounced downward trend, with media accounts becoming less central to the Twitter discourse in both Egypt and Syria over time. It is worth nothing that

Figure 6.1: Media retweets as a percentage of all top 200 retweets by month

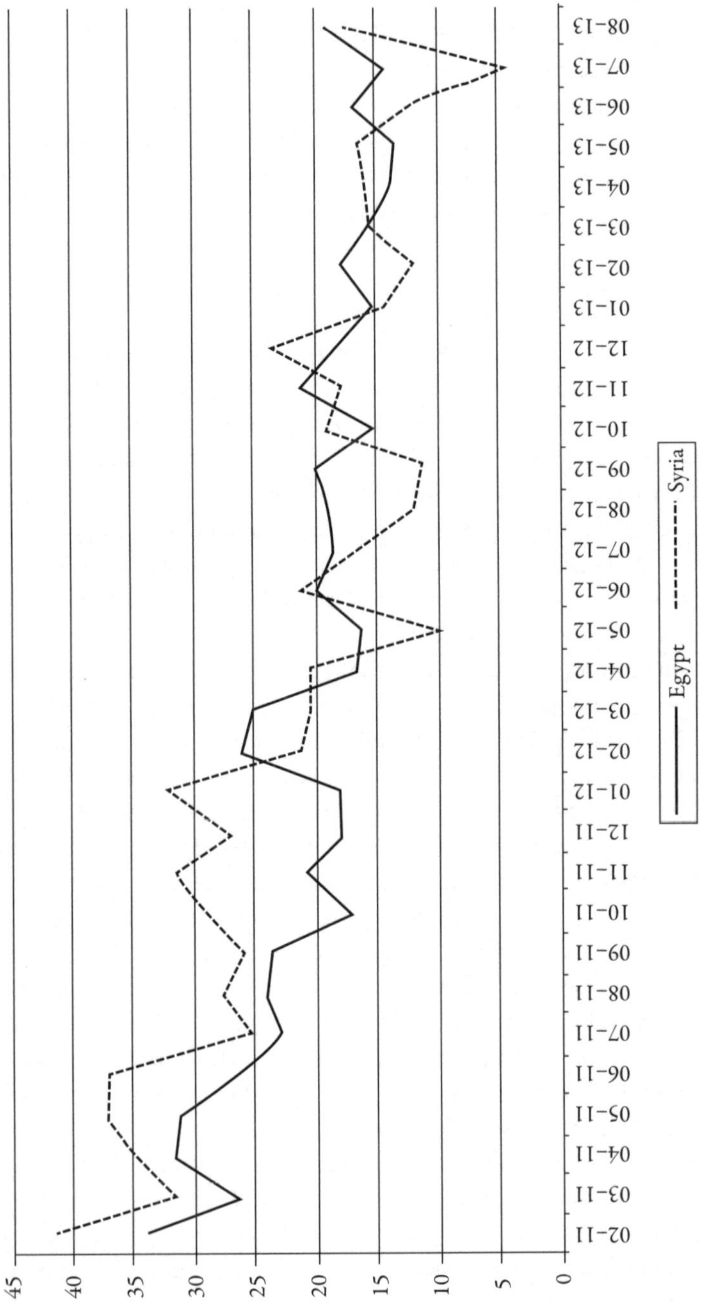

Egypt ——— Syria -------

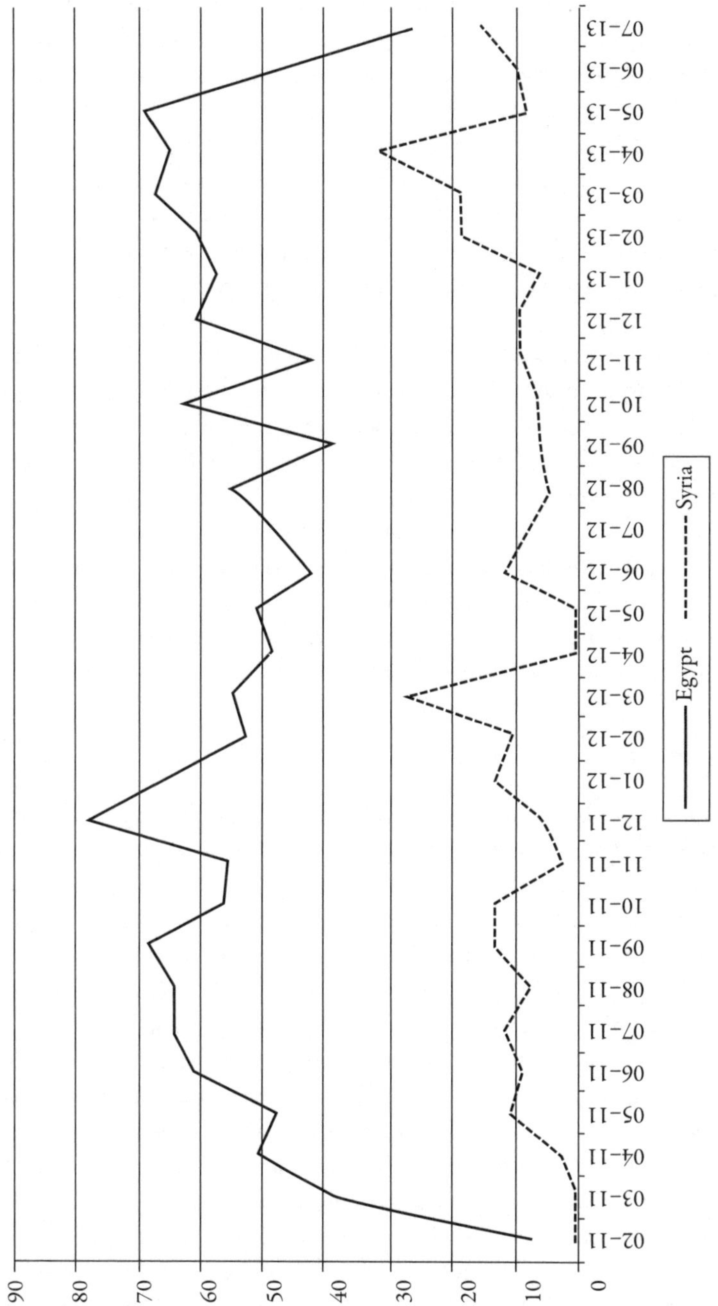

Figure 6.2: National Media as Percentage of All Media Retweets

these totals likely understate the actual significance of these media accounts in the Twitter political sphere, since it captures only retweets of the media accounts themselves and not the subsequent discussion of the content of the stories reported through those accounts.

Figure 6.2 presents the relative significance of national media outlets compared with global or pan-Arab media outlets. Egypt had a far more robust national media ecosystem than Syria, with a dense array of newspapers, online news portals and television stations. This can be seen in the retweeting patterns presented in Figure 6.2, where local Egyptian media accounts receive the large majority of total media retweets compared with transnational Arab or international media platforms. In Syria, by contrast, global and pan-Arab media make up by far the largest share of the retweets. It should also be noted that the key role of social media activists in the Syrian online ecosystem can make the coding of what counts as a 'media account' somewhat tricky.[17] For the purposes of this analysis, I included accounts from collective online news portals such as @shaamnews, but not individual accounts.

This Twitter analysis offers some empirical support for the claim that broadcast, print and social media must be understood as single informational ecosystem, and that each country's ecosystem features a distinctive configuration of domestic and foreign media.

Transitional National Patterns

Integration between different types of media looks different across each national context, however, with some countries offering robust national media and others far more dependent on regional and international platforms.

Egypt has always had a more robust and contentious public sphere than other more tightly controlled Arab authoritarian regimes.[18] The Mubarak regime maintained tight control over broadcast media and the intelligence services enforced certain red lines, but Egyptian newspapers featured regular criticism, independent columnists, and critical journalists. Well before the revolution, Egypt's media had evolved into a complex hybrid ecosystem of enormous state-run dinosaurs, respected private daily newspapers, and pugnacious tabloids alongside activist blogs and social media.

Most of these independent media rallied to the side of the revolution in early 2011. Independent television stations such as ONTV hosted highly influential political talk shows and programs which drove the national agenda.[19] The sight of top generals being grilled on live TV by a revolution-sympathising talk show host seemed like an early sign of the emergence of a public sphere in the classical sense. So did the robust, critical debate in the opinion pages of leading independent newspapers, which opened themselves to a wide range of new voices and relaxed the red lines constraining political criticism.

Those Egyptian media outlets soon found themselves facing regulatory pressure, capture by powerful social groups, and attachment to local political trends. The state media sector remained largely intact. The Supreme Council of the Armed Forces, which ruled Egypt from February 2011 until the June 2012 Presidential election, resisted any scrutiny of the military. Unreformed state media institutions quickly resumed their old habits, as the media became the vehicle for a sustained attack on the challengers to the old regime.[20] Activists and protesters were soon targeted by the military-controlled media, demonised as foreign-backed agents of destabilisation and blamed for the country's ills.[21] Legislation, personnel, and practices carried over from the old regime with few major changes.[22] This was exemplified by the inflammatory and misleading coverage of protests in October 2011 outside Maspero, the headquarters of Egyptian state broadcasting, which led to a bloody attack on Coptic Christian demonstrators. Activists continued to find ways to creatively use media to advance their agendas and critiques, but they were shouting into the abyss or preaching to a dwindling choir of activists.[23]

The Muslim Brotherhood's victory in the June 2012 Presidential election created a new set of circumstances. Efforts to reform state institutions, including the media, now triggered intense fears of 'Islamisation'. Both public and private media mounted massive anti-Muslim Brotherhood campaigns along with constant reporting of economic and social breakdowns, which fueled popular discontent and shaped the popular support for the July 2013 military coup. Real violence interacted with sensationalist media to produce widespread fear and fury, with narratives rapidly hardening and dialogue across ideological lines becoming rare. Outlets that had once been critical, such as Ibrahim Eissa's *Al-Tahrir*, emerged as spokesmen for the revived security state, while popular websites and tabloids eagerly peddled pro-regime and anti-Brotherhood rumors. Figures such as right-wing conspiracy theorist Tawfik Okasha and regime attack dog Ahmed Moussa rose to the center of the Egyptian public sphere. Businessman and al-Sisi advisor Tarek Nour's *Cairo and the People* promoted the regime's line, including the controversial but regular broadcasting of secret wiretaps of activists obviously leaked by the intelligence apparatus. The 'Tamarod' campaign which culminated in the 30 June protests against Morsi received lavish, supportive coverage, which almost certainly helped pave the way for the popular support for the 3 July coup. In early December 2012, leading Arab journalist Jamal al-Rayyan tweeted that 'most of the Egyptian media is an instrument for incitement to the anarchy in which Egypt is living today.'

Following the coup, the regime formed an even tighter symbiosis with the media, which focused on mobilising support for General al-Sisi and demonising the Muslim Brotherhood.[24] Journalists and television hosts dropped any pretense of objectivity, instead competing with each other over who could most enthusiastically support the regime.[25] The Muslim Brotherhood's encampment at Rabaa received extremely alarming coverage, while the massacre of over 1000 people in August was portrayed in a highly sympathetic light. Pro-revolution voices were forced from the air, arrested or harassed. Most famously, Bassem Youssef's political comedy program, which had been so effective in subverting the Morsi Presidency, could not survive a month in the post-coup political environment. Discontent with the 'unprecedented crisis in Egyptian journalism' came to the fore in the second half of 2014, as the extent of its contributions to the restoration of a neo-authoritarian regime became clear.[26] Liberal politician Amr Hamzawy scathingly described it as a 'neo-fascist' period for the Egyptian media, while a veteran Egyptian journalist describes today's media as in its worst condition ever seen.[27]

Tunisia

Tunisia's national media followed a similar path, despite beginning from less robust foundations. Its pre-revolutionary media was far more rigidly controlled than Egypt's.[28] The 2000s witnessed some important experiments such as Radio Mosaique, Shams FM, and Zeituna, and television stations such as Hanibal TV (launched in 2004) in the years leading up to the uprising.[29] During and after the revolution, long-frustrated journalists and citizens leaped at the opportunity to develop a real media sector. A new press code adopted in 2011 scaled back the most restrictive aspects of the Ben Ali regime's media control. In November 2012, Tunisia established a new oversight body outside the Ministry of Information, with responsibility for the media.[30] Finally, the new Constitution adopted in 2014 offers robust protections for freedom of speech and the media.

These reforms went further than in Egypt, but still fell far short. National television and radio remained dominated by the old guard from the Ben Ali period.[31] Meanwhile, private media outlets, many of which had been established in the Ben Ali period, went smoothly from 'serving the regime to serving agendas.'[32] Previously existing private television stations adapted quickly to the new market, with their owners often using them to promote their personal profile and advance their political agendas. Ennahda, meanwhile, created its own television and radio stations, such as Zaytouna TV, in an effort to compete.[33] Businessmen close to the anti-Ennahda political party Nidaa Tounes set up Al-Hiwar TV, which broadcasts a steady stream of anti-Islamist content. This proliferation of partisan media led, as in Egypt, to the fragmentation and self-segregation of the public into hostile, mutually incomprehensible camps. By the summer of 2016, six of the top ten television stations in the country were under political control.[34]

Tunisia's transition nearly broke down in mid-2013. As in Egypt, the media served a key function in the mobilisation of discontent against the elected Islamist government. Abd al-Salam al-Obaydi, media advisor to PM Ali Larayedh, complained in late 2013 that 'the media which was a weapon in the hands of the Ben Ali regime has turned itself into a weapon to attack the current government.'[35] The media fanned the discontent and rage which nearly derailed Tunisia's transition. Sensational reporting of events like the assassination of opposition figure Chokri Belaid or allegations of Ennahda corruption galvanised popular mistrust and rage. Over the course of 2012 and 2013, both broadcast and online media were flooded with a stream of sensational stories of Ennahda infiltration of state institutions. Retired police officers and 'security experts' appeared frequently on television and the radio, consistently warning of Ennahda plots and calling for them to be unseated.[36] During the Tunisian Presidential campaign in the winter of 2014, a furious President Moncef Marzouki lashed out at the media as 'sleeping remnants of the old party' and lambasted National TV as a 'lying and corrupt media which doesn't have the right to speak in the name of Tunisians.'[37]

Beyond Egypt and Tunisia

The Egyptian and Tunisian experiences each illustrate how unreformed and un-institutionalised national media sectors undermined democratic transitions. In Morocco and Jordan, the regimes increased direct and indirect controls over the media in order to rebuild support for the political order and market limited constitutional reforms while demonising protestors and raising fears of the bloody potential consequences of civic unrest. Regimes in the Gulf adopted increasingly draconian measures of control against both the formal media sector and against individual online activists. Kuwait, which had long enjoyed one of the most open and contentious media spaces in the region, witnessed severe crackdowns after 2011, with citizens imprisoned for tweets criticising the Emir and newspapers experiencing unusual governmental pressure. Bahrain fiercely attacked independent media and oppositional online networks. Most Arab regimes proved able to use familiar media methods, from censorship to undermining opposition to mobilizing nationalist passions, to help them survive the uprisings.

These mechanisms were exacerbated in countries where state institutions failed more dramatically and violent anarchy had become a reality rather than a concern. In Syria, the near-complete absence of credible national media opened the door to a more central role for transnational and social media, almost all of which quickly aligned with one faction or another. Television stations such as the pro-rebellion Gulf stations Al-Jazeera and Al-Arabiya, the extreme Islamist Al-Wesal, and the pro-'Resistance' (in practice, pro-Assad) Lebanon-based Al-Mayadeen, anchored their respective narratives for or against the Syrian uprising. Syrian rebels worked through their online networks to distribute supportive images, videos, information and quotes to the Arab and international media.

In Libya, the proliferation of national and local television stations aligned with particular political factions contributed to polarisation, fear, and insecurity.[38] Again, the lack of a pre-existing media ecosystem, after decades of Gaddafi's autocratic rule, opened the door to highly partisan transnational media and social media to define the information space. Collapsing political institutions, the absence of reliable non-partisan media, and the very real violence magnified the impact of the information circulating through these media platforms.

Can transitions survive the media?

The role of the media should not be viewed in isolation from the underlying political challenges, of course. The pernicious effects of the Arab media took root in transitional environments characterised by institutional uncertainty, personal insecurity, and ideological or sectarian divisions. Such uncertainty, fear and anger created a fertile environment and eager audience for sensationalist media which fanned rumors, incited against political adversaries, and fueled divisive and demonising narratives. In particular, transitional moments in most Arab cases revealed profound disagreements about national identity and deep fears about the future. Long delays and highly contested processes in the drafting of constitutions contributed to the intensity of these identity conflicts. Initial moments of unity consistently gave way to growing polarisation around regional, ethnic, sectarian or ideological identities, and between Islamists and anti-Islamists. Populist, mobilisational media interacted with partisan, polarised social networks to drive discourse to the extremes and intensify divisions between groups.

The role of the media in the regional autocratic retrenchment of the last few years has proven profoundly dispiriting to those who put faith in the emergence of a new Arab public sphere. Regimes and old elites proved quite capable of adapting to the challenge and turning the new media environment to their advantage. The same media which helped to drive the diffusion of protest during the early Arab uprisings proved equally effective at driving resentment, fear, division and demobilisation of exhausted publics. But despair is premature. The underlying transformations in the media environment which originally empowered the Arab uprisings have not disappeared. Nor have the deep grievances which originally sparked the protest wave. When political conditions change, the media will likely once again accelerate and intensify episodic protests and political challenges to the brittle new authoritarian regimes in the region.

7

NOT READY FOR DEMOCRACY

MODERNISATION, PLURALISM, AND THE ARAB SPRING[1]

Tarek Masoud

In 2011, Egypt and Tunisia overthrew their dictators and ushered in periods of democratic competition and governance. Five years later, Tunisia appears to have consolidated its democracy, while Egypt is back to authoritarian rule. What explains this difference? Eschewing existing explanations that focus on the differing stances and interests of the countries' militaries or the different normative commitments of the two countries' Islamists, this chapter will argue that the source of the divergence lies in socio-economic differences of the kind long highlighted by modernisation theorists such as Seymour Martin Lipset, and Carles Boix and Susan C. Stokes.[2] Wealthier, more urban, and more industrialised Tunisia was always more propitious terrain for democracy than poorer, more rural, and more agrarian Egypt. However, in contrast to much of the literature linking economic development to the emergence of democracy—which holds that development makes democracy more likely by changing individual habits and values—this chapter suggests that it does so by multiplying the forms of social and political organisation within which citizens are embedded (what I call 'empirical pluralism'). The empirical pluralism of more developed societies generates the 'inconclusive political struggle' that so many

111

democratisation theorists believed essential to the emergence and maintenance of democratic regimes.[3] I make this argument drawing on a variety of local and global data on democracy, military coups, civil society, and economic development—comparing Egypt and Tunisia not just to each other, but to a broader set of global dictatorships and democracies.

Introduction

Five years after the beginning of the so-called Arab Spring, only two of the twenty-two member states of the Arab League have managed to meet Juan Linz and Alfred Stepan's (rather minimal) criteria for a 'completed' democratic transition:[4] in Egypt and Tunisia, free and fair elections gave rise to democratic governments with the requisite state capacity and coherence to actually govern the territories under their ambit.[5] However, mere months after getting democracy, Egypt lost it, as the military overthrew the country's first freely-elected president (who to some seemed poised to extinguish Egypt's democratic experiment). Tunisia, in contrast, held new presidential and parliamentary elections in 2014 that saw the country's first elected government transfer power peacefully to another elected government, thus fulfilling Samuel Huntington's famous 'two turnovers' test for democratic consolidation.[6]

Scholars have offered two main explanations for the divergence between Egypt's and Tunisia's post-Arab Spring trajectories. The first focuses on differences between the two countries' military apparatuses. In these accounts, Tunisia's small and historically quiescent army is presented as having been unable and unwilling to insert itself into the political tussles of civilian politicians, while Egypt's large and historically influential army is thought to have been unable and unwilling to stay out of them. The second explanation for the divergence focuses on the characteristics and behaviours of the civilian politicians themselves, and their commitments to democracy and to political compromise. In this telling, Tunisian democracy has survived because the country was blessed with Islamists and non-Islamists who exhibited a greater fund of democratic values than their Egyptian counterparts, who were unruly, uncompromising, and mutually suspicious.

However, these two broad narratives—highlighting the deeds and decisions of officers and civilians, respectively—are unsatisfying. For even if the behaviours of officers and politicians determined the outcomes of transitions, a complete understanding of these behaviours requires us to attend to the incentives and constraints facing them. As political scientist Jeffrey Kopstein noted in an essay on the 1989 revolutions in Eastern Europe, if the success or failure of a democratic transition is truly a function of the choices made by individuals, we still must explain the causes of those choices.[7] That is what this chapter will attempt to do: to move us beyond testimonials to the good or bad behaviours of political actors during transitions and to uncover the deeper, structural factors that made actors behave in the ways that they did.

My argument is that differences in economic development generated the observed differences in Egypt's and Tunisia's democratic transitions. The causal chain by which development (or its absence) leads to democratic transition (or transition breakdown) is long, but to render it digestible, let us begin at the end, with the question of whether or not a military decides to abrogate a transition and initiate an authoritarian restoration. Where most scholars attribute military coups against fledgling democracies to the characteristics and histories of the militaries that undertake them, I argue that they have much more to do with the characteristics of the political landscapes in which the militaries are embedded. Specifically, building on prior theoretical work on military coups, I contend that militaries wishing to intervene in politics are more likely to be able to do so when civilian political forces are unable to cement their commitment to democracy. In turn, I argue, the ability of civilian politicians to commit to democracy is a function of the capabilities of 'losers' in founding democratic elections, as has been pointed out by several scholars, most notably Adam Przeworski.[8] Where losers were reasonably assured of their ability to win (or at least be competitive in) future elections, they continued to uphold the fledgling political system. Where they had little faith in their ability to emerge victorious in future contests, losing parties went, in Stepan's words, 'knocking on the barracks door'—calling for the military to undo at bayonet point what they could not themselves undo at the ballot box.[9]

But what determines the electoral fortunes of political losers in new democracies—and, in turn, whether they precipitate military involvement? Here, I argue for renewed attention to the makeup of civil society at moments of democratic transitions. Since political parties in newly democratising systems frequently lack well-defined mass organisations, they must tap into pre-existing civic networks in order to mobilise voters.[10] Consequently, countries with more diverse social networks and forms of civic life are more likely to give rise to multiple credible competitors in founding elections. I call this situation 'empirical pluralism,' in order to distinguish it from 'normative' pluralism (which I take to mean the belief of actors in the necessity of freedom of association and the expression of multiple worldviews in political life). Where civil society was stunted or limited, elections tended to give rise to monolithic party systems in which losers had little hope of winning in future rounds. In such circumstances, losing parties thus turned from elections to protest, revolution, and to the call for military intervention.

If military coups are determined by the democratic commitments of losers in founding elections, and the commitments of losers are determined by their electoral fortunes (i.e. the existence of 'empirical pluralism'), and 'empirical pluralism' is determined by the structure of civil society at the time of transition, what determines the structure of civil society? This brings us to the role of economic development. Scholars of the so-called 'modernisation' school have long recognised that economic development processes are essential for transforming traditional societies into modern ones. However, this article emphasises a different feature of modernisation than has typically been highlighted by those earlier scholars. It makes no claim about how modernity changes the values or cognition of individuals (a view that has been ably criticised by Kurzman among others).[11] Instead, this chapter highlights the ways in which modernisation leads to a proliferation of the kinds of social networks in which individuals are embedded, moving them beyond the faith and the kin group toward a wider array of affiliations based on such factors as class and occupation.[12] The richer, more diverse civil societies of more developed economies in turn generate richer, more diverse party systems in new democracies, which in turn possess the requisite pluralism and dispersion of political power long deemed necessary to sustain democratic institutions. The full logic of the argument is diagrammed in Figure 7.1.

The structure of this chapter follows the structure of the argument outlined above. At each step in the argument, I attempt to adduce as much evidence as possible, comparing Egypt and Tunisia not just to each other, but to a broader set of countries that have undergone democratic transitions and military coups. First, the article takes on the most prominent agent-centric accounts of the divergence between Egypt and Tunisia—i.e. the differing natures of the countries' militaries. It argues that theories that locate Tunisia's democratic success in the small size and historical quiescence of its coercive apparatus miss important empirical facts both about military coups in general and the incentives and capabilities of Tunisia's armed state agents in particular. Comparing Tunisia to the universe of cases of attempted coups in the latter half of the twentieth century, I find that the characteristics of that country's military cannot explain its relative political quiescence during the

Figure 7.1: Logic of the argument: Linking development to party system pluralism to democratic consolidation

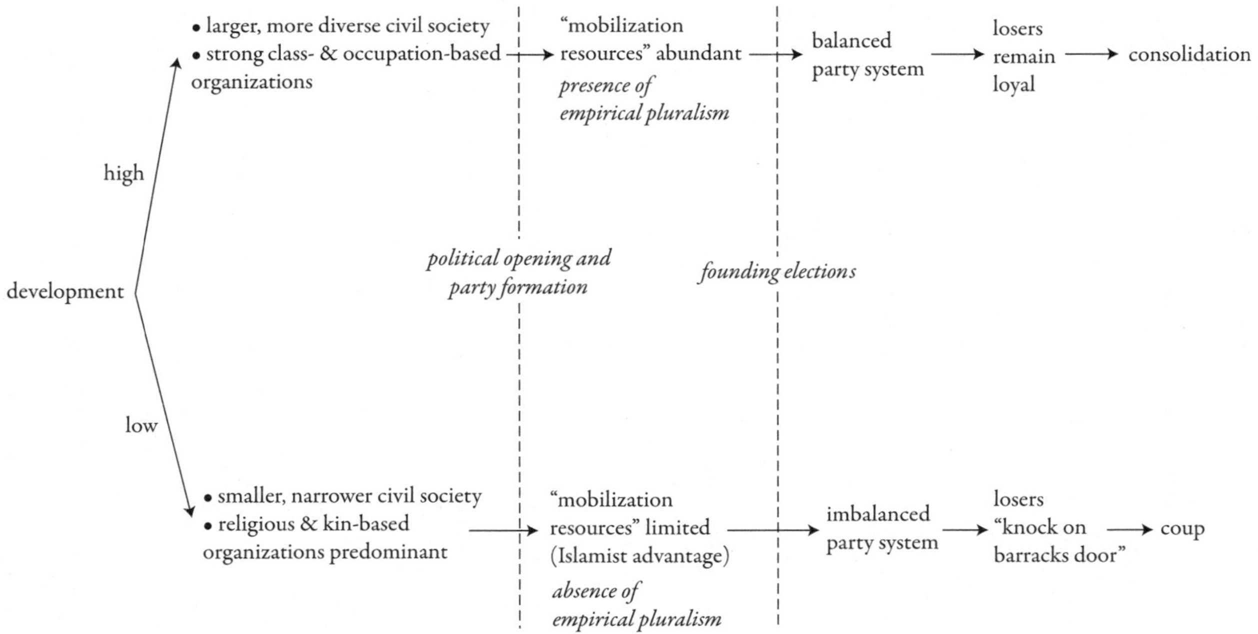

2011–13 democratic transition. Instead, I argue, following previous theorists of military coups, that we should focus on the relative absence in Tunisia of powerful calls for military intervention from non-Islamist political parties. I then turn to explaining the political loyalty of Tunisia's secular parties, attributing this to their superior performance in the country's founding elections. I offer a combination of aggregate and individual level evidence to suggest that the superior performance of secularists in Tunisia (relative to their counterparts in the Egyptian case) is a function of that country's denser, secular civil society, which provided secular parties with more resources for mobilising newly available voters in 2011. Egypt, in contrast, had a much narrower civic space, dominated by religious institutions, as is characteristic of less developed countries. Finally, I attempt to explain the differences in Tunisia's and Egypt's civic landscape, demonstrating with aggregate evidence that these differences reflect logics of civil society formation long articulated by modernisation theorists. The article concludes with a consideration of the normative implications of the argument presented here, and by distinguishing it from other strains of modernisation theory.

Military Quiescence and Rebellion

Scholars have long recognised that the greatest threat to democratic transition is abrogation by the armed forces.[13] As Naunihal Singh puts it, 'coup attempts are the basic mechanism for most of the regime change and irregular leadership removal in the world.'[14] Why was Tunisia able to elude this distressingly common danger, and why did Egypt so readily fall victim to it? The conventional answer to this question emphasises the diminutive size of Tunisia's military in comparison to Egypt's. For example, James Gelvin notes, '[in] Tunisia, the military has historically been relatively small compared to militaries in the rest of the Arab world—about 36,000 officers and men at the time of the uprising.'[15] In contrast, he tells us, 'The Egyptian military is the polar opposite of its Tunisian counterpart. It is huge: the army alone includes 900,000 men (including reservists).' Moreover, Michelle Penner Angrist suggests that only 18,000 of the Tunisian army's personnel were soldiers, the rest being administrators.[16] These differences in size supposedly point to a difference in capabilities: in this account, the large Egyptian army was simply more capable of asserting its political will than the diminutive Tunisian one. Philippe Droz-Vincent argues that 'the small size of the military was a guarantee against military coups.'[17] In fact, so feeble does Angrist believe the Tunisian army to be that she argues that its decision to back the protesters in 2011 was basically inconsequential: 'Not only was the Tunisian army small [...] it was also under-supplied and poorly equipped.'[18]

However, the evidence suggests that ascribing the Tunisian military's political quiescence to its small size is a mistake. Small armies conduct coups all the time. Consider Egypt. In 1952, a group of self-described 'Free Officers' (al-ḍubbāṭ al-ʾaḥrār) overthrew a monarchy that had been in place since 1804, and inaugurated a regime that lasted until the overthrow of Hosni Mubarak in 2011. Egypt's population at the time was approximately 20 million, but according to Hazem Kandil and Anthony McDermott, respectively, its army numbered between only 35,000 and 65,000 men.[19] In other words, Tunisia's army in 2011 was larger (relative to its population) than Egypt's was in 1952. Moreover, the Egyptian military at the time of its coup against the monarchy was not deemed to be especially capable. According to Kandil, the British 'kept the army understaffed, unequipped, and trained for little more than parade ground marches.'[20] And yet this parade ground army was still able to seize power in a country of more than 20 million people. It does not take a large, well-equipped army to carry out a coup.

In order to probe this point more systematically, we must look beyond the two cases at hand, to examine the average sizes and other characteristics of armies throughout recent history that have conducted military coups. We need to know if Tunisia's army is especially small not just relative to Egypt's, but to others that have seized (or attempted to seize) power. If it is, then this would constitute evidence in favour of the proposition that the diminutive size of Tunisia's army was an important determinant of its behaviour. I employ data on military coups from Jonathan Powell and Clayton Thyne, who have enumerated every attempted and successful military coup from 1950 to the present.[21] They count 471 coups in ninety-seven countries from 1950 to 2014. Of those, 236 (50.11 per cent) were successful, meaning that the officers held power for at least a week. These constitute the units for this analysis.[22]

To explore the relationship between coups and military size, I combine these data with information on the size of the armed forces from the International Institute of Strategic Studies' annual Military Balance assessments. The IISS data, which run from 1961 to the present, includes information on active and reserve personnel in national militaries and paramilitaries. I add these four quantities to arrive at a single estimate of total military personnel per country-coup-year. I note here that this data is available for only 269 of the 471 coups in the database, representing seventy-six countries from

1961 to 2014. Of these, 123 (45.72 per cent) were successful by Powell and Thyne's definition, which means our data is slightly skewed toward unsuccessful coups. In order to render the figures comparable across countries, I employ population data for each country-year from the World Bank's World Development Indicators to calculate an estimate of the number of military personnel per 1,000 inhabitants for each coup attempt in the database.[23]

What do these data show us? The median number of soldiers per 1,000 for these 269 coups and attempted coups is 4.75. For successful coups, the median is 4.89, for unsuccessful ones it is 4.62. Tunisia comes in at just under this, at 4.45.[24] Of the 125 coups conducted by militaries with fewer than 4.45 soldiers per 1,000 inhabitants, sixty-nine failed and fifty-six (44.8 per cent) were successful. This is only a little under the average rate of coup success (50.11 per cent for the 471 coups conducted between 1955 and 2014; 45.72 per cent success rate for the cases for which Military Balance data are available). The point here is simple: Tunisia's military may have been small relative to Egypt's, but it was not small relative to other militaries that have conducted coups. This is illustrated in Figure 7.2, which is a smoothed histogram of military personnel per 1,000 inhabitants for the countries in our data, with a vertical line representing Tunisia's 2013 value on this variable.

Before proceeding, it is important to be aware of the shortcomings of the foregoing analysis. By analysing only those countries that have experienced coups, I am of course selecting the dependent variable. Although small militaries are healthily represented among those that conduct coups, it may be that they are still less likely to conduct coups than big militaries. To test this proposition I would need data on military size per capita for every country for every year, not just countries or years in which coups took place. That said, the fact that roughly half of the coups in the dataset were conducted by militaries the size of Tunisia's or smaller suggests at the very least that the probability that small militaries engage in coups is not insignificant relative to that of large ones. In fact, one might argue that by selecting on the dependent variable, I am likely to underestimate the propensity of small militaries to engage in coups. Furthermore, Singh gives us reasons to believe that, all else being equal, small militaries might be more likely to conduct coups. Singh draws our attention to 'what happens within the military once the coup attempt begins'— that is, whether the military fractures in response to a coup. It could be argued that larger militaries are more likely to contain within them competing factions that could defect in response to a seizure of power by a segment of the officer corps, while smaller ones are easier to hold together under such circum-

Figure 7.2: Military size, relative to population, in 269 cases of attempted and successful coups, 1961–2014

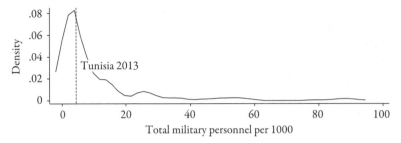

Total military personnel per 1000

stances. Knowing this, officers in larger militaries might be more reluctant to initiate coups in the first place. A full discussion of coup dynamics is beyond the scope of this article. The point of the foregoing is merely to suggest that the data limitations outlined above do not undermine the conclusion of our analysis: that the absolute size of the Tunisian and Egyptian militaries is insufficient to explain variation in their behaviour.

We cannot yet dispense with military-centric explanations of Egypt's and Tunisia's divergence, however. An alternative, and more sophisticated, argument is that the two militaries' behaviours were determined not by their relative sizes, but by their histories of political involvement. Jenkins and Kposowa and Bratton and Van de Walle argue that certain types of militaries—characterised by control over big chunks of the economy and, most importantly, by previous interventions in domestic politics—are those most likely to cut a democratic transition short with a military coup.[25]

Much of the pre-existing scholarship on Egypt's and Tunisia's militaries validates this perspective, emphasising the former's history of political control.[26] As the scholar Yasser El-Shimy argues, post-1952 Egypt constituted a 'praetorian state' in which the military was not just predominant, but powerful enough to singlehandedly determine the shape of the Egyptian political system.[27] Others have documented the military's sway over large segments of the economy (and have noted how the military populates local governments as well as the boards of major state-owned companies with retired officers).[28] By contrast, Tunisia's military is thought to have been systematically averse to political engagement and willingly subject to civilian control.[29] Philip Droz-Vincent points out that 'in Tunisia, the military has always been distant from the regime.' In a recent restatement of the conventional wisdom, we read that 'The military in Tunisia has historically played a much less prominent role in politics than its Egyptian counterpart [...] [and] never developed the economic or institutional interests that would drive it into politics.'[30]

There are, however, reasons to believe such testimonials are overstated. Prior to Tunisia's 2011 constituent assembly election, one former minister of the Interior, Farḥat al-Rajḥi, was reported to have declared that a victory by the Islamist party Ennahda would result in a military coup (allegedly due to the strong opposition of remnants of the prior regime concentrated in coastal cities). Although this obviously did not take place, the fact that rumours of this nature were circulating among Tunisia's political elite underline the danger of assuming that the Tunisian military was incapable of conceiving of, let alone executing, a coup.[31] After all, it is not as if Tunisian history is entirely bereft of military intervention in politics. Most notably, the dictator who was ousted in 2011, Zine el-Abidine Ben Ali, was himself a general and a former minister of the Interior who took power from his predecessor, Habib Bourguiba, in what has been described as a 'bloodless coup'.[32] In fact, according to Hicham Bou Nassif, the Tunisian military should be properly considered a co-conspirator in the 1987 coup, through which it hoped to achieve more political influence in that country.[33] Although the Tunisian military's hopes for increased influence in Ben Ali's regime did not come to pass, this history naturally undermines testimonials to the allegedly inherent political neutrality of the Tunisian military.

But even putting aside the 1987 coup and the military's role in it, the question is not whether Tunisia's military was less politically central than Egypt's, but rather whether it was less politically central than other militaries that have undertaken military coups. In order to answer this question, I try to compare the political centrality of the Tunisian military to others in the database of coups assembled by Powell and Thyne.[34] There is, however, no direct measure of 'political centrality'. Therefore, for the purposes of this chapter, I rely on the measure of 'militarisation' compiled by the Bonn International Center for Conversion.[35] This data series, which runs from 1990 to 2013, is comprised of an index of six key variables that capture the relative importance and power of the national militaries. These are (1) military expenditure as a share of GDP, (2) military spending versus health spending, (3) military and paramilitary personnel in relation to the total population, (4) military reservists compared to the population, (5) military and paramilitary personnel compared to the number of physicians, and (6) the number of heavy weapons relative to the population.[36] Country scores are normalised from 0 to 1,000. Given the truncated time frame for which we have this data (1990 to 2013), our data comprises just seventy-three coup attempts in thirty-two countries (43.84 per cent of which were successful). Country scores in our data range from 340.62 for Papua New Guinea in 2012 to 835.05 for Azerbaijan in 1994. We reason that countries with higher GMI scores are ones in which the military is more politically central, as evidenced by their ability to capture a greater share of national resources and by their physical presence in a country's everyday life.

How does Tunisia stack up against these coup-enacting countries in terms of militarisation (our proxy for a military's 'political centrality')? Tunisia's GMI score in 2013 was 580.16, ranking 76th in the world. (For comparison's sake, Egypt's GMI score for 2013 is 683.86, making it 26th in the world.) The average GMI score for the seventy-three coup attempts in our data (1990 to 2013) is 611.41 (lower than Egypt, higher than Tunisia), while the median is 624.147. To give you a sense of what these numbers mean: a country with the average GMI score in our data would have ranked between 55th and 54th in 2013 (between Australia and Kyrgyzstan, respectively), while a country with the median GMI score in our data would have ranked between 45th and 46th in 2013 (between Angola and Sri Lanka). On this measure, then, Tunisia is considerably less militarised than either the average or median coup-enacting country (at least for the years 1990 to 2013).[37] That said, for twenty-eight attempted coups (of which fourteen were successful) conducted in thirteen countries, we observe lower GMI scores than Tunisia's 2013 score. So, Tunisia may be less militarised than the average place in which we observe a military coup, but it is more militarised than many countries that have experienced coups. This is illustrated in Figure 7.3, which is a kernel density plot of GMI scores for seventy-three coup attempts from 1990 to 2013, with a vertical line at Tunisia's 2013 score.

The above analysis, as cursory as it is, represents the first attempt I know of to put the military's behaviour in Egypt and Tunisia in broader comparative perspective, comparing the attributes of those militaries to others that undertook forceful seizures of power. What the data seems to show is that both Egypt and Tunisia were credible candidates for military coups, and that the political quiescence of the military in the latter country could not have been predicted solely on the basis of that army's size or the relative militarisation of Tunisian society.

Beyond the army

Finally, even if we grant that the Tunisian army was too small and too apolitical to follow the Egyptian model, it was not the only armed agent of the

Tunisian state capable of doing so. The large Ministry of Interior, with its strong ideological opposition to the Islamists who controlled the Tunisian government after Ben Ali's fall, could plausibly have undertaken a forceful seizure of power.[38] According to Hicham Bou Nassif, the ratio of police officers to citizens in Tunisia ranged between one officer for every 67–112 citizens—that is, between nine and fifteen policemen per thousand inhabitants—rendering the Tunisian Ministry of Interior comparable in size, relative to the country's population, to the Egyptian army.[39] In fact, there are reports that in the summer of 2013, as Tunisia was wracked by mass protests after the assassination of leftist party leader Mohamed Brahmi, a coup by the security forces was a distinct possibility. Presidential spokesman Adnān Munṣir alleged that 'the presidency of the republic has thwarted on more than one occasion attempted political, security, and military coups', although he later denied that the leadership of the army or the Ministry of Interior had been involved in these attempts.[40] Everything said about the Egyptian army to explain its coup-proneness could thus also have been said about the Tunisian Ministry of Interior.

However, the primary reason that a coup by the Ministry of Interior would not have worked is because the most powerful anti-Islamist forces in Tunisia were also opposed to it. Where opponents of the Muslim Brotherhood in Egypt called to dismantle democratically elected institutions and the installation of military tutelage, in Tunisia, Ennahda's opponents called for a reconfiguration of government and new legislative elections, not the dissolution of the entire democratic edifice. For example, on 8 July 2013, Maya Jribi of the PDP—which in early 2012 merged with Tunisian Horizons into a new, centrist, Republican Party (*al-Ḥizb al-Jumhūrī*)—declared that the 'dissolution

Figure 7.3: Country-level militarisation in seventy-three cases of attempted and successful coups, 1990–2013

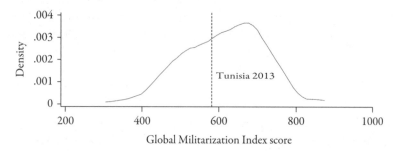

of the National Constituent Assembly would lead directly to civil war,' and that, while Ennahda should be rejected, rejections should take place at the ballot box.[41] Similarly, though the UGTT called a general strike for 26 July 2013 and demanded a government of national unity, it explicitly refrained from calling for the dissolution of the constituent assembly.[42] The head of the union, Ḥussayn ʿAbbāsī, explained, 'We propose maintaining the Constituent Assembly but with a time-frame to speed up completion of its work.'[43] In short, whereas in Egypt, opponents of the Brotherhood were united in their call for military intervention, in Tunisia most consequential non-Islamists wished to remain within the country's new and hard-won electoral framework. There was simply no room for the Ministry of Interior or the army to intervene, even if they wished to do so.

What the above analysis suggests is that, in our search for answers for why Tunisian democracy has so far held together, we must look beyond the characteristics and decision-making processes of the national coercive apparatuses. In what follows, I suggest that we can gain more purchase by redirecting our attentions to the actions and behaviours of civilian politicians during moments of transition.

'Knocking on the Barracks Door'

The proposed analytical shift from militaries to civilians is validated by much of the literature on military seizures of power. Scholars of democratic transitions and coups have long highlighted the role of civilian politicians in enabling military intrusions into the political sphere. Steven R. David tells us that one 'factor promoting coups d'état is a weak public commitment to civilian institutions' and a civil society that is too weak to stand up to the army.[44] Terry Lynn Karl suggests that military interventions in democratic transitions take place when political conflicts become so acute that a segment of the political elite 'call[s] upon the military to protect its vital interests.'[45] In his magisterial study of militaries in Latin American politics, Alfred Stepan tells us that 'the capacity of the military as a complex institution to develop a consensus for intervention is greatly aided to the extent that civil society "knocks on the doors" of the barracks'.[46] In short, the scholarly consensus has held that military abrogations of democratic transitions of the kind we observed in Egypt in 2013 are functions of political conflicts among civilian politicians that cause one faction to seek the army's intervention on their behalf. In the absence of this type of conflict, it is much more difficult for the army to justify political interventions, either to its external patrons (such as, in the Egyptian case, the United States), or internally, to factions of the military that might be hesitant to wade into the political sphere.[47]

This scholarship naturally redirects our attention to the nature of conflict among civilian politicians in the two countries. And here, too, scholars have identified important differences. For example, scholars have hypothesised that Tunisia differed from Egypt in the extent to which its elites—Islamist and non-Islamist—believed in the necessity of compromise.[48] In contrast, the conventional wisdom holds that Egypt was marked by intense polarisation between Islamists (who had long constituted the most electorally successful opposition bloc in Egyptian politics) and non-Islamists, and an insufficient commitment to democracy and to the need for compromise.[49] In this telling, Egyptian secular elites went 'knocking on the barracks door' because they required rescue from heavy-handed and undemocratic Islamists, while Tunisian secular elites refrained from this because both they and their Islamist rivals were more committed to democracy in the first place.

Assuming for a moment that this story is an accurate reflection of empirical reality in both countries, we must ask why Egyptian and Tunisian elites exhibited such different beliefs and commitments. This has not been well explored. Stepan and Linz report that 'secular liberals and Islamists began meeting regularly eight years before Ben Ali's fall to see whether they could reduce mutual fears and agree upon rules for democratic governance.'[50] The result of these meetings, they report, was that the two parties arrived at 'highly innovative 'pacts'' that smoothed the course of the transition. The idea here is that sustained contact between Islamists and secularists during the authoritarian period enabled them to build trust with each other and to outline the contours of the future political system. The problem with this narrative is that oppositionists in Egypt also cooperated with each other during Mubarak's rule; the warmth that this cooperation would have generated dissipated quickly once the man was overthrown. For example, during the uprising against Mubarak, Islamists and non-Islamists formed an opposition coordinating committee that included one prominent member of the Muslim Brotherhood, Muḥammad al-Biltāgī, currently in prison on terrorism charges and widely reviled by his erstwhile allies as a villain.[51] Another example of the failure of cross-ideological cooperation to generate post-revolutionary comity in the Egyptian case can be observed in the makeup of the prominent anti-Mubarak Kifāya (Enough) movement (*al-Ḥaraka al-Miṣriyya min ajl al-Taghyīr*). The coordinators of this group included the staunch leftist ʿAbd al-Ḥalīm Qandīl, and the staunch Islamist politician Magdī Aḥmad Ḥussayn. In fact, when the Islamist Ḥussayn—then in prison—put forth his candidacy in January 2011 to become the general coordinator (*munassaq ʿām*) of the movement, the secular Qandīl defended his right to run despite being in prison, declared that Ḥussayn's detention was a mark of 'pride, not shame,' and compared him to Nelson Mandela, 'who remained the president of his party throughout his imprisonment.'[52] However, this cross-ideological closeness did not prevent both men from becoming avid combatants on either side of the divide separating Islamists and non-Islamists that emerged after the 2011 elections.

Empirical Pluralism, or 'A Sufficiently Even Balance of Political Power'

Where does this leave us? In the remainder of this section, I present an alternative argument for why Egyptian non-Islamists went 'knocking on the barracks door,' while Tunisian non-Islamists stuck with the democratic game. Here, I focus less on ideology and values and more on political necessity. The key analytical difference between Egypt and Tunisia, I argue, lies in the different outcomes of the two countries' founding elections. In Tunisia's constituent assembly elections, concluded in October 2011, Ennahda captured approximately 41 per cent of the seats, with the remainder (59 per cent) going to a collection of secular parties. In Egypt, by contrast, the first post-Mubarak elections, concluded in January 2012, brought an Islamist supermajority to the legislature, with the Muslim Brotherhood's Freedom and Justice Party capturing approximately 47 per cent of the seats, and the ultra-orthodox Nour Party (Party of Light) capturing 24 per cent.[53] In other words, Tunisia's post authoritarian period was marked by what I call 'empirical pluralism'—the existence of a variety of political parties who were credible claimants on power—while Egypt's was marked by a lack of such pluralism.[54]

The existence of empirical pluralism in Tunisia meant that Islamists needed to compromise with secularists to govern, and secularists remained committed to democratic procedures (which continued to hold out the promise of acquiring power). In contrast, the absence of empirical pluralism in Egypt meant that Islamists—who possessed a supermajority—felt no need to compromise with their opponents (whom they felt were too electorally weak to matter). And Egypt's non-Islamists, believing elections to be a fool's game that would only deliver continued Islamist majorities, felt no compunction about calling upon the army to dismantle the entire electoral edifice.

Figure 7.4: Founding election outcomes in Tunisia (a) and Egypt (b) Light bars represent Islamist seat shares (% of total seats)

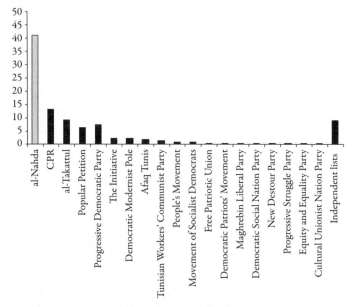

7.4a: Tunisia, October 2011

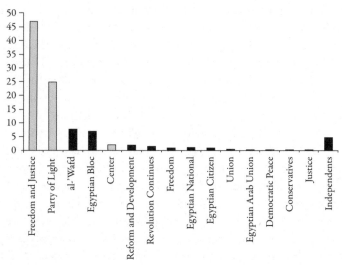

7.4b: Egypt, November 2011–January 2012

This chapter's focus on the existence of pluralism and of a balance of power between political factions as an essential ingredient of successful democratic transitions is consistent with a long tradition of democratic theorising.[55] After all, Adam Przeworski has famously argued that democracy survives only when losers in electoral contests can be reasonably assured of the probability of winning some future election.[56] This probability is a function not just of the fairness of the electoral procedure, but of the loser's own societal strength and reach. When losing parties in founding elections are strong, they are less likely to conclude that democracy is a hopeless errand and consequently, to once again use Stepan's evocative phrase, they are less likely to go 'knocking on the barracks door.'

The importance of pluralism as a prerequisite to democratic consolidation appears even in studies that explicitly disavow the idea that democracy can be said to have any prerequisites at all. In 1970, Dankwart Rustow posited that democratisation requires only 'a prolonged and inconclusive political struggle' that eventually compels political leaders 'to institutionalise some crucial aspect of democratic procedure' as a means of settling their differences. This article highlights the inconclusive nature of the political struggle as the key feature that enables a democratic settlement. After all, if one side can win the struggle, there is no need to strike a democratic compromise. The greater the degree of pre-existing pluralism, the greater the probability that political struggles will be 'inconclusive' and thus the greater the potential for democratic settlements. A similar insight comes to us from O'Donnell, Schmitter and Whitehead, who declare that democracy can result from political situations in which 'no social or political group is sufficiently dominant to impose its 'ideal project', and all groups are thus forced to accept 'a second-best solution which none of the actors wanted or identified with completely but which all of them can agree to and share in.'[57] An even earlier, albeit non-scholarly, expression of this idea comes from Walter Lippmann, who argued that the survival of democracy 'depends upon a sufficiently even balance of political power to make it impracticable for the administration to be arbitrary and for the opposition to be revolutionary and irreconcilable.'[58] According to Lippmann, 'unless all the citizens of a state are forced by circumstances to compromise, unless they feel that they can affect policy but that no one can wholly dominate it, unless by habit and necessity they have to give and take, freedom cannot be maintained.'[59] Indeed, this idea of the salutary effect of empirical pluralism even appears in early debates about the US constitution. In Federalist 10, James Madison argued that a large, diverse polity like the proposed United States of America, far from being inimical to democracy (as some thought), was actually most conducive to it, due to 'the greater security afforded by a greater variety of parties, against the event of any one party being able to outnumber and oppress the rest.'[60]

Comparing political outcomes in Tunisia and Egypt after the resignations of Ben Ali and Mubarak (see Figure 7.4), it is evident that Tunisia exhibited Madison's 'greater variety of parties', Lippmann's 'sufficiently even balance of power', O'Donnell, Schmitter and Whitehead's lack of 'sufficient dominance', and Rostow's 'inconclusive struggle', but that Egypt did not. The importance of this difference to the transition outcomes in both countries has not been ignored by scholars and analysts. In recent contributions, Eva Bellin and Alfred Stepan both note the positive effects of Tunisia's relatively 'leveled' political playing field (and the comparatively dismal effects of Egypt's lopsided one).[61] The natural question this analysis raises, however, is why these countries exhibited such different degrees of pluralism in the first place.

Scholars have hazarded multiple potential explanations for the difference in the outcomes of Tunisia's and Egypt's initial post-authoritarian elections. Some have pointed to fortuitous choices of electoral rules (see Brownlee et al. for a discussion). An emblematic statement is that of Stepan, who tells us that the choice of proportional representation in Tunisia had 'crucial anti-majoritarian, democracy-facilitating, and coalition-encouraging implications.'[62] According to Stepan, '[h]ad a Westminster-style 'first-past-the-post' system of plurality elections in single-member districts been chosen, Ennahda would have swept almost nine of every ten seats, instead of the slightly more than four in ten it was able to win under PR.' Bellin makes a similar argument. These testimonials to the importance of electoral engineering, however, obscure a simple fact: the precise electoral formula that was used in Tunisia (proportional representation using the Hare quota) was also employed for two-thirds of the legislative seats in Egypt's founding election (with the remaining third being elected in nominal, majoritarian districts). And in Egypt, Islamists captured a supermajority (around two thirds) of seats in the list PR tier. In short: if we want to explain why Islamists dominated in Egypt and not in Tunisia, we cannot explain the difference with respect to electoral institutions.

Others would direct our attention to policies of previous authoritarian regimes that inhibited or enabled the emergence of parties that could be credible contestants in the post-authoritarian period. Bratton and Van de Walle contend that 'neopatrimonial' regimes thwarted political parties, while Brownlee demonstrates that more competitive authoritarian regimes, which allowed a modicum of political competition, tended to generate pluralism and give way to democracies.[63] Lust and Waldner make an alternative argument, suggesting that Tunisia's more repressive authoritarian environment leveled the playing field among contestants in the post-authoritarian period.[64] Surveying the data, however, it is difficult to conclude that Egypt and Tunisia were meaningfully different in this regard. Figure 7.5 is a chart of Freedom House scores for Egypt and Tunisia from 1990 to 2010 (higher scores on Freedom House's 14-point scale connote fewer political and civil liberties). Both countries ranked in 'not free' territory prior to their uprisings, with little in the way of meaningful differences between the two over the past twenty years.

This is not to say that the values of actors, the rules governing elections, or the policies of prior regimes do not matter. But here I want to argue, following Brownlee, Masoud, and Reynolds, that we are more likely to gain purchase on the sources of Egypt's absence of pluralism, and Tunisia's relative abundance of it, by attending to initial conditions and underlying socioeconomic structures rather than to these more proximate and contingent factors.[65]

The Roots of Empirical Pluralism

So far, this chapter has asked why Egypt's democratic transition was reversed by coup while Tunisia's has (formally, at least) achieved consolidation. It has argued that attention to the actions of particular players should instead be refocused on the structures that shaped their choices. I focused on two intermediate differences between Egypt and Tunisia that scholars have deemed consequential for their ultimate transition outcomes. The first are differences in the degree of 'military centrality'—that is, the political importance of the military. I have made three arguments. First, although Egypt's military was

Figure 7.5: Freedom House scores for Egypt and Tunisia, 1990–2010

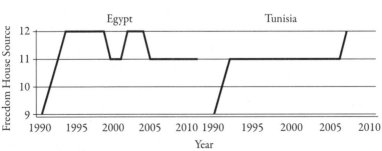

129

larger and more of a political player than Tunisia's, the latter country's army was not significantly smaller or more socially marginal than those of other coup-prone countries. Second, when one factors in Tunisia's Ministry of Interior, which was both large and hostile to the Islamists who had come to run the country, it is evident that Tunisia had no shortage of armed agents of the state that were willing and able to conduct an armed coup against demo-cratically-elected leaders. Third, and most importantly, the literature on mili-tary coups demonstrates that the inability of civilian politicians to conclude power-sharing agreements is an important enabling condition for military interventions into politics. This third point suggests that, when trying to explain the presence (or absence) of military abrogations of democratic experi-ments, the focus must be on the factors inhibiting (or favoring) political compromise during the transition period.

This brings us to what several scholars consider to have been the most important difference between the Tunisian and Egyptian transitions: The relative balance between Islamist and non-Islamist political parties in Tunisia, and the electoral dominance of Islamist parties in Egypt.[66] The rest of this chapter attempts to explain where this difference came from. It argues, following Brownlee, Masoud, and Reynolds that variation in the pluralism of party systems is a function of longue durée socio-economic factors.[67] To rehearse the argument here: in both Egypt and Tunisia, new political parties had to get off the ground quickly and build mass connec-tions to voters. In both places, parties attempted to build upon pre-existing civil society networks in which voters were already embedded. In Egypt, what Stepan and Linz refer to as 'the hegemony [...] of religious forces over much of civil society' meant that Islamist parties were able to become much stronger than secular ones, which lacked access to equivalent civic net-works.[68] Thus, as Daniel Brumberg has noted, the Egyptian opposition's demand for military intervention was 'a metaphor for [its] structural weak-ness' and its lack of 'capacity for sustained mobilisation.'[69] In Tunisia, in contrast, the strong non-Islamic civil society sector—especially the powerful national labour union—provided a source of organisational ballast to non-Islamists that allowed them to match Ennahda at the ballot box, and thus remain committed to the democratic game.

New Parties and Civil Society

My analysis of the differences between Egypt and Tunisia focuses on the opportunities that Islamist and non-Islamist parties in each country faced for reaching voters, and thus winning seats, in founding elections. It begins from the observation that the principal challenge for new political parties in new democracies is building face-to-face connections with voters.[70] When the collapse of the autocrat is followed by hastily convened 'founding elections' political parties lack the time necessary to build up voter mobilisation apparatuses.[71] Consequently, as several scholars have noted, parties reach voters by 'piggybacking'[72] on already-extant social networks such as labour unions, peasant associations, extended clan or tribal networks, religious associations, and the like.[73] Where there are few such pre-existing structures, few strong parties can emerge. Where many such structures exist, we expect a variety of political parties—religious conservatives, leftists, and others—to be able to build linkages to citizens and erect mass bases.

Comparing Tunisian and Egyptian civil societies on the eve of the Arab Spring reveals genuine differences in the diversity of their civil societies. Egypt featured dense and 'encompassing' religious civil society networks.[74] Carrie Rosefsky Wickham, for example, has described the existence of a large 'parallel Islamic sector' that comprises charitable societies, cultural organisations, and businesses.[75] The 'social embeddedness of Islamic networks,' as Wickham puts it, constituted a major asset for Islamist movements: 'The presence of Islamist networks at the local level where people lived, studied, and worked made them highly accessible and minimized the social distance between participants and nonparticipants.'[76] Come election time, Islamists were able to use these pre-existing forms of social life to reach voters and capture seats. In contrast, Egypt's secular political parties and activists lacked equivalents to Egypt's dense religious civil society. Scholars have described Egypt's non-Islamic civil realm as limited and tightly controlled by the state.[77] Egyptian secularists consequently had fewer 'mobilisation resources' during founding elections than their Islamist counterparts.[78] The result of this 'mobilisational asymmetry' was an Islamist supermajority observed in the first post-Mubarak legislature.[79]

Tunisia represents an alternative scenario. Here, both religious and non-religious civic networks appear to have been strong. For instance, Tunisia famously possessed the Arab world's first human rights organisation, the Tunisian League for Human Rights, established in 1976.[80] This stronger non-religious civic space provided non-Islamists with opportunities equivalent to those of Islamists for building capable electoral vehicles in the country's October 2011 Constituent Assembly elections.

A particularly important distinction between the Egyptian and Tunisian civil societies can be observed in differences between the two countries' labour movements. The literature on trade unionism in both countries has noted the weakness and state-control of Egypt's major labour-based association, and the comparative strength and independence of Tunisia's.[81] In fact, as several observers have noted, Ben Ali's resignation could not have been brought about without mobilisation by the UGTT.[82] The status and power of organised labour in Egypt was considerably diminished by comparison. In that country, the state-controlled labour movement lacked the organisational capacity to serve as a foundation for non-Islamist political organisation in the post-Mubarak era. For instance, Mostafa Hefny's interviews with Egyptian labour leaders reveal their own sense of marginality to the Egyptian revolution: 'We made a lot of calls,' one of them reports, 'but it was the kids in Tahrir who were crucial. Our people were not very responsive.'[83]

A broader snapshot of the weakness of Egypt's civil society and the strength of Tunisian civil society is offered by comparing the density of registered private voluntary associations in each country on the eve of the Arab Spring. In 2010, Tunisia had 9,969 associations registered with the Ministry of Interior, according to a database maintained by the governmental organisation Ifāda (*Markaz al-ʾIʿlām wa al-takwīn wa al-dirāsāt wa al-tawthīq ḥawl al-jamʿiyāt*, Center for Information, Establishment, and Documentation on Associations).[84] Assuming a population of 10.6 million (according to World Bank figures from 2010), that comes to 0.94 civic associations per 10,000 inhabitants. Egypt, in contrast, featured approximately 26,000 registered civic organisations in 2010.[85] Assuming a population of 78.08 million, that comes to a civic association density approximately of 0.33 per 10,000 Egyptians—or around one third that of Tunisia's.

To offer an individual-level comparison of the density of Tunisian and Egyptian civil societies, I follow Howard's study of civil society in the post-Soviet world, and analyse responses from the most recent wave of the World Values Survey, which included both Egypt and Tunisia (in addition to 58 other countries).[86] As in the earlier period covered by Howard, the World Values Survey's sixth wave (2010–2014) asks respondents whether they are an 'active' or 'inactive' member of one of the following five types of organisations: church or religious groups; sport or recreational organisations; art, music, or educational organisations; labour unions; and political parties. For most of these groups, a greater percentage of Tunisians report present or past membership than do Egyptians.[87] To simplify the presentation of these data, I further follow Howard, and construct a measure of the average number of organisational memberships per person. Tunisia's and Egypt's scores are presented in

Figure 7.6. On average, Tunisians have about four times as many organisational memberships as the average Egyptian. Tunisia's relatively stronger civil society, I argue, constituted the basis for a stronger and more diverse partisan landscape than the monolithically religious Egyptian landscape.

Figure 7.6: Organisational memberships per person for Egypt and Tunisia, based on 2012 and 2013 World Values Surveys (www.worldvaluessurvey.org)[88]

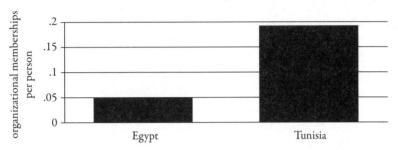

As with our discussion of the two countries' militaries, it is one thing to compare Tunisia's and Egypt's civil societies to each other, but a proper analysis of the role of civil society in sustaining Tunisian democracy requires that we situate both countries within a broader, worldwide comparison. Such a comparison using the World Values Survey data reveals that Egypt and Tunisia feature the lowest rates of civic membership in the entire sample. Thus, though Tunisia appears to have a more diverse civil society than Egypt, widening our lens to include all sixty countries in the World Values Survey's sixth wave would not lead us to identify that country's civil society as particularly vibrant. This is puzzling, since both countries' average associational membership scores are surpassed in the World Values Survey by polities in which we might a priori expect to have lower rates of associational membership, such as oil-rich Qatar (see Michael Ross on the weakness of civil society in rentier states) and tribal Jordan.[89] Without being able to determine the reason why Egypt and Tunisia perform so poorly in the survey, I use more objective, country-level data on non-governmental organisation density compiled by Jeremy Scott Forbis to explore how Tunisia's and Egypt's civil societies compare not only to each other, but to civil societies in a global set of democracies and dictatorships.[90]

Forbis' data comprise 158 countries and are drawn from an annual yearbook of non-governmental organisations by country. Although he compiles the data for a number of years, I employ the 2004 data. The number of NGOs is divided by the population to arrive at a measure of NGOs per 100,000 inhabitants. The average number of NGOs per 100,000 citizens in the data range from 0 (Mauritius) to 146.6 (St. Vincent and the Grenadines), with a mean of 8.9 and a median of 2.7.[91] Egypt's NGO density in this data is 0.575 NGOs per 100,000 citizens (placing it in the bottom 25th percentile), whereas Tunisia's is approximately six times this number, at 3.4 (placing it in the top half of countries in the dataset).

But how do Egypt's and Tunisia's civic densities compare to the average electoral democracy? In order to answer this question, I combine Forbis' civil society data with Freedom House scores for each country in 2004. As is well known by most consumers of the scholarly literature on democracy, Freedom House rates countries on a scale from 1 to 7 on civil liberties and political rights, where a score of 1 on a given dimension connotes an assessment of the country as 'free' and a score of 7 means that it is 'not free.' The scores are added to generate an index that ranges from 2 to 14 (where any score above 10 is considered 'not free'). Figure 7 is a smoothed histogram of civil society densities of the 112 countries in the sample with Freedom House scores from 2 to 10 (comprising countries that are considered 'free' or 'partly free' and excluding those considered 'not free'). The dashed line represents Tunisia's 2004 civil society density score. Although the country's score of 3.4 NGOs per 100,000 is much less than the average for this subset (10.7), it is close to the median of 3.6. In other words, almost half of the countries in the 'free' or 'partly free' sample displayed less dense civil societies than Tunisia. In contrast, Egypt's civil society density puts it just above the 10th percentile in the Forbis data.

Religious versus Non-Religious Civil Society

A key point of my analysis is that it is not simply that Tunisia had a stronger and more diverse civil society overall, but that Egypt's weaker civil society was more religious in nature than Tunisia's. This meant that Egypt's founding elections would produce a monolithic partisan landscape dominated by religious parties. The assumption I make here is that religious parties are more able to co-opt religious organisations for voter mobilisation during founding elections, while non-religious parties have an advantage with respect to non-religious forms of social organisation (such as labor unions or occupational associations). Consequently, countries whose civil societies are dominated by religious institutions will tend to produce party systems

Figure 7.7: Distribution of civil society density in countries rated 'Free' or 'Partly Free' by Freedom House, 2004 (Data from Forbis 2008)

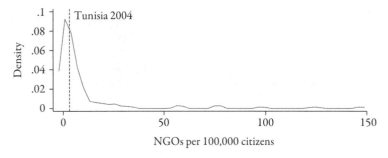

in which religious actors predominate, while those in which secular forms of organisation are prominent will produce party systems with large secular, or at least non-religious, parties. To establish this at the cross-national level would require detailed data on the types of civic organisations that obtain in transitioning countries throughout the world, as well as the ideological makeup of the party systems that emerge from founding elections. Until such data are available, I must restrict myself to comparing Egypt and Tunisia with each other, rather than with a global set of transitioning countries. Consequently, the analysis in this section must be viewed as provisional, even as I hope it will be convincing.

The thesis advanced here is that Egypt's more religious civil society advantaged Islamist parties in founding elections, while Tunisia's more secular one gave opportunities to secular parties. My task, then, is to demonstrate that these two countries' civil landscapes were different in the hypothesised ways. First, I compare mosque density in Tunisia to mosque density in Egypt. According to data from the Tunisian Ministry of Religious Affairs, Tunisia had 4,655 mosques and prayer spaces (*jawāmi'* and *masājid*) by December of 2009.[92] Assuming a population of 10.5 million, this gives us a mosque density of 0.44 mosques per 10,000 citizens. Egypt, in contrast, in 2009/10 reported 107,265 mosques and prayer spaces (*masājid* and *zawāyā*).[93] Assuming a population of 78.08 million, this comes to 1.37 mosques per 10,000 people, or more than three times greater than Tunisia's mosque density. Figure 7.8 compares the number of mosques and civil society organisations per 10,000 inhabitants in both countries.

This greater density of religious civil society also appears in the individual-level, World Values Survey data analyzed earlier in this section. In order to

Figure 7.8: Density of mosques versus civic associations, Egypt and Tunisia, 2009/10

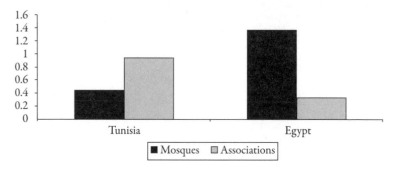

arrive at an estimate of the density of religious civic memberships in each country relative to other forms of civic engagement, I construct a new variable which is the share of the average number of civic memberships that is accounted for by 'active' or 'inactive' membership in 'church or religious organisations' in the World Values Survey data for the two countries (see Figure 7.9). For Egyptian respondents—who report many fewer civic memberships than their Tunisian counterparts—approximately 22.37 per cent of the average organisational memberships is made up of membership in religious institutions. In the Tunisian data, religious memberships make up only 8.19 per cent of the total, reflecting the much stronger fund of secular 'social capital' in that society compared to Egypt.[94]

The upshot of this section is twofold: first, I showed using a variety of individual-level and aggregate data that Tunisia had a much stronger civil society than Egypt. Second, I also showed that Egypt's civic landscape, though generally weaker than Tunisia's, featured a much higher density of religious

Figure 7.9: Religious memberships as percentage of average memberships per person in Egypt and Tunisia, based on 2012 and 2013 World Values Surveys

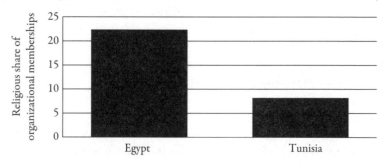

associations and institutions. The result is that in Egypt, religious parties had a massive, inborn organisational advantage over their secular counterparts, whereas in Tunisia, non-religious parties possessed mobilisation resources equal to those of Islamists. Social scientists have long argued that more diverse, pluralistic civil societies ensure democratic survival by making 'domination' by a single faction less likely.[95] As the foregoing has attempted to show, this salutary pluralism was present in Tunisia and decisively absent in Egypt.

Development and Civil Society

Where does pluralism in civil society come from? The natural candidate is economic development—if a long line of literature on 'modernisation' is to be believed.[96] Scholars have long hypothesised that diverse civil societies emerge as a result of industrialisation and developmental processes that compel peasants to move from the countryside to the cities and develop such institutions as labor unions, mutual benefit associations, and other manifestations of modern social life.[97] In contrast, in less developed, more agrarian societies (such as Egypt), associational life is likely to be less diverse, primarily rooted in the extended family and in the religious community.[98]

It is beyond the scope of this chapter to re-litigate this underlying proposition, but a preliminary examination of the civil society density data examined in section 4 suggests that this element of social science wisdom has considerable validity. Figure 7.10 is a binned scatterplot of the relationship between the logged per capita GDP of each country in 2004, and its civil society density for that year, as measured by Forbis.[99] What we expect to find, according to the standard social science theories, is a monotonically increasing relationship between development and civil society density. The general pattern conveyed by the data suggests that, for the most part, the modernisation theorists were correct: more developed countries have richer, more diverse civil societies.

By these lights, the divergence between Tunisia and Egypt is perhaps to be expected. By almost any measure, Tunisia is more developed than Egypt. Nearly 67 per cent of Tunisians live in cities compared to 43.1 per cent of Egyptians, industry is a greater share of the Tunisian labor force than of the Egyptian one (33.2 per cent of Tunisia's labor force versus 24 per cent of Egypt's); and Tunisia's GDP per capita is almost 30 per cent higher than Egypt's ($4,317 versus $3,314).[100] Egypt's diminished economic development may be a function of the long term effects of Nasser's program of Arab

Figure 7.10: Civil society density and economic development, 2004

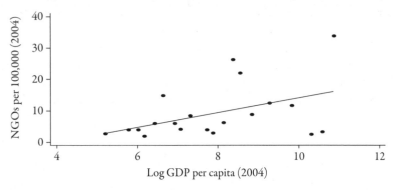

Sources: Forbis 2008 and World Bank Development Indicators.

Socialism that involved heavy state interventions in the economy, guaranteed employment, and a robust program of subsidies.[101] In contrast, according to Eva Bellin Tunisia's leader, Habib Bourguiba, never pursued the same strategy, and always maintained a relatively vibrant private sector.[102] To the extent, then, that the actions of agents impacted the democratisation outcomes in Egypt and Tunisia after the so-called Arab Spring, the evidence suggests that we should attend as much to the economic development strategies adopted by leaders at early moments of state-building, as to the more proximate strategies of politicians and activists during transitional periods.

The upshot of this discussion is simple: the partisan pluralism necessary to the maintenance of democracy is a function of civic pluralism, which is in turn a function of economic development. Or, to put it another way: Tunisia featured a more diverse partisan landscape because its more diverse civic landscape generated opportunities for new political parties to build mass bases in that country's founding elections. And Tunisia enjoyed a more diverse civic landscape because of its higher levels of urbanisation, industrialisation, and economic development than Egypt.

Conclusion: Redeeming Modernisation

In this chapter, I have argued that understanding why Tunisia and Egypt diverged requires us to look beyond their militaries and at the structures of their civil societies on the eve of their transitions. Tunisia had a more diverse civic landscape than Egypt's, which was dominated by religious groups. Consequently, Tunisia's one party state gave way to genuine pluralism, while Egypt's gave way to another one party state (but this time dominated by religious actors). I have argued, moreover, that we are likely to find the roots of these differences in modernisation processes that could have been observed long before the Arab Spring began.

This reaffirmation of modernisation theory might appear a theoretical and normative step backward. As Clark, Golder, and Golder have noted, 'for many people, the terminology used by modernisation theory and its implications are unsettling and troubling. After all, it suggests that all countries, once they mature, will eventually come to look like the United States and Western Europe. In effect, countries just need to grow up—rather like a baby growing into a responsible adult.'[103] An example of the low esteem in which much of modernisation theory is held comes to us from Coleman and Halisi, who quote one African critic's declaration that modernisation theory 'is a simplistic theory which quite arbitrarily picks out certain characteristics as desirable and assumes that some polities (the developed countries) more or less have them while others, the poor slobs (the underdeveloped countries), more or less lack them. The scientific value of such a theory is hard to see. What is not so hard to see is the consequence of the theory for the sense of superiority of some peoples and the sense of inferiority of others.'[104]

It is my hope, however, that the account offered here avoids these charges. The argument presented here—that economic development determines the pluralism of the political landscape during transitional periods—is analytically distinct from more traditional theories of modernisation that believe democracy emerges when increasing wealth turns individuals into democrats. An example of such reasoning is the recent contribution by Inglehart and Welzel, who argue that 'economic development tends to bring enduring changes in a society's values that, at high levels of development, make the emergence and survival of democratic institutions increasingly likely.'[105] More can be said about the analytic shortcomings of these values-centric accounts of democratisation, but the persistence of democracy in societies where normative beliefs in democracy are weak or attenuated—that is, the existence of 'democracy without democrats'—militates against the conclusion that national-level democracy is a function of individual-level values.[106] Democracy, in my account, is a function of the structurally-given incentives, capacities, and constraints of political actors, not of their deepest, most heartfelt beliefs. The distinction between the story offered here, and the more traditional modernisation accounts, is diagrammed in Figure 7.11. (In order to distinguish the argument of this chapter from classic modernisation arguments, I have indicated the alternative pathway in a lighter shade.)

Finally, an additional virtue of the argument presented here is that it eludes another, non-normative critique of modernisation theory. In their classic contribution to the debate over modernisation and democracy, Przeworski and Limongi criticise modernisation theory for its utter disregard for the actual agents of politics. 'In the modernisation theory,' they claim, 'no one does anything to bring democracy about; it is secreted by economic development and the corollary social transformations.'[107] Instead of falling from the sky when conditions are propitious, the authors argue, 'democracy is or is not established by political actors pursuing their goals.' This is almost certainly true. But the account advanced here is not blind to the importance of purposive political actors. On the contrary, political actors are central to it. But instead of conceiving of those actors as completely free to do what they like, constrained only by their beliefs and normative commitments, this essay encourages us to take seriously an observation made by Karl Marx more than 150 years ago. People, he declared, 'make their own history, but they do not make it as they please. They do not make it under self-selected circumstances, but under circumstances existing already, given and transmitted from the past.'

Figure 7.11: Pathways from Modernisation to Democracy

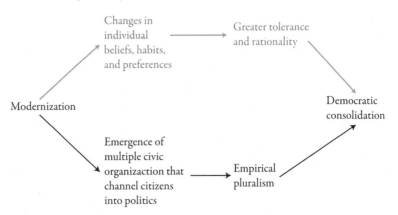

8

INTERNATIONAL ASSISTANCE TO ARAB SPRING TRANSITIONS

Zaid Al-Ali

One of the many unique features of the transitions that followed the popular uprisings that swept across the Arab region in 2011 was the near complete absence of a transition plan that policy makers could pick up and follow to guide their respective countries to safer and more democratic shores.[1] As a result, policy makers in each of these countries suddenly found that they had to decide a number of key issues, all of which were extraordinarily consequential, within an extremely short timeframe and within a constantly changing set of factual circumstances. These included the specific type of electoral framework that each country should adopt (in the knowledge that each option would favour and hinder certain outcomes and specific groups and would therefore have to be considered carefully), the electoral calendar, the process through which the pre-existing constitution should be replaced, and subsequent legal and regulatory reform.

A number of principles underpin each of these issues, some of which are very general and which are not usually challenged publicly. These include the view that elections should be free and fair, that the constitutional drafting process should be inclusive and transparent and that systems of government should be based on the separation of powers, judicial independence, and the protection of fundamental rights, including socio-economic rights.[2] There is, however, a significant lack of knowledge and understanding on many of the other key issues that policy makers in a post-dictatorial environment have to decide, particularly how transitions should be managed from a constitutional, electoral and legal perspective.[3]

National institutions in the Arab region were not in a position in 2011 to offer many ideas on any of these key issues. The uprisings and the departure of so many regimes and dictators had taken everyone by surprise, which meant that almost no thought had been dedicated to planning the transitions beforehand. Even if the uprisings could have been anticipated, the almost complete absence of free expression, particularly on issues of democratic transition, would have made a planning effort completely impossible.[4] Finally, the individuals who were in a position to determine their countries' transitions following the uprisings were often closely linked to the defunct regimes and were therefore not necessarily culturally or politically in favour of political and legal revolution. Policy makers scrambled to devise transitions while balancing all these concerns. As the ground shook under the feet of thousands of protesters throughout 2011, many national officials buckled under the pressure and were desperate for assistance. Clearly, international actors had an enormous role to play. Responding to this significant need should have been straightforward in the circumstances given that the community of international experts, scholars and institutions was in any event fully focused on the highly dramatic events that were unfolding throughout the region.

The interaction that took place between the international community and national policy makers in Arab countries had an important impact (often by omission) and is so far not very well understood. This chapter seeks to partially fill that knowledge gap, by addressing two key aims. The first is to examine what role the international community actually played in Arab Spring countries, with a particular focus on two case studies—Libya and Yemen. And the second is to analyse the manner in which international assistance in democratic transitions was and continues to be delivered in the Arab region. This involves discussion of international organisations' mandates, and the extent to which they actually curtail international involvement in transition countries. I also discuss the manner in which the international community formulates the advice that they give to individual countries, with a view to determining the factors that are taken into consideration during that process.

Given the nature of the issues being considered, much of the discussion that follows focuses on the United Nations and on the various agencies that played a key role in our two case study countries. The United Nations is the region's most important and influential international actor by far, and it therefore provides the greatest amount of material for discussion and is the most deserving of attention. It must be said, however, that most of the conclusions I reach at the end of this chapter apply just as much to other international actors.

Libya

On the eve of its 2011 revolution, Libya's political system was markedly undemocratic, even by regional standards. Whereas most Arab countries had nominal experience with elections, Libya had none. Its state institutions were extremely fragile, subject to the whims of a small number of unelected officials. It also had no experience with political parties, which had been banned for decades, which contributed to a poor post-war political atmosphere. As a result, when elections were eventually organised after the uprising, they were contested by hundreds and parliament was populated by dozens of political forces and parties, many of which suffered from a lack of experience, ideology and/or vision for how their country should be managed. This was made worse by the fact that many of these parties were connected to militias who were more than willing to use force, exacerbating an already fragile security situation. In the context of all of the above, any attempt to reverse the country's situation would necessarily face significant challenges.

After the fall of both Ben Ali in Tunisia and Hosni Mubarak in Egypt in early 2011, an initial round of protests in eastern Libya quickly evolved into a full blown civil war. A coalition of opponents and defectors from Gaddafi's regime formed a National Transitional Council (NTC) in March 2011 and a number of western powers intervened militarily on their behalf. The conflict eventually ended with Gaddafi's capture and death on 20 October 2011, at which point the entirety of Libya's territory formally fell under the NTC's control.

One of the NTC's first actions was to produce an interim constitution, which would necessarily sweep away a large part of Gaddafi's institutional arrangements.[5] A draft was first published during the summer of 2011 and was eventually finalised on 3 August 2011. The document sought to satisfy two objectives: firstly to establish a framework for the functioning of state institutions during the interim period, and secondly to establish a road map for

Libya to transition to democracy. Without stating so explicitly, the document provided that the interim period should consist of two phases, the first which would start immediately upon the interim constitution's publication, and the second which would commence after 'liberation', which would trigger a succession of events (including elections, the drafting of a new permanent constitution and yet another election).

The document starts by setting out a number of basic rights, including freedom of speech and association (important precedents for Libya). It quickly moves on to organise both legislative and executive power. Article 17 provides that legislative authority was to be exercised by the NTC, which was responsible for enacting legislation, for 'establishing the State's general policy' and for 'guaranteeing national unity, the safety of the national territory, embodying and propagating values and morals, ensuring the safety of citizens and expatriates', etc. Meanwhile, Article 24 provides that authority during the interim period was to be exercised by an 'executive office' which was to be appointed by the NTC and would enjoy strong oversight powers over the executive.

The bulk of the interim constitution's transitional provisions are included in a single provision (Article 30). It details that the NTC should form a government within thirty days of Libya's 'liberation', and that the government would have at most ninety days to promulgate an electoral law, appoint the members of an electoral commission, and commence the procedure for organising the elections. It also provides that the elected legislature (the General National Congress, or GNC) should appoint a constitutional drafting committee which would have sixty days to prepare a final draft constitution. The draft would then have to be approved by the GNC and would be submitted to a referendum within thirty days. Were the draft to be rejected by the Libyan people, the drafting committee would then have thirty days to prepare a new version. After the constitution is approved, the GNC would be required to enact a new electoral law within thirty days, and elections should be organised within 180 days of the approval of the electoral law.

The text was so deficient that it was bound to have long term consequences: it simply did not provide enough guidance on how the interim period should be managed, as a result of which the GNC would have no choice but to add to it and amend it on a regular basis, whether because it was necessary to do so or merely because it considered that it would be convenient to do so. The result was that the only standard that would guide the GNC's behavior were its own instincts, which should have been a major cause for concern given how inexperienced its members were likely to be and the total absence of democratic traditions.

Finally, and perhaps most importantly, the bulk of the interim constitution was drafted by the NTC well before the civil war was over. This meant that it was not the result of a negotiation between the country's various communities and groups, and that a large proportion of the population would not even have been aware that an interim constitution was being drafted. This had a number of immediate consequences: apart from preventing some of the country's leading jurists and thinkers from commenting on the document's contents, it also established a precedent of incomplete consultation and elitism that would not serve the country well in years to come.

Meanwhile, and despite all of the above, the international community was busy clearing a path for the NTC. The United Nations General Assembly awarded it Libya's seat on 16 September 2011 and the African Union granted it recognition on 20 September 2011. The United Nations also established a mission for Libya on 16 September (the United Nations Assistance Mission to Libya or 'UNSMIL'), and appointed Ian Martin as the Special Representative of the Secretary General ('SRSG') on 19 September.[6] The Security Council provided that UNSMIL's mandate was to 'assist and support Libyan national efforts to [...] undertake inclusive political dialogue, promote national reconciliation, and embark upon the constitution-making and electoral process.'[7] UN Secretary-General Ban Ki Moon also issued a report to the Security Council on Libya on 22 November, in which he commented on the transition plan for the first time, albeit very briefly.[8] The timetable, he noted, was 'challenging' particularly 'in a country where there has been limited or no electoral experience in over forty-five years.' As regards specific measures, he urged the Libyan authorities to 'enhance the representation of women and to engage in consultation with civil society, including young people and women.' Finally, in line with a long tradition of non-intervention in domestic issues, he described the elections as a 'Libyan-led process', indicating that the UN 'could only provide assistance and support in line with its mandate, [given that] it is the Libyans who must agree on the electoral system and other essential elements of the electoral legislation.' UN Special Representative Ian Martin's own view was that the United Nations should adopt a 'light footprint' approach and proceed with 'humility'.[9]

Pursuant to the interim constitution, the NTC drafted an electoral law in January 2012 which provided for a mixed parallel system according to which 120 seats should be allocated under a majoritarian system and another eighty would be allocated through proportional representation. The drafters were primarily motivated by a desire to allow a wide spectrum of political actors to be represented in the GNC, and to reduce the likelihood that significant proportions of the population might feel disenfranchised. The disadvantage of the chosen system, however, was that it was extremely complicated, and was likely to lead to a deeply fragmented legislature that would have significant difficulty composing a government, let alone formulating coherent policy, as required under the interim constitution. That was likely to be compounded by the fact that the NTC did not appear to make any provision for assistance to the GNC once it assumed its function.

Perhaps even more seriously, almost no thought had gone into how the electoral process was likely to interact with the interim constitution's provisions relating to the constitutional process. The GNC, once elected, was likely to represent Libya's makeup on a proportional basis, which necessarily meant that the western Tripolitana province was likely to have the most representatives by far.[10] Given that the interim constitution provided that the GNC was to appoint the constitution drafting committee, it was inevitable that the committee would be dominated by members from the west of the country as well. Many Libyans from the eastern Cyrenaica were unhappy with this arrangement, particularly given that their province was widely considered to have been the most deprived under the previous regime. They might have satisfied themselves that the GNC was a temporary body whose work could be undone by a subsequent legislature, but they could not accept that the country's permanent constitution would be dominated by western interests with no guarantees that their own perspective would be taken into account. After a series of boycott threats in eastern Libya, the NTC finally relented and two days before the election, voted to amend the interim constitution to provide that the constitutional drafting committee should be directly elected. The NTC's last minute amendment had a series of negative consequences. Firstly, it created a sense of confusion for voters on what they were voting for: whereas they had originally understood that the elections were to determine the contents of the final constitution, voters were now no longer certain. Secondly, and perhaps more importantly, the NTC firmly established the idea that the interim constitution could be amended, and that one could do so suddenly, without significant prior notice, and even on a poorly thought out whim.

The elections eventually took place on 7 July 2012, with a delay of less than three weeks, and were generally regarded as very successful from a technical point of view.[11] UNSMIL and other organisations provided significant support to the electoral process, although no effort was made to resolve the very serious substantive problems set out above. As a result, it did not take long for Libya's political process to unravel. Of the eighty party seats, thirty-nine were won by the National Forces Alliance (which fragmented shortly after its apparently strong showing), and the remaining forty-one seats were divided up between twenty different parties, many of which had only one seat each. Meanwhile, the 120 individual members were fractured by design.[12] Considering the tremendous challenges that Libya faced at the time—the GNC's lack of capacity, its inexperience, poor work ethic and internal divisions, combined with the interim constitution's lack of clarity—proved extremely problematic.[13] The GNC only finally managed to grant confidence to its first government in November 2012, which itself was considered to be highly ineffectual.[14] On the constitutional issue, the GNC had to decide whether to adhere to the NTC's last minute amendments of the constitutional declaration and organise elections for a constituent assembly, or whether to reverse it and simply appoint a drafting body itself. The matter was only resolved in February 2013 (seven months after the July 2012 elections), when the GNC announced that it had opted in favour of an elected Constitution Drafting Assembly (CDA) after all. A new CDA electoral law (with a majoritarian system and single seat constituencies) was approved in July 2013 and the elections themselves finally took place on 20 February 2014. In the meantime, the GNC's popularity declined markedly, given the ruling authorities' lack of action on declining security and worsening services and a growing perception that politicians were all self-serving.[15] The GNC was prompted into deciding in favour of electing a new legislature that could take over its own responsibilities as well.

The UN, as always, provided technical support to the elections, by organising meetings, conferences and training sessions and also by reviewing drafts of the electoral law. While they were, once again, technically deemed to be a success, the context in which the CDA elections took place was highly problematic.[16] Firstly, the turnout was modest in comparison to the 2012 GNC elections. Some 1,102,000 people registered to vote in 2014, which was far lower than the 2.8 million who had registered and the 1.76 million who had voted in the GNC elections. The low turnout immediately had a negative impact on the CDA's popular legitimacy within the country. Secondly, although the interim constitution was amended to extend the constitutional drafting process to 120 days (from 60),[17] the deadline for completion nevertheless remained far too ambitious. Considering the slow pace of reform and the absence of progress on constitutional dialogue at the highest levels, it was impossible to imagine that the CDA could come close to completing its work within that short timeframe. Inevitably, the deadline was missed, further undermining any chance that the country might have had to strengthen the rule of law. Most seriously however, no provision had been made for dealing with the country's most contentious political disputes; instead the CDA, which was originally intended to function as a non-political body of experts saw political positions imposed on many of its members by their constituencies, with no mechanism to reach a negotiated settlement.

The CDA eventually started work in April 2014, and published a first partial draft of the constitution in December 2014, for which it was severely criticised as it showed little progress.[18] A second draft was published in October 2015, by which time the CDA itself had also lost significant credibility in the country.[19] The final draft was published in April 2016, not without significant controversy, given that it did not enjoy the support of more than a third of the CDA's members, in apparent violation of its rules of procedure.[20]

The GNC's new law to elect a new House of Representatives (HoR) provided that (contrary to the 2012 elections) all candidates would run in single member constituencies as individual candidates (often referred to as 'first past the post'). The elections took place on 25 June 2014, with the usual support from the UN and other international actors, and while they were once again technically a success, turn-out was estimated at 42 per cent of the 1.5 million registered voters. Also, because of the electoral framework that was applied, the HoR's membership actually represented a small minority of Libya's population. Following a number of disputes, the GNC and Tripoli-based armed groups refused to recognise the HoR, and the country has been living with rival parliaments since, with the GNC based in Tripoli and the HoR based in Tobruk (a city in eastern Libya), neither recognising the legitimacy of the other.[21]

On 14 August 2014, the UN's Secretary-General appointed Bernardino León, a Spanish diplomat, to serve as his new Special Representative. After an aborted and failed attempt in June 2014, UNSMIL successfully launched a political dialogue on 14 January 2015 between the GNC, the HoR and other key players in the hope that a resolution to the conflict could be reached.[22] On 11 July 2015, most of the participants to the political dialogue initialed an agreement that provided for the formation of a government of national unity and which paved the way to new elections. A number of difficulties arose over the coming months, including resistance to the agreement by various factions within both the GNC and the HoR and also corruption allegations surrounding Mr León.[23] At the time of writing, the UN-brokered agreement appeared to be back on track, although its application was still in its initial phase and was proceeding only haltingly.[24] The constitutional process meanwhile continued to start and sputter.

Yemen

On the eve of the 2011 uprising, Yemen was in a desperate situation. The little oil resources that it had were declining, worsening an already serious budgetary crisis, which itself led to an increase in poverty. Resentment amongst southern Yemenis against the central government had increased considerably. Both the Houthi movement and Al-Qaeda in the Arabian Peninsula were growing in prominence and strength, worsening security risks in much of the country. Demonstrations against then-president Ali Abdallah Saleh's rule quickly turned violent, until June 2011 when Saleh himself was seriously wounded in an attack on the presidential compound, forcing him to leave the country for three months to receive medical treatment.

As the country edged closer to civil war, a number of international initiatives were launched, mainly with the aim of reducing tensions and contributing to a solution. Indeed, various components of the international community, including Yemen's immediate neighbors, were increasingly alarmed at Yemen's prospects for survival.[25] The Gulf Cooperation Council (GCC) tabled an initiative in May 2011 to resolve the crisis. That document, which consisted of a single page of bullet points, provided for the formation of a national government, 50 per cent of which should be derived from the ruling party, 40 per cent from the opposition, and 10 per cent from 'other political forces'; that Saleh should be granted immunity within one month from the Initiative's signature and that he should resign in favor of his vice president; that a presidential election should be organised in which the vice president would be the only candidate; that a new constitution should be written and adopted; and that parliamentary elections should follow. At the time it was first issued, Saleh refused to sign the GCC Initiative as it would have required him to leave office—something that he was clearly not prepared to contemplate at that point.

Simultaneously, the Secretary-General of the United Nations dispatched Jamal Benomar, one of his Special Advisers, to Sanaa to engage with the various actors and to explore whether a political solution to the crisis might be possible. Benomar, a Moroccan citizen, had previously been imprisoned for eight years in Morocco for his political activities and for demanding greater freedom of expression and association.[26] After escaping from Morocco, he eventually joined the United Nations, working in various capacities. In 2003, he was appointed senior political adviser to the United Nations Assistance Mission in Iraq and later as the Secretary General's envoy to facilitate a national dialogue conference. Benomar visited Yemen for the first time in April 2011, at a time when the country was on the brink of civil war. Under his guidance, a small team of United Nations officials in Sanaa decided to draft a document that would supplement the GCC Initiative, and which provided significantly more detail on how the transition process would be managed. Remarkably, Benomar's involvement in Yemen was not specifically mandated by the United Nations' Security Council. Its members were made aware of his presence after the fact, and only provided him with a mandate after he had already been there for six months.

Resolution 2014, adopted on 21 October 2011, was the start of a more aggressive international policy on Yemen. Amongst other things, the resolution endorsed the GCC Initiative, which meant that the Security Council was essentially declaring its desire for Saleh to be removed from office— something that it had not done in any other country in the region. The Resolution ended by requiring that the Secretary-General report back on the implementation of the resolution within thirty days, which gave Yemeni actors (most importantly, president Saleh) very little time to fall in line. The deadline and threat of action was in fact an effective tool to force Saleh's hand; during a November 2011 meeting with Benomar, Saleh requested that he should delay his briefing to the Security Council to give him more time to negotiate a settlement with his Yemeni colleagues and rivals.[27] The result was that, on 23 November 2011, all of Yemen's main political actors signed both the GCC Initiative and a shorter version of the document that Benomar's team had drafted. That document became known as the Implementation Mechanism for the GCC Agreement.

That document provided that the transition should take place in two phases, the first of which was generally already provided for in the GCC Initiative. During the second phase, which would start after the new president was elected (by virtue of a referendum and not a competitive election), the main task was to convene and organise a National Dialogue Conference (NDC), which was tasked with addressing the country's major institutional issues and was to include 'all forces and political actors, including the youth, the Southern Movement, the Houthis, other political parties, civil society representatives and women'. The Implementation Mechanism also set out a list of all the issues that should be discussed by the Conference, including the process through which the constitution should be drafted, the state's structure and political system, reform of the civil service, the judiciary and local governance, national reconciliation and transitional justice, human rights, the protection of vulnerable groups, etc. After the completion of the National Dialogue, a Constitutional Drafting Commission (CDC) was to be composed to prepare a new draft constitution within three months of the date of its establishment. Parliamentary elections would only take place after a new constitution is approved in a referendum.

In comparison with other transition processes in the region, the GCC Initiative and its Implementation Mechanism were by far the most ambitious and sophisticated for at least two reasons. Firstly, in virtually every other country affected by the Arab spring, constitutional drafting was conceived in an entirely one-dimensional manner. In all cases, drafting bodies would be dominated by one or two political viewpoints at most, and would not create sufficient space for vulnerable groups or progressives. In some countries, the executive appointed drafting committees (as was the case in Morocco, Algeria, Egypt in 2013, Syria and Jordan) and made sure that their appointments were dominated by loyalists. In other countries, constitutional drafting bodies were either directly (Tunisia and Libya) or indirectly elected (Egypt in 2012). Elections typically ensured that a small number of parties would dominate by virtue of some specific political advantage that was temporary in nature (populist platforms, external assistance, or the prior existence of strong organisational party structures by virtue of the previous regime's tolerance towards specific parties). The NDC was specifically designed to overcome that problem. By virtue of being an appointed body, whose membership would be selected by consensus and through involvement of the international community, a broad cross section of Yemen's population was tapped for membership. This included individuals and groups that would never have been granted a seat at the table through an electoral process, including progressives, youth groups and women.

Secondly, the constitutional processes in the rest of the region were always a one-step process. Whether an appointed committee or an elected assembly was responsible for the drafting process, the relevant bodies were always solely responsible for drafting the text; and as soon as they were finished, their drafts would be submitted for approval either to the people via a referendum or to the legislature. Once again, Yemen was the only exception to that rule: according to the plan's initial design, the NDC would debate the constitution's substantive issues and the CDC would be responsible for consolidating all of the NDC's outcomes into a single constitutional draft.

At the same time, the design also suffered from a number of important flaws that were very likely to impair the final outcome of the process. National Dialogue sessions are by their very nature designed to resolve broad issues of national concern, such as whether to adopt a federal system of government, whether to opt in favour of presidentialism, or what forms of transitional justice should be adopted, if any. Dialogue sessions often include many participants who do not have sufficient background or comparative information on each of the topics to make an informed decision on specific technical issues, and Yemen was no exception in that regard. In Yemen, the NDC was required to discuss and resolve a large number of technical issues that would have been better off in the hands of a committee of experts (including for example, mechanisms for protecting judicial independence; enforcement mechanisms for fundamental rights; the design of oversight frameworks, etc.). This overburdening of the NDC, coupled with an absence of adequate resources, was likely to have two consequences:

(i) It would be almost impossible for the NDC to formulate workable solutions on such a large number of technical topics. That, in turn, meant that the CDC would most likely have to ignore a large number of the NDC's outcomes which would necessarily damage the process' legitimacy; and

(ii) Because of the huge list of topics that it was asked to resolve, the NDC would inevitably leave many areas open for lack of time. It also meant that any major political issues that were left unresolved by the NDC would then inevitably be passed on to the CDC. That raised a major difficulty given that the CDC was not conceived of as a political body, but the overburdening of the NDC was likely to push the CDC in that direction.

Also likely to cause difficulty down the line was the fact that the NDC's sessions all took place in the capital's only five star hotel, which created an immediate disconnect between many participants and the needs of ordinary citizens. In that context, and given what was likely to be the chaotic nature of the discussions, it was bound to be extremely difficult to remain focused on the concerns of ordinary people, including poverty and corruption. One consequence was that the individuals who designed the process appeared to prioritise certain issues over others.

Finally, and perhaps most importantly, the transition plan's worst vulnerability was that it allowed for Yemen's most negative political actors (including former president Saleh) to remain active in the country and to influence the process through their party colleagues and other proxies. Although there is little question that this could not have been avoided at the transition's earlier stages, a strategy could have been developed to marginalise these actors as discussions progressed. Sanctions were the only tool that was utilised, and they were employed far too late to have any real impact.[28]

The National Dialogue Conference's internal rules and its makeup were carefully negotiated from May 2012 to February 2013. The newly elected president first appointed a Liaison Committee, which was required to engage with the country's many components to better understand their views on how the Conference should be organised. The Liaison Committee was eventually replaced by a Technical Committee in July 2012, which was tasked with agreeing procedures for the conference, and determining selection procedures. In the end, the Conference included 565 members, 56 per cent of whom were southerners, 28 per cent women, 20 per cent youth; forty seats were reserved for civil society, with eighty-five members for the southern separatists and thirty-five for the Houthis.

The Conference opened on 18 March 2013 and closed on 25 January 2014, which was after its original deadline of September 2013. It managed to reach detailed agreements on many issues, including the improvement of oversight and anti-corruption mechanisms, the enforcement of political and human rights, and the improvement of representation for women. The final published versions included close to 2,000 outcomes, all of which were theoretically binding on the state and would have to form the basis of the new constitutional arrangement. The NDC left many issues undecided, including the type of federation that should be established and the number of regions. A new presidential committee was established to decide the issue, and announced in February 2014 that the country should have six regions. The announcement was immediately rejected by the Houthi movement, on the basis that it 'divides Yemen into poor and wealthy regions', as well as by a number of political parties.[29] Nevertheless, the transition process continued without even acknowledging that the proposed federal arrangement had been rejected by some of the country's principal political actors.[30]

The constitutional drafting committee was formed in March 2014 and was initially given a period of a few months to prepare a draft constitution that would have to be based on the outcomes. The CDC eventually completed its work in January 2015, far later than expected.[31] Apart from the CDC's poor work ethic, and the fact that many of its members lacked expertise on a large number of issues, the delay was in large part due to the CDC's mandate as well as the contradictions and gaps in the NDC's outcomes.[32] By way of example, the NDC included two different outcomes on appointment mechanisms to the Constitutional Court. The Good Governance Working Group decided that the Constitutional Court's members should be 'elected by a general assembly of judges.' At the same time, the State Building Working Group decided that 70 per cent of the Court's judges should be elected by the 'general assembly of judges', 15 per cent by the Bar Association, and the remaining 15 per cent by the Council of Faculties of Sharia and Law in state universities. Apart from the fact that these outcomes were contradictory, the CDC was faced with an important dilemma: many of its members were acutely aware that the judiciary was replete with regressive and corrupt judges, and so held the view that either version of the NDC's decision on this specific issue would cause the newly formed Constitutional Court to be dominated by those same elements, and so decided not to follow either outcome. Instead, and only after significant debate, the CDC eventually decided that '[t]he President of the Republic shall nominate half of the [fourteen] members and the Supreme Judicial Council, universities and the Bar Association shall nominate the remaining half' (Article 329). All of the nominees to the Court would have to be confirmed by a three-fifths majority in the upper chamber of parliament. In a clear illustration of what was wrong with the NDC's organisation and working methods, its deliberations and decisions on this issue had close to no impact on the final outcome.

In addition, close to a quarter of the CDC's final draft relates to details of the federal system of government that the NDC never even considered. The division of labour under the draft constitution was entirely the work of the CDC, mainly because the NDC had never considered how these responsibilities should be allocated in a federal system of government. That approach was highly problematic, mainly because the CDC was far less representative and enjoyed less legitimacy than the NDC, certainly as a decision-making body.[33] The result was that some of those actors who were not involved at the CDC stage, and who did not agree with the outcome, took to alternative means to scuttle the process.

By the time the CDC completed its draft on 15 January 2015, security had deteriorated significantly in the country. In particular, gunmen loyal to the powerful Houthi movement had taken control over large parts of the country, including the capital. On 20 January 2015, which is to say only days after the draft was completed, they occupied the presidential palace, and demanded amongst other things that the draft constitution be amended to reflect their position on federalism.[34] By March 2015, the president fled the country. Saudi Arabia and other countries in the region initiated a blockade and bombing campaign against Yemen, citing the need to break the Houthi's control over the capital as one of their motivating factors.[35]

Assessing international assistance to transition countries

Scope of action in transition countries

Taken together, these two case studies teach us a number of important lessons about international intervention in developing countries. The first relates to the international community's scope of action, and the circumstances which lead it to vary from country to country. Theoretically, in countries that are not experiencing a severe political or security crisis the UN usually limits itself to what is referred to as 'technical support' (which is generally understood to mean the provision of expert and material support on matters of a non-political nature) and avoids entering into the realm of 'substantive support' (usually understood to mean providing opinions on sensitive and political matters). National officials, particularly those who monopolise access to power and policy making, employ a number of mechanisms to prevent international organisations from engaging in any meaningful activity. Apart from simply preventing certain organisations and their staff members from entering the country, governments insist that whatever work an international organisation carries out must be based on a programme that itself must be negotiated and approved by the national authorities.[36] The government then uses that leverage to remove any activity that could potentially threaten its monopoly on power.[37] If any of the agencies or individual staff members step out of bounds, they run the risk of being ejected from the country by the national authorities. In one relatively prominent case that took place in Algeria in 2003, a senior official from UNDP was declared *persona non grata* formally on the basis that he had acted beyond his mandate and encroached on national sovereignty issues.[38] In post-conflict situations (e.g. Libya in 2011 and Iraq in 2003) or states that are particularly fragile (e.g. Yemen in 2011), the Security Council can however broaden the UN's traditional mandate to include political support, usually through the establishment of a 'mission'.[39]

In practice, this understanding of responsibility based on a country's situation bears little relationship to the international community's true scope of action, mainly because the various categories of assistance that countries can receive have not been properly set. In fact, based on all of the available evidence, it is fair to say that the division between technical support and substantive advice is not always clear and is often illusory. Firstly, there is in fact no agreed definition of what constitutes 'technical support', leaving the term to be determined on a case by case basis by the national and international officials who happen to be involved in the process in question. It is generally understood that international organisations should not be involved in making political decisions on behalf of the national authorities. National authorities usually welcome and international organisations are happy to provide a restrictive form of technical support, which can take the form of training sessions for staff (including electoral workers; parliamentary staff; court staff), the procurement of materials on behalf of institutions (e.g. computers and other equipment), and the provision of expertise on scientific matters that have no connection to political considerations (e.g. improving agricultural yields; improving transport; demining). But that is where consensus ends. There are other possible forms of support, some of which could be qualified as technical in some contexts, but which are sometimes considered to be controversial and therefore inappropriate by some bodies. In some cases, ruling authorities can consider that purely technical support to specific institutions represents a threat to their authority and are not shy about blocking specific initiatives. For example, in countries where the judiciary has been utilised by ruling authorities for political purposes, initiatives that are designed to improve judicial independence or to improve transparency in the judicial sector can be blocked, despite the fact that judicial independence is a constitutionally recognised norm in all Arab countries.[40]

Technical support can even on occasion be stretched to include the provision of substantive advice on key policy issues (while making sure not to lobby in favour of any particular outcome). For example, where a state is considering what type of decentralised model of government it should adopt, international organisations can present options based on comparative practice.[41] Although this approach is often considered to be technical, it is actually far from innocent, as comparative studies and examples are never comprehensive and the examples that are used to make particular points are typically drawn from the author's biases.[42] This should not come as a surprise, as the opposite approach can lead to perverse results.[43] On occasion, national authorities are happy to allow for the provision of options on sensitive policy issues, but in other circumstances, they will not even allow international organisations in the drafting chamber and will block any formal communication with them, specifically to prevent this type of involvement.[44] Finally, international organisations have been known to provide substantive advice on key issues to national offices, including by providing commentary to draft constitutions or legislation. This is typically considered to be substantive support, and is not usually regarded as being technical in nature, but many countries actually welcome this type of support and sometimes even seek it out.

Secondly, there is no agreement on what constitutes political support either. Indeed, in Libya, when UNSMIL was first established by virtue of Resolution 2009 (2011) it was provided with an incredibly vague mandate by the Security Council, which requested it to 'assist and support Libyan national efforts to [...] undertake political dialogue, promote national reconciliation and embark upon the constitution-making and electoral process.'[45] The Security Council pointedly did not request that UNSMIL should limit itself to supporting national authorities, and also did not specifically state that the support should be technical in nature. In its second resolution on the matter, the Security Council clarified the mandate somewhat by virtue of its Resolution 2040 (2012) when it stated that UNSMIL should 'assist the Libyan authorities to define national needs and priorities throughout Libya, and to match these with offers of strategic and technical advice [...] including through technical advice and assistance to the Libyan electoral process and the process of preparing and establishing a new Libyan constitution.'[46] Superficially, Resolution 2040 appeared to limit UNSMIL's mandate when it provided that all assistance should be limited to providing 'strategic and technical advice', but the use of the term 'strategic' in this context added significant confusion given the term's absence of a clear definition. However, the main difference in fact between these two versions of UNSMIL's mandate was that Resolution 2040 provided that UNSMIL should assist Libya's national authorities to 'define national needs' which was tantamount to stating that the Libyans were unsure of what direction they hoped to move in, and that UNSMIL should have as part of its job to help identify Libya's priorities. Vitally however, UNSMIL's amended mandate did not appear to have any impact on the work that it was doing on the ground, which remained highly technical in nature, and which eschewed any and all political issues even as Libya's crisis intensified.[47]

The United Nations Assistance Mission for Iraq, which was established in 2003, was mandated by the Security Council by virtue of its Resolution 1546

(2004) to 'promote national dialogue and consensus building on the drafting of a national constitution by the people of Iraq.'[48] Despite the almost identical wording with UNSMIL's mandate, the two missions adopted completely different approaches. While UNSMIL favored a 'light footprint' approach, UNAMI involved itself very heavily in political negotiations from 2003 onwards, to the extent that it argued in favour of particular options during the drafting of Iraq's constitution.[49] Even more strikingly, the UN's heavy involvement in Yemen was carried out without a Security Council mandate at all. Even when a mandate was finally granted in October 2011, it was incredibly vague in comparison to the UN's missions in countries where the UN played almost no role.

We are therefore brought to two separate conclusions. The first is that mandates are more often than not used as an excuse for inaction rather than being a genuine impediment to providing substantive support. Those situations in which international organisations, in particular the United Nations, were actually prevented from implementing genuine reforms are the result of particular circumstances from which it is impossible to draw any broad conclusions.[50] To take but one example, what transpired in 2003 in Algeria was the result of a lopsided political dispute between some segments in the then government on the one hand and the president and the country's entire security establishment on the other, in which there was essentially no contest. The UN official who was declared *persona non grata* was a major casualty to that dispute, and his expulsion from the country was a circumstance that is highly unlikely to be replicated elsewhere, particularly in transition countries.[51] Indeed, one of the defining characteristics of a political transition is intense political competition between rival groups in parliament, most of whom are eager for knowledge of comparative experiences. In many cases (as was the case in Tunisia, Yemen, Libya, Iraq and others), national parliaments and state institutions shift from being under the control of a single party to being in a state of genuine plurality. Some parties can be relatively new with very little experience to draw from, and many seek out knowledge and information on comparative experiences to bolster their own positions.[52] Thus, whatever the circumstances that led to the crisis in Algeria, they were never considered to apply to Yemen, and almost certainly would not have prevented substantive support in Libya and in Tunisia from as early as 2011.[53]

The second conclusion is that, whereas international involvement in transition countries should be determined by each individual country's needs, it is actually determined by the preferences and biases of whichever international officials happen to be based in the country in question and whichever national officials happen to be in control. This explains the UN's different levels of involvement in Libya and Yemen. It also explains why, in countries such as Tunisia, where the UN sought to limit itself to a restrictive form of technical support, other inter-governmental organisations such as IDEA and the Venice Commission, and non-governmental organisations such as Democracy Reporting International, the Carter Center and Human Rights Watch were able to provide significant substantive support, which was generally positively received by Tunisian institutions. Based on the circumstances, it would be fair to say that the UN's limited involvement in substantive matters was more a product of its own preferences rather than a genuine restriction imposed by Tunisia's national authorities.

If anything, the involvement of international organisations in transitions should be based on need rather than anything else.[54] The stakes in transition countries are incredibly high. The potential for disaster is significant, and knowledge about the possible consequences tends to be sparse, since transition countries emerging from dictatorial rule have not had much opportunity to engage in study and debate on democratic transition.[55] Libya's interim constitution provides an excellent illustration of this point: it was entirely drafted by national actors, and was never questioned by the international community, despite the fact that it clearly set the country on a negative trajectory.[56] By remaining silent on the interim constitution's very many flaws, the international community was essentially contributing to the difficulties that would inevitably emerge. In the meantime, while the international community remained silent on decisive issues, significant efforts were made to encourage the Libyan authorities to include gender and youth (technical issues *par excellence*) in all aspects of their work, to the extent that this was mentioned in just about every Security Council Resolution relating to Libya as being a key area of concern from 2011 onwards.[57]

The outcome of a more deliberate and strategic approach to substantive advice should not be construed as political interference, for a number of reasons. The first is that, although the UN Charter and other international instruments prevent international organisations from 'intervening' in 'the domestic jurisdiction of any state', the provision of advice does not necessarily constitute an 'intervention' unless it is imposed as a condition in the context of a negotiation, which is not what is suggested here.[58] My goal here is to indicate that the scope for the provision of (non-prescriptive) advice in transition countries is much larger than it is generally considered to be, and I am not suggesting that advice can be imposed in the same way that economic reforms are imposed as conditions by institutions such as the World Bank. In addition, it must be noted that the cost of silence can be so high that it should override any concerns relating to sovereignty. As already noted elsewhere, a defective constitutional framework can contribute to a deteriorating security environment not only for the country in question but also for the neighboring countries.[59]

Developing country specific strategies

In countries where the international community does decide in favour of providing substantive advice, there does not appear to be a coherent approach to determining what advice should be given. This is apparent if we compare the different approaches that were taken in our two case study countries. In Yemen, the UN played a significant role in shaping the Implementation Mechanism. One of the key aspects of that document was the heavy emphasis on national dialogue, and the lack of emphasis on parliamentary elections, which (had the transition plan been allowed to play out in full) would have taken place five years after Yemen's uprising had begun. Meanwhile, there is no record of the UN ever advising the Libyan authorities not to rush to elections in 2012 and 2014, even after the UN became progressively more active on substantive issues in 2013 and 2014. On the contrary, the UN does not appear ever to have questioned whether any of Libya's three elections were well timed, whether they applied the best electoral models, or whether they contributed to increased tension and insecurity.

The fact that the UN adopted such radically different approaches would be entirely justifiable if they were actually based on a sound understanding of each country's circumstances. But were they? An analysis of the various factors surrounding each country would suggest not. If we examine our two case studies, particularly with a view to determining their capacity to organise elections in 2011, we are brought to the opposite conclusion. Table 8.1 is illustrative of that point.

We know from our two case studies and from our broader knowledge of the region that of all the Arab Spring countries, Libya was probably the least well placed to organise early elections. It did not have any useful experience with putting together such a large scale effort (not even of the fraudulent kind). It did not maintain its main policy-making institutions, it did not have any experience with political parties, and it did not maintain a single aspect of its pre-

2011 political process. This should have suggested to any national or international officials who were involved in designing the transition process back in 2011, or who were in a position to influence its contents, that Libya should have been the last country in the region to organise elections. Instead, Libya had three separate polls within two years, the most recent of which was based on 'first past the post', which was perhaps the worst of all possible options for a country with such poor democratic traditions. Because of all the factors set out above, elections were highly likely to return a large number of parliamentarians with little relevant experience. The NTC largely consisted of former regime loyalists, some of whom at least had the benefit of governance experience, but it nevertheless found the business of governing revolutionary Libya to be extremely challenging. Having said that, it should have been obvious that, if the NTC suffered because of inexperience, any elected assembly that would replace the NTC would have even more trouble. Democratic legitimacy only buys elected parliaments a small amount of leeway, particularly if they are lacking capacity to formulate sound policy, while the general population suffers.

Table 8.1

	Were state institutions maintained?	Did the country have any experience with elections?	Did political parties/groups survive?	Did the political process survive?
Yemen	Yes	Yes	Yes	No
Libya	No	No	No	No

A convincing argument could be made that, given Libya's particular circumstances and the population's thirst for an immediate opportunity to exercise their basic democratic rights, it was simply impossible to resist the call for early elections. Even so, the NTC and the international community could have taken a number of specific approaches that might have mitigated some of the obvious risks that the country was facing. At the very least, Libya's situation in 2011 should have indicated that a solid institutional framework should have been established prior to any elections. One of the first issues that could and should have been addressed was the interim constitution, which (as already stated) was painfully inadequate. A serious effort at designing international policy on Libya should have involved a detailed study of that document and an analysis of what should have been done to remedy its inadequacies.

Not only is there no evidence that such a study was carried out, but there is also no indication that it would have had any impact on the international community's strategies in relation to Libya. In 2011 and early 2012, the only interest appeared to be to ensure that the 2012 elections were organised in accordance with international standards and that a sufficient number of women and younger Libyans participated.[60]

All this reinforces a number of important conclusions, the first of which is that the UN (as well as other international organisations) does not have a mechanism in place to formulate what advice should be given to each specific country. Indeed, country-specific approaches were decided upon in each country by the individuals who happened to be present, and based on each of these individual's preferences and biases, many of which had nothing to do with the circumstances of the country in question. In 2011, the stakes for the region were so high that one could have expected a major brainstorming effort on the part of national and international experts with experience in democratic transitions. This was particularly true in places such as Libya after the interim constitution was published. A meeting of minds between key national officials and some of the world's leading authorities on democratic transitions in coordination with the leadership of major international organisations such as the United Nations, with a focus on the Secretary General's office, might have led to the formulation of country-specific approaches that would have averted many of the mistakes and omissions that were made. At this stage, it is impossible to say whether this more deliberate and consultative approach could have made a difference, but it would at least have involved far more reflection and planning than what actually took place.

The UN's highly decentralised approach to international assistance might be justifiable if the individuals who were chosen to lead each specific mission or office in our two countries were picked on the basis of their particular aptitude to supporting democratic transitions in a revolutionary context. Research on this question reveals that, on the contrary, individuals are retained more on the basis of who happens to be available when a position is vacant. One senior UN official described the selection process as 'musical chairs', while another said slightly more charitably that 'there is some logic to the recruitment process, but it is not the type of logic that you would have liked for it to adopt.'[61] Even in Yemen, where for a time it seemed that Mr Benomar was having a majorly positive impact, a similar dynamic was in place. There is no evidence to suggest that Mr Benomar was selected to be the UNSG's Special Adviser because his abilities and knowledge were considered to be particularly well suited to that country. Nor is there any evidence to suggest that his strong preference in favour of national dialogue sessions, or the particular way in which Yemen's NDC was structured, were conceived based on an analysis of Yemen's situation. On the contrary, and as noted above, Mr Benomar's writings suggest that he had been advocating in favor of that strategy for close to a decade before arriving in Yemen in 2011. His role at the early stages of the process might have been fortuitous, but it also appears to have been largely coincidental.

Responsibility and accountability

A final concern of international involvement is the lack of accountability for failures at both the institutional and individual levels. There is obviously a natural tendency to attribute responsibility for the outbreak of civil conflict to national authorities, but given how involved international actors have been in some contexts (including in Libya, Yemen, Iraq, etc.) the question of responsibility and accountability for external actors is a serious one.

Picking apart this issue would first require an examination of whether specific actions, policies or omissions by international actors in a given country were a contributing factor in the outbreak of a conflict. Iraq (not one of our case studies, but an important example of external involvement) is a case that is essentially beyond dispute: external actors pushed the Iraqis to draft and adopt a final constitution well before the Iraqis were ready to do so, and violence quadrupled in the country immediately after the new text was adopted. Specific external actors (mainly US and UK officials) were clearly culpable for having contributed to this outcome. It can also reasonably be argued that other actors such as the United Nations were culpable through omission, in particular for not having publicly raised any concerns about the constitutional negotiation process.[62] Responsibility is not as easily established in Libya, but a strong argument can be made that the international community's failure to issue warnings about the interim constitution's inadequacies, as well as its enthusiastic approach to early elections contributed to the new ruling authority's inability to govern the country and to the eventual emergence of rival centers of authority. In Yemen, it is unclear whether much could have been done to improve the transition process' initial design, but at the very least formal objections should have been registered as to the manner in which the presidential commission decided the country's federal arrangement, which ended up being one of the main drivers of the conflict.

Assuming one can trace some form of causality between the actions or omissions taken by external actors and deteriorating political and security conditions within a particular country, one should examine whether there should be some form of institutional or individual accountability. At this stage, there do not appear to be any accountability mechanisms in place at all, at any level. For international officials, there is rarely any path but upwards, regardless of their actual performance on the ground. There also does not appear to have been any serious attempt to hold international organisations accountable for their own failures, whether from within or without.

What types of accountability measures can be used to increase the likelihood that major international players will invest greater effort to offer more constructive advice on constitution building? At the very least, one should expect an attempt to rationalise the experiences of the past few years with a view to improving performance over the coming period. One possible result of such an effort could be a clear and specific declaration of policy at the international level in relation to specific countries that moves beyond obvious generalities such as human rights, transparency and gender. Another could be a common acceptance that democratic transitions are extremely sensitive, that policy failures during transitions can lead to major conflicts which can easily spill across borders, and therefore that there is an international responsibility to contribute in as positive manner as possible to issues of process design, with a view to preventing conflict.

9

CONFRONTING THE DICTATORIAL PAST IN TUNISIA

TOWARDS A POLITICAL UNDERSTANDING OF TRANSITIONAL JUSTICE

Kora Andrieu

'Transitional justice' is the term given to a relatively recent field of human rights which considers that if societies are to move peacefully forward towards democracy, they must first confront the gross human rights violations in their past, repair the rights of victims, and put an end to impunity, so as to build a state truly based on the rule of law. Four measures, or 'pillars' are usually cited: trials, truth-seeking mechanisms, reparations—both material and symbolic, and administrative reforms meant to prevent the recurrence of violence and promote democratisation. According to United Nations transitional justice expert Pablo de Greiff, there are four aims of transitional justice: recognition, civic trust, the rule of law, and, ultimately, reconciliation. Indeed, the first assumption of transitional justice is that the coordinated and complementary implementation of these four 'pillars' will contribute not only to the pacification of post-conflict or post-dictatorial societies, but also will reinforce the democratisation process. 'Justice', in this context, means not only criminal prosecutions, but extends to include truth-seeking, public apologies, human development, and memorialisation or history-teaching reforms, which are all posited as new forms of 'accountability' that, in transitional contexts, contribute to the process of recognising victims and reestablishing their rights after periods of mass violations.

If the goals of transitional justice thus appear to encompass much more than the rule of law, the field has nonetheless long been dominated by a legalist paradigm that sees its origins in the Nuremberg trials and defines it, for the most part, as a judicial answer to mass atrocities.[1] Ruti Teitel, for instance, defines transitional justice as 'a concept of justice, intervening in a period of political change, characterised by a juridical answer to the wrongs of past repressive regimes.'[2] Born first in the context of Latin American transitions, transitional justice was 'exported' to South Africa and, from there, became an almost universal and systematic tool of the international community in post-conflict or post-dictatorial contexts. Transitional justice was first globally disseminated as a set of human rights norms related to liberalism and the international discourse that links development to peace-building and liberal state-building.[3] The field thus became increasingly judicialised, centering on a set of international human rights laws—such as the right to justice, the right to reparations, and the so-called 'right to truth'—and on the recently created office of a UN Special Rapporteur with a mandate for 'the promotion of justice, truth, reparations, and guarantees of non-repetition.' Through this legalistic, liberal approach, the field of transitional justice "has defined" itself in explicit opposition to 'politics' and has tended to underscore its 'depoliticisation'.

In this chapter, I will explore, through an analysis of the Tunisian case, the limits of the field's detachment from political issues. The judicial character of transitional justice is certainly essential, but this must not obscure the fact that its measures are also, fundamentally, political tools. Indeed, born in a specific, post–Cold War context, the field and its network of 'experts' are bound together by a definite consensus as to what constitutes a 'good' political regime. In the words of Paige Arthur, it is 'an international web of individuals and institutions whose internal coherence is held together by common concepts, practical aims, and distinctive claims for legitimacy.'[4] This shared conception of legitimacy is manifest, for instance, in the way transitional justice has progressively become attached to liberal peace-building operations.[5] It has in the process developed into an apparatus within the wider peace-building 'package' of democratisation, for confronting the past is considered essential to building a culture of human rights, to reforming a state's institutions, and to re-creating civil society after mass violence. Indeed, it seems safe to say that there is agreement in the field on the fact that democracy is, or should be, among the 'final ends' of transitional justice: if its measures cannot be directly said to promote democratisation, it is expected that they will, in the longer-term, have a positive impact on the democratic process overall.[6] In cases where a transitional justice process took place outside of an actual political transition (such in Canada, Brazil, Morocco, or Spain), it is asserted that the process will, at the very least, contribute to a 'consolidation' of democracy. Viewed through this paradigm, transitional justice appears as part of a global post–Cold War trend that sees political liberalism as the only criteria of political acceptability, the goal of any 'normal' political progress. This, in itself, is a political assertion. Indeed, in Francis Fukuyama's words, 'the assertion that we have reached the end of history is not a statement about the empirical condition of the world, but a normative argument concerning the justice or adequacy of liberal demo-cratic political institutions.'[7]

In Tunisia, soon after the fall of the Ben Ali regime, the toolkit of transi-tional justice was almost immediately adopted and, with the help of an extremely proactive international community, put into operation. Countless conferences, workshops, and seminars were organised after the revolution to sensitise the temporary government and civil society organisations to the importance of transitional justice, and to 'sell' its tools to local actors.[8] However, despite official attempts to present it as a depoliticised and purely legal approach to dealing with a legacy of gross human rights violations, I will demonstrate that discourses on 'facing the past' in Tunisia were rapidly instru-mentalised to serve political ends. By putting forward one specific type of victim, or by promoting certain kinds of reparations, it was possible to tell a particular story about the past and to serve a particular political project. Transitional justice thus appeared in Tunisia, in spite of the efforts of the international community to 'legalise' it, as an intrinsically political instrument of legitimisation. This chapter, based on my own experience working on the ground since 2012, will present the main elements of the Tunisian process, define its limits and its political meaning, and attempt to discover the best means by which transitional justice can truly serve the democratic project initiated by the 2010–2011 revolution. As a case study, it will raise essential questions about the very nature of transitional justice and its relations to poli-tics, and will defend a more substantial, foundational approach to transitional justice, as opposed to the current and dominant 'problem-solving' approach.

The Legacy of Human Rights Violations in Tunisia

Since transitional justice is concerned with facing the past, it is important first to recall what the legacy of political violence is in Tunisia. Zine el-Abidine Ben Ali took power on 7 November 1987, in the course of a peaceful coup officially justified for 'medical reasons' against eighty-four-year-old President Habib Bourguiba, who had governed the country since its independence in 1956. Although he had never abandoned the idea that Tunisia was a Muslim country, Bourguiba and his 'Destour' (Constitution) party were inspired by a generally secular and modernist conception of the country's identity, which excluded any public recourse to religion and turned the country resolutely towards the West, at the expense of other Pan-Arabist movements which had shared in the struggle for independence, such as that of Salah Ben Youssef. Ben Youssef led a faction of the nationalist movement, more radical in its demands and defensive of Tunisia's Arabic–Islamic identity. After the country's independence, he was condemned to death, forced into exile, and finally assassinated in Germany in 1961.[9] His supporters were persecuted during the years that followed independence, and more than 900 were killed.[10] Bourguiba was also allegedly responsible for crimes committed during the violent evacuation of French soldiers from Bizerte. Due to his stark opposition to Bourguiba, and despite the fact that he was just as 'westernised' and francophone as the latter, Ben Youssef was soon to become a heroic figure for the losers of the independence and the victims of Bourguiba's authoritarian rule.

Finally freed from his opponents, Bourguiba pursued his modernising project, radically accelerating reforms in the fields of economy, education and society—this to the point that he was sometimes called the 'Arabic Atatürk'.[11] The Personal Status Code granted important rights to women, including in areas of divorce, inheritance, and contraception: a first in the Arab world.[12] It also prohibited polygamy and set a minimum age for marriage. The country's Muslim identity was carefully circumscribed by the president, who tried to suppress the feast of Ramadan for economic reasons, fought against women wearing the veil, and put an end to the traditional religious '*sharia*' tribunals by unifying the national judicial system under a secular model. Islamic institutions, such as the famous 'Zitouna' mosque and religious school in Tunis were strictly controlled by the state.[13] Bourguiba's priority was to consolidate the state and to break the feudalist and tribal dynamics that he thought were preventing the country's development. This stance contributed to solidifying the 'Bourguiba myth' in the national memory, where he often appears as the sole architect of the Tunisian modern state and a liberator of women.

Many human rights violations were committed during this period, both against the leftist opposition (for instance the 'Perspectives' movement in the 1960s) and against the Islamists, including the Youssefists who fomented a *coup d'Etat* in 1963.[14] The different experiments of that period (*dirigisme*, forced collectivisation, and rapid liberalisation) built a fragile national economy and had very negative social impacts: for many Tunisians purchasing power remained extremely low, while unemployment and job insecurity increased, leading to tragic events, notably in 1978[15] and 1984.[16]

However, it was not until the late 1970s, with the economic crisis and Bourguiba's reinforcing of the authoritarian nature of the regime by proclaiming himself 'president for life', that the opposition would organise itself in earnest.[17] Leftist student movements and labour unions were the first victims of a bloody cycle of repressions in 1971, 1972, and 1978, which almost completely dismantled them, leaving more room for the Islamists to reorganise themselves as a genuinely political movement.[15] Reinforced by the context of the Iranian revolution, they unified themselves under the banner of the 'Movement of the Islamist Tendency' (MTI). Confrontation between the regime and the MTI escalated in the 1980s, when a series of attacks against tourist hotels and coffee shops throughout the country set off a spiral of violence. MTI activists were arrested en masse and some were judged in show trials, while others were tortured or forced into exile. All Islamist publications were forbidden.[18] Between 1984 and 1987, following a new series of bombing attacks on tourist attractions in Sousse and Monastir, thousands of Islamists, including the present president of Ennahda, Rached Ghannouchi, were arrested for 'plots against the safety of the state.'[19] Most of these opponents would later benefit from a general amnesty promulgated in 2011.

On the surface, the first years of the Ben Ali era were characterised by a form of opening and a relative political liberalisation, which aimed at projecting a better image of the country on the international scene. Several international treaties, including the Convention against Torture, were ratified. Thousands of political prisoners were released. Under its new name of 'Ennahda' ('rebirth'), the MTI was legalised and allowed to participate in the 1989 elections. This opening would be limited, however: as soon as Ben Ali consolidated his own power within the Democratic Constitutional Rally (RCD), purging it of the pro-Bourguiba elements that had opposed his 1987 coup, he turned against the Islamists once again. Ennahda was banned; its members imprisoned, persecuted, or forced into exile.[20] The eruption of the civil war in neighboring Algeria accelerated and radicalised this anti-Islamist impulse, legitimising it as a part of the so-called 'fight against terror', so that it received the unequivocal support of the international community. Supporters of Ennahda were systematically harassed and arrested for threatening national security, and all forms of political association were forbidden. Several show trials were held against the Islamists, without benefit of due process or fair judicial guarantees.[21] Torture became more and more systematic, in the secret prisons of the regime as well as the underground cells of the Ministry of the Interior. The majority of victims, during that period, were Islamists, but other political opponents were targeted by the repression as well.[22] The army itself was not spared: in 1991, Ben Ali responded to suspicions of a military coup with a campaign of detention and torture directed at more than 300 officers, in the so-called 'Baraket Essahel' affair.[23]

In the 1990s, despite a favourable international image, Tunisia became a police state—one of the most authoritarian in the world, violating a wide range of human rights, from freedom of expression and information to freedom from torture and arbitrary execution.[24] People lived in a general atmosphere of suspicion and self-censorship, although the 'political police' was in fact less powerful than generally described, with secret services comprising around 50,000 agents.[25] In the post-9/11 world, Tunisia quickly became an important global actor in the new 'War on Terror', especially after a terrorist attack on the Djerba synagogue in 2003 enabled the government to justify the arbitrary arrest and repression of Islamists and political opponents. Thus it could continue its persecutions with complete impunity. In 2009, a report by Amnesty International documented cases of torture, forced disappearances, and unfair trials, and stated that 'security concerns and anti-terrorist preoccupations are being used to justify arbitrary arrest, and the repression of Islamists and political opponents in general'.[26] Tunisia's severe 2003 anti-terrorism law allowed security forces to arrest and try civilians who had allegedly committed acts of terrorism. Cases appeared before a military court, where proceedings were closed to outside observation and, defendants claimed, convictions were often based on confessions obtained through the use of torture.

Structural violations of social, economic, and cultural rights were also of great consequence during this period. Under Ben Ali's rule, especially after he married hairdresser Leila Trabelsi, corruption became systemic, and the regime came to resemble more and more a mafia state. According to the International Crisis Group, 'their tactics included marriages of convenience with the leading bussiness families, use of threats by the security services, and extortion of varying degrees of legality'.[27] This takeover of the country's economy operated according to a regional strategy, with coastal cities such as Sousse or Monastir privileged, while the industrial heart of the country was left behind—in particular the governorates of Gafsa, Sidi Bouzid, and Kasserine, which the ruling elites always looked upon with suspicion because of their unionist traditions and tribal tendencies.

Regional inequalities are also explained by the fact that the Tunisian economy is built around tourism and exports, prompting many companies to settle on the coast, the more attractive location for both sectors. The industrialisation model chosen by Tunisia after 1970 greatly encouraged private investment, which gave further impetus to opening towards the outside world for the benefit of the few coastal areas at the expense of the interior. As highlighted in the 'White Paper' of the Ministry of Regional Development, as a result of this policy, 'the interior areas are constrained, either in agro-rural development schemes or in a logic of domestic migration for the benefit of coastal cities ... and have been placed, by political choice, at the margins of any modernisation dynamic, their main function being to provide cheap labour for jobs considered low status.'[28] This marginalisation prompted the legislators after the revolution to include regions as possible 'victims' of past repression within transitional justice law, although in practice, demonstrating the intentionality and systematic character of this regional exclusion has proven very difficult.

At a political level, the centralisation of power in Tunis fed these inequalities. Regional councils, predominantly, and sometimes exclusively composed of members of the RCD, were run on a patronage basis, and were in fact deprived of any decision-making power. There was no mechanism to promote the accountability of the regions in the use of public funds, and long-standing loyalty to the regime was the main criterion for being granted money. Tourism, one of the country's primary sources of revenue, was not developed according to any long-term national strategy either: it remained confined to the coastal regions of the Sahel and greater Tunis, on a low-cost 'all inclusive' model that excluded important archaeological sites in the inner regions, such as the ruins of Sbeitla, the Roman pools of Gafsa, or the amphitheatre of El Jem. Tourism thus did not become a significant source of long-term economic, ecological, and human development.[29] The inequality this created was one of the main causes of the 2011 revolution. It is estimated that corruption cost Tunisia approximatively $1 billion dollars each year. The natural resources of the country, in particular the phosphate mines in the Gafsa region, were not exploited fairly, and the income derived from them did not benefit the wider Tunisian society. In 2008, demonstrations against a corrupt and unfair recruitment process for employment in the mining company were severely repressed, with hundreds of people arrested and wounded, and four deaths. It marked a first turning point and a telltale sign of the regime's fragility.[30]

These various factors, combined with the economic crisis and a significant rise in unemployment, in particular among young graduates, were at the heart of the twenty-eight days of turmoil that saw the death of hundreds, thousands wounded, and the escape of President Ben Ali and of his family on 14 January 2011, opening a new page in Tunisia's history.

The First Measures of Transitional Justice (January–October 2011): A Fragmented Approach

Truth-seeking

He was probably unaware of it himself, but Ben Ali opened the debate on transitional justice in Tunisia during his last speech on national television. Trying in vain to ease social tensions, he announced, on 13 January, the opening of a fair and transparent investigation into crimes committed by the security forces against demonstrators. Three commissions would thus be created after the revolution: a commission of inquiry on human rights violations committed during the demonstrations; a commission of investigation on corruption and embezzlement; and a commission for political reform. Despite severe criticism, these commissions would nevertheless produce significant results that would inform the rest of the transitional justice process.

a) The inquiry commission on crimes and abuses committed during the revolution

The work of this first fact-finding commission, presided over by human rights advocate Taoufik Bouderbala, consisted mostly of hearing the accounts of victims and their relatives, but included also the testimonies of alleged perpetrators and witnesses collected by the commissioners across the entire country over a period of several months. A hotline was installed to receive victims' testimonies or witnesses's accounts of the violence. An archive system was created and a database established with the names, details, and contact information on all victims. In total, the commission documented 2,489 cases of violation, including those of 338 individuals who were killed and 2,147 who were wounded. The mandate of this commission, however, was limited to documenting abuses committed between 17 December 2010 and the first free elections of 23 October 2011.[31] The timeframe was narrow and resources were limited, which made this an important but insufficient step in the transitional justice process. The final report was not widely distributed and its conclusions disappointing, as it failed clearly to identify those responsible for abuses among the security forces. Committee members report that they were submitted to various pressures from the authorities when drafting the report, and forced to modify their conclusions.[32]

b) The inquiry commission on corruption and embezzlement

On 14 March 2011, the newly created National Confiscation Commission took control of more than 285 companies and 320 properties belonging to Ben Ali and his entourage. The Ministry of Finance then established the Commission for the Recovery of Assets Looted and Hidden Abroad and the Commission for the Management of Funds and Confiscated Properties. An inquiry commission was also created, in parallel, to shed light on the general patterns of corruption and embezzlement, and to establish responsibility.

This inquiry commission was innovative in the framework of transitional justice, for it functioned like a typical truth commission, though its mandate was limited to affairs of corruption and economic crimes. As in other 'typical' truth commissions, citizens were invited to testify before the panel and file complaints on relevant cases. A 'green line' was created to receive phone calls. By this means more than 5,000 cases were documented, of which several hundreds were transmitted to the courts. These cases often linked corruption to other forms of human rights violations, such as police beatings or day-to-day humiliations. To that extent, the commission also functioned as a tool to effect social inclusion, recognising and reintegrating people previously considered 'outsiders', while dismantling networks of connivance.[33] It was an interesting step toward defining the limits and potential for including corruption in the mandate of transitional justice mechanisms. The commission on corruption and embezzlement, however, was prey to political pressure: its members received several death threats, and their headquarters eventually had to be guarded by the army. The death by sudden heart attack of its respected President Abdelfattah Amor, which according to his family was the direct consequence of this work pressure, seriously impeded the advancement of the commission's research. After the release of its report, the commission was transformed into a permanent anti-corruption institution. However, very few out of the 550 corruption cases transmitted to courts have led to trials, let alone convictions.[34]

Reparations

As early as 2011, debates on transitional justice in Tunisia were focusing on the sole issue of reparations, before truth-seeking, an order of events that contributed to the politicisation and fragmentation that I will later describe. Two decrees promulgated in 2011, before any in-depth investigations on past violations, are partly responsible for this focus.

Decree-law No. 1, promulgated on 19 February 2011, granted amnesty to all individuals who had been arrested or condemned for political reasons since 1989, including those brought up on charges of violating the protest law or belonging to an illegal organisation. In 2011, more than 12,000 former political prisoners were released from prison, amidst a general turmoil due to several uprisings and escapes from the country's prisons during the revolution itself. The decree also provided for important reparations and a rehabilitation scheme that included the recruitment into the public sector and the administration of all beneficiaries of the amnesty program, as well as financial compensations. This decree raised several issues, and it was accordingly widely criticised by the Tunisian public, by international experts, and by the victims themselves. Since many beneficiaries of the amnesty were Islamists, as they were the group most targeted and arrested during the last years of the regime, segments of the public came to regard the reparations with suspicion, perceiving them as a device whereby the ruling Islamist party could reward its troops, rather than as the legal entitlements of victims of gross human rights violations. Several abuses were observed as well. No distinction was made among beneficiaries, with the result that many extremists who joined the Salafi group Ansar al-Sharia, which was later listed as a terrorist organisation, were freed during the amnesty and even recruited into the public administration.[35] Finally, from a transitional justice point of view, promising financial reparations before any actual truth-seeking process is completed, and thus before there is an estimate of the number of beneficiaries and an assessment of the state's financial capacity to actually live up to its promises, seems problematic. The payment of compensations was indeed slow, uneven, and incomplete, and many victims were excluded from recognition altogether as they did not have the court decision that was necessary for them to make their claims. In protest, associations organized repeated hunger strikes and staged several public demonstrations. By 2016, 18,850 citizens had received an amnesty certificate.[36] Politically, the process was damaging, as the implementation of decree-law No. 1 fed suspicions that Ennahda was using the general amnesty to reward its supporters and to take over the public administration by distributing key positions to its members. It also contributed heavily to the popular sentiment that transitional justice itself was an 'Islamist' entitlement, and that Ennahda was dangling it over the heads of businessmen and former regime officials like a 'sword of Damocles' to make political gains during the transition period.[37]

Another decree-law on reparations was promulgated by the interim government of Beji Caid Essebsi on 24 October 2011. It granted the 'martyrs and wounded of the revolution' a set of material and symbolic reparations that included the public commemoration of 14 January as a new national holiday, the creation of a museum of the revolution, the changing of street names to honor martyrs, and amendments to history books. The decree defined 'martyrs of the revolution' as those who had 'risked their lives to concretise the goals of the revolution, and died as martyrs or were physically wounded (...) between 17 December 2010 and 28 February 2011'. In order to benefit from the financial reparations scheme, victims had to go to the headquarters of their governorate with a medical certificate that confirmed their status and detailed the harm suffered. Financial reparations were allocated in two payments, in February and December 2011: 6,000 Dinars for the 2,749 wounded, and 40,000 Dinars for the families of 347 martyrs. These payments were partially financed by a gift of 20 million dollars made by the government of Qatar.[38] Decree-law No. 98 also provided for reimbursement of the transportation and medical expenses of victims who were 'incapacitated at more than 6 per cent', but without further adjusting the allocated amounts according to the gravity of the wounds and the expense of the necessitated care. This created inequities, as some victims who had been left paraplegic needed constant medical care costing far in excess of the allocated sums. Public sector recruitment of these victims was also planned by the government as a form of rehabilitation, and as compensation for the loss of income generally associated with victimisation. In October 2013, more than 2,700 wounded had been recruited to the public sector, as well as 200 family members of martyrs.[39]

However, several abuses were observed in implementing this program as well, as the required medical certificate cost approximately 80 Tunisian Dinars (less than 40 Euros). Many victims could not afford this amount, while others were able to obtain false certificates by bribing doctors. The lack of transparency regarding the definition of victims and difficulties in establishing a final, uncontested list of victims also impeded the process, feeding competition. Several institutions were charged with establishing the list: the inquiry commission presided over by M. Bouderbala, the 'Committee of Martyrs and Wounded' at the National Constituent Assembly, and in addition the Ministry of Human Rights and Transitional Justice and the National Human Rights Institution. To date, there is still no final number or definitive list of the victims of the 2010–2011 revolution.

In the process, the symbolic aspect of reparations detailed in the decree was left by the wayside, and, apart from the many '14 January 2011' streets and avenues that have replaced '7 November 1987' signs, there is no official recognition of the victims in the public space. Following the 2014 elections, victims of the former regime and the 'wounded of the revolution' gradually faded from the Tunisian collective memory, as the various terrorist attacks committed between 2012 and 2016 made, paradoxically, the security forces appear to be the new 'martyrs', along with the two assassinated leftist figures, Chokri Belaïd and Mohamed Brahmi. Accepting the 'victimhood' of Islamist activists became even more difficult in this fragile context, which saw a revival of the earlier stigmatisation and even harassment of persons seen as ideologically associated with terrorism, or categorised as such.[40]

Transitional versus revolutionary dynamics

The Tunisian context is exceptional on many grounds, as it represents an interesting example of transition without negotiation, quite different from more classical cases, such as Poland or South Africa. What is unique about the Tunisian revolution is that it occurred at what Mark Freeman calls the beginning of 'second-generation' thinking about transitions. That is, it took place at a time when international support was based on a better understanding of local factors, and democratic openings were no longer seen as technocratic exercises but rather as 'social contract-formation moments.'[41] Moreover, the Tunisian transition benefitted from many advantages: the army was not an enemy to reckon with, as it was in South America; the economy would not have to transition from communism to capitalism, as it did in Eastern Europe; and the previous regime was not totalitarian and allowed for the development of some sort of civil society; there were no deep racial or ethnic cleavages as in South Africa; and the transition was not imposed from the outside, as happened in Iraq and Afghanistan, but was spurred instead by an internal and legitimate revolt. This positive context encouraged and facilitated the transmission of international expertise, towards which Tunisia adopted an open-door policy to the point of soon becoming a 'model' for other Arab Spring countries. This 'flood' of international assistance explains the rapid pace at which the transitional justice lexicon, unknown to most before 2011, was adopted by Tunisians and integrated into the national discourse—becoming even a key guarantee of the new constitution of January 2014.[42] To protect and ensure the complete implementation of transitional justice, the final dispositions of the constitution state that, in all matters related to it, the non-retroactivity of laws, previous amnesties, prescriptions, or double jeopardy arguments cannot be opposed. This radical statement was strongly criticised by various lawyers and constitutional experts, who saw it, paradoxically, as a way to 'constitutionalise anti-constitutionality', and to place, *de facto*, transitional justice under a regime of exception.

The Tunisian context was a revolutionary one in which the term 'breaking with the past' would acquire an entirely new meaning: defining Tunisia's relationship to the 'old regime' would crucially influence the entire process of transitional justice from its earliest stage. This transfer of revolutionary hopes onto the transitional justice process, which turned that process into a form of 'revolutionary justice', became a strong argument for its opponents, who came to see it as a remnant of an out-dated political context and an obstacle to economic development. This revolutionary understanding of transitional justice is surprising to some extent, for it contradicts the dominant narrative that sees transitional justice as a 'reforming' tool, for the peaceful reintegration of former regime officials through fair 'vetting processes', leading eventually to some form of 'reconciliation-with-justice'. By contrast, in Tunisia a strong revolutionary dynamic, intent on dismantling all 'counter-revolutionary' forces, at first competed with a 'soft' transitional justice discourse, which was perceived as too lenient towards the former regime. Fears of a comeback overshadowed the entire Tunisian transition, influencing many post–14 January political decisions. The spectre of counter-revolution also influenced choices made in the course of the transitional justice process. Indeed, after Ben Ali's departure, several members of his RCD party joined the new interim government. The interim president himself, Mohamed Ghannouchi, was Ben Ali's prime minister from 1999 to 2011. Popular opposition to such comebacks of former 'RCD-ists' was strong, and, following the 'Kasbah 1' and 'Kasbah 2' demonstrations, Ghannouchi was forced to resign on 27 February 2011.[43] He was replaced, however, by another figure from the former regime: Beji Caid Essebsi, who had been a minister under Bourguiba and President of the

Assembly under Ben Ali, and was now aged eighty-six. Public opinion, however, saw Essebsi as representing a more consensual form of 'Bourguibism', closer to the independence movement of the 'Destour', which remains, in some sectors of Tunisian collective memory, associated with modernism and progressivism. Essebsi's government lasted until the first elections of 23 October 2011, a period during which several measures from the toolbox of transitional justice were adopted: key former regime representatives were tried, and the basis of a complete 'lustration' or vetting process was put in place. However, as will be demonstrated below, these measures hovered at the margins of transitional justice *per se*, often flirting with revenge and resembling more a form of revolutionary, or exceptional, justice.

The trials of the former regime

As with reparations, accountability was pursued in Tunisia in a fragmented, somewhat incoherent, and politicised manner. Several trials of highly placed dignitaries from the former regime took place before the drafting of a comprehensive transitional justice law, and before any attempts to reform the justice system. Consequently, these trials were generally considered unfair, lacking fundamental judicial guarantees. Contradictions would arise from this fragmentation, as the transitional justice organic law of December 2013 also included provisions for the judgement of presumed perpetrators: it created 'Specialised Judicial Chambers' that could, in theory, have the power to reopen these cases. Establishing links between these diverse steps, commissions, and trials will prove difficult, and it will certainly be one of the main challenges for the future coherence of transitional justice in Tunisia. Disconnected from a comprehensive transitional justice framework, the early criminal prosecutions were indeed highly politicised.

In accordance with a Tunisian law on the status of security forces, military justice was considered the legitimate tribunal for dealing with any crime committed in the exercise of their functions by the security forces, the police, or the army.[44] In fact, many victims felt reassured by this decision, as civilian justice was fully discredited and in need of deep structural reform, tainted by its collaboration with Ben Ali's regime. The courts opened their investigations in July 2011, and grouped the cases geographically: the military courts of Tunis, Sfax, and Le Kef started their hearings in November and December 2011. Defendants included two former interior ministers, five general directors of the ministry, and several high and mid-level security forces commanders. Sentences were pronounced during the summer of 2012, condemning Ben Ali *in absentia* to life imprisonment and sentencing other key figures for murder, manslaughter, or complicity in both. However, other key actors, such as the head of the security forces in the city of Thala, where most of the victims were shot during the deadly days of 8–10 January, were acquitted and even promoted. The defendants appealed against the verdict before the Military Court of Appeals, which, on 12 April 2014, confirmed the first verdict finding Ben Ali guilty of murder and complicity in murder. The Court then reduced the sentences for all other high-ranking officials, leading to the release of most of Ben Ali's national security and presidential guard chiefs. Their sentences were reduced to three years for 'failure to render assistance', and those three years had already passed since their arrest. Military judges were of the opinion that Tunisian law did not recognise any sort of responsibility for 'complicity' to murder, and that the chain of command could not be established. The military trials were generally considered as having respected the rights of the defense and the main judicial guarantees, but they nonetheless faced important challenges. Major shortcomings included their failure to build evidence to identify those directly responsible for crimes, and the lack of penal code articles that would make possible the prosecution of senior officers for crimes that their subordinates had committed. This demonstrates that, in transitional justice processes, the state of existing laws is often one of the biggest obstacles to fighting impunity. The government's failure to press effectively for Ben Ali's extradition from Saudi Arabia also undermined accountability.

The verdict of the military appeals court in April 2014 provoked outrage among civil society organisations and the families of the martyrs, who staged several demonstrations in protest. One year later, the Court of Cassation annulled the decision of the military appeals court and referred the case of the 'martyrs and wounded of the revolution' (Tunis, Thala, and Kasserine) back to the court of First Instance. Victims and civil society organisations have repeatedly asked that the case be transferred to civilian justice or to the Specialised Judicial Chambers that were later created in each of Tunisia's First Instance courts as a provision of the 2013 organic law on Transitional Justice. But the Chambers were slow to be established, and technical issues still arise as a result of this transfer. Will the jurisdiction of the Specialised Chambers trump that of military justice, which still, under the new constitution, has jurisdiction over abuses by security forces? Such a transfer could also be in violation of the constitutional principle of *non bis in idem*, or double jeopardy, according to which no one can be judged twice for the same crime. Legally, the only way these trials could be re-opened would be if the recently established Truth and Dignity Commission, through its investigations, were to find new, crucial evidence that was not considered by the military tribunals.

The previous case also reflects common judicial difficulties that arise in dealing with gross human rights violations in transitional periods. Indeed, only a handful of human rights cases have gone to court, mostly for deaths and injuries inflicted by the security forces when they were trying to suppress the uprising. Military judges faced important obstacles, both judicial and practical, due in part to the absence of the principle of command responsibility in Tunisian national law. This established principle of international law holds senior officers liable for crimes that their subordinates committed with their explicit or tacit approval.[45] According to Human Rights Watch, the lack of provisions criminalising command responsibility in Tunisia made possible the military courts' light sentences for Ben Ali and senior commanders for their role in commanding the troops that killed scores of protesters during the Tunisian uprising.[46] But impunity is also a threat when it comes to torture-related affairs. Out of the thousands of reported cases only one has gone to trial, resulting in the sentencing of a former interior minister and other high-level security personnel to only two years in prison. In the case, known as the 'Barraket Essahel affair', a military court convicted former interior minister Abdallah Kallel and three security officials for 'using violence against others either directly or through others,' and sentenced them to four-year prison terms. The case arose from the arrest and detention of seventeen senior military officers in 1991, in connection with an alleged plot by the military against Ben Ali. The charge of torture was dismissed on the basis of the non-retroactivity principle: the military judges considered that, while Tunisia did ratify the Convention against Torture in 1991, it had not yet incorporated it into its national law at the time of the affair. The appeals court later reduced the sentences by half, and Abdallah Kallel was finally released in July 2013.

These affairs had only a limited impact on the greater public, even though the wider participation of victims was made possible thanks to a reform of military justice permitted by a 2011 decree. Ben Ali's absence, however, is certainly an important factor explaining the lack of public involvement in the process, for without him the trials lost some of the cathartic and almost ritual impact that they often impart to transitional justice processes. The defence rapidly denounced these trials as 'show trials' targeting only a few scapegoats: Tunisia still awaits its Nuremberg, and impunity gaps remain, exacerbated by the absence of any deep justice or security sector reforms.

Guarantees of non-repetition

Vetting the administration is the main function of this final 'pillar' of transitional justice, which aims at reforming state institutions to prevent the future recurrence of violence. The idea is that if the same people are left in the administration, some of whom may have been involved in gross violations in the past, civic trust may be difficult to establish, and in its absence reconciliation will not be possible.

In Tunisia, early scrutiny was given to the two sectors most responsible for the former regime's political oppression: justice and security. Under Ben Ali the judicial sector was entirely controlled by the executive. Members of the 'Supreme Judicial Council'—in charge of the nomination, promotion, and dismissal of judges—were handpicked by presidential decree under Law 67–29 of 1967. Any judge who opposed their decisions would be dismissed or transferred to other regions, his salary blocked and his passport revoked, with no possibility of appeal. After 14 January, demands for reform of the judicial sector were made by various actors, unsurprisingly given the important role played by lawyers in the 2010/2011 uprising. But the vetting and reform process was slow and incoherent. After the October 2011 elections, the Constituent Assembly suspended the Supreme Judicial Council and created an interim judicial authority to serve until a High Institute for Judicial Independence could be established. After more than one year of inaction, in May 2012, the Ministry of Justice decided to dismiss, unilaterally, eighty-two judges with no notice or explicit justification.[47] The judges complained that they had been denied access to their files, did not know the grounds for their dismissal, and therefore could not effectively appeal it. Officially, the decision was based on vague allegations of 'corruption' and 'loyalty to the former regime'. This lack of transparency and the collective punishment violate fundamental judicial guarantees and contradict the very principle of transitional justice, which stipulates that, on the contrary, vetting should be based on the principle of individual responsibility and should encourage social inclusion and national reconciliation. Thanks in part to intense international pressure and mounting criticisms, some of the judges have since been reinstated, but with this exception, no actual vetting of the judicial sector has yet been undertaken. The judicial oversight body was finally created in May 2015, but it fell short of international standards as it failed the test of full independence from the executive.[48]

In the security sector too, structural institutional reforms were implemented in a hasty manner. During the months that followed the departure of Ben Ali, minister of the interior Ferhat Rajhi, under pressure from human rights associations, ordered the dismissal of forty-two high-level officials of the Interior Security Forces, a gesture which was inaccurately presented as a dissolution of the 'political police'.[49] In parallel, 2,200 officers of the Ministry of the Interior who had lost their jobs under the former regime, were unilaterally reintegrated. Under Ben Ali, agents could indeed be removed for political reasons—for instance if they were too religiously rigorous and were therefore considered potential supporters of the Islamists. Others, however, had been dismissed because they had actually committed crimes. This collective reintegration was therefore highly criticised, and the debates on security sector reforms became highly politicized. Anti-Islamists accused Ennahda of trying to create a new, parallel security structure, and of being responsible for the rise of jihadism after 2012. Revolutionaries on the other hand, in particular among the 'Troïka', tended to see security institutions as inherently 'counter-revolutionary' and therefore refused to put security issues at the top of the political agenda. Some, finally, suspected the former regime, still present within the deeper structures of the Ministry of Interior, of encouraging jihadism in order to legitimate new, repressive security measures.[50] In the absence of real reform, the security forces themselves tended to see Ennahda, and Islamists more generally, through the eyes of the former regime, and they became increasingly unwilling to embrace change. The first public hearings of the Truth and Dignity Commission, where victims of torture and police brutality testified, could contribute to easing these tensions, provided that the security forces understand that the goal of transitional justice is not to settle scores but to restore trust and enable structural reform. Otherwise, in a context marked by a state of emergency and the rise of terrorism, the risk of a return to authoritarianism remains.[51]

Debates about vetting, however, were much more passionate in the electoral sector, clear evidence of the politicisation of the Tunisian transitional justice process. In March 2011, following the protests of Kasbah 1 and 2, the RCD was dissolved by a judicial decision that was highly popular and generally acclaimed. All the party's assets, including its headquarters in the center of Tunis, were confiscated by the state. The Commission on Political Reform, headed by constitutionalist Yadh Ben Achour and installed during that same period, was responsible for establishing criteria for candidacy in the future elections for the National Constituent Assembly (NCA). The Commission suggested, in article 15, that three types of candidates should be excluded: former ministers under Ben Ali's successive governments; persons who had occupied positions of high responsibility in the RCD; and anyone who had publicly called for Ben Ali's reelection in 2014.[52] The High Commission to Supervise Elections (ISIE) compiled a list of 3,100 names, on the basis of archives and the press, to which were added the 5,000 names identified by the Ben Achour Commission.[53]

A draft law on the so-called 'immunisation of the revolution' was later, in April of 2012, submitted to the NCA by the Republican Congress (CPR) of President Marzouki. The draft law proposed excluding from all participation in political life (elections, key administration or security sector positions, embassies, and the like) for a period of ten years anyone who had occupied, between 2 April 1989 and 14 January 2011, a function within the government or the RCD, or who had publicly called for Ben Ali's reelection in 2009.[54] The defenders of the law affirmed that this initiative was in line with 'lustration' and 'vetting' processes employed in Eastern Europe, and that such political exclusion was necessary to preserve the objectives of the revolution and 'protect the blood of martyrs'. This draft, however, met with severe criticism from some civil society organisations, political actors, and the international community, as it risked depriving 20,000 citizens of their political rights.[55] The draft, moreover, contradicted many human rights principles, including the right to political participation. Excluding candidates on the sole basis of their past political affiliation is a form of political discrimination based on opinion, and is contrary to the principle of the non-retroactivity of the law. Indeed, being a member of the RCD was not considered as a crime during the period under consideration. In fact, membership to the RCD was often imposed externally, as it conditioned access to employment, health care, free transportation, universities, and public service. The immunisation law therefore was more like a purge or a witch-hunt than a vetting process in a fair transitional justice framework. The latter would require an individual and case-by-case evaluation of the integrity and responsibility of each civil servant, before there could be any question of banning a person from public participation. However, this draft law was paradoxically presented by its defenders as a truly revolutionary alternative to transitional justice, and the two projects competed at the NCA for several months, which partly explains the delays in the adoption of the organic transitional justice law.[56] The electoral context can also explain the need to resort to political exclusion, for it was based on a mistaken idea within the main opposition party Nidaa Tounes that vetting and 'lustration' were tools to get rid of one's adversary, especially given the rapid return to the political scene of personalities associated to the regimes of Ben Ali and Bourguiba.

The draft law on the immunisation of the revolution was finally rejected, partly due to the experience of neighboring Libya, where a similar law had precipitated a relapse into violence,[57] and partly to the counter-example of de-Baathification in Iraq.[58] However, the debates surrounding it brought to light tensions within Tunisia's transition: the dynamic of revolution seemed once again to contradict that of transition. The immunisation law belonged to a radical revolutionary process that relies on the principle of collective responsibility to undergird a *tabula rasa* of the past: anyone even remotely associated with a former regime is deemed guilty. Transitional justice, on the contrary, should rest on the individualisation of guilt, and should look forward, in the end, to national reconciliation. After a complete and fair accountability and vetting process, based on adequate truth-seeking and a recognition of past abuses, it should allow for the peaceful reintegration of some 'former regime' representatives into the fabric of a new state. To that extent, transitional justice contradicts the very logic of revolution.

Recent political developments demonstrate the limits of the revolutionary understanding of transitional justice in Tunisia: generally deemed unfair, trials and vetting measures were rapidly overturned, and even, in some cases, created political opportunities for former regime representatives to come back into the political arena. They were glorified now by the perception that they were themselves victims and benefitted from a sense of nostalgia for the past, in what was a difficult social and security context. Following the 2014 elections, in which—unlike in 2011—former regime officials could participate without constraint, Nidaa Tounes formed a political alliance with Ennahda and turned against the very basis of transitional justice. After the attacks in Tunis and Sousse in March and June 2015, which caused killed sixty-two people including fifty-nine foreign tourists, President Caïd Essebsi declared a state of emergency and announced a radical ban against the non-violent Islamist party Hizb ut-Tahrir.[59] He also proposed an 'economic reconciliation law' offering amnesty to businessmen, public officials, and state employees for acts related to financial corruption and embezzlement, thus effectively sabotaging the mechanisms in place to address economic crimes through truth-telling, restitution, and prosecutions, in particular the work of the Truth and Dignity Commission.[60] These individuals could now negotiate a 'reconciliation agreement' with another commission run directly by the executive, repaying the money they had obtained illegally in exchange for a halt to prosecutions or the annulment of sentences pronounced against them. The law would 'improve the environment for investment', according to the president, and increase asset recovery to be used in future development projects in marginalised regions. Strongly opposed by civil society, this proposition would effectively mean the end of the transitional process begun in 2011, which in many ways looked like a perfect example of the international community's general approach to 'dealing with the past'. Opponents of the reconciliation law see it as a way to absolve corrupt officials without the intervention of any truth or accountability mechanisms, while its supporters considered transitional justice a threat to the country's economic and political stability and feel that Tunisia cannot afford to wait for the final report of the Truth and Dignity Commission's conciliation procedures (possibly in 2018–2019). They argue that businessmen must be freed from the machinations of 'revolutionary justice' that have oppressed them since 2011, and have stood in the way of investments. Ennahda itself is divided, between its ideals as a supporter of the revolution and a former opposition movement, and its need to preserve a fragile ruling coalition with Nidaa Tounes. If adopted, the economic reconciliation law will dramatically reduce the Truth and Dignity Commission's prerogative in arbitration and in the investigation of economic crimes, while seriously impeding the truth-seeking and memorial process.[61]

Transitional Justice after the 23 October 2011 Elections: Institutionalising a Process

The temporal mandate of transitional justice mechanisms is another highly contentious issue in Tunisia, and has become the subject of intense debates and memorial contestations. The secular fringe of society tends to prefer limiting the mandate of the Truth Commission to investigating abuses of the Ben Ali era only, in order to preserve Bourguiba's legacy. Islamists, on the other hand, prefer to go back to the pre-independence period, or even to the French protectorate, in order to question the founding myth of the Tunisian state, and to underline instead its religious and pan-Arab origins as represented by Ben Youssef's movement. Transitional justice in Tunisia thus impinges on deep identity and memorial issues, particularly as regards the state's relation to religion.[62] Ennahda's victory in the 2011 elections helped the Islamists move their own memorial agenda forward. The government of national unity created by a coalition comprised of the Islamists, the Congress for the Republic (Moncef Marzouki), and Ettakatol (Mustapha Ben Jaafar), which is known as the 'Troïka', promulgated a decree law on the temporary organisation of power. Also known as the 'small constitution', it charged the NCA to vote for an organic law on transitional justice. To that end, a Ministry of Human Rights and Transitional Justice was created in January of 2012. This initiative was entirely new in the field and history of transitional justice—no country had ever decided to institutionalise the process to the extent of dedicating an entire ministry to it.[63] This decision was not widely accepted. Both civil society and victims' organisations feared that such a ministry would threaten the neutrality of the process and thereby steal transitional justice out from under them. The fact that the first minister of human rights and transitional justice, Samir Dilou, a lawyer who had spent a decade in prison, was a member of Ennahda, reinforced this perception. Officially however, the role of this minister was only to facilitate a national dialogue and to promote consensus between various sectors of civil society, as well as national and international actors involved in the process—and not to dictate from the top a state policy of transitional justice. The ministry was supposed to give coherence to what had so far been a rather fragmented process, and to act merely as a mediator.

In reality, the Tunisian Ministry of Human Rights and Transitional Justice did play an important part in organising the national consultations that led to the drafting, by a specially nominated 'technical committee', of an organic law on transitional justice. This technical committee was composed of representatives from five different coalitions of civil society organisations, each more or less affiliated with a particular political bent, and a representative of the ministry. National consultations took place in each region of the country between 16 September and 7 October 2012. During that period, twenty-four dialogue sessions were organised in each governorate, where representatives of civil society and victims' organisations were invited to discuss the principles of transitional justice, outline their expectations of the process, and make their requirements known. A national sensitisation campaign was organised beforehand, which featured short cartoons broadcast on national television explaining in simple terms the principles of the 'right to reparations', 'the right to truth', and the 'right to justice'. Participants were invited, at the end of each dialogue session, to fill out a questionnaire asking them about their preferences regarding the future transitional justice law: When should the mandate of the Tunisian Truth Commission begin? What should reparations be composed of (symbolic measures or financial compensation)? What type of human rights violations should be included in the Truth Commission's mandate? Can amnesty be granted in exchange for truth-telling? Should economic crimes and corruption be considered on a par with gross human rights violations? The official line is that the technical committee drafted the organic law on the sole basis of the answers received. However, the timeframe between the end of the consultations and the publication of the first draft was only one week, which raises suspicion as to the extent to which those results were taken into account. Moreover, despite a clear effort to engage with civil society and promote a participatory approach, the consultation had only a limited impact. Many associations complained that they had not been properly informed about the time and place of the dialogues. Moreover, participation in the sessions was based on nominative invitations, and the selection process for attendees was unclear. Individual victims and citizens who did not belong to any network or association were *de facto* excluded. The over-representation of Islamist organisations in the conversations was also noted. Finally, the reach of the consultations was limited, as only a total of 1,200 forms were filled out.

The Organic Law on Transitional Justice and the Mandate of the Tunisian Truth and Dignity Commission

After several months of discussions, setbacks, and revisions, the National Constituent Assembly adopted the Law on Establishing and Organising Transitional Justice on 14 December 2014. The law created a Truth and Dignity Commission (Instance Vérité et Dignité—IVD, TDC in English) composed of fifteen independent members with four-year terms, tasked with ferreting out the truth about the abuses perpetrated in Tunisia since 1 July 1955. The Law on Establishing and Organising Transitional Justice set out a comprehensive approach to addressing past human rights abuses. The Truth and Dignity Commission was to address issues of reparations, accountability, institutional reform, vetting, collective memory, and national reconciliation. All gross human rights violations committed systematically by an organised group since 1 July of 1955 would be examined. The TDC's investigations were to be based on victims' testimonies and on targeted research and legal investigations, with the goal of creating a comprehensive database of human rights violations. The TDC was also tasked with providing a list of all victims, recording their testimonies, identifying public responsibilities, identifying the root causes of all violations, and providing urgent reparations to victims in need. It was also to make recommendations for collective reparations, institutional reforms and vetting, and to promote reconciliation and the safeguarding of national memory.[64]

To fulfil this ambitious mandate, the TDC was handed important powers, including the authority to summon people to testify; to access public archives;

and to organise confidential or public hearings. It was also given license to make onsite visits, to request forensic examinations, and to take all necessary measures to protect witnesses and victims. Within the TDC there was to be an arbitration and reconciliation committee that would consider all cases relating to corruption and gross violations of human rights, were it to receive a request for arbitration from the victim, from the alleged perpetrator, or from the national commission on corruption. Leniency or amnesty could thus be exchanged for honest truth-telling. The inclusion of economic crimes and corruption in the TDC's mandate, considered on a par with other gross human rights violations such as deliberate killing, arbitrary detention, sexual violence, or torture, is original and remains quite rare in the field of transitional justice.[65] Electoral fraud and forced exile are also on the list of gross human rights violations. Finally, the definition of 'victim' adopted by the law is unprecedented, as it includes 'any region that has been systematically marginalised and excluded', thereby opening the door to collective reparations or affirmative action programs for the inner regions of Gafsa, Sidi Bouzid, and Kasserine, where economic and social inequalities, arguably government-induced, were among the root causes of the uprising.

The law also created Specialised Judicial Chambers with judges trained in transitional justice to deal with cases of serious human rights violations. Article 8 of the law states that these Specialised Judicial Chambers should be created by a decree within courts of first instance in the headquarters of appeals courts, and be composed of judges chosen among 'those who have never participated in trials of a political nature.' The law outlined the material jurisdiction of the Specialised Judicial Chambers as follows: they are to adjudicate cases related to gross violations of human rights as specified in international agreements ratified by Tunisia. It further entrusted the Specialised Judicial Chambers with adjudicating cases referred to it by the Truth and Dignity Commission: cases of electoral fraud, financial corruption, the misuse of public funds, and of driving individuals to forced migration for political reasons. In August 2014, a decree-law was issued establishing eight Specialised Judicial Chambers. The TDC, acting under the final disposition of the 2014 Constitution, was also given the power of reopening certain cases and transferring them to the Chambers if its investigations should expose important new evidence. This possibility represents a last hope for justice for the case of the so-called" 'martyrs and wounded of the revolution', after the April 2014 verdict of the military appeal court—even if reopening cases before of the Special Chambers would also entail significant judicial and constitutional complications.

Members of the Truth and Dignity Commission were selected by a specific committee within the National Constituent Assembly, which was dominated by Ennahda representatives, reflecting the assembly's political balance at the time. The committee selected candidates from 288 approved applicants"—the criteria being no previous political involvement, and a reputation for neutrality, independence, and impartiality. The participation of civil society in the nomination process was limited, however, which diminished the perceived legitimacy of the selection. Theoretically any citizen had the right to oppose an individual's nomination, but the selecting committee did not respond to those objections. Moreover, the list was not widely disseminated, and the law provided no right to appeal. This lack of transparency impacted consensus on the final list of commissioners. Nevertheless, the TDC was officially installed in June of 2014, with a female president, Sihem Bensedrine—a journalist and long-time opponent of Ben Ali, who was herself a victim of his regime. The members were given six months to begin their work. During this period, they received intensive training, drafted internal regulations and procedural standards, recruited their executive and investigative staffs, established statement-taking forms, and developed an outreach and communication strategy. Between 2014 and 2015, the commission received 22 million Dinars (11 million dollars) of public funds for operating expenses, including 2 million Dinars (1 million dollars) that could be used as a compensation fund for urgent cases. By 2016, when the period for depositions closed, 3,150 arbitration claims for financial crimes had been filed, while more than 60,000 cases were registered, three quarters of which concerned violations of political and civic rights.[66] Some thirty collective files for 'victim zones'[67] (region, city, neighborhood or governorate), demanding reparations in the form of affirmative action or preferential development programs, were also recorded.[68] Several public hearings were organised in Tunis, beginning in November of 2016, each one focusing on a specific category of victims (martyrs of the revolution, women), a type of violation (corruption, torture), or a period (the fight for independence, the bread strikes). During highly emotional moments broadcast live, thousands followed the public hearings of the TDC and many discovered, for the first time, the true nature of the former regime. The hearings certainly contributed to reinforcing the TDC's legitimacy and rendered regime nostalgia more difficult to sustain. Even the myth of Bourguiba was seriously affected when victims of the Youssefist movement publicly testified.

But the TDC hearings have also re-awakened old reflexes and dark methods, and provoked violent personal attacks against TDC president Sihem

Bensedrine, who is still today depicted as representing an outdated revolutionary spirit, and accused of being responsible for the dismissal of dozens of security officials in March 2011, when she was Ferhat Rajhi's adviser. In the summer of 2015, a coalition of deputies even signed a petition demanding the establishment of a commission of inquiry into the TDC itself, in particular into the alleged corruption of Sihem Bensedrine. Nonetheless, and even more so since the public hearings, the TDC continues to be a stronghold, perhaps the last one, of the revolutionary spirit, and 'a bulwark against the general disillusionment with politics.'[69] By publicly recognizing the damages inflicted by the state on its citizens, the TDC may even be able to short-circuit the radicalisation of young people.[70]

Breaking the 'Categories' of Victims and Unifying the Process: Making Transitional Justice Work in Tunisia

The problem-solving approach to transitional justice and its pitfalls

The Tunisian case is revealing of the limits of what I will call here the 'problem-solving approach to transitional justice', which sees it as a purely judicial and technical tool for helping post-conflict societies deal with a past of repression. From the beginning, transitional justice in Tunisia was highly politicised, and debates surrounding it raised fundamental issues of memory and identity that went well beyond such a purely technical approach.[71] The 'problem-solving' approach sees transitional justice as only one element of a larger 'democratic transition package', which also includes economic liberalisation and free elections. It thereby avoids the complexities involved in defining concepts like 'justice' and 'transition', and limits itself to specifying the steps a society needs to take if it is to efficiently 'deal' with its past. To that extent, transitional justice appears related to 'transitology', a field of research which became very popular during the third wave of democracy, and which sees democratic transition as resulting from the sequential implementation of a series of steps and conditions. By establishing causal links between certain ideas (truth encourages reconciliation, justice is a condition for peace), by claiming its 'neutrality' and its 'depoliticisation', transitional justice too pretends to be a species of science.

However, as I will demonstrate here, avoiding the political dimension of any transitional justice initiative entirely is problematic at best, and perhaps impossible. As the Tunisian example demonstrates, transitional justice is at its core a politically performative, or definitional, experience. By recognising a certain category of victims, it necessarily excludes others, and thereby puts forward a particular narrative about the past that serves particular political ends.[72] This partly explains why in Tunisia defining the dates of its mandate and the type of crimes covered by its investigations was so controversial, and why changes in the political landscape so deeply impacted the transitional justice process. To some extent, the technocratic tendency of the field is the result of its own history, which was built in stark opposition to politics and always looked upon politics with suspicion. In a landmark book on the topic, Ruti Teitel defines transitional justice as 'a judicial answer to mass atrocity', expressly suppressing its political dimension in the name of a certain legalism.[73] Politics thus appears to be the domain of narrow personal interests, while transitional justice aims at more noble, collective and altruistic goals. This legalistic depoliticisation of transitional justice strongly influenced the field, as demonstrated by its use of a distinctive moral discourse about 'healing', 'reconciliation', and 'forgiveness', by the frequent reliance on 'experts' and 'civil society', by the positivistic belief in an absolute impartiality of laws, and by the monetisation of suffering through financial reparations. Revealingly, Pablo de Greiff, the UN special rapporteur on the promotion of the right to truth, justice, reparations, and guarantees of non-repetition, built what he called a 'complete, normative and self-sufficient' theory of transitional justice. He assigned two medium-term goals (recognition and civic trust) and two final goals (democracy and reconciliation) goals to it.[74] For him, such a theoretical construction was a way to counter the idea that transitional justice is in fact an 'exceptional justice', or a 'transactional justice'—a view defended by scholars such as Ruti Teitel, for whom 'justice in times of political change is extraordinary, contextualised, and partial', since 'what is considered as just is contingent and determined by the injustices that precede it'.[75] On the other hand, Pablo de Greiff considers transitional justice to be a generic form of justice applied in the particular context of transitions, characterised by imperfections and marked by the collapse of a society's normative universe. For de Greiff, the possible theorisation of transitional justice is clearly demonstrated by the fact that all four of its 'pillars' are intrinsically related: trials reinforce the efficiency of truth commissions; truth-seeking contributes to the implementation of reparation programs; accountability is a step towards reforming institutions, etc. The condition for a real theory is indeed 'a comprehensive conception' which 'articulates the relationship that the different measures have to one another, the relationship between these measures and the normative goals (...) the measures should seek, or the relationship between these different goals, some of which may clash.'[76] According to him there is, therefore, 'a thick network of mutual relations' that links together all measures of transitional justice, which, the reasoning goes, appears as a complete and self-sufficient theory—almost a scientific one.

While this perspective is appealing on many grounds, the risk exists that transitional justice may end up looking like a collection of recipes. De Greiff talks, for instance, of 'the best way to obtain expected results', or of the need to 'reinforce synergies' between all mechanisms, to better contribute to a society's democratisation.[77] In light of the Tunisian experience, I will defend here what I call a 'foundational' perspective on transitional justice that is far different from De Greiff's problem-solving approach—one which, by contrast, sees transitional justice as an intrinsically political moment of redefining a society's social contract through its relationship with its own past. According to this conception, the goals of transitional justice are more ambitious than simply 'dealing' with the past. Transitional justice is not about simply promoting justice and repairing past abuses but rather aims, by raising deep questions about the meanings of this past and the inclusion of a society's victims, at rethinking the very nature of political ties.

In Tunisia, transitional justice became bound up with a revolutionary legitimacy that was both its strength and its weakness. After the 2014 elections, official support for the TDC began to fade. Transitional justice was the first victim of the political alliance between Nidaa Tounes and Ennahda, which came at the price of a selective amnesia. In fact, this abandonment of the revolutionary and transformative aspirations of transitional justice seemed like the necessary condition for this counter-natural alliance between a secular movement composed of former regime officials and an Islamist party that was one of the main opponents of the same regime. This 'Islamo-Destourian' ideology worked both ways, with Islamists becoming more nationalistic until Ennahda eventually distanced itself from political Islam,[78] while Destourians slowly 'Islamicised'.[79] Ennahda now barely refers to the 2010–2011 revolution in its official statements, and by publicly calling for reconciliation it has abandoned part of its political base of supporters who, for so long, fought against the regime's persecution and hoped through transitional justice to win some form of official recognition.

Transitional justice and politics: a complicated relationship

The Tunisian example demonstrates the concrete difficulties that stand in the way of a 'pure', depoliticised and strictly judicial vision of transitional justice, especially in a revolutionary context marked by a strong desire to break with the former regime. As we have seen, debates on transitional justice in Tunisia were highly politicised from the outset, and aroused deep social tensions, leading even to a form of competition between victims. The names of 'victim', or 'martyr' were glorified, and thus became the object of important symbolic contestations. The fact that the Islamists agreed to call Mohamed Bouazizi a 'martyr', despite strong Muslim beliefs against suicide, is revealing of their intention to recapture a revolution in which they were for the most part, *de facto*, absent.[80]

Even before the drafting and adoption of the organic transitional justice law, this politicisation was encouraged by the adoption of both decree-laws No. 1 and No. 97 on reparations. According to good practice and international standards, financial and symbolic reparations should follow a truth-seeking process, not precede it. Truth-seeking mechanisms help establish lists of victims and assist in estimating a state's actual capacity to fulfil its promises. In Tunisia however, the order was inverted: reparations were promised and distributed before an inquiry commission had defined the exact number and identities of beneficiaries, thus leading to countless abuses. The establishment of a final, definitive list of victims remains a highly contentious issue in the country, partly due to the financial interests involved, but also for memorial and symbolic reasons. A 'Committee of Martyrs and Wounded of the Revolution' was created within the NCA and tasked with receiving victims' files and registering their complaints in order to establish a comprehensive list of all victims. However, other institutions were given the exact same assignment, further complicating the process of payments. The Ministry of Justice, Human Rights and Transitional Justice established its own list, while the Superior Council of Human Rights and Fundamental Freedoms and the Inquiry Commission on Abuses Committed Since 17 December 2010 did likewise. Because of this multiplication of institutions, victims were greatly confused as to what procedures they should follow in order to file their complaints and receive reparations. This fragmentation also contributed to deepening divisions between victims, segregating them into various 'categories' and thus encouraging competition between them. This confusion appears to be a consequence of the fact that, until the adoption of the organic transitional justice law, Tunisia had undertaken a plethora of largely unrelated transitional justice initiatives, each an *ad hoc* response rather than a part of an integrated policy. The challenge and risk of politicisation was only heightened by the fact that these various initiatives were essentially 'event-based': each of them were established in response to a specific event, and therefore targeted only at the victims of those events, thus creating a class of victims.[81]

The application of decree-law No. 1, in particular, was compromised by politics: granting reparations to former political prisoners who were, in their vast majority, close to the Islamist movement was a move that could only be badly received by the majority of the population. For large parts of the public indeed, the fact that Ennahda had seized power after the first free elections of 2011 was enough in in the way of compensation. Asking for more was considered greedy and unjustified.[82] Today, despite rumours affirming that the beneficiaries of this decree have received thousands of dinars in reparations from the government of Qatar, the reality is that no payment has been made. The only compensation has been recruitment to public office, a process which was incoherently implemented: many former political prisoners were put in positions that did not match their knowledge or expertise, and they therefore continued to be stigmatised by their colleagues. In other cases, individuals were given positions that were far beneath their qualifications and salary prior to their arrest, and the supposed reparation was thus experienced as a humiliation. Several demonstrations and hunger strikes were organised in protest. Decree-law No. 97 also directly politicised the issue of reparations, making a pledge to 'sacrifice one's life to serve the goals of the revolution' a condition of payment. This criterion, explicit in the law, is problematic in that it makes reparations contingent on a form of heroism, thereby excluding many collateral victims, such as a the seven-month-old baby who died in Kasserine after inhaling tear gas. As a consequence, it remains unclear whether the goal of this decree is to repair past human rights violations or to reward political activists. In theory the right to reparation should not depend on the heroism or even the 'justness' of the causes defended by the victims. The simple fact of having suffered a gross violation of their rights is enough to entitle victims to reparations. To avoid such politicisation, it is important that reparation policies and the documents that embody those policies are coherent and include all victims, with no consideration of their political affiliation or of the event during which the violation happened. Fragmenting the process and focusing on periods instead of types of violations have, *de facto*, excluded from the program other victims, such as those of the 2008 uprising in the mining region. Indeed, decree-law No. 97 makes a strong historical statement in saying that the revolution began on 17 December 2010; the protesters of Gafsa and Redeyef consider that their 2008 movement was the real turning point. In reaction they staged several demonstrations and the decree was finally modified in December 2012. However, this example shows that challenges raised by reparations run deep: their time and scope and the definition of victims are more than purely judicial matters. They have to do with fundamentals, with history and memory.

The main requirement if the transitional justice process in Tunisia is to succeed thus lies in its mechanisms' ability to truly 'de-fragment' the categories of victims created by the largely incoherent and *ad hoc* approach that has dominated since the revolution.

This fragmentation inevitably raises doubts about equality of treatment among the different categories of victims thus created. As Special Rapporteur Pablo de Greiff rightly stressed in his report on Tunisia, this is even clearer in a context characterised by the low levels of trust that are typical in the wake of repression, and 'failing to stem this problem would undermine the whole transitional justice project, which in the end has as one of its explicit aims contributing to mending social fragmentation, or achieving reconciliation by means of both judicial and non-judicial measures.'[83] However, according to Pablo de Greiff, the best way to counter this 'event-based' and political approach to transitional justice is 'to put the concept of human rights unambiguously at the center of all efforts' and, therefore, to depoliticise it.[84] According to the Special Rapporteur, structuring all measures solely around the concept of human rights would lessen the risk of fragmentation by avoiding the creation of different 'types' of victims, thereby making the system structurally less prone to a segregation that promotes and deepens divisions within society". Politics, once again, needs to be removed from the equation.

The politics of victimhood and its dangers

As we have seen, the category of 'victim' in Tunisia rapidly took on a dignified and heroic status, capable of implicitly legitimising anyone who benefitted from it. From the point of view of the Islamists, transitional justice, which was imported as a 'toolkit' by international actors after the revolution, had a certain attraction: its mechanisms could be used to put forward their own narrative of victimhood, and to rewrite the Tunisian past in a way that would be favourable to their 'rebirth' (*ennahda*). Transitional justice thus seemed a useful political and social instrument, a means to reinforce their symbolic capital and to promote contested visions of the state's history. The goal was to put an end to the secular and modernist narrative dominant in Bourguibist

Tunisia, not the least by reviving past violations against the 'Youssefist' move-ment. This explains why in the constitutional debates they insisted that the temporal mandate of the TDC begin in 1955. The Destourians, on the other hand, were keen to have the investigations begin in 1987, so as to focus on Ben Ali while preserving the Bourguiba legacy. At the same time, the Islamists were much more present on the scene of transitional justice. They had well-organised civil society associations and networks, and they attended confer-ences, workshops, and training on the topic, while the victims of the left, and even the martyrs and wounded of the revolution, were much more circum-spect in those public debates. As a consequence, the secular fringe of civil society became even more suspicious of transitional justice, seeing it as a tool of the Islamists that did not recognise their own past of suffering and oppres-sion. A large part of Tunisian society continues to equate political Islamism to terrorism, and to believe, to a greater or lesser extent, that those victims 'deserved' what was done to them. The impact of the public hearings of the TDC on this popular understanding remains to be measured.[85] In any case, demands for reparations emanating from political prisoners close to the Islamists were often considered by the secular opposition as a mark of their 'venality', an expression of their narrow interest, rather than the simple claim-ing of a legal entitlement. Ennahda's victory in the 2011 elections reinforced this suspicion: the politicisation of victims and their efficient level of organisa-tion contributed to delegitimising their aspirations. Since they now had access to power, it was expected that these victims should be content and remain silent. This mind-set reflects an attitude to victims that can be observed in several contexts: a proactive victim who makes political calculations and claims his/her rights loud and clear inevitably becomes a doubtful or cynical victim, whose claims seem less than legitimate. It seems as though what is expected from victims is passivity and vulnerability. This may explain the tendency of transitional justice's actors to 'depoliticise' their discourse and to adopt a strictly legal, moral, or humanitarian vocabulary to describe victims. In the end, the victims are no longer true actors in the process: their trauma and pathology should, it is expected, make them incapable of actively organis-ing themselves so as to obtain for themselves that to which they have a right. As a consequence, the political sphere is once again removed from the domain of transitional justice, to the profit of a purely sentimental and charitable con-ception of justice.

As the Tunisian example has demonstrated, if transitional justice is to remain true to the goal that it was initially designed to serve (promoting democracy, reestablishing the rule of law, recreating trust and an open social sphere), it cannot deny the political dimension inherent to any transition. To that end, victims, but also survivors and perpetrators, should all be considered as agents in their full capacity. Considered in this way, transitional justice will cease to be a temporary toolkit and become instead a truly formative moment and a means by which a society can come to terms with a legacy of gross human rights violations and raise essential questions about its nature, its identity and sovereignty, without negating its past but instead transforming and integrating it into its national myth. Transitional justice is an inherently definitional project which determines 'who may now speak', who is a victim, and what was the nature of the violence that created this victim.[86] To that extent, choosing whether to include corruption in its mandate and deciding what dates its investigations will cover are not trivial questions. Their answers have important consequences for a society's understanding of the past it seeks to face, and how that past will be remembered. Transitional justice as we have observed it in Tunisia forces us to reconsider transitional justice *per se*, and it has moved us away from a problem-solving approach in 'dealing with the past' and towards seeing the process as a complex political struggle over the meaning of a country's past—over the interpretation of its modern history, and the definition of its future identity.

10

WITH OR WITHOUT YOU?

TRANSITIONAL JUSTICE AND POLITICAL TRANSITIONS IN MOROCCO AND TUNISIA

Frédéric Vairel

Transitional justice is a hot topic, in the Arab world as elsewhere, and Morocco and Tunisia are flagship examples. Because of their contrasted regimes' trajectories, these two countries constitute an excellent starting point to help us understand how transitional justice has been imported to the region.

For more than twenty years, various reconciliation enterprises, usually organised as NGOs—of which the best example is the International Center for Transitional Justice (ICTJ)—have aimed at diffusing an institutional model of conflict resolution worldwide: the Truth and Reconciliation Commission (TRC).[1] Such institutional models transform the definition of justice: the rehabilitation of victims, partly through reparations, generally comes before the judgment of the perpetrators. Global 'reconcilers' use the methods of any social engineering project: they build up a model through a 'one-size-fits-all approach', enriched from experience to experience.[2] In their ambition to achieve reconciliation, however, voluntarist models come up against the impossibility of reaching 'states that are essentially by-products', as Jon Elster has described them. These states cannot be reached by a simple exercise of will: reconciliation 'can never be brought about intelligently or intentionally' even if positive incentive or coercion is added.[3] Paradoxically, those involved in reconciliation share the same difficulty as the authoritarian regimes from which they seek 'closure'. If the former aim to bring people together through a political formula I will address further on in this chapter, the latter encourage forgetfulness, by means of amnesty.[4]

TRCs are the flagship of an emerging international field of practices, knowledge and professional careers organised around the constitution and implementation of 'post-conflict best practices': namely, transitional justice. The use of truth commissions can be explained as a tool for bypassing obstacles to the organisation of trials against former torturers. These obstacles are both political (the large number of perpetrators, former torturers' power in the new political setting, links between the judges and the apparatuses involved in violations) and juridical (the weak coercive power of international law, the state of the law, or general principles of law like *nulla poena sine lege*— no punishment without a law—which prevent the application of international law).[5] These obstacles also explain how, in practice, the complementarities between TRC and legal procedures (civil, administrative, or criminal) are transformed into a mere substitution of justice with truth and reconciliation. This is what happened in South Africa, Chile, Sierra Leone, and El Salvador. The Moroccan experience fuels this trend. These mechanisms of 'transitional' justice are seen to present various advantages over the procedures of so-called 'classical' justice. They ostensibly offer a deeper and more precise description of violations; individual and collective access to the right to know the truth; greater involvement of civil society and victims; broader reparations beyond just punishing torturers and providing indemnities for victims; better cooperation between politicians and perpetrators; more independent work; and a more accurate presentation of the state's problems which contributed to violations in the past.[6]

Morocco and Tunisia are the two Arab countries where transitional justice, as a public discourse and a political practice, has gained a real foothold and received a fair trying.[7] In both countries a TRC has been built. And their commissioners are facing common obstacles. Despite 'ready-to-use solutions' provided by international aid and expertise,[8] their task nonetheless consists in setting up and operating institutions whose functioning depends upon trial and error experiments and inventiveness, while working under huge time constraints, political pressures, and in the face of victims' expectations that are hard to satisfy.

In this chapter I will show that the commission's vicissitudes cannot be fully explained by the differences between the Moroccan and Tunisian political systems. It is impossible to draw conclusions from a mere autocratic/transitional division. Rather than following an argument of path-dependence, therefore, this chapter will present a comparison that is attentive to the full contexts of the two countries. While there is in this field a large body of literature concerned with drawing lessons from previous experience,[9] the aim of this chapter is more modest. I will pay attention to what kind of political actors are trying to take advantage of transitional justice, and how political struggles around the uses, meaning and scope of transitional justice shape its definition. That Tunisia enjoyed a 'democratic transition' does not necessarily ease the work of its Truth and Dignity Commission's (TDC), while authoritarianism in Morocco does not necessarily complicate the task of its Equity and Reconciliation Commission (ERC). To understand the differences between the two commissions' trajectories, one needs to focus on the political struggles and the state of power relationships in the two countries. In Morocco, incumbents were the first actors and beneficiaries of human rights violations, but the ERC was only made possible by the will of King Mohammed VI. In Tunisia, the TDC is a by-product of a popular uprising.[10] At the same time, the breadth of the mandate and jurisdiction of the Tunisian commission is a direct threat to actors of the authoritarian regime, who seek to restore their reputation and to find a new place in post-uprising politics.

First, we should examine the way global reconcilers understand their contexts of action. Reconciliation devices maintain a tautological relation with the contexts of their implementation. These contexts are thought of not as comparable but as equivalent: the 'transition' requires restorative justice procedures which, in turn, are the best indication that a transition is under way. This necessary condition for the diffusion of TRCs in countries as different as Paraguay, Morocco, Colombia and Ghana, or Tunisia relates to knowledge (of, for example 'transitology') shared in various social contexts. We will then insist on the fact that comparison is not only a social scientist's tool, it is also a social practice which facilitates the transmittal of transitional justice from one country to another. Finally, we will look at how legacies of past violence are addressed in Morocco and Tunisia, and how the elaboration of reconciliation policies is context-dependent.

Model Building and Restorative Justice

The origins of transitional justice date back to the 1990s, when actors from various backgrounds undertook, in an increasingly international and institutionalised manner, to write an authoritative handbook on 'post conflict best practices'. Its chapters present sometimes contradictory conclusions that in some instances concentrate on society's 'upper level' (the elites' capacity to mutually tolerate one another, or the form and function of institutions) and in others, the 'bottom' (the tolerance, or the frequency of interactions between 'ordinary people' belonging to the warring parties). Those promoting this approach nonetheless tend to rely on an all-purpose manual designed to guide the actions of the actors involved, such as international institutions confronted with post-war or post-state repression dilemmas.[11] One of the manual's chapters is about 'transitional' justice and, especially, truth and reconciliation commissions.[12] Though it was neither the first transitional justice experience nor the first truth and reconciliation commission charged with shedding light on a violent episode involving political authorities, the South African TRC enjoyed considerable success and has earned an unparalleled place in political history. It occupies a unique position in the making of the TRC model because it systematised and detailed various features of how such a commission must perform, including the stipulation that former judicial practices must be replaced by the work of a TRC and that a form of justice sometimes called 'restorative justice' must be formulated and implemented.

Even if 'prosecuting perpetrators' is among the five key 'strategies for transitional justice' put forward by the ICTJ and among the criteria defining the very notion, TRCs document human rights abuses by non-jurisdictional means.[13] There are political and legal reasons why formal judicial practice fails as a means of investigating those in charge, the perpetrators, and the beneficiaries of violence. The balance of political power and the state of the existing judicial system often prohibit the criminalisation or political marginalisation of silent partners and agents of political violence, while the cost of trials seems disproportionate to state resources.[14] From a political point of view, the strength of former authoritarian rulers in the political setting and the inability of judicial institutions to carry out their mission given their involvement or their attachment to the regime—and especially to the police forces which would be in charge of the investigations—make it very difficult to use preexisting legal practices and institutions.[15]

The joint emphasis on the non-judicial dimension and the recourse to non-jurisdictional solutions in the administration of justice leads to a 'broadened'

definition of the task at hand.[16] Establishing the truth, implementing reparations, constructing memorials, developing initiatives of reconciliation, and
reforming institutions responsible for the violations, take the place of mere
sanctions against perpetrators.[17] These reparation policies are subject to innovation: today, the practitioners of reconciliation are according increasing
attention to gendered human rights violations and to the collective or 'community' dimension of political violence. In Morocco, a National Forum on
Reparations—which was held from 30 September to 2 October 2005 and
brought together 170 local and national associations—was organised by the
Equity and Reconciliation Commission (known by its French acronym IER
or Instance Équité et Réconciliation).[18] This forum designed a reparation
program for regions in which the population perceived their economic and
social marginalisation to be linked to the perpetration of human rights abuses.
The program was, it is important to note, financed by the EU and the UNDP,
the funds being managed by the largest public sector bank, the Caisse de
Dépôt et de Gestion. In Tunisia, law 53–2013 considers a victim 'any region
that has suffered organised marginalisation or exclusion'. As a helpful step
toward the international success of the truth commission model, this change
in the meaning of 'justice' has practical utility: the absence of recourse to
criminal justice makes telling the truth less difficult for perpetrators. Obstacles
like this partly explain the use of TRCs. They also help us understand how,
practically, the complementarity between TRCs and judicial procedures (civil,
administrative or criminal) can become merely a matter of substituting one
for the other. Such was the case in South Africa (with a few exceptions), in
Chile, Sierra Leone, Salvador and Morocco.

Used first in the work of the South African TRC, victims' public hearings
are a reconciliatory panacea.[19] They are promoted by various international
NGOs, the first of them being the ICTJ, but also by Human Rights Watch
(HRW), Amnesty International and the International Federation for Human
Rights (FIDH). They aim to restore victims' dignity by providing them with
an official platform, and thus putting an end to enforced silence for fear of
retaliation or exclusion. These public hearings lend credibility to political
authorities' willingness to break with the past and contribute to building a new
relationship between the state and its citizens. By providing opportunities for
debates about the past, public hearings allow for the examination of how violations worked and for this very reason have the potential to prevent new violations. Even though hearings aim to promote debate, one should notice that
they do not deviate from 'exemplary demonstrations of the recognition of the

truth centered on the victims.'[20] The ICTJ's first operational guideline confirms this point: 'Give priority to the interests and perspectives of victims and survivors. ICTJ always assesses and respects the interests of victims, often working closely with victims' organisations and human rights advocacy groups.'[21]

As ERC members understood them, public hearings had all the virtues attributed to TRCs. In the Moroccan context, 'public hearings would allow victims to recover their dignity, arouse a public and official recognition of their sorrow and entrench human rights values.'[22] By paying nearly obsessive attention to victims, ERC commissioners, like their counterparts at other TRCs, have also made the choice to not name the torturers. This choice, which might appear at first glance to be directly linked to local circumstances, is explained by ERC president Driss Benzekri: 'The victim is the hero of the story.'[23] At play in the hearings is the conformity of the Moroccan experience to the model and its capacity to become a model in turn. The role of Morocco in diffusing the model throughout the Arab region in a missionary way is indicated explicitly by international NGOs reports.[24] The same is true for the Peruvian TRC, which was the first in Latin America to organise public hearings for victims.[25] In this perspective, it is not surprising that the law on the Tunisian TDC provides for the organisation of public hearings.

Comparing the Two Experiences

It is important to note that the two experiences came at very different stages. Following the Consultative Council on Human Rights' (CCDH) twentieth recommendation of November 2003, Mohammed VI set up, on 7 January 2004, the Equity and Reconciliation Commission (ERC)—a national commission for truth, equity and reconciliation. The commission aimed to get to the bottom of more than four decades of state crimes and released its report in January of 2006. This Moroccan experience has been internationally acclaimed as a pioneering effort in the Middle East and North Africa and a 'success'.[26] A follow-up committee of the National Council for Human Rights, established in 2011 by King Mohammed VI to replace the CCDH, is now implementing the ERC recommendations.[27] In Tunisia, the Ministry of Human Rights and Transitional Justice was installed in January of 2012, and after nearly two years the Organic Law on Establishing and Organising Transitional Justice was voted in on 24 December 2013. Tunisia's Truth and Dignity Commission was established in June of 2014. Its work began on 10 December 2014, and the Commission had by the late summer of 2016 already received more than 62,000 victims' complaints.[28]

The two commissions vary considerably in terms of the way they were established and the mandates they were given. The Moroccan experience of transitional justice 'took place within the same system that was responsible for the abuses of the past'[29] or 'without rupture in governance' as Driss Benzekri, the ERC president, explained in an interview: 'The monarchy is still there; we've maintained continuity.' The Moroccan ERC was installed independent of parliamentary procedures by a royal decree (*dahir*) on 10 April 2004. Transitional justice arrived in Tunisia after Ben Ali's flight to Saudi Arabia in 2011, and the Tunisian TDC was created by Organic law 2013–53 on 24 December 2013. Its members were appointed by the National Constituent Assembly (NCA), while Moroccan commissioners were named by the king. Members of the Moroccan commission insisted on its 'extra-judiciary' dimension; the TDC is linked to Special Chambers and to a broader program of judicial reform.[30] In Morocco, the most prominent issue was public hearings of former victims. In Tunisia, the lustration law and the judgment of central actors in the former regime of Ben Ali are enshrined in the law (Art. 8, Organic law 2013–53).

While Morocco was in an existing authoritarian situation and Tunisia was in transition away from Ben Ali's authoritarian rule after a popular uprising, various elements were common to the two transitional programs.[31] First, in both countries transitional justice procedures took the now-fashionable form of a Truth Commission, named respectively the Equity and Reconciliation Commission (ERC, Morocco) and the Truth and Dignity Commission (TDC, Tunisia), as if such a commission is now the only way of dealing with violent pasts.[32] The historical periods considered (forty-three years for Morocco and fifty-eight years in Tunisia) are among the longest periods of operation of any TRCs around the world.

When it comes to transitional justice in Morocco and Tunisia, the 'native' form of comparison (in the sense of Clifford Geertz's 'native knowledge') is a core question. Since Moroccan actors in the transitional justice process have become exporters of their practical knowledge on this matter, Moroccan and Tunisian actors are comparing their experiences. What is more, the ICTJ is offering Tunisian commissioners ready-to-use and Moroccan tried-and-tested solutions.[33] Ironically, Morocco, an authoritarian country, has become a model and an exporter of 'transitional' solutions and devices to a country on the road towards democracy. In September of 2014, Sihem Bensedrine, an opponent to Ben Ali's regime and a well-known Tunisian human rights activist, now TDC president, went to Morocco in order to share experiences about reparations.[34] However, earlier in 2014, at a conference held in Rabat, Abderrahim Berrada, a renowned lawyer who was close to leftist movements during the 1970s and has been involved with opposition movements ever since, told his Tunisian comrades: 'If you want to do a good job, do not draw inspiration from the Moroccan experience!'. Cooperation between Morocco and Tunisia around transitional justice started soon after the uprising on the occasion of a March 2011 FIDH seminar on democratic transition, which was attended by a counselor to the president of the Moroccan Conseil Consultatif des Droits de l'Homme (CCDH, National Human Rights Council), and an international conference which was held in Tunis in April of 2011 entitled 'Addressing the Past, Building the Future: Justice in Times of Transition'. There have since been repeated meetings at various levels—from Tunisian delegations visiting Morocco to public lectures and visits to Tunisia by former Moroccan ERC members or executives.[35]

Finally, various indications demonstrate the strong internationalisation of both transitional justice programs: the selection of experts' profiles; the emphasis on victims and on reparations procedures, together with a common celebration of 'civil society'; the transformation of human rights advocacy; and, last but not least, the role of international donors and agencies, especially the International Center for Transitional Justice (ICTJ), the European Union, the United Nations Development Program, and the Office of the United Nations High Commissioner for Human Rights (Tunis). In Tunisia, former political opponents and human rights activists are labelling their activities as 'transitional justice': it has become a remarkably fashionable way to self-define, but it has consequences on the way actors position themselves, since transitional justice is not human rights advocacy, which in turn is different from political opposition.

An Emergence from Political Struggles

In both countries, transitional justice is a by-product of contentious politics. Compared to other countries' experiences with settling the legacies of past abuses, the Moroccan case stands out because the international Truth and Reconciliation Commission model was first imported there as a result of street mobilisations. In November 1999, some human rights activists—mostly but not only former far-left activists who had suffered from the security forces' coercive policies in the 1970s—created an organisation to gather and protect victims of the 'black years' (*al-sanawât al-sawda*) or the 'years of lead' (*sanawât alrasâs*): the Moroccan Truth and Justice Forum (TJF, *al-Muntadâ al-maghribî min ajli al-haqîqa wal-'insâf*). The establishment of a TRC was one of its main objectives. In a completely novel way, the TJF gathered together victims from all the groups that had suffered under repression, without regard for their ideological stances: nationalists, socialists, Marxist-Leninists, Islamists or Sahrawi freedom fighters, and army officers involved in the 1971 and 1973 coup attempts. The TJF's founders parted company with established human rights organisations that they considered unable to take a stand over the way the king intended to settle the human rights violations file. The relevant tools of public policy—resorting to a TRC to deal with the past—have been imposed under pressure from the TJF. Inspired by contentious practices observed in Latin America, the association has routinely demonstrated, between 2000 and 2003, in front of former secret detention centres. Its first sit-in took place on 4 March 2000, at Derb Moulay Cherif, a police station used as a secret detention facility in the 1970s and the 1980s. The Truth and Justice Forum's mobilisations, and those of its allies and rivals the Moroccan Association for Human Rights and the Moroccan Organisation for Human Rights occasioned a number of virulent debates which culminated in the imposition of a TRC. In other words, their actions made it clear that any settlement would have to be not only a technical and financial one, but would also need to conform to international standards if it was to achieve legitimacy.

The Moroccan ERC resulted from a social movement against impunity and, in a way, was representative of a dense network of associations that provided support, outreach assistance and competencies. It was also a consequence of the monarchy's pragmatic strategy of adapting to relatively unified claims.[36] As for the Truth and Dignity Commission in Tunisia, it emerged on a devastated political landscape where NGOs worthy of the name might be counted on one hand, and where networks of mobilisation had been seriously damaged by decades-long repression.

In Tunisia, transitional justice appeared as a discourse and as an institutional toolkit for dealing with the past after the 2010–2011 uprising.[37] Only three months after Ben Ali was forced out of the country by protests, an international conference ('Addressing the Past, Building the Future') was organised in Tunis, on 14–15 April 2011, by the Arab Institute for Human Rights, the ICTJ, the Tunisian League for Human Rights, and the UN Office of the High Commission for Human Rights.[38] Throughout the discussions, one major aim of the conference was to root transitional justice in the Tunisian context.[39] The new authorities reaffirmed their interest in transitional justice during a meeting between the justice minister, Lazhar Karoui Chebbi, and ICTJ experts (on 21 September 2011).

During the period of the interim governments, two initiatives for addressing the past are worth noting: the work of the National Fact-Finding Commission on crimes and abuses committed during the revolution (since 17 December 2010), and the National Committee to investigate cases of corruption and embezzlement.[40] But these initiatives to confront the past through judicial processes (lawsuits) and heal wounds (through the distribution of reparations) were limited and un-coordinated. The 23 October 2011, elections introduced a shift in the trajectory of transitional justice in Tunisia. Various debates and seminars were organised around transitional justice and Truth Commissions.[41] The National Constituent Assembly adopted a Constitutional Law relating to the Provisional Organisation of Public Authorities (No. 6–2011, 16 December 2011), sometimes described as the 'small constitution'. Article 24 states that the NCA 'shall enact an organic law regulating transitional justice, its foundations, and its area of competence' (Title VI, Transitional justice). The law followed the transitional justice model of 'civil society participation'. A 'national dialogue' was organised, with debates in regions that shed light on political struggles around victims' representation and 'organised' access to the debates.[42] While in Morocco one organisation alone was able to represent the victims of repression, the Tunisian political landscape was fragmented between at least five groups, from various political backgrounds: the Tunisian Network for Transitional Justice, the Tunisia Center for Transitional Justice, the Tunisian Center for Human Rights and Transitional Justice, the Al Kawakibi Democracy Transition Center, and the National Independent Coordination for Transitional Justice. These NGOs bloomed after Ben Ali's ouster. Their self-definition demonstrates how transitional justice had become, in just a few months, a legitimate field of action and funding.

Commissions in their Political Context

The two commissions stand in different relationships with their political environment and they deal with very different political situations. The ERC works in a political environment where power relationships and the hierarchy of actors have been stabilised after the monarchical succession. The TDC was created in a context of relative power dispersion and one in which, since the 2014 elections, the new power balance is unfavourable to the commission.

At the same time, the existing power equilibrium is very unstable, depending on the life expectancy of an elderly man, Beji Caid Essebsi, and on Rached Ghannouchi's leadership of Ennahda. In the cases of Nidaa Tounes, with Caid Essebsi, and of Ennahda, with Ghannouchi, reference to the patriarch holds things together, since both are leading political organisations facing internal tensions.

In Morocco, political legitimisation works 'from above'. The relative ease with which the ERC was imposed in the Moroccan context can be explained by the king's domination on the political scene—in others words, by the authoritarian character of the political setting. The installation of the ERC, as announced by a November 2003 recommendation of the CCDH (Conseil Consultatif des Droits de l'Homme—National Human Rights Council), reads as follows: 'In accordance to the most high will of his Majesty the King Mohammed VI, may God assist him, to uphold the values, culture and spirit of human rights as a constant choice of the Kingdom of Morocco, firmly and oftentimes asserted by his Majesty (...)'. One should not see here only the mark of an old-fashioned decorum, but the very definite assertion of royal prerogative. The ERC is installed by the king and its 'experts' appointed by him. The Commission statutes are approved by royal decree (*dahir*), which officially launches the ERC's work. This explains why the commission appears 'neutral' to many commentators and political actors: with the exception of a few commissioners, its members are not political party members, but are appointed instead on the basis of their expertise in human rights, as explained by official biographies that were published alongside the ERC statutes. At the institutional level, the ERC is part of a series of experts' commissions, under the king's authority, aimed at defusing conflict around particular public problems. The aim is to thwart the representation mechanisms of parliament by resorting to what amounts to a form of representation that leverages expertise in the place of political allegiances. This re-composition of political pluralism dilutes the influence of various special interest groups. The committee follows international standards, employing them as a tool and in an ad hoc manner. In this way knowledge and technical skills override ideology. As far as reforming the regime is concerned, the ERC demonstrates the efficiency of a mechanism constructed without the government or parliament and operating outside of their control. As a result, the government is 'reduced to signing checks', as the ERC president said to mark his independence.[43]

The extra-judiciary dimension of the process and the non-revelation of torturers' names during public hearings of victims, for example (constraints one can link to the authoritarian situation and to the presence of former torturers in the regime's architecture), make the ERC tolerable to various actors. Some procedural constraints aside, the scope of violations examined by the ERC—arbitrary detention and enforced disappearance—has been criticised by Moroccan and international associations because extra-judicial executions, torture and iniquitous trials were not taken into consideration. Despite all this, on the basis of their mission statement, which articulated the ERC's aim as establishing 'the nature and the extent of the violations' (Article 9.1), commission members interpreted their mandate broadly, as shown by the 'ERC statutes Presentation', formulated by members on 15 April 2004, and by their final report. The ERC's members, members of the administration and all those collaborating with them are subject to confidentiality. Whereas 'all state authorities and institutions bring their support to the commission and provide it with all information and data allowing it to accomplish its missions' (Article 10, ERC statutes), ERC members have no power of constraint or sanction that would allow them to independently obtain information useful to their work. Cooperation in this area was limited. While different departments of the Ministry of Interior have collaborated in a way said to be satisfactory by ERC members, the same does not hold true for the Royal Gendarmerie and the Army.[44] Some high-ranking officers have refused any cooperation with the ERC. One should note that fewer than ten perpetrators have testified during its hearings.

In Tunisia, the transitional justice law and the commissioners' appointment happened in a context where the rules of the game and the distribution of power were in a state of flux. The drafting of relevant laws has been very sensitive to the broader political context and its fluidity. While the government reviewed the organic law on transitional justice on 12 November 2012, and submitted it to the NCA Legislation committee in January of 2013, it took nearly a year for the law to be voted on by the NCA. What happened in the meantime? On 6 February 2013, Chokri Belaid, a leader of the Popular Front's leftist coalition, was murdered. The crime was denounced in a one-day general strike organised by the Tunisian General Labour Union (UGGT). Crowds attended the funeral, marches were organised, and riots broke out in various places. Some Ennahda offices were attacked and torched. Following the assassination, the first Ennahda-led government resigned on 19 February 2013. But Ennahda refused to cede the floor to a government of technocrats. With the assassination of Mohamed Brahimi, a member of the NCA and a leader of the Popular Front, on 25 July 2013, the country was propelled into a severe political crisis. Polarisation of the political scene, which had already worsened during 2012, reached its peak with marches and counter-marches, rumours of a military coup, and calls for the dissolution of the Assembly by Nidaa Tounes, a coalition bringing together some former members of Ben Ali's party and the Popular Front, and led by Beji Caid Essebsi, a former director of national security and the Ministry of Interior under Bourguiba, and president of parliament under Ben Ali.[45] On 6 August 2013, Mustapha Ben Jaafar, president of the NCA announced the suspension of its work. Following a call from UGTT, a foursome gathered. The group included the UTICA (the businessmen's organisation), the Tunisian League for Human Rights, and the Bar association.[46] These 'arbitrators' from 'civil society', as local actors called them, asked Ennahda to leave power. The Islamist party eventually renounced its position and opened the way to a government of technocrats. At the very same moment, Egypt was moving from polarisation to a military coup and violent confrontation that saw the crushing of the sit-in on Rabaa al-Adawiyya Square in Cairo. This Egyptian scenario—which showcased the risk of losing everything (power and liberty both)—pushed all Tunisian players, including Ennahda, into favouring negotiations over the possible consequences of a worsening security situation[47] During the political crisis, compensation for people wounded during the 'Revolution' was the only element related to transitional justice that was discussed. The 24 December 2013 Law establishing the Truth and Dignity Commission was finally voted in by 125 of 217 MPs in a chamber dominated by the Troïka parties: Ennahda, Ettakatol, and the Congress for the Republic. All opposition parties abstained. Before the commissioners' selection began, critiques were aimed largely against the immunisation of nominations from administrative courts' control. An NCA committee, composed of ten members recruited by proportional representation, prepared a list of thirty names from a total of 430 candidates. Fifteen names were chosen in a plenary session.

Depending on the actors and the circumstances of the moment, the law and the commission members have been criticised for their 'politicisation'. In struggles like these, politicisation takes on different meanings. The way in which the appointments were made, and, later, the TDC's composition have sparked debate because of their links to party politics. Seven candidates were challenged in numerous appeals because of their possible 'non-neutrality'. Sihem Bensedrine's links with President Moncef Marzouki and Ennahda were denounced. Objections were raised about other candidates as well: Ibtihel Abdellatif was a member of Ennahda; Khaled Krichi, a founding member and spokesperson of Al-Chaab party. Reactivating old rivalries, CPR members of the NCA boycotted the vote, noting that Khemais Chammari, a famous human rights activist, was a former member of parliament (1994–1995). The make-up of the TDC was challenged by several NGOs at the beginning of the selection of its members and again after the NCA vote on the list. In February of 2014, the Tunisian League for Human Rights, transitional justice NGOs and the '25 Lawyers' group lodged appeals before the administrative court. In May, transitional justice NGOs repeated their complaints before the administrative court: the nomination process, they claimed, was unconstitutional because the decisions of the hiring committee were not subject to appeal, and those on the list were not independent of political parties. They expressed publicly their professional belief in the 'strength of the law'. It is noteworthy that this option of using the law as a political tool and resource is also a feature of the transitional context: it demonstrates the new confidence of these groups in the administrative courts. For some, the committee's composition was merely a reflection of power sharing between the 'troïka' parties: Ennahda, CPR and Ettakatol. These parties dominated the Nomination Committee 'in proportion to their representation at the Constituent Assembly.'[48] The NGOs' opposition to the composition of the Committee and to what they referred to as its 'non-independence' was also a way to protest their removal from the hiring process. At least until the October and November 2014 parliamentary and presidential elections, the hierarchy of actors was relatively fluid. In this situation, transitional justice and reparations, the parameters of the law, the commission's mandate and the identity of commissioners were issues at stake in political struggles. Indeed, both personal and political disputes went on after the TDC's creation, and several resignations interfered with the functioning of the commission. Only ten days after his installation, Khemais Chemmari stepped down for health reasons and because he had expected to lead the TDC. The NCA replaced him with Lilia Brik Bouguerra. Between September 2014 and September 2015, three other commissioners resigned. In August 2015, Zouhair Makhlouf, vice-president of the TDC, wrote a letter to the president of the Assembly complaining about Bensedrine's mismanagement. The letter leaked to the press, and Makhlouf was dismissed from the TDC. A legal battle began: while administrative courts annulled the dismissal, the TDC repeated the action several times. An actor and an observer of the process notes and regrets that 'these conflicts weakened the TDC's public standing and worsened the tense internal dynamics that have undermined the commission's ability to obtain a minimum consensus to implement its mandate'.[49]

Another feature sheds light on the different trajectories of the two commissions. In Morocco, the political field is rather consensual and the king's decisions are not contested. In Tunisia, because of the legacy of Ben Ali's rule, actors behave as enemies and become mere adversaries only with difficulty.

The ERC took root in a broader context where activists had abandoned revolution—whether socialist or Islamic—and the goal of overthrowing the Moroccan regime, preferring instead to reform it from within. Authoritarian reform provides opportunities for those activists willing to participate to public policies. Symbolically, the ERC was signifying a rupture with the past, since its mandate covered the period from Independence to the end of Hassan II's rule. Most of the struggles around the setting up and implementation of a TRC happened before the reform was set in motion. Discussions took place between Driss Benzekri and the king's advisors about possible ways to bring the CCDH closer to the Paris principles as they applied to to the status and functioning of national institutions for the protection and promotion of human rights. The implementation of a TRC was included 'in the deal'. These discussions ended with Benzekri's nomination as CCDH general secretary on 10 December 2002. Benzekri was joined by a new team, including feminist activists, children's rights activists, and famous human rights activists, many of them former victims of political detention. Omar Azziman, a law professor, former OMDH president and former minister of justice, as well as a legal advisor to the king, became president of the council. This reformed version of the CCDH helped in the creation of an ad hoc institution: the Equity and Reconciliation Commission. On 6 November 2003, in its twentieth recommendation, the CCDH suggested that the king should create the ERC. It stipulated that debates should be confined to the CCDH assembly. During their review of the recommendation, some CCDH members cast doubt on the usefulness of such a commission and tried to reduce its political ambition and scope, in particular by rejecting its working title of 'Equity and Reconciliation Commission'.[50] In January 2004, the inauguration speech by the king gave the ERC full legitimacy, at least among political actors strongly linked to the monarchy. The harshest criticisms dealt with the cooptation of human rights activists by the *makhzen*, the native name for the Moroccan autocracy. The launch of public hearings saw the ERC again subject to harsh rebukes. Abdelkrim Al-Khatib and Mahjoubi Aherdane publicly voiced their staunch opposition, arguing that it was destabilising the monarchy. The king's support was key in the decision to continue with public hearings. One story is revealing: during dinner following the first public hearing, the ERC president received a phone call from the king. He hung up and announced: 'We won!' Some commissioners then asked what they had won and Benzekri added: 'It was the king. He said: "very good! Go on!"'[51]

The TDC has triggered much debate and controversy in Tunisia, a sign of the vitality of the press—which makes full use of its newly recovered freedom—but also a sign of the various hurdles facing the commission and of a public arena dominated by suspicion.[52] The critiques and defiance directed towards the TDC are also a consequence of its jurisdiction. The TDC mandate is comprehensive in terms of the kind of violations it investigates and in terms of powers.[53] It can 'resort to any procedure or mechanism which may contribute to revealing the truth' (Article 40, Law on Transitional Justice) and the commission enjoys police powers like the right to search and seize evidence, documents and information, to hear witnesses linked to violations and to 'summon every person whose testimony it deems useful'. The law not only states this solemnly: 'Nobody may interfere in the Commission's works or influence its decisions', (Article 38) but also prescribes criminal penalties for anyone standing in the way of the commission's work (by hindering its investigations, refusing to testify or refusing to disclose information). The TDC's powers make it a direct threat for a variety of political actors, first and foremost any who would have been compromised under Ben Ali's rule. It is not surprising that former prime minister and now president of the republic, Beji Caid Essebsi, is wary of the TDC. He was minister of the interior, minister of defence, and minister of foreign affairs under Bourguiba's rule. He was also president of parliament under Ben Ali (1990–1991). In June 2014, when asked his opinion on the TDC he replied: 'I do not have a lot of expectations about it. When you see that they will start in 1955, you understand that their goal (*qasd*) is an act of revenge, it is vitiated since the beginning of the story'. Invited to comment on Sihem Bensedrine's appointment as head of the commission, he added: 'I prefer not to talk about people. My position concerns the foundation of the commission. But the commission is a reality. The fact that the commission is a reality does not mean it is a good thing.'[54] Soon after his election as president, he declared 'We have to turn the page and look toward the future'.

The bitter enmity between Sihem Bensedrine and the newly elected president, Beji Caid Essebsi, is best illustrated by controversies over the president's archives and the draft law on economic reconciliation. Both demonstrate the politicisation of transitional justice, which is not only a major issue in the political struggle but can also be used as a tool. On 26 December 2014, between Beji Caid Essebsi's election and the handover of power, Bensedrine went to the Carthage Palace with six trucks asking to remove the president's archives in order to put them in 'a secure place', under TDC control. Members of the presidential security trade union denied the trucks access to the Palace, angering Bensedrine. A serious controversy ensued, in which both juridical and political arguments swirled around the usefulness and the legality of the TDC project. The timing is quite revealing here, since Bensedrine clearly was trying to take advantage of the interim period while her strongest supporters at the presidency and the NCA were still in office. Apparently Bensedrine thought she would be able to create a *fait accompli* while still in power. While the president's archives could provide substantial information given the centralisation of Bourguiba and Ben Ali's regimes, some observers point out that the Ministry of the Interior's archives could also have been chosen, given its central position in the history of repression.[55] In suggesting that 'truth' lay in the archives, where it might be hidden as in a safe or sequestered space, the organisers of the attempt to seize the president's archives showed naïveté. Torturers do not leave traces, and it is less than obvious that each one of them acted as a 'torturer'. Proof of torture would be quite difficult to find among the twenty thousand boxes stored in the Carthage Palace basement. Producing a narrative to tell the story of fifty years of repression and arbitrary rule is not like trying to discover the grave of a disappeared relative: 'truth' is not a substance; it is a process, and in the case at hand, it is a very political process. There is a good chance that the narration of violent episodes will in the end depend on individual testimonies.

President Beji Caid Essebsi made his career under the regimes of Bourguiba and Ben Ali. It is not surprising, therefore, that he called for 'reconciliation' in his investiture speech.[56] His speech marking Independence Day, on 20 March 2015, developed the same theme. On the one hand, he called for modalities of 'economic reconciliation' with businessmen facing lawsuits for corruption. On the other, he framed ways to deal with the past. He expressed fears lest transitional justice turn into an avenging justice.[57] Approved on 14 July 2015, the draft law on 'Reconciliation in the Economic and Financial Sectors' created a new controversy about the past. In the name of reconciliation and transitional justice, and on the pretext of stimulating the economy and reassuring investors, President Essebsi proposed an amnesty for civil servants, public officials and businessmen accused of bribery and money laundering. The draft explicitly provided for 'the abolishment of all provisions relating to financial corruption and embezzlement of public funds set out in the Basic

Law No. 53 of 2013, dated 24 December 2013, on establishing and regulating transitional justice' (Chapter 12). In other words, this project aimed to limit the Truth and Dignity Commission's prerogatives to human rights violations. Local actors, political parties from the left, the opposition in parliament, the UGTT, the Bar and the TLHR, and international actors like HRW, the ICTJ, the Venice Commission and the UN Special Rapporteur on the promotion of truth, justice, reparation and guarantees of non-recurrence, all firmly opposed the project. In August, leftist activists launched a protest campaign under the motto Mânîch Msâmah ('I do not forgive'). Despite police violence, they organised demonstrations in various cities, and a national march in Tunis on 12 September 2015. In October, the bill's examination was postponed. The government integrated its provisions within the 2016 finance law, but the articles were declared unconstitutional by the provisional authority for the review of constitutionality in December of 2015.[58] At the end of June 2016, the government decided to resume debate over the draft law on economic reconciliation. It was a clear indication of the government's determination to reintegrate businessmen close to Ben Ali into the economic and political game, and a demonstration of how much the trajectory of transitional justice depends on various political confrontations. Loaded with revolutionary meaning, the notion is not only a key stake in political struggle but also used as a tool. When substituted for revolutionary justice, as the TDC comprehensive mandate reveals, it can be a bargaining chip for dealing with former incumbents.[59] It is thus not surprising that actors linked to the former regime, when back in power, decided to target transitional justice as an idea and as a set of actors and institutions.

Conclusion

The plasticity of transitional justice appears to serve various purposes in different contexts. The term 'transitional justice' is accordingly applied to a variety of political games, in a wide range of situations, and with diverse outcomes. Ambiguities in confronting the violent past turn out to be quite different from what one might expect from a transition between the dichotomies of authoritarianism and democracy.

In Morocco, the Palace was the principal instigator and beneficiary of repression. Its domination over society was both an asset to and a constraint on the ERC's activity. The relative ease with which the commission was imposed on political society was due to its endorsement by the king. At the same time, the

Table 10.1: Truth Commissions in Morocco and Tunisia: An Overview

Country	Name	Sponsor	Mode of establishment	Period covered by report	Length of work	Number of members
Morocco	Equity and Reconciliation Instance	The King	Royal decree	2 March 1956–July 1999	7 January 2004 to 30 November 2005 (23 months, earlier 9 months, renewable 3 months)	15
Tunisia	Truth and Dignity Instance	The Constituent Assembly	Organic Law	1 July 1955–24 December 2013	4 years beginning 9 June 2014 (with a renewable period of 1 year)	15

Mandate (type of HRV investigated)	Judicial dimension	Change of regime	Public audiences	Access to information	Naming of perpetrators	Staff
Forced disappearance and arbitrary detention	Extra-judiciary settlement	No	8	Recommended (but not sanctioned)	No	60 permanent
Gross or organised violation of human rights perpetrated by organs of government or individuals acting on his behalf/gross violations of human rights (murder, rape and any other form of sexual violence, torture, forced disappearance, death penalty without guaranty of a fair trial)	Special chambers	Yes	Enshrined in the law	Mandatory	Yes	about 100

ERC's promoters shied away from anything which might destabilise the regime's architecture. This explains why none of the perpetrators were named during the process. The main obstacle to the commissioners' investigations was not the limits to their mandate, which was restricted to planning investigations on 'forced disappearance and arbitrary detention'. The state of the archives—scattered or fallen into decay or even missing—and the 'uneven cooperation of security services', with the exception of the Ministry of Interior (ERC report), diminished the precision of the narrative. Victims considered the 'truth' that emerged from the ERC process to be unsatisfactory.

In Tunisia, the nature of the 'transition' has made drafting a transitional justice law into an obstacle course. And the 2014 elections brought to power a man who had made his political career in the old regime: Beji Caid Essebsi has no interest in the TDC's smooth working or in revisiting the past. At every step, from his investiture speech to the different stages in the examination of the draft law on reconciliation, he tried as hard as he could to delegitimise transitional justice and its defenders. It is obvious then, that democratic functioning and the (at least temporary) institutional stabilisation factors one would think of as facilitating the transitional justice process in Tunisia, are in fact undermining it.

Far from providing ready-to-use solutions on how to deal with past violence, transitional justice is a highly debated and conflict-ridden issue. In both Tunisia and Morocco, victims and their relatives are still confronting a past which has not been forgotten—despite the efforts of those who, from various positions and out of various motives, would like to 'close the book' as if a sufficient 'amount' of truth has already been revealed.

11

TRANSITIONAL JUSTICE
IN POST-REVOLUTIONARY EGYPT

Nathalie Bernard-Maugiron

In May 2015 former Egyptian president Mohamed Morsi was sentenced to death on a charge of escaping from prison in early 2011.[1] Six months earlier, in November of 2014, former president Hosni Mubarak had been cleared of charges of killing protesters during the January 2011 upheaval.[2] In between, a prominent activist had been sentenced in February 2015 to five years in prison for participating in a peaceful demonstration in November 2013 against military trials of civilians.

In the aftermath of the Arab Spring, hopes and expectations regarding the contribution Arab countries could make to the theory and practice of transitional justice were high. Would transitional justice, 'the full range of processes and mechanisms associated with a society's attempts to come to terms with a legacy of large-scale past abuses, in order to ensure accountability, serve justice and achieve reconciliation', be able to rebuild the Egyptian state and Egyptian society on stable foundations, and would mechanisms be put in place to prevent similar occurrences in the future?[3] What measures were going to be employed to cope with the legacies of past human rights abuses? Would justice be offered to victims of human rights violations committed under the former regime, and would the individuals responsible be held accountable? Would such processes nudge the field of transitional justice forward on a different path and demand new ways of thinking?

There was general optimism after the fall of Mubarak. Conferences were organised around transitional justice mechanisms.[4] More than five years later, however, little progress has been made in the implementation of transitional justice in Egypt. Calls have been ignored by all of the successive governments following the revolution of 25 January 2011. Each government has failed to prosecute cases of human rights violations and has committed new crimes that have remained largely unaddressed. Hundreds of unlawful killings and other human rights violations have been committed with impunity, and Egyptian authorities have consistently shown themselves unwilling to investigate such abuses.[5]

Transitional justice can incorporate a number of judicial and non-judicial mechanisms. Among the range of measures associated with transitional justice in Egypt, the primary focus has been criminal justice. But the charges against former president Mubarak for abuses committed during the 2011 events have been lifted, and he has not been prosecuted for other crimes committed during his thirty years in power. Conversely, former President Morsi and the Muslim Brotherhood have received harsh penalties for abuses committed while they were in power or after having lost power, and young revolutionaries have been sentenced to years in jail for taking part in demonstrations against the new military regime. Fact-finding commissions, a non-judicial means of reconciliation, either failed to produce objective reports or adopted recommendations that were not implemented. If these two mechanisms did not manage to secure redress, other transitional justice mechanisms have not been more successful.

Failed Prosecutions

One mechanism of transitional justice is to ensure that perpetrators are brought to justice and held accountable for their past crimes:

Investigations and trials of powerful leaders (whether political or military) help strengthen the rule of law and send a strong signal that such crimes will not be tolerated in a rights-respecting society. Trials remain a key demand of victims. When conducted in ways that reflect victims' needs and expectations, they can play a vital role in restoring their dignity and delivering justice.[6]

Prosecutions can take place before national courts, but reconciliation will be difficult to achieve if the judicial process fails to dispense impartial justice or does not have the capacity to protect the rights of the accused.

After the overthrow of Hosni Mubarak in February 2011, courts were asked to pass judgment on several charges against the former Egyptian president. Those included accusations relating to the death and injury of hundreds of demonstrators, as well as to the misappropriation of public funds not only by the president but also by a number of high officials. After clearing Mubarak and his top officials of all charges and failing to investigate members of the security forces on charges of killing protesters, the criminal courts sentenced Muslim Brothers and prominent secular opponents to jail for participating in peaceful street protests.[7] Judges were among the main actors responsible for the fall of Mohamed Morsi, and they now face accusations of delivering selective justice.

Mubarak-era abuses

The salient aspect of the prosecutions against Mubarak and his former top officials before the criminal courts has been the impunity of the main perpetrators. In November 2014, the Cairo Court of Appeals ruled Mubarak not guilty of killing protesters in January of 2011. He and his former minister of the interior had, however, been found guilty in June 2012 of failing to prevent the killing of peaceful protesters between 25 and 28 January 2011 and had been sentenced to life in prison.[8] That conviction was overturned by the Court of Cassation in January of 2013 on points of law, and a retrial was ordered and opened in April 2013. In November 2014, all charges were dropped on procedural grounds and the Court of Cassation upheld that ruling in March 2017. Mubarak was then released, as the Court of Cassation had in January of 2015 overturned another conviction sentencing him to three years in prison for embezzling public funds.[9] The cases brought against the former president were limited in scope and time (to the period between 25 and 28 January 2011), and all crimes perpetrated during decades of abuses remain unpunished. Victims of the last thirty years of human rights violations have been denied justice and remedy.

Almost all Mubarak-era government officials who stood trial for corruption and squandering public funds have also been cleared. Some of them, who had been indicted for their role in economic crimes and on corruption charges, managed to negotiate a financial settlement with the court thanks to amendments to the 1975 Law on Illicit Gains that allowed reconciliation for officials charged with extorting public money so long as they repaid the money stolen.

Deals granting impunity in exchange for cash have also been made with a number of Mubarak-era businessmen and investors.[10] In the words of Christoph Wilcke, 'if money can buy impunity, then not only will justice be for sale and owned by the rich, but incentives for accumulating illicit wealth will mount. It is a great irony and slap in the face for the people of Egypt that the corrupt can buy impunity with money first stolen from the people.'[11]

A political isolation law adopted in April 2012 by the Parliament to exclude those who had been officials of the dissolved National Democratic Party (NDP) during the last ten years of Mubarak's rule from running in the 2012 presidential elections, or for public office for the next five years, was deemed unconstitutional by the Supreme Constitutional Court. Prohibition of former top members of the NDP from running in elections for ten years was included in the 2012 constitution, but the 2014 constitution is silent in this regard.

Courts also exonerated members of security forces involved in the killing of demonstrators, and public opinion attributed this leniency to a failure of will on the part of the judiciary to punish associates of the former regime. Only one policeman served a (three-year) sentence for shooting at protestors during the 25 January revolution. Other police officers involved in killing protesters during the same period were not brought to trial; or, in the few cases where charges were brought against them, they were acquitted on the grounds of insufficient evidence.

Only three soldiers involved in killings and abusing protesters during the rule of the Supreme Council of the Armed Forces (SCAF) (from February 2011 to June 2012) were sentenced by a military court (to two and three years in jail) after they were charged with involuntary manslaughter for driving military vehicles into the protesters during the Maspero clashes with Coptic Christians in October 2011, in which twenty-seven protesters were killed. Other police officers were set free and the military failed to investigate incidents involving army officers. Most members of the security forces implicated in the killing or wounding of protesters remained in their positions or were transferred to administrative positions. Only four police officers were convicted after the removal of Morsi for killing protesters: a police captain was sentenced in March 2014 to ten years in jail, and three lower-ranking officers were given one-year suspended sentence for their roles in the deaths of thirty-seven prisoners gassed to death in a crowded police van during their transfer to a prison in August of 2013. The sentence was overturned on appeal in June

2014. Other security forces responsible for killing hundreds of protesters when dispersing Morsi supporters' sit-ins were not investigated or held accountable. 'The prosecution has yet to charge a single member of the security forces with involvement in human rights violations in relation to the hundreds of deaths at the Rabaa al-Adawiya protest camp in August 2013, or at other protests since Mohamed Morsi's ousting. By contrast, thousands of Mohamed Morsi's supporters are currently detained on various accusations.'[12]

Judges have complained that the files sent to them by the prosecution in charge of investigating criminal complaints are almost empty and that they cannot issue convictions backed by insufficient concrete evidence.[13] The prosecution, for their part, accuses the police of failing to gather the necessary material evidence and blames the minister of the interior for failing to cooperate and deliver the records of central security forces. Families of victims and their lawyers also accuse the police of destroying evidence, and of using pressure and intimidation to convince them to withdraw their complaints.

Police officers who are to gather evidence belong to the very same administration as those who participated in the crimes being investigated. This exposes deep flaws in the Egyptian Code of Criminal Procedures. Even in cases of alleged police abuse, evidence-gathering is entrusted to the police, giving them opportunity to tamper with the evidence or to withhold it to escape accountability. There are no independent bodies investigating cases of police brutality. As for members of the armed forces, they enjoy *de facto* immunity, since they appear before military courts controlled by the military leadership.

A fund was established by the SCAF in June of 2011 to compensate victims of state repression. However, the fund seems to have lacked financial resources and '[f]amilies of the victims also reported having been mistreated by the state officials in charge of issuing their monetary compensation and complained of increased bureaucratic procedures and difficulties when applying for their compensations. The fund has no clear vision or mechanism to maintain the scope of its work, especially in light of the continuation of the violence and the addition of new victims.'[14]

Prosecution of Supporters of Morsi and Selective Justice

By contrast, the supporters of Morsi has been much more forcefully prosecuted. 'The prosecutorial record over the last three years shows a persistent lack of accountability in relation to crimes allegedly committed by public security forces, alongside selective prosecutions targeting government critics or opponents.'[15] Thousands have been arrested since Morsi's ouster and put in preventive detention pending the outcome of investigations on accusations that they took part in violent protests, belonged to a banned terrorist group, or on other charges.

Morsi himself and other prominent Brotherhood figures have been referred to trial for escaping from prison during the opening days of the 25 January Revolution; for inciting violence and killing peaceful demonstrators near the Presidential Palace in December of 2012; and for espionage, treason and conspiring with foreign groups to carry out terrorist acts in Egypt. In April 2015, Morsi was sentenced to twenty years in prison for conspiring in the 2012 Presidential Palace killing, and one month later was sentenced to life in prison for collaborating with Hamas, Hezbollah and the Iranian Revolutionary Guard. In the same month (May 2015), he received a death sentence for escaping from prison in January 2011, and in June 2016 he was convicted of spying for Qatar and of stealing documents concerning state security and sentenced to life in prison once again. In November of 2016, the Court of Cassation overturned his death sentence and ordered a retrial.

In cases tried in March and April 2014, a judge in the province of Minya handed down more than 1,200 death sentences against members of the Muslim Brotherhood for killing police officers. As the Egyptian Initiative for Personal Rights wrote, 'the court argued that criminal intent to kill any member of the police forces and presence at the crime scene constituted sufficient evidence for murder or attempted murder convictions. At the same time, courts have consistently acquitted police officers present at the scenes of protester killings, citing lack of evidence linking individual officers to protester deaths or accepting arguments of self-defence.'[16] Even if the number of death sentences in the March case was later reduced to thirty-seven, with the other sentences commuted to life, and in the April case to 183 death sentences out of 682, such draconian sentences have cost the courts' credibility.[17] Both cases were criticised for violating the right to a fair trial and to due process. In February 2015, the Giza Criminal Court handed down a death penalty against 183 defendants on charges of killing police officers during an attack on a police station in August 2013. This led to accusations that judges were displaying bias against the Muslim Brothers and seeking revenge for their conflict with Morsi. The rulings were not criticised by other judges. The removal from their positions of judges suspected of affiliation with the Muslim Brotherhood may have deterred them from speaking out against colleagues.

Secular activists, human rights defenders and bloggers critical of the government have also been put on trial and sentenced to heavy prison time and fines for breaking the anti-protest law adopted in November 2013 by protesting without a permit. All these controversial rulings have led to an 'alarmingly selective justice system in Egypt, which appears more intent on settling political scores and punishing dissent than establishing justice.'[18] While Morsi supporters and political activists have been prosecuted and referred to trial, security forces and political officials responsible for human rights violations have been able to walk free.

Judges—Actors of the Transition Process

Judges have been at the centre of political struggles and have emerged as among the most dynamic players in the post-revolutionary period. Under Mubarak, the judiciary had already played an active political role as an arena in which to pursue political objectives in defiance of the regime in power. The courts challenged the authoritarian regime by issuing rulings guaranteeing a variety of political rights and freedoms.[19]

During Morsi's year in power, courts increasingly weighed in on sensitive political issues, often in conflict with the executive and legislative branches. In retaliation, the executive and legislature took steps to discipline the judiciary, reduce its political influence, and even purge political opponents from its ranks. Since Morsi's ouster in July 2013, judges have been accused by the opposition and by NGOs of being used by the military regime to quash any kind of dissent and of taking their revenge by prosecuting Morsi and his supporters.[20]

There is no evidence that such embarrassing rulings were due to direct interference from the executive authority in the rulings of the courts. On the contrary, judges may have felt strong enough to let their vision of politics and society drive their decisions. As Ibrahim al-Houdaybi argues, 'in many cases, the judiciary feels independent from the law. Judges replace their role as jurists with that of statesmen; their rulings fail to reflect prevailing interpretations of legal texts and are instead based on what they perceive as the interests of the state, based on their position in the legal structure and their own beliefs.'[21]

As to members of the prosecution, 'anecdotal evidence provided to the International Bar Association Human Rights Institute [IBAHRI] suggests that it is accepted that the President or executive will sometimes attempt to influence the Office of Public Prosecution by "suggesting" that they should either drop an investigation or start one against a particular individual. One senior diplomat suggested that this situation has indeed deteriorated since Mubarak because at least under Mubarak the prosecutor would sometimes say "no". Others suggested that the pressure a prosecutor might face is more subtle, with no direct command received but a clear understanding of what he is expected to do.'[22]

Many judges may be convinced that they are defending the stability of their country and condemning criminals who deserve heavy sentences. As Nathan Brown writes, 'the judiciary as a body shows real willingness to distance itself from the executive but little interest or willingness to distance itself from the state. And, for many judges, that state has just come under severe attack by an alien force. The invaders managed to temporarily seize the presidency; for a while key institutions of state—including, most shockingly to judges, courts themselves—were quite literally besieged by these outsiders. Of course, not all judges feel this way, but many do seem to share the sense of crisis that perhaps has led to some of the brutal efficiency displayed when trying some cases.'[23] This politicisation of the judiciary has had damaging consequences for the judges themselves. The harsh rulings led to a general perception that the courts were issuing decisions with an implicit political leaning: in conformity with the army's priorities. The judiciary, which once enjoyed high prestige and respect within society, has seen its status diminished.

That most judges display a conservative bent can be traced to the recruitment process used in picking judiciary personnel and the demographic profile this imposes on the institution. The criteria for appointment delineated by the judiciary law, are as follows: a candidate must have Egyptian nationality and hold a law degree. He must possess a good reputation, enjoy civil rights, and present various guarantees of morality. State security agencies monitor the appointment process and investigate the social and political background of every candidate. They ensure that anyone with origins in the poor social strata or who has relatives known to be Islamists, criminals, or leftists will be excluded from consideration.[24] Social standing has always been a main criterion in appointment. Sons of judges have a better chance of appointment to the judiciary than other law graduates. In fact, a widespread complaint is that sons of counselors or well-known personalities close to the government manage to get hired even when their exam results at the law faculty are inferior to those of other candidates. 'Egypt's politics of patronage and clientelism, Sahar Aziz writes, have further compromised judicial independence. Like other state institutions, the judiciary is wrought with nepotism, and the appointment process is far from meritocratic. Judges' family members and relations are often appointed to judgeships despite poor academic records that [should] disqualify them.'[25]

Most Egyptian judges, therefore, have a rather conservative, nationalistic and patriarchal mindset.[26] They are part of a social elite; they value hierarchy, seniority, and order, and oppose radical changes in politics and society. They are trained in the faculties of law of Egyptian universities and most see themselves as the mentors of a modern liberal state based on respect for the rule of law and the separation of powers. In 2016, the nationalistic tendency amongst judges led the State Council to unexpectedly declare unconstitutional the controversial maritime border demarcation deal concluded between Egypt and Saudi Arabia, under which Egypt would transfer sovereignty over the two Red Sea islands of Tiran and Sanafir to Saudi Arabia.[27] The Court of Administrative Justice upheld that ruling on appeal in January 2017.[28]

The Failure of Fact-Finding Commissions to Bring Truth and Reconciliation

Fact-finding commissions, like truth and reconciliation commissions, are a non-judicial means of transitional justice. They seek to uncover the truth behind allegations of past human rights abuses, to establish an accurate historical record, and to replace retribution by truth-telling. Repressive regimes 'deliberately rewrite history and deny atrocities to legitimise themselves. Truth-seeking contributes to the creation of a historical record that prevents this kind of manipulation. It can help victims find closure by learning more about the events they suffered, such as the fate of disappeared individuals, or why certain people were targeted for abuse.'[29]

Several fact-finding commissions have been mandated by successive governments to carry out independent investigations into human rights violations and to expose the truth about such incidents. None, though, has covered the decades of Mubarak's rule, and none has proven efficient, sincere, or transparent. All failed to provide accountability, truth and reconciliation.

By Shafiq in 2011: Police Forces Responsible for Killing Protestors

The first fact-finding commission was set up in February 2011 by Ahmed Shafiq, then prime minister, to investigate the killing of protesters in January and February of 2011. A summary of its findings and recommendations, made public in April 2011, held police forces responsible for many of the deaths of protesters during the 25 January uprising and also implicated members of the

National Democratic Party, accusing them of orchestrating violence against protestors by hiring thugs to attack peaceful demonstrators:

> The fact-finding commission concluded that at least 825 protesters were killed and over 6,000 injured during the uprising and that the police forces were responsible for many of those deaths. Among the commission's key findings was the use of snipers by the Ministry of Interior. As opposed to injuries and deaths resulting from clashes between protesters and security forces, the use of snipers is unambiguously indicative of premeditated plans to kill and injure protesters. As such, this issue continues to prove contentious, with Ministry of Interior officials denying the use of snipers during the eighteen-day uprising and, in some statements, denying that the ministry employed snipers at all. The commission also implicated NDP figures with orchestrating violence against protesters, including the 2 February attack on Tahrir Square when armed thugs descended on protesters on camel and horseback. In addition to its limited scope, the work of the commission has not been highlighted by the transitional government or accompanied by public outreach, undermining the usefulness of the exercise and its impact.[30]

The complete report was never released and no follow-up was provided by the transitional government.

By Morsi in 2012: Use of Excessive Force by the Police and the Army

One of Morsi's first actions after he took office in June 2012 was to set up a fact-finding commission to investigate all incidents in which protestors had been killed or injured between 25 January 2011 and the beginning of his presidency on 30 June 2012. The commission was comprised of senior dignitaries, including judges, doctors and members of the security forces and of the Ministry of Interior.

The commission submitted its report to Morsi at the end of December 2012, but the president refused to make it public, claiming that he wanted to 'ensure that neither the course of the investigation nor the outcome [be] politicised.'[31] He was probably more concerned, though, by the political costs the release of a report containing allegations against the armed forces would have for him and his regime.

The committee mentioned on its website that it had identified nineteen separate incidents where the military and the police had used excessive force or committed other violations of human rights against protesters.[32] In March and April 2013, the Egyptian daily *Al Shorouk* and *The Guardian* published part of the report leaked to them, highlighting its finding that the police and the armed forces had participated in various crimes, including killings, forced disappearances, torture and sexual violence throughout the country during the 2011 uprising.[33] Morsi forwarded the report to the public prosecutor who appointed a team to investigate its findings in 'absolute secrecy'.[34] The prosecutor, however, did not bring charges against any of the police or army personnel accused in the report of being involved in killing protesters. Human Rights Watch launched a campaign for the publication of the report, but with no result: 'Publication of the new report would be a step towards addressing the right of victims' families to know the truth about the circumstances in which their relatives died (...). That should be possible without compromising the interests of justice—for example by withholding the names of those allegedly responsible while the allegations against them are rigorously investigated.'[35] A 'Where is the Report' campaign was launched in Egypt by activists, advocating more transparency as regards the report's findings, but those findings remained secret.[36]

By Adly Mansour in 2013: Primary Responsibility for the Deaths Lies with Islamist Leaders

The commission appointed by interim president Adly Mansour in December 2013 was given six months to investigate all incidents of violence that had occurred since 30 June 2013. It was made up of judges and legal professionals but included no members of civil society or human rights organisations. In addition, its mandate failed to establish enforcement and accountability mechanisms that would compel state institutions to cooperate with the commission; neither did it specify whether the commission had the powers of subpoena and search and seizure.[37]

The commission missed the original deadline of June 2014, blaming a lack of cooperation by the security forces as well as the refusal of the Muslim Brotherhood to collaborate (after they had first agreed to do so). The deadline was extended to September and then to November 2014. An executive summary of the report was made public in November of 2014, but not the full report, 'to protect witnesses.' The commission concluded that 'the primary responsibility for the deaths that occurred during and after the violent dispersal of the Rabaa al-Adawiya sit-in lay with Islamist leaders, not the government.'[38] The report added that leaders of anti-government protests had armed the crowds and refused to abide by the government's calls for dispersal.[39] 'The report says that the police were justified in violently dispersing the protest, although it blames security forces for failing to target those carrying arms amongst the crowd, thereby increasing the casualties.'[40] It places the blame for the violence on Islamist groups, 'for ruling in an undemocratic manner, undermining legal institutions and making enemies out of the police, military and other institutions. The report says that the Brotherhood chose the path of confrontation when it lost its popular backing. However, it adds, the transitional government and society at large were also responsible for the current situation for failing to live up to demands for reform raised in 2011.'[41]

No follow-up mechanism was established to implement the recommendations of the commission.

The Egyptian Initiative for Personal Rights (EIPR), which had published its own report on the events of 30 June and thereafter, reached the conclusion that the commission had not considered its findings.[42] For instance, as far as the Rabaa al-Adawiya sit-in dispersal is concerned:

> The Fact-Finding Commission placed the primary blame for the heavy casualty toll during the dispersal of the Rabaa al-Adawiya sit-in and other political violence in the summer of 2013 on the leadership of the Muslim Brotherhood and the protesters themselves. For Rabaa al-Adawiya, the bloodiest incident investigated, the Commission concluded that security forces had used graduated force and were compelled to use lethal force only in response to the use of firearms by some protesters. The report argued that security forces had taken sufficient steps to minimise casualties and provide a safe exit to protesters. The Commission only faulted the security forces with not targeting armed elements within the protest efficiently, therefore increasing casualties. However, it also blamed unarmed protesters for insisting on remaining at the site of the violence and serving as 'human shields' for those using violence. EIPR's own investigation and witness testimonies it gathered concluded that security forces used excessive lethal force, showed a blatant disregard to the right to life, and failed most of the time to provide a safe exit to protesters. Evidence collected by EIPR suggested that some protesters were killed while fleeing and that security forces consistently resorted to the use of lethal force when it was not strictly necessary to protect life or prevent serious injury. Even though the Commission's report indicated that eight members of the security forces were killed during the dispersal compared to 607 civilians according to the Commission's findings, it maintained that the use of lethal force by security forces was legal and proportionate to the risk posed.[43]

The government report also differs from that released by Human Rights Watch in August of 2014.[44] It claims that 624 protesters died in Rabaa al-Adawiya Square and approximately 150 in the dispersal of Nahda Square (where another pro-Morsi protest was held), while Human Rights Watch had documented approximately 1,150 deaths. Human Rights Watch's report had found also that the military had planned and executed the systematic killing of demonstrators in what 'likely amounted to a crime against humanity', while the report of the fact-finding commission blamed the leadership of the Muslim Brotherhood for inciting violence and claimed that the fault of the government consisted only in delaying the dispersal of the sit-ins.

The Failure of Other Transitional Justice Mechanisms

The failure of these fact-finding commissions to establish the truth and to effect redress and accountability was compounded by the failure of other mechanisms. Reforms of government institutions, in particular of the security system and the judiciary, are also crucial to the transitional justice process as they lay the groundwork for national reconciliation. Successive transitional governments however have failed so far to initiate judicial and security sector reform. The cost of reforms has been deemed too high.

All successive governments that have ruled Egypt following the revolution of January 2011, even Morsi's, have failed to initiate a reform of the judiciary.[45] A Justice Conference scheduled to work out a reform acceptable to all sides was cancelled in June 2013.[46] Judges oppose by nature any radical change in their traditional working methods. Any amendment to the judiciary laws is viewed as driven by a hidden political agenda: in the words of Yussef Auf, 'full reform will not unfold in the near future, since the current leadership is old and resistant to change, in addition to the fact that the current landscape in Egypt is not conducive to significant change.'[47] Any change in inherited traditions that have developed over the decades will need internal support: 'the judiciary has a perpetual sensitivity toward reform, especially when it does not come from within the judicial establishment. This leads to an important conclusion: the judiciary itself must be involved in the reform process. Otherwise, the process will be fraught with risks and prone to failure. The confrontation between the judiciary and the Muslim Brotherhood under the rule of former president Mohamed Morsi is an example of this kind of failure.'[48]

Only judges who publicly supported the ousted president Mohamed Morsi were dismissed from their positions for breaking the judicial authority law that prohibits engaging in politics.[49] In March 2016, the former head of the Judges Club, a reformist who had been one of the most fervent opponents of Mubarak, was forced into retirement by a disciplinary committee over charges of participating in the storming of the state security headquarters in March 2011.[50]

No effective measures have been taken to reform the Ministry of Interior or the state security services either.[51] Most agents have retained in their positions, which may encourage a feeling of impunity among them. In the words of Yezid Sayegh:

> The Ministry of Interior has emerged as a major partner in the coalition of state institutions that now rules Egypt, and often takes the lead in shaping the manner in which state power is exercised in the daily lives of citizens. The Mubarak-era securocratic state, in which the president maintained checks and balances and civilian political elites exercised significant influence from their base in the ruling National Democratic Party, is being replaced with an overt police state. With radicalisation on both sides taking Egypt further into political violence, the opportunity for security sector reform will remain closed until national reconciliation can be achieved.[52]

New hopes for a serious commitment to accountability were raised when, in July of 2013, interim President Adly Mansour appointed for the first time a minister for transitional justice charged with the 'political management of the transitional period' with the goal of achieving 'comprehensive national reconciliation.' However, his approach has been to focus solely on Morsi's year in power rather than to seek justice and accountability for all past crimes. In January of 2014, he declared that it was not the right time to talk about transitional justice because there was no legislative support for it.[53] He also stated that the Muslim Brotherhood was 'indirectly responsible for all the chaos in Egypt in recent times', having obviously already passed judgment on who was guilty and accountable for the crimes of the past.[54] He was replaced in June by a new minister, who defended the controversial protest law in a meeting with the US chargé d'affaires to Egypt, stating that its aim was to protect public order.[55] In September of 2015, the ministry for transitional justice disappeared after a government reshuffle. The transitional justice law which the 2014 constitution required the House of Representatives to adopt during its first session had not been adopted by June 2017.

After the resignation of the new government's two most prominent liberal figures, vice president Mohamed ElBaradei in August 2013, and deputy prime minister Ziad Bahaa-Eldin in January 2014, no official reconciliation efforts were conducted by members of the government. Both sides seem to exclude reconciliation and do not appear ready to provide concessions.[56] The government, moreover, has adopted far-reaching repressive measures that leave very little room for reconciliation. Members of the Muslim Brotherhood have been arrested, and their assets have been frozen, as well as the funds of NGOs affiliated with them. Their schools have been put under government supervision and they have been banned from carrying out any activities in the country. The group has been designated as a terrorist organisation and the Freedom and Justice Party has been dissolved. Reconciliation, therefore, is unlikely to occur in the short term: as Ashraf el-Sherif argues, 'both sides have invested heavily in demonising the other—making the prospects of reconciliation remote. Brotherhood leaders in particular would have difficulty persuading their grass roots to forgo seeking retribution for those killed by the regime. Angry Islamist youth may then be won over by the Islamic State model in Iraq and Syria that involves forgoing electoral democracy and peaceful and inclusive political activism, and instead raising arms in a violent struggle against their own states in the name of the Islamist cause; that is, the exact opposite of reconciliation. For the regime, reconciliation could result in the loss of credibility in the eyes of large swaths of society that had been mobilised by unprecedented anti-Islamist propaganda in addition to the avowedly anti-Islamist segments of the police and judiciary.'[57]

Conclusion

Transitional justice in Egypt has been particularly difficult to achieve, because of the chaotic aftermath of the fall of Mubarak. The different ruling systems that have been in charge have all been involved in various human rights violations and have demonstrated their disregard for ensuring genuine accountability for past abuses and establishing the rule of law. All of these successive governments committed abuses against their political opposition, leaving new victims and new cases to be investigated.

In spite of the appointment of a minister for transitional justice in July 2013, and the inclusion in the 2014 constitution of a provision requiring the next parliament to pass a transitional justice law, the current government continues to resort to repressive measures against Muslim Brothers and young secular activists while other perpetrators still enjoy impunity. Transitional justice is no longer a priority.

'Transitional justice in Egypt, Rowida Omar writes, needs the proper psychological climate and community support for reconciliation to take place, which necessitates transparency and inclusion at every stage. Justice in Egypt must start with a political decision to reform state institutions and with an end to the spread of hatred and violent speech through the media.'[58]

In addition, the few transitional justice mechanisms so far have focused only on the prosecution of former officials for killing or injuring protesters, though, as the Tahrir Institute for Middle East Policy argues:

limiting the scope of transitional justice to these events allows the current al-Sisi government to avoid any scrutiny of the role of the SCAF and any of its political and security allies in Egyptian politics for the previous fifty years. By co-opting the language of transitional justice and making limited gestures in this regard, al-Sisi seeks to establish the government's legitimacy and deflect demands for more wide-ranging reforms. This sets inherent limits on the capacity of transitional justice to address broader issues, including demands for equality and the reform of the state apparatus. As it currently stands, the head of state has changed, but the practices of the government remain the same.[59]

The lack of progress in the area of transitional justice is mostly due to a lack of political will on the part of Egypt's successive governments to engage with the process and establish measures of truth-telling and accountability. In the words of another expert, 'justice will only be achieved if there is sufficient political will to make a clean break with the past, hold those responsible for violating Egyptians' rights to account, and compensate the victims of these abuses.'[60]

This lack of accountability has led to a significant increase in both peaceful and violent protests. It can also, and easily, generate vengeance and destabilise the new political order, turning opponents to radicalisation and driving them into the arms of extremist groups by eroding their faith in justice and democracy. Democratisation and progress in social and economic development in Egypt 'will not happen until the grievances of the recent past and present are resolved for good. Only under a system of accountability, efficiency, and equality will Egypt be able to move forward with its transition'.[61]

NOTES

INTRODUCTION: TAKING THE ARAB TRANSITIONS SERIOUSLY

1. See for instance Filiu, Jean-Pierre, *The Arab Revolution: Ten Lessons from the Democratic Uprising*, London: Hurst, 2011; Achcar, Gilbert, *The People Want: A Radical Exploration of the Arab Spring*, Berkeley, CA: University of California Press, 2013; Gerges, Fawaz (ed.), *The New Middle East: Protest and Revolution in the Arab World*, Cambridge: Cambridge University Press, 2013; Lynch, Marc (ed.), *The Arab Uprisings Explained: New Contentious Politics in the Middle East*, New York: Columbia University Press, 2014; Brownlee, Jason, Masoud, Tarek and Reynolds, Andrew (eds), *The Arab Spring: Pathways of Repression and Reform*, Oxford: Oxford University Press, 2015; Beinin, Joel, *Workers and Thiis: Labor Movements and Popular Uprisings in Tunisia and Egypt*, Palo Alto: Stanford University Press, 2015; Kienle, Eberhard and Sika, Nadine (eds), *The Arab Uprisings: Transforming and Challenging State Power*, London: I. B. Tauris, 2015. On Egypt more specifically, see Korany, Bahgat and El-Mahdi, Rabab (eds), *Arab Spring in Egypt: Revolution and Beyond*, Cairo: AUC Press, 2012; Lacroix, Stéphane and Rougier, Bernard (eds), *Egypt's Revolutions: Politics, Religion and Social Movements*, London: Palgrave Macmillan, 2015.
2. Dobry, Michel, *Sociologie des crises politiques: La dynamique des mobilisations multisectorielles*, Paris: Presses de Sciences Po, 2009.
3. O'Donnell, Guillermo; Schmitter, Philippe C., and Whitehead, Laurence, *Transitions from Authoritarian Rule: Southern Europe, Vol. 1*, Baltimore, MD: Johns Hopkins University Press, 1986.
4. Salamé, Ghassan (ed.), *Democracy without Democrats: The Renewal of Politics in the Muslim World*, London: I. B. Tauris, 1994.

1. TOWARDS A 'DEMOCRACY WITH DEMOCRATS' IN TUNISIA: MUTUAL ACCOMMODATION BETWEEN ISLAMIC AND SECULAR ACTIVISTS

1. There is no discussion of secularism in Dahl, Robert, *Polyarchy: Participation and*

Opposition, New Haven, CT: Yale University Press, 1971, or in Lijphart, Arend, *Patterns of Democracy: Government Forms and Performance in Thirty-Six Countries*, New Haven, CT: Yale University Press, 1999. Juan J. Linz and I devote Chapter 3 in our *Problems of Democratic Transitions and Consolidation: Southern Europe, South America, and Post-Communist Europe*, Baltimore, MA: Johns Hopkins University Press, 1996, to a typology of democratic, authoritarian, sultanistic, post-totalitarian, and totalitarian regimes, but we do not use 'secularism' as part of our classification.

2. I define and discuss the 'twin tolerations' in much greater detail in a chapter titled 'The World's Religious Systems and Democracy: Crafting the "Twin Tolerations"' in *Arguing Comparative Politics*, Oxford: Oxford University Press, 2000, pp. 213–254; a much shorter version is available in Stepan, Alfred, 'Religion, Democracy and the "Twin Tolerations"', *The Journal of Democracy*, Vol. 11, 2000, pp. 32–52.

3. Kalyvas, Stathis N., *The Rise of Christian Democracy in Europe*, Ithaca, NY: Cornell University Press, 1996.

4. For more details on these points see Stepan, Alfred, 'The Multiple Secularisms of Modern Democratic and Non-Democratic Regimes', in Calhoun, Craig; Juergensmeyer, Mark; and Van Antwerpen, Jonathan (eds), *Rethinking Secularism*, New York: Oxford University Press, 2011, pp. 114–144.

5. Salamé, Ghassan (ed.), *Democracy Without Democrats? The Renewal of Politics in the Muslim World*, London: I. B. Tauris, 1994.

6. Islam is not discussed in the classic, four-volume work edited by O'Donnell, Guillermo; Schmitter, Philippe C., and Whitehead, Laurence, *Transitions From Authoritarian Rule*, Baltimore, MA: Johns Hopkins University Press, 1986, nor in my *Problems of Democratic Transition*.

7. I have made six research trips to Tunisia since the fall of Ben Ali on 14 January 2011. Among other research activities I have interviewed the presidents of five of the largest political parties.

8. See their article, 'Our Country of the Year: Hope Springs', *The Economist*, 20 December 2014. Interestingly, the 'runner-up' for Country of the Year was Indonesia, and Senegal was praised for responding 'with alacrity to its Ebola outbreak.'

9. On its seven-point scale where 1 is the best score, and 7 is the worst, Tunisia received a 1 for 'political rights' in 2015. To be sure, Tunisia is still far from what Linz and I would classify as a 'consolidated democracy'. For example, Freedom House correctly only gives Tunisia a 3 for 'civil liberties' due to continuing problems (many related to legacies of the previous authoritarian 'deep state' of 55 years' duration) with establishing the rule of law, a reformed judiciary and a rights-respecting police force, but some problems such as the presence of Salafi violence really only became serious during the post-Ben Ali period.

10. See Künkler, Mirjam and Stepan, Alfred, 'Indonesian Democratization in

Theoretical Perspective' in Künkler, Mirjam and Stepan, Alfred (eds), *Democracy and Islam in Indonesia*. New York: Columbia University Press, 2013, pp. 3–23.

11. See Stepan, Alfred, 'Rituals of Respect: Sufis and Secularists in Senegal in Comparative Perspective' *Comparative Politics*, Vol. 44, No. 4, July 2012, pp. 379–401.

12. I compare Indonesia, Senegal and India from the perspective of Muslims and the successful achievement of democracy and their active participation in public space in 'Muslims and Toleration: Unexamined Contributions to the Multiple Secularisms of Modern Democracies' in Stepan, Alfred and Taylor, Charles (eds), *The Boundaries of Toleration*, New York: Columbia University Press, 2014, pp. 267–296.

13. For the 'scope conditions' for a four-player game see Linz and Stepan, *Problems of Democratic Transition and Consolidation*, pp. 55–65.

14. See Ortega Frei, Eugenio, *Historia de una Alianza Política*, Santiago: CED/CESOC, 1992.

15. See Künkler, Mirjam, 'How Pluralist Democracy Became the Consensual Discourse Among Secular and Nonsecular Muslims in Indonesia' in Künkler and Stepan (eds), *Democracy and Islam in Indonesia*, pp. 53–72.

16. Horowitz, Donald L., *Constitutional Change and Democracy in Indonesia*, Cambridge: Cambridge University Press, 2013, p. 293.

17. For a discussion of 'aggressive secularism' in France and Turkey, in contrast to a religious friendly 'passive secularism' in the United States see Kuru, Ahmet T., *Secularism and State Policies Toward Religion: The United States, France and Turkey*, Cambridge: Cambridge University Press, 2009, and his 'Passive and Assertive Secularism: Historical Conditions, Ideological Struggles, and State Policies Toward Religion', *World Politics*, Vol. 59, 2007, pp. 568–594.

18. See the excellent chapter on Tunisia in Filiu, Jean-Pierre, *The Arab Revolution: Ten Lessons from the Democratic Uprising*, London: Hurst, 2011, p. 14.

19. See Hourani, Albert, *Arabic Thought in the Liberal Age, 1798–1939*, Cambridge: Cambridge University Press, 1983, p. 65. The university is sometimes spelled Zaytuna as in this quote from Hourani, but often it is now spelled in English, Zeitouna.

20. See Stepan, Alfred, 'Tunisia's Transition and the Twin Tolerations', *Journal of Democracy*, Vol. 23, 2012, pp. 89–103, especially, pp. 99–102.

21. See Charrad, Mounira, *States and Women's Rights in the Making of Post-Colonial Tunisia, Algeria, and Morocco*, Berkeley, CA: University of California Press, 2001.

22. See Kepel, Gilles, *Jihad: The Trail of Political Islam*, Cambridge, MA: Harvard University Press, 2002, pp. 254–275.

23. House of Commons Speech on 11 November 1947.

24. 'Appel de Tunis', 6 June 2003, three-page document, one copy given to me with the names of the twenty-three signatories by a participant from Ettakatol, and an

identical copy with the same names given to me by a participant from Ennahda in May 2011.

25. Some of the other twenty-two signatories were civil society and political society leaders or organisations such as PDP (a political party), Le Bâtonnier (a barristers' organisation), various human rights organisations, and some prominent journalists and intellectuals in their personal capacity.

26. I received a copy of this document on 11 November 2011 while visiting the Tunis headquarters of the most secular party in the CNA ruling coalition, Ettakatol. The person who gave it to me was one of the drafters, Zied Daoulatli. The Arabic-to-English translation is the work of Mostafa Hefny. For a discussion of this document eight years later see Sami, Farah, 'Eight Years Ago Today, When Leftists and Islamists got Along', 2013, available online: http://www.tunisia-live.net/2013/10/18

27. Interview with Marzouki in Tunis and a separate confirmatory interview with Ghannouchi in Tunis, both in May 2013.

28. Tarek Masoud's chapter in this volume, which is impressively fact-filled, points out that I claim that the difference between Tunisia and Egypt in the Arab Spring is that 'secular liberals and Islamists in Tunisia began meeting regularly eight years before the fall of Ben Ali, to see whether they could reduce mutual fears and agree upon rules of democratic government.' My argument is that these meetings helped make the transition to democracy in Tunisia. For Masoud, 'The problem with this narrative is that oppositionists in Egypt also cooperated with each other during Mubarak's rule', yet the transition to democracy did not occur in Egypt. He writes: 'The divergence between Tunisia and Egypt is perhaps to be expected. By about any measure Tunisia is more developed than Egypt.' The fact that Tunisia has 'the partisan pluralism necessary to the maintenance of democracy,' he maintains, 'is a function of civic pluralism, which in turn is a function of economic development.' I have two fundamental disagreements with these critiques. First, I did not merely document cooperation, but 'mutual accommodation' and eventual agreements between the moderate Muslim Ennahda party and two secular center-left parties. Between them, these three moderate Tunisian parties won a coalitional majority in the Constituent Assembly. In Egypt there were a few talks between secularists and Islamists such as the 'Fairmont Group' in 2012 but as Carrie Wickham shows in her work, they did not manage to create mutually agreed democratic procedures. Second, on the economic argument, since the early 1950s Tunisia indeed had a more developed civic society than Egypt, but Masoud should be more cautious about socio-economic determinism. Tunisia never held a single free and fair election, from independence in 1951 to the fall of Ben Ali in 2011. Indeed, in the sixty-year lead up to the democratic transition, the country had a somewhat lower civil liberty average than Egypt, according to the NGO Freedom House. The cause of the democratic transition in Tunisia is not the long-standing, pre-existing civil

society, but the creation of strong elements of a democratic political society in eight years of crafting by secularists and Islamist parties, something completely absent in Egypt.

29. For example, Monica Marks and I recently found an important February 2006 document 'À propos d'une dérive' which criticises those secularists who signed the accords: 'What can we say about the haste with which some political formations and associations ... known for their commitment to secularism and democracy have signed this so-called manifesto of alliance with the movement of Mr. Rached Ghannouchi? This approach ... blurs the boundaries between the secular view of politics and fanaticism ... between religion and theocracy; in a word between democracy and non-democracy.' The statement had 109 signatories including some prominent feminists from ATFD, unionists, and human rights activists.

30. Wickham, Carrie R., *The Muslim Brotherhood: Evolution of an Islamist Organization*, Princeton, NJ: Princeton University Press, 2013, p. 286.

31. Data supplied to me by Stephen Whitefield of Oxford University based on a poll he and his colleagues gave in Egypt in December 2011 with 2001 respondents. They repeated this question with 2051 respondents in March 2014 after the 3 July 2013 coup against the Morsi government and an eradication campaign against the Muslim Brotherhood, and 78 per cent of respondents affirmed that the military 'should continue to intervene when it thinks necessary.'

32. This was written by Samir El-Ayed on 23 September 2011. In a March 2011 seminar I had with one of the most progressive and important parts of youth-led civil society, the April 6 Movement, one of their leaders told me emphatically that one of their most important projects was to figure out how they could get the military to write the constitution before elections. For more like this see my 'The Recurrent Temptation to Abdicate to the Military in Egypt', 13 January 2012. available online: http://blog.freedomhouse.org/weblog/2012/01/two-perspectives-on-egypts-transition.html

33. This survey data is quite evocative of Karl Marx's, *The Eighteenth Brumaire of Louis Bonaparte* in which Marx lists as a characteristic of Bonapartist regimes the abdication of the right to rule in exchange for other kinds of protection by the ensuing strong state.

34. The Tunisia data is from the previously cited Whitefield survey. For data from surveys of democratising polities in Spain (1992), in Uruguay, Chile and Brazil (1996), India (2004), and South Korea (2004), see Stepan, Alfred; Linz, Juan J. and Yadav, Yogendra, *Crafting State Nations: India and Other Multinational Democracies*, Baltimore, MA: Johns Hopkins University Press, 2011, p. 65, Table 2.5.

35. I discuss this Commission in my article 'Tunisia's Transition and the Twin Tolerations', pp. 91–94.

36. Linz and Stepan, Alfred, *Problems of Democratic Transition and Consolidation*, p. xiii. Adam Przeworski and Philippe C. Schmitter, in their writings on demo-

cratic transition, also insist on, and document, the 'indeterminacy' of outcomes and the frequency of failures.

37. For the individual leadership contributions in Spain of seven major figures, most importantly Adolfo Suárez, see Linz and Stepan, Ibid., pp. 87–115, especially 92–99. For Cardoso's innovative leadership against inflation, see Stepan, Alfred, 'Fernando Henrique Cardoso: The Structural-Historical Scholar-President of Brazil' in Rueschemeyer, Dietrich and Snyder, Richard (eds), *Cardoso and Approaches to Inequality*, Boulder, CO: Lynne Rienner, Forthcoming. For how the many different groups and leaders in Indonesia's constituent assembly consensually came to numerous crisis ameliorating (or avoiding) decisions see Horowitz, Donald L., *Constitutional Change and Democracy in Indonesia*.

38. This fascinating period deserves a book and was shrouded in secrecy and somewhat conflicting accounts. At this time, however, I will attempt to make tentative arguments based on nineteen interviews with most of the major participants and a few key analysts between 28 October and 3 November 2015. I conducted these interviews with Monica Marks, a doctoral candidate at St Antony's College, Oxford, associated with the ERC WAFAW Program, who is writing her PhD on the role of Ennahda in the Tunisian democratic transition and is a fluent Arabic speaker.

39. For more on these events see the Carter Center's 2013 report, 'The Carter Center Congratulates Tunisia's National Constituent Assembly on Final Draft of Constitution and Urges Safeguards for Human Rights', https://www.cartercenter. org/news/pr/tunisia-061213.html.

40. What follows concerning the new style of internal work of the CNA is based largely, but not exclusively, on a long interview Monica Marks and I had with Mustapha Ben Jaafar, on 4 November 2014 in his CNA presidential office in Tunis.

41. Ibid.

42. Whereas the Egyptian Tamarod knew it was being listened to closely by the military which Tamarod activists felt would eventually overthrow Morsi, the Tunisian prime minister Ali Larayedh (who the Tunisian Tamarod campaign was insisting leave office) told us that the Tunisian military appeared to him to have completely ignored the Tunisian Tamarod, and that he never felt threatened by the Tunisian military. Interview in Tunis, on 4 November 2014.

43. Monica Marks and I talked to the President of UTICA, Mouldi Jendoubi at his UTICA headquarters in Tunis, 4 November 2014, the President of the Tunisian Bar Association, Mohamed Fadhel Mahfoudh at his office in the Justice Palace on 30 October 2014, the President of the Tunisian League of Human Rights, Mokhtar Trifi, 30 October 2014, and the Vice President of UGTT and the editor of their newspaper, *Chebab*, on 3 November 2014, and 30 October 2014, respectively.

44. For a deeper analysis of the motivations for and mistranslations surrounding this language, see Marks, Monica, 'Complementary Status for Tunisian Women',

Foreign Policy, 20 August 2012, http://foreignpolicy.com/2012/08/20/comple-
mentary-status-for-tunisian-women/

45. For Ennahda's votes in their *shûrâ* against containing any reference to Sharia in
    the constitution see Marks, Monica, 'Convince, Coerce, or Compromise?
    Ennahda's Approach to Tunisia's Constitution', Brookings Doha Center paper,
    2014, https://www.brookings.edu/research/convince-coerce-or-compromise-
    ennahdas-approach-to-tunisias-constitution/. For the role of compromise in the
    constitution, see Marzouki, Nadia, 'Dancing by the Cliff: Constitution Writing
    in Post-Revolutionary Tunisia; 2011–2014', in Bali, Asli and Lerner, Hanna (eds),
    Constitution Writing, Religion and Democracy, Cambridge: Cambridge University
    Press, 2017.

46. Guellali, Amna, 'The Problem with Tunisia's New Constitution', *Human Rights
    Watch*, 2014, https://www.hrw.org/news/2014/02/03/problem-tunisias-new-
    constitution

47. Interview with Rached Ghannouchi, 29 October 2014, Tunis.

48. For more of Ghannouchi's reflections, see his op-ed in *The Wall Street Journal*,
    'Tunisia's Perilous Path to Freedom', 15 January 2015, https://www.wsj.com/arti-
    cles/rached-ghannouchi-tunisias-perilous-path-to-freedom-1421353952. I find
    it significant that he now normally identifies himself as the president of the
    Ennahda Party in Tunisia. Sometimes in the past he stressed Ennahda as a move-
    ment. It is still both, but like the history of the Christian Democrats in Germany,
    Ennahda is increasingly becoming a political party.

49. For a balanced and informative eight-page political analysis of this coalition see
    Monica Marks, 'Tunisia Opts for an Inclusive Coalition', Monkey Cage blog, *The
    Washington Post*, 3 February 2015, https://www.washingtonpost.com/news/mon-
    key-cage/wp/2015/02/03/tunisia-opts-for-an-inclusive-new-government/?utm_
    term=.37621a310afd

50. For example, the secretary-general of Nidaa Tounes, Taïeb Baccouche, who is a
    champion of the anti-Ennahda, 'erradicationist' wing of the party, publicly
    denounced the inclusion of Ennahda in the coalition. Ibid.

2. CONSTITUTING CONSTITUTIONALISM: LESSONS FROM THE ARAB
WORLD

1. I have considered some of the ideas in this section in greater length in Brown, Nathan
   J., 'Reason, Interest, Rationality, and Passion in Constitution Drafting', *Perspectives
   on Politics*, Vol. 6, No. 4, December 2008, pp. 675–689.

2. See, for instance, the report by Vivien Hart, an academic associated with a major
   project spearheaded by the United States Institute of Peace and the United Nations
   Development Program: 'Democratic Constitution Making', United States Institute
   of Peace Special Report 107, July 2003, https://www.usip.org/publications/
   2003/07/democratic-constitution-making, p. 5.

3. See, for instance, Ackerman, Bruce, *We the People: Foundations*, Cambridge, MA: Harvard University Press, 1993.

4. Hart, 'Democratic Constitution Making', p. 3.

5. Arato, Andrew, *Civil Society, Constitution, and Legitimacy*, Lanham, MD: Rowman and Littlefield, 2000.

6. Ibid, p. 229.

7. Ibid, p. 230.

8. Ibid, p. 250.

9. Ibid, pp. 250–255.

10. Arato, Andrew, *Constitution Making Under Occupation*, New York: Columbia University Press, 2009.

11. Widner, Jennifer, 'Constitution Writing in Post-conflict Settings: An Overview', *William and Mary Law Review*, 49, 2008, http://scholarship.law.wm.edu/wmlr/vol49/iss4/16, p. 1514.

12. Ginsburg, Tom; Elkins, Zachary; and Blount, Justin, 'Does the Process of Constitution-Making Matter?', *Annual Review of Law and Social Science*, 5, 2009, p. 219.

13. See, for example, the forthcoming work of Todd A. Eisenstadt, A. Carl LeVan, and Tofigh Maboudi. Also of interest is the scholarhip of Tali Mendelburg on the actual effects of deliberation, though that work does not focus primarily on constitution writing.

14. Elkins, Zachary; Ginsburg, Tom; and Melton, James, *The Endurance of National Constitutions*, Cambridge: Cambridge University Press, 2009, p. 211.

15. Krasner, Stephen, 'State Power and the Structure of International Trade', *World Politics*, Vol. 28, No. 3, April 1976, p. 319.

16. See Brown, Nathan J., 'Reason, Interest, Rationality, and Passion in Constitution Drafting', *Perspectives on Politics*, Vol. 6, No. 4, December 2008, pp. 675–689; I have relied on that earlier article for portions of this section.

17. Zolberg, Aristide R., 'Moments of Madness', *Politics and Society*, Vol. 2, Issue 2, 1972, p. 183.

18. See Kuran, Timur, *Public Truth, Private Lies*, Cambridge, MA: Harvard University Press, 1995.

19. Elster, Jon; Offe, Claus; and Preuss, Ulrich K., *Institutional Design in Post-Communist Societies: Rebuilding the Ship at Sea*, Cambridge: Cambridge University Press, 1998, p. 25.

20. Elster, Jon, *Ulysses Unbound: Studies in Rationality, Precommitment, and Constraints*, Cambridge: Cambridge University Press, 2000, p. 159.

21. Elster, Jon (ed.), *Deliberative Democracy*, Cambridge: Cambridge University Press, 1998, pp. 117–118.

22. Przeworski, Adam, *Democracy and the Market: Political and Economic Reforms in Eastern Europe and Latin America*, Cambridge: Cambridge University Press, 1991, p. 87.

23. The subtitle of Elster et al., *Institutional Design in Post-Communist Societies*.
24. Browers, Michaelle L., *Political Ideology in the Arab World: Accommodation and Transformation*, Cambridge: Cambridge University Press, 2009.
25. Brown, Nathan J., *Palestinian Politics after the Oslo Accords: Resuming Arab Palestine*, Berkeley, CA: University of California Press, 2003.
26. Grazin, Igor, 'The Rule of Law: But of Which Law? Natural and Positive Law in Post-Communist Transformation', *John Marshall Law Review*, Vol. 26, 1993.
27. Loveman, Brian, *The Constitution of Tyranny: Regimes of Exception in Spanish America*, Pittsburgh, PA: University of Pittsburgh Press, 1993.
28. Przeworski, Adam, 'Democracy as a Contingent Outcome of Conflicts', in Jon Elster and Rune Slagstad (eds), *Constitutionalism and Democracy*, Cambridge: Cambridge University Press, 1988, p. 60.

3. BULLETS BEAT BALLOTS: THE ARAB UPRISINGS AND CIVIL–MILITARY RELATIONS IN EGYPT

1. See 'Sirri wa khatir: al-fariq al-Sisi wa niyyat al-'askar lil saitara 'ala al-i'lam wa hurriyat ma ba'd al-thawra ["Secret and dangerous: Team Sisi and the military's plan to control the media and freedoms after the revolution"]', posted by 'Mohammed Salah', 2 October 2013, http://www.youtube.com/watch?v=4OI6iL3VpyM
2. Ashour, Omar, 'Egypt: Return to a generals' republic?', BBC News, 21 August 2013, http://www.bbc.co.uk/news/world-middle-east-23780839
3. The author was one of seven organisers of this series of meetings and interactions.
4. Sharp, Jeremy, 'Egypt: Background and U.S. Relations', Congressional Research Service, 24 March 2017, http://fas.org/sgp/crs/mideast/RL33003.pdf
5. Ashour, Omar and Ünlücayakı, Emre, 'Islamists, Soldiers and Conditional Democrats: Behaviors of Islamists and the Military in Algeria and Turkey', *Journal of Conflict Studies*, Vol. 26, No. 2, 2006, pp. 104–132.
6. Sayigh, Yezid, '*Above the State: The Officers' Republic in Egypt*', Carnegie Endowment for International Peace, August 2012, http://carnegieendowment.org/files/officers_republic1.pdf. See also Harb, Imad, 'The Egyptian Military in Politics: Disengagement or Accommodation', *Middle East Journal*, Vol. 57, No. 2, 2003, pp. 269–290.
7. Interview with the author, Cairo, 21 May 2011.
8. BBC Online, 'Egypt's Army Backs Sisi as a Presidential Candidate', 24 January 2014, http://www.bbc.co.uk/news/world-middle-east-25917452
9. See full recording: https://www.youtube.com/watch?v=I-LhCcutKXc&hd=1
10. Those conclusions are based on several conversations with more than twenty army and police officers, as well as the author's observation of the SCAF's behavioural patterns between February 2011 and July 2012.
11. See for example: Al-Ali, Zaid et al. 'The Egyptian Constitutional Declaration Dated 17 June 2012: A Commentary.' *IDEA*, June 2012, http://www.constitu-

tionnet.org/files/commentary_to_june_2012_constitutional_declaration_final. pdf. After a tug-of-war, a 100-member constituent assembly was formed in June 2012 to draft a new constitution.

12. 'Yehia al-Gamal: Mubarak talaba min al-jaysh darb al-mutazhahirin...wa rafd al-jaysh ajbarahu 'ala al-tanhi' [Mubarak asked the army to crack down on demonstrators...and the army's refusal forced him to step down], *Al-Ahram*, 10 September 2011, online: http://gate.ahram.org.eg/News/113877.aspx

13. Interview with the author, Cairo, 16 January 2012.

14. Lieutenant Colonel in Egyptian Armed Forces, interview with the author, Cairo, April 2013.

15. On how SOPs impact decision-making in times of crises see: Allison, Graham, *Essence of Decision: Explaining the Cuban Missile Crisis*, Longman, 1971; Bendor, Jonathan and Hammond, Thomas, 'Rethinking Allison's Models', *American Political Science Review*, Vol. 86, No. 2, 1992, pp. 301–322; Dutton, Jane E., 'The Making of Organizational Opportunities', *Research in Organizational Behaviour*, No. 15, 1993, pp. 1995–226.

16. See, for example, Ashour, Omar, 'From Bad Cop to Good Cop? The Challenge of Security Sector Reform in Egypt', Brookings Doha Center–Stanford University Project on Arab Transitions, Paper Series No. 4, 2012, http://www.brookings.edu/research/papers/2012/11/19-security-sector-reform-ashour

17. 'Al-Sisi: al-dabit illay yadrub qanabil gaz wa khartoush wahd yamut yahsaluh haja fi 'ainuh mish haithakum' [Al-Sisi: Officer using gas canisters and shotguns, somebody dies, something happens to his eye, won't be tried], posted by Shabka Rasd, 3 October 2013, https://www.youtube.com/watch?v=rF8Yz8J3MHI

18. Al-Jazeera America, 'In Egypt, Demonstrations, Death Mark Anniversary of 1973 War,' 7 October 2013, http://america.aljazeera.com/articles/2013/10/6/egypt-warns-brotherhoodagainstanniversaryprotests.html; Police Captain, Skype interview with the author, 31 October 2013.

19. O'Donnell, Guillermo; Schmitter Philippe C., and Whitehead, Laurence, *Transitions from Authoritarian Rule: Southern Europe, Vol. 1*, Baltimore, MD: Johns Hopkins University Press, 1986, p. 16.

20. Ashour, Omar, 'Disarming Egypt's Militarized State', Project Syndicate, July 2013, http://www.project-syndicate.org/commentary/disarming-egypt-s-militarized-state-by-omar-ashour

21. Kirkpatrick, David, 'Ousted general in Egypt is back, as Islamists' foe', *The New York Times*, 30 October 2013, http://www.nytimes.com/2013/10/30/world/middleeast/ousted-general-in-egypt-is-back-as-islamists-foe.html

22. After the overthrow of President Mohamed Morsi on 3 July 2013, anti-coup protestors sat-in in two Squares in Cairo and Giza. The military cracked down a few times but the worst crackdown ensued on 14 August 2013. The military stormed the sit-ins in Cairo's Rabaa Square and Giza's Al-Nahda Square, and carried out

what Human Rights Watch called the 'worst mass unlawful killings in Egypt's modern history' and 'a likely crime against humanity.' More than 1,000 demonstrators died in less than ten hours. The Egyptian Centre for Social and Economic Rights recorded 932 fully documented bodies, 294 partly documented bodies, and 29 undocumented bodies, including 17 women and 30 teenage girls and boys.

23. Fletcher Forum Staff, 'An Interview with Bernardino León, EU Special Representative for the Southern Mediterranean,' The Fletcher Forum for World Affairs, 18 September 2014, http://www.fletcherforum.org/2013/09/18/leon/

24. 'Amr Darrag yakshif tafasil al-mufawadat munthu al-inqilab hatta fad Rab'a' [Amr Darrag reveals the details of the negotiations from the coup until the breakup of the rabaa sit-in], posted by Al-Jazeera's Mubasher Misr, 15 August 2014, https://www.youtube.com/watch?v=7q9z_kGwV58.

25. Ibid.

26. Taylor, Paul, 'West Warned Egypt's Sisi to the End: Don't Do It,' Reuters, 14 August 2013, http://uk.reuters.com/article/2013/08/14/uk-egypt-protests-west-id UKBRE97D16E20130814

27. Kirkpatrick, David, 'Prominent Egyptian Liberal Says He Sought West's Support for Uprising', The New York Times, 4 July 2013, https://mobile.nytimes.com/2013/07/05/world/middleeast/elbaradei-seeks-to-justify-ouster-of-egypts-president.html; Parvaz, Dorothy, 'Nasr City: What Remains after a Massacre', Al-Jazeera, 27 July 2013, http://www.aljazeera.com/indepth/features/2013/07/2013727182042553247.html; Human Rights Watch, 'Egypt: Many Protestors Shot in Head or Chest', 28 July 2013, http://www.hrw.org/news/2013/07/28/egypt-many-protesters-shot-head-or-chest

28. See for example: 'Fadihat Muhammad al-Ghaiti ...adrabu ikhwan al-Azhar bi 'aid min hadid li'annahum khawanat abna' al-jasus Hassan al-Banna wa Mahmud Hussain' [The scandal of Muhammad al-Ghaiyi ... the Brothers hit al-Azhar with an iron fist because they are the treacherous sons of spies Hassan al-Banna and Mahmud Hussain], posted by TheXMediaWar, 19 October 2013, http://www.youtube.com/watch?v=y0HgdoGILok; Kirkpartick, David, 'Egypt Military Enlists Religion to Quell Ranks,' The New York Times, 25 August 2013, http://www.nytimes.com/2013/08/26/world/middleeast/egypt.html

29. Kamel, Ahmed, 'Saad Eddine Ibrahim yutalibu bitahwil al-mudaris wa al-musajid ila ma'taqalat "mu'aqata"' [Saad Eddine Ibrahim demands the transfer of schools and mosques to 'temporary' prisons], Al-Watan, 24 January 2014, http://www.elwatannews.com/news/details/403381; Al-Maseryoon, 'Saad Eddine Ibrahim yutalibu bitahwil al-mudaris wa al-musajid ila ma'taqalat lil-Ikhwan' [Saad Eddine Ibrahim demands the transforming of mosques into detention centers for the Brothers], 24 January 2014, http://bit.ly/1wz6giZ

30. Telephone interview with the author, March 2014.

31. Hammad, interview, part 4, 8 December 2008, online: http://www.aljazeera.net/programs/pages/70e6c2b1-f62c-4a28-94e6-32abda60ea65#L4

32. Interview with the author, Cairo, 16 April 2013.

33. Interview with the author, Cairo, 14 April 2014.

34. See 'Sirri wa khatir: al-fariq al-Sisi wa niyyat al-ʿaskar lil saitara ʿala al-iʾlam wa hurriyat ma baʿd al-thawra' [Secret and dangerous: Team Sisi and the military's plan to control the media and freedoms after the revolution], posted by Mohammed Salah, 2 October 2013, http://www.youtube.com/watch?v=4OI6iL3VpyM

35. Al-Araby al-Jadeed, 'Misr: al-jaysh wa al-shurta laysu "yad wahida"' [Egypt: the army and the police are not 'one hand'], 23 November 2014, http://www.alaraby.co.uk/politics/6f231f24-6bda-4515-ac53-452ca8e80e04

36. Human Rights Watch, 'Egypt: Rash Deaths in Custody', HRW Reports, 21 January 2015, http://www.hrw.org/news/2015/01/21/egypt-rash-deaths-custody

37. This conclusion is based on the author's observations, interactions and meetings with MPs involved in SSR initiatives (from both the upper and lower chambers) between February 2012 and April 2013.

38. Ali Larayedh, (former interior minister of Tunisia), conversation with the author, Geneva. 22 November 2012.

4. MILITARIES AND DEMOCRACY IN THE MIDDLE EAST: TOO MUCH AND TOO LITTLE

1. Goldberg, Ellis, 'Mubarakism Without Mubarak: Why Egypt's Military Will Not Embrace Democracy', *Foreign Affairs*, 11 February 2011.

2. Cook, Steven A., *Ruling but not Governing: The Military and Political Development in Egypt, Algeria, and Turkey*, Baltimore, MD: Johns Hopkins University Press, 2007, p. 15.

3. See Cronin, Stephanie, *Armies and State-Building in the Middle East: Politics, Nationalism and Military Reform*, London: I. B. Tauris, 2014; and Kandil, Hazem, *Soldiers, Spies, and Statesmen: Egypt's Road to Revolt*, London: Verso, 2012.

4. Rutherford, Bruce, *Egypt After Mubarak: Liberalism, Islam, and Democracy in the Arab World*, Princeton, NJ: Princeton University Press, 2013, p. 253.

5. Sayigh, Yezid, 'Above the State: The Officers' Republic in Egypt', Carnegie Endowment for International Peace, August 2012, http://carnegieendowment.org/files/officers_republic1.pdf

6. Bertelsmann Stiftung, 'BTI 2016—Egypt Country Report', No. 18, 2016; Harding, Henry, 'ANALYSIS: Egypt's Military-Economic Empire', *Middle East Eye*, 26 March 2016; Farid, Doaa, 'Egyptian Army's Economic Empire: Unidentified Market Share Yet High Impact', *Daily News Egypt*, 7 November 2015; Ottaway, Marina, 'Al-Sisi's Egypt: The Military Moves on the Economy,' Middle East Program Occasional Paper Series, Woodrow Wilson International Center for Scholars, 4–5, 2015; Wickberg, Sofia, 'Overview of Corruption and Anti-Corruption in Egypt', Transparency International, No. 4, 2015; Abdel Razek, Sherine, 'Military Inc.?' Al-Ahram Weekly, 1 January 2015; Hauslohner, Abigail, 'Egypt's Military Expands

Its Control of the Country's Economy', *Washington Post*, 16 March 2014; Kholaif, Dalia, 'The Egyptian Army's Economic Juggernaut', Al-Jazeera, 5 August 2013; Marshall, Shana, and Stacher, Joshua, 'Egypt's Generals and Transnational Capital,' *Middle East Report*, No. 262, 2012, p. 12; and Abul-Magd, Zeinab, 'The Generals' Secret: Egypt's Ambivalent Market', Sada, Carnegie Endowment for International Peace, 9 February 2012.

7. Linz, Juan J., *Totalitarianism and Authoritarian Regimes*, Boulder, CO: Lynne Rienner Publishers, 2006, p. 170.

8. Quinliven, James T., 'Coup Proofing: Its Practice and Consequences in the Middle East,' *International Security*, Vol. 24, No. 2, 1999, pp. 131–165.

9. The literature on the Turkish military is vast. Among the most prominent English-language works are: Lerner, Daniel and Robinson, Richard D., 'Swords into Ploughshares: The Turkish Army as a Modernizing Force', *World Politics*, Vol. 13, No. 1, 1960, pp. 19–44; Harris, George S., 'The Role of the Military in Turkish Politics, Part I', *Middle East Journal*, Vol. 19, No. 1, 1965, pp. 54–66; Brown, James, 'The Military and Society: The Turkish Case', *Middle Eastern Studies*, Vol. 25, No. 3, 1989, pp. 387–404; Hale, William, *Turkish Politics and the Military*, New York: Routledge, 1994; and Sakallıoğlu, Ümit Cizre, 'The Anatomy of the Turkish Military's Political Autonomy', *Comparative Politics* Vol. 29, No. 2, 1977, pp. 151–166.

10. Cook, Steven A., 'Where the Turkish Military Fails, Egypt's Succeds', *Foreign Affairs*, 19 July 2016, https://www.foreignaffairs.com/articles/turkey/2016-07-19/where-turkish-military-fails-egypts-succeeds

11. Gunay, Niyazi, 'Implementing the "February 28" Recommendations: A Scorecard', Research Notes No. 10, Washington Institute for Near East Policy, 2001.

12. As Peter D. Feaver has written, 'A military could never coup and yet still systematically undermine civilian control.' See Feaver, Peter D., 'The Civil-Military Problematique: Huntington, Janowitz, and the Question of Civil Control', *Armed Forces and Society*, Vol. 23, No. 2, 1996, p. 154.

13. Malinowski, Tom, 'Jefferson in Benghazi', *The New Republic*, 9 June 2011, https://newrepublic.com/article/89645/benghazi-libya-rebels

14. Huntington, Samuel P., *The Soldier and the State: The Theory and Politics of Civil-Military Relations*, Cambridge, MA: Harvard Belknap, 2002.

5. MODERN MAMLUKS AND ARAB COUNTER-REVOLUTION

1. Hourani, Albert, *Arabic Thought in the Liberal Age*, Oxford: Oxford University Press, 1962.

2. Filiu, Jean-Pierre, *The Arab Revolution: Ten Lessons from the Democratic Uprising*. London: Hurst, 2011.

3. Clot, André, *L'Egypte des Mamluks 1250–1517: L'empire des esclaves*, Paris: Tempus, 2009, pp. 41 and 70.

4. El Azhary Sonbol, Amira, *The New Mamluks: Egyptian Society and Modern Feudalism*, Ithaca, NY: Syracuse University Press, 2000.

5. Batatu, Hanna, *Syria's Peasantry, the Descendants of its Lesser Rural Notables and their Politics*. Princeton, NJ: Princeton University Press, 1999.

6. Cook, Steven, *Ruling but not Governing: The Military and Political Development in Egypt, Algeria and Turkey*, Baltimore, MD: Johns Hopkins University Press, 2007, p. 14.

7. The expression 'warlords' was first used by Jonathan Randal in his seminal 1983 *Going All the Way: Christian Warlords, Israeli Adventurers and American Bunglers*, reprinted in an updated edition in Randal, Jonathan, *The Tragedy of Lebanon*, New York: Just Books, 2012.

8. The reference book on that topic is Owen, Roger, *The Rise and Fall of Arab Presidencies for Life*, Cambridge, MA: Harvard University Press, 2012.

9. Front de libération nationale (FLN); Front islamique du salut (FIS).

10. *Décideurs* in French.

11. Haut comité d'État (HCE).

12. Groupe islamique armé (GIA).

13. Union générale du travail tunisien (UGTT).

6. TRASHING TRANSITIONS: THE ROLE OF ARAB MEDIA AFTER THE UPRISINGS

1. Lynch, Marc, *Voices of a New Arab Public: Iraq, Al-Jazeera, and Middle East Politics Today*, New York: Columbia University Press, 2006; Lynch, Marc, *The Arab Uprising: The Unfinished Revolutions of the New Middle East*, New York: Public Affairs, 2012; Eickelman, Dale and Anderson, Jon W. (eds), *New Media in the Muslim World: The Emerging Public Sphere*, Bloomington: Indiana University Press, 2003.

2. Portions of this chapter appeared previously in an earlier form in *Current History*, December 2015 and *The Journal of Democracy*, October 2014.

3. Khan, Zafrullah and Joseph, Brian, 'Pakistan After Musharraf: The Media Take Center Stage', *Journal of Democracy*, Vol. 19, Issue 4, 2008, pp. 32–37; Voltmer, Katrin, *The Media in Transitional Democracies*, New York: Polity Press, 2013, p. 6; also see Plattner, Marc F., 'Media and Democracy: The Long View', *Journal of Democracy*, Vol. 23, 2012, pp. 62–73.

4. Masoud, Tarek, 'Has the Door Closed on Arab Democracy?', *Journal of Democracy*, Volume 26, No. 1, 2015, pp. 74–87; El-Issawi, Fatima and Cammaerts, Bart, 'Shifting Journalistic Rules in Democratic Transitions: Lessons from Egypt', *Journalism*, Volume 17, No. 5, 2016, pp. 549–66.

5. Brumberg, Daniel, 'Transforming the Arab World's Protection-Racket Politics', *Journal of Democracy*, Volume 24, 2013, pp. 88–103.

6. Lynch, Marc; Freelon, Deen; and Aday, Sean, *Blogs and Bullets V: How Social Media Undermined Egypt's Transition*, Washington, DC: Peacetech Lab, 2016.

7. Brown, Nathan J., 'Egypt's Failed Transition', *Journal of Democracy*, Volume 24, No. 4, 2013, pp. 45–58.

8. Rugh, William, *Arab Mass Media*, New York: Praeger, 2004; Hafez, Kai (ed.), *Arab Media: Power and Weakness*, London: Bloomsbury Academic, 2008; Sakr, Naomi, *Arab Television Today*, New York: I. B. Tauris, 2007.

9. Lynch, Marc, *Voices of a New Arab Public*.

10. Lynch, Marc; Freelon, Deen; and Aday, Sean, 'Syria's Socially Mediated Civil War', United States Intitute of Peace, Peaceworks No. 91.

11. Lynch, Marc (ed.), *The Arab Uprisings Explained: New Contentious Politics in the Middle East*, New York: Columbia University Press, 2014.

12. Milton, Andrew K., 'Bound but Not Gagged: Media Reform in Democratic Transitions', *Comparative Political Studies*, Vol. 34, 2001, pp. 493–526.

13. Quoted by Kerim Bouzouita in Longo, Pietro and Meringolo, Azzurra (eds), *Tunisian Media Between Polarization and Compromise*, Rome: Reset Doc, 2015, p. 28.

14. Diamond, Larry, 'Liberation Technology', *Journal of Democracy*, Vol. 21, 2010, pp. 69–83; Howard, Philip and Hussain, Muzammil, 'The Role of Digital Media', *Journal of Democracy*, Vol. 22, 2011, pp. 35–48.

15. Lynch, Marc, 'After Egypt: The Promise and Limits of Social Media, *Perspectives on Politics*, Vol. 9, No. 2, 2011, pp. 301–310.

16. For a detailed discussion of this dataset, see Lynch, Marc; Freelon, Deen; and Aday, Sean, 'Syria in the Arab Spring', *Research and Politics*, Vol. 1, No. 3, 2014, DOI: 10.1177/2053168014549091; and Freelon, Deen; Lynch, Marc; and Aday, Sean, 'Online Fragmentation in Wartime: A Longitudinal Analysis of Tweets About Syria, 2011–13', *Annals of the American Academy of Political and Social Sciences*, Vol. 659, 2014, pp. 166–79. This subsection draws on data produced for a broader forthcoming research project conducted with Deen Freelon.

17. For more on the Syrian online ecosystem, see Lynch, Marc; Freelon, Deen; and Aday, Sean, 'Syria's Socially Mediated Civil War', United States Intitute of Peace, Peaceworks No. 91, 2014; O'Callaghan, Derek; Prucha, Nico; Greene, Derek; Conway, Maura; Carthy, Joe and Cunningham, Pádraig, 'Online Social Media in the Syria Conflict: Encompassing the Extremes and the In-Betweens', arXiv:1401.7535v3 [cs.SI] August, 2014, https://arxiv.org/abs/1401.7535.

18. Sakr, Naomi, *Transformations in Egyptian Journalism*. London: I. B. Tauris, 2013; Webb, Edward, *The Media in Tunisia and Egypt*, New York: Palgrave Pivots, 2014.

19. Aly, Ramy, 'Rebuilding Egyptian Media for a Democratic Future', *Arab Media and Society*, 31 May 2011, http://www.arabmediasociety.com/articles/downloads/20110531104306_Aly.pdf; Peterson, Mark A., 'Egypt's Media Ecology in a Time of Revolution', *Arab Media and Society*, 2011, http://www.arabmediasociety.com/?article=770.

20. Berger, Miriam, 'A Revolutionary Role or a Remnant of the Past? The Future of the Egyptian Journalist Syndicate after the January 25 Revolution', *Arab Media and Society*, Vol. 18, 10 June 2013, http://www.arabmediasociety.com/articles/downloads/20130612130820_Berger_Miriam.pdf; Maslin, Jared, 'Pro-regime journalists are shaping public opinion in Egypt', *Columbia Journalism Review*, 22 January 2015, http://www.cjr.org/b-roll/egypt_sisi_mona_iraqi.php.

21. Howeydi, Fahmy, 'Al-laʻb fi al-iʻlam ["Playing with the Media"]', *Al-Shorouk*, 20 August 2014.

22. Abdulla, Rasha, 'Egypt's Media in the Midst of Revolution', Carnegie Endowment for International Peace, July 2014, http://carnegieendowment.org/files/egypt_media_revolution.pdf

23. Alexander, Anne and Aoragh, Miriyam, 'Egypt's Unfinished Revolution: The Role of the Media Revisited', *International Journal of Communication*, Vol. 8, 2014, pp. 890–915.

24. Qallash, Yahya, 'Al-iʻlam al-masri baʻd 25 Yanayir wa 30 Yunyu ["The Egyptian Media After 25 January and 30 June"]', *Al-Ahram*, 19 October 2014.

25. Elmashed, Mohamed, 'We completely agree: Egyptian media in the era of President el-Sisi', Committee to Protect Journalists, 2015, https://cpj.org/x/5fe4

26. See the report of the Egypt Media Forum, 'Striving for Excellence in the Egyptian Media', 1–3 October 2014, published by *Arab Media and Society*, 12 January 2015, http://www.arabmediasociety.com/?article=853

27. Hamzawy, Amr, 'Asnaf al-ʻarab hasab iʻlam fashi ["Types of Arabs according to the Fascist Media"]', *Al-Masry al-Youm*, 19 July 2014; Egyptian journalist interviewed in Washington, DC, November 2014.

28. Haugbolle, Rikke H. and Cavatorta, Francesco, '"Vive la grande famille des médias tunisiens": Media reform, authoritarian resilience and societal responses in Tunisia', *Journal of North African Studies*, Vol. 17, No 1, 2012, pp. 97–112.

29. El-Issawi, Fatima, 'Tunisian Media in Transition', Carnegie Endowment for International Peace, 10 July 2012, http://carnegieendowment.org/2012/07/10/tunisian-media-in-transition-pub-48817; Longo and Meringolo (eds), *The Tunisian Media*.

30. Longo and Meringolo (eds), *The Tunisian Media*, pp. 9–10

31. Krishan, Mohamed, 'Al-iʻlam al-tunisi wa huma al-intikhabat ["The Tunisian Media and Election Fever"]', *Al-Quds al-Arabi*, 21 October 2014.

32. Bin Yusif, Tahir, 'Al-iʻlam al-tunisi min khadmat al-nizam ila khadmat al-ajandat ["Tunisia's Media From Serving the Regime to Serving Agendas"]', Tunis, 2013.

33. Baltayib, Nur al-Din, 'Al-iʻlam al-tunisi fi qalb al-maʻraka ["The Tunisian media in the heart of the battle"]', *Al-Akhbar*, 27 September 2014.

34. Younes, Najwa, 'Six of Tunisia's Ten Leading Television Networks Under Political Ownership', Tunisia Live, 13 July 2016, http://www.tunisia-live.net/2016/07/13/six-of-tunisias-ten-leading-television-networks-under-political-ownership/

35. Quoted by Rania Al-Zu'ubi, Al-Jazeera, 4 November 2013 (Arabic).
36. Personal interview, Tunis, 8 November 2014.
37. Quoted in *Al-Balad*, 3 November 2014 (Arabic).
38. Wollenberg, Anja and Pack, Jason, 'Rebels With a Pen: Observations on the Newly Emergent Media Landscape in Libya', *Journal of North African Studies*, Vol. 18, No. 3, 2013, pp. 191–210; El-Issawi, Fatima, 'Transitional Libyan Media: Free at Last?', Carnegie Endowment for International Peace, 14 May 2013, http://carnegieendowment.org/2013/05/14/transitional-libyan-media-free-at-last-pub-51747; Abou-Khalil, Naji and Hargreaves, Laurence, 'Libyan Television and its Influence on the Security Sector', US Institute of Peace Special Report, No. 364, 2015, https://www.usip.org/sites/default/files/SR364-The-Role-of-Media-in-Shaping-Libya%E2%80%99s-Security-Sector-Narratives.pdf

7. NOT READY FOR DEMOCRACY: MODERNISATION, PLURALISM, AND THE ARAB SPRING

1. The author thanks Jason Brownlee, Candelaria Garay, Ellen Lust, Amaney Jamal, Jeffrey Nugent, Jonah Schulhofer-Wohl, Andrew Reynolds, and Hassan Aly for helpful discussions and comments on this chapter, which develops arguments initially advanced in Brownlee, Jason; Masoud, Tarek; and Reynolds, Andrew, *The Arab Spring: Pathways of Repression and Reform*, Oxford: Oxford University Press, 2015. The title deliberately echoes the work of Charles Kurzman, with whom I respectfully disagree: Kurzman, Charles, 'Not Ready for Democracy? Theoretical and Historical Objections to the Concept of Prerequisites', *Sociological Analysis*, Vol. 1, 1998, pp. 1–12.
2. Lipset, Seymour Martin, 'Some Social Requisites of Democracy: Economic Development and Political Legitimacy', *American Political Science Review*, Vol. 53, No. 1, 1959, pp. 69–105; Boix, Carles and Stokes, Susan C., 'Endogenous Democratisation', *World Politics*, Vol. 55, No. 4, 2003, pp. 517–549.
3. Rustow, Dankwart A., 'Transitions to democracy: Toward a dynamic model', *Comparative Politics*, 1970, pp. 337–363.
4. Linz, Juan J. and Stepan, Alfred, *Problems of Democratic Transition and Consolidation: Southern Europe, South America, and Post-Communist Europe*, Baltimore, MD: Johns Hopkins University Press, 1996.
5. Brownlee, Masoud and Reynolds, *The Arab Spring*. A definition of transition completion similar to that of Linz and Stepan is offered by Bratton and Van de Walle: 'A transition to democracy can be said to have occurred only when a regime has been installed on the basis of a competitive election, freely and fairly conducted within a matrix of civil liberties, with results accepted by all participants.' Bratton, Michael and Van de Walle, Nicholas, *Democratic Experiments in Africa: Regime Transitions in Comparative Perspective*, Cambridge: Cambridge University Press, 1997, p. 194.

6. Huntington, Samuel P., *The Third Wave: Democratisation in the Late Twentieth Century*, Norman, OK: University of Oklahoma Press, 1993, pp. 266–267; Zakaria, Fareed, "'Why democracy took root in Tunisia and not Egypt,'" *Washington Post*, 30 October 2014, https://www.washingtonpost.com/opinions/fareed-zakaria-why-democracy-took-root-in-tunisia-and-not-egypt/2014/10/30/c5205adc-606a-11e4–9f3a-7e28799e0549_story.html

7. Kopstein, Jeffrey, '1989 as a Lens for the Communist Past and Post-Communist Future', *Contemporary European History*, Vol. 18, No. 3, 2009, pp. 289–302.

8. Przeworski, Adam, *Democracy and the Market: Political and Economic Reforms in Eastern Europe and Latin America, Cambridge: Cambridge University Press*, 1991.

9. Stepan, Alfred, *Rethinking Military Politics: Brazil and the Southern Cone*, Princeton, NJ: Princeton University Press, 1998.

10. LeBas, Adrienne, *From Protest to Parties: Party-building and Democratisation in Africa*, Oxford: Oxford University Press, 2011; Riedl, Rachel Beatty, *Authoritarian Origins of Democratic Party Systems in Africa*, Cambridge: Cambridge University Press, 2014.

11. Kurzman, Charles, 'Not Ready for Democracy? Theoretical and Historical Objections to the Concept of Prerequisites', *Sociological Analysis*, Vol. 1, 1998, pp. 1–12.

12. Kornhauser, William, *The Politics of Mass Society*, Abingdon: Routledge, 2013; Rueschemeyer, Dietrich; Stephens, Evelyne Huber; and Stephens, John D., *Capitalist Development and Democracy*, Cambridge: Cambridge University Press, 1992; Cohen, Jean L. and Arato, Andrew, *Civil Society and Political Theory*, Boston, MA: MIT Press, 1994; and Hechter, Michael C., 'From Class to Culture', *American Journal of Sociology*, Vol. 110, No. 2, 2004, pp. 400–445.

13. Power, Timothy, "'Theorizing a Moving Target: O'Donnell's Changing Views of Postauthoritarian Regimes'", University of Oxford, unpublished working paper, 19 March 2012. http://kellogg.nd.edu/odonnell/papers/power.pdf.

14. Singh, Naunihal, *Seizing Power: The Strategic Logic of Military Coups*, Baltimore, MD: Johns Hopkins University Press, 2014, p. 3. See also Marinov, Nikolay and Goemans, Hein, 'Coups and Democracy', *British Journal of Political Science*, Vol. 44, No. 4, 2014, pp. 799–825.

15. Gelvin, James L., *The Arab Uprisings: What Everyone Needs to Know*, Oxford: Oxford University Press, 2015, p. 68.

16. Angrist, Michele Penner, 'Understanding the Success of Mass Civic Protest in Tunisia', *The Middle East Journal*, Vol. 67, No. 4, 2013, pp. 547–564.

17. Droz-Vincent, Philippe, 'Authoritarianism, Revolutions, Armies and Arab Regime Transitions', *The International Spectator*, Vol. 46, No. 2, 2011, p. 5.

18. Angrist, 'Understanding the Success of Mass Civic Protest in Tunisia', p. 551.

19. Kandil, Hazem, *Soldiers, Spies and Statesmen: Egypt's Road to Revolt*, London: Verso, 2012, p. 9; McDermott, Anthony, *Egypt from Nasser to Mubarak: A Flawed Revolution, Vol. 3*, Abingdon: Routledge, 2012, p. 16.

20. Kandil, *Soldiers, Spies and Statesmen*, p. 7

21. Powell, Jonathan M. and Thyne, Clayton L., 'Global Instances of Coups from 1950 to 2010: A New Dataset', *Journal of Peace Research*, Vol. 48, No. 2, 2011, 249–259. The data has been updated to 2014 and is available at: http://www.jonathanmpowell.com/coup-detat-dataset.html

22. Naunihal Singh analyses coups from 1950 to 2000 (*Seizing Power*, 2014). His data for that shorter period also comprises 471 cases, meaning that the Powell and Thyne data is missing some cases that Singh picks up.

23. Data available at: http://data.worldbank.org/data-catalog/world-development-indicators

24. The *Military Balance* for 2013 has Tunisia at a population of 10,732,900, with a total armed forces of 47,800 (35,800 active duty, and 12,000 paramilitaries). No figure on reservists is recorded.

25. Jenkins, J. Craig and Kposowa, Augustine J., 'Explaining Military Coups d'État: Black Africa, 1957–1984', *American Sociological Review*, 1990, pp. 861–875; Bratton, Michael and Van de Walle, Nicholas, *Democratic Experiments in Africa: Regime Transitions in Comparative Perspective*, Cambridge: Cambridge University Press, 1997, p. 215.

26. Abdel-Malek, Anouar, *Egypt—Military Society: The Army Regime, the Left, and Social Change Under Nasser*, New York: Random House, 1968; Harb, Imad, 'The Egyptian Military in Politics: Disengagement or Accommodation?' *The Middle East Journal*, 2003, pp. 269–290; Cook, Steven A., *Ruling but not Governing: The Military and Political Development in Egypt, Algeria, and Turkey*, Baltimore, MD: Johns Hopkins University Press, 2007, p. 8.

27. El-Shimy, Yasser Magdy, 'Fumbled Democracy: Why Egypt's Transition Floundered', Presentation, Midwestern Political Science Association, 2015.

28. Soliman, Samer, *The Autumn of Dictatorship: Fiscal Crisis and Political Change in Egypt Under Mubarak*, Stanford, CA: Stanford University Press, 2011; Springborg, Robert D., 'Egypt's Future: Yet Another Turkish Model?', *The International Spectator*, Vol. 49, No. 1, 2014, pp. 1–6; Abul-Magd, Zeinab, '"The Egyptian Republic of Retired Generals"', *Foreign Policy*, Middle East Channel, 28 May 2012, http://foreignpolicy.com/2012/05/08/the-egyptian-republic-of-retired-generals/

29. Brownlee, Jason, *Democracy Prevention: The Politics of the US-Egyptian Alliance*, Cambridge: Cambridge University Press, 2012, p. 169; Stepan, Alfred; Linz, Juan J. and Yadav, Yogendra, *Crafting State Nations: India and Other Multinational Democracies*, Baltimore, MA: Johns Hopkins University Press, 2011; Ware, L. B, 'The Role of the Tunisian Military in the Post-Bourguiba Era', *Middle East Journal*, Vol. 39, No. 1, 1985, pp. 27–47.

30. Droz-Vincent, Philippe, 'Authoritarianism, Revolutions, Armies and Arab Regime Transitions', *The International Spectator*, Vol. 46, No. 2, 2011, p. 18; Grewal, Sharan, '"Why Tunisia Didn't Follow Egypt's Path"', *The Monkey Cage*, 4 February

2015, http://www.washingtonpost.com/blogs/monkey-cage/wp/2015/02/04/why-egypt-didnt-follow-tunisias-path/

31. See "'Wazīr al-dākhiliya al-sābiq yuhadid bi-inqilāb 'askarī idhā fāzat al-nahḍa fi al-intikhābāt ('Former interior minister threatens military coup if Ennahda wins elections')'", France 24, 6 May 2011, http://www.france24.com/ar/20110505-tunisia-minister-interior-army-coup-d-etat-nahda-islamist-election

32. Boulby, Marion, 'The Islamic Challenge: Tunisia Since Independence', Third World Quarterly, Vol. 10, No. 2, 1988, pp. 590–614; Marzouki, Moncef. 'Winning Freedom', Index on Censorship, Vol. 18, No. 1, 1989, pp. 23–25.

33. Nassif, Hicham Bou, 'A Military Besieged: The Armed Forces, the Police, and the Party in Bin 'Ali's Tunisia, 1987–2011', International Journal of Middle East Studies, Vol. 47, No. 1, 2015, pp. 65–87.

34. Powell and Thyne, 'Global Instances of Coups from 1950 to 2010'.

35. Global Militarization Index, Bonn International Center for Conversion, 2015, http://gmi.bicc.de

36. Details of the index's construction, data sources, and the relative weighting of each of the six factors is available at: http://gmi.bicc.de

37. 2013 Global Militarization Index rankings, sorted by GMI scores, can be viewed at: http://gmi.bicc.de/index.php?page=ranking-table?year=2013&sort=index_asc

38. Brooks, Risa, 'Abandoned at the Palace: Why the Tunisian Military Defected from the Ben Ali Regime in January 2011', Journal of Strategic Studies, Vol. 36, No. 2, 2003, pp. 205–220.

39. Nassif, Hicham Bou, 'Generals and Autocrats: How Coup-Proofing Predetermined the Military Elite's Behavior in the Arab Spring', Political Science Quarterly, Vol. 130, No. 2, 2015, pp. 245–275.

40. 'Ba'd hadīthahu 'an muḥāwla inqilāb siyāsī 'askarī amnī: 'adnān munṣir yanfi itihāmahu liljaysh' ('After speaking of attempted political, military, and security coup,' 'Adnān Munṣir denies accusing the army,' al-Ṣabāḥ News (Tunis), 28 February 2014.

41. 'Maya Jribi: La dissolution de l'ANC mènera tout droit à la guerre civile,' African Manager, 8 July 2013, http://www.africanmanager.com/152998.html

42. Joyce, Robert, "'Live Blog: NCA Member Mohamed Brahmi Assassinated'", Tunisia Live, 25 July 2013, http://www.tunisia-live.net/2013/07/25/nca-member-mohamed-brahmi-assassinated. Key paragraph: "'Contrary to a Mosaique FM report, Najwa Makhlouf of the UGTT labor union says that the union has not called for the dissolution of the NCA, but has only called a general strike.'"

43. Amara, Tarek, 'Tunisia's Biggest Union Tells Islamist-Led Government to Quit', Reuters, 30 July 2013, http://www.reuters.com/article/2013/07/30/us-tunisia-protests-idUSBRE96T0WM20130730. See also, al-Aswad, Ḥabīb, 'Wazīr al-dākhiliya al-Tūnisī musta'id lil-istiqāla' ('The Tunisian Interior Minister is Ready

to Resign'), al-Bayān, 30 July 2013, http://www.albayan.ae/one-world/arabs/2013-07-30-1.1932963

44. David, Steven R., *Third World Coups d'État and International Security*, Baltimore, MD: Johns Hopkins University Press, 1987, p. 5.

45. Karl, Terry Lynn., 'Dilemmas of Democratisation in Latin America', *Comparative Politics*, Vol. 23, No. 1, 1990, pp. 1–21.

46. Stepan, *Rethinking Military Politics*, p. 128. See also Rubin, Humberto, 'One Step Away from Democracy', *Journal of Democracy*, Vol. 1, No. 4, 1990, pp. 59–61; King, Daniel and LoGerfo, Jim, 'Thailand: Toward Democratic Stability', *Journal of Democracy*, Vol. 7, No. 1, 1996, pp. 102–117; Trinkunas, Harold A., 'Ensuring Democratic Civilian Control of the Armed Forces in Asia', East-West Center Occasional Papers, 1999; and Tudor, Maya, 'Renewed Hope in Pakistan?', *Journal of Democracy*, Vol. 25, No. 2, 2014, pp. 105–118.

47. Stepan, *Rethinking Military Politics*.

48. Esposito, John L.; Sonn, Tamara; and Voll, John O. *Islam and Democracy After the Arab Spring*, Oxford: Oxford University Press, 2015; Bellin, Eva Rana, 'Drivers of Democracy: Lessons from Tunisia', Crown Center Middle East Brief, No. 25, 2013, p. 3.

49. Brown, Nathan J., 'Egypt's Failed Transition', *Journal of Democracy*, Vol. 24, No. 4, 2013, pp. 45–58; Brumberg, Daniel, 'Transforming the Arab World's Protection-Racket Politics', *Journal of Democracy*, Vol. 24, No. 3, 2013, pp. 88–103.

50. Stepan and Linz, *Problems of Democratic Transition and Consolidation*, p. 23.

51. 'Lajna waṭaniyya limufāwaḍat niẓām Mubārak (National committee to negotiate with the Mubarak regime)', *Al-Jazeera* (Doha, Qatar), 30 January 2011. Available at: http://goo.gl/RSUfAP

52. Nūrā Fakhrī, "Abd al-Ḥalīm Qandīl: Min ḥaq Magdī Ḥussayn khawḍ intikhābāt Kifāya ('Abd al-Ḥalīm Qandīl: it is Magdī Ḥussayn's right to run in Enough's elections)', al-Yawm al-Sābi' (Cairo), 12 January 2011, http://goo.gl/axAfEC

53. Tunisian results available at: http://www.tunisia-live.net/2011/11/14/tunisian-election-final-results-tables. Egyptian seat breakdowns drawn from Mamdūḥ Sha'bān, Su'ād Ṭanṭāwī, and 'Alī Muḥammad 'Alī, '235 maq'adan lil-ḥurriya wa al-'adāla wa ḥulafā'ahu wa 123 lil-nūr wa 38 lil-wafd wa 34 lil-kutla fi barlamān al-thawra (235 seats for Freeedom and Justice and its allies and 123 for [Party of] Light and 38 for the Wafd and 34 for the [Egyptian] Bloc in the parliament of the revolution)', *al-Aḥrām al-Raqamī* (al-Ahrām Digital), 22 January 2012. Available at: http://digital.ahram.org.eg/Policy.aspx?Serial=774569. See also the website of the Higher Elections Commission (http://www.elections.eg/, http://elections2011.eg).

54. The importance of empirical pluralism as a determinant of democratic consolidation *may* seem to run contrary to earlier research that showed that increasing party system fractionalisation—a measure of pluralism—was correlated with democratic

breakdown, at least in presidential systems such as Egypt (see, for example, Stepan, Alfred and Skach, Cindy, 'Constitutional Frameworks and Democratic Consolidation: Parliamentarianism versus Presidentialism', *World Politics*, Vol. 46, No. 1, 1993, pp. 1–22). However, research by Cheibub and Mainwaring and Perez-Linan does not find this to be the case. As Mainwairing and Perez-Linan report, 'In presidential systems, party system fragmentation might help explain the *stability* of democratic and semi-democratic regimes.' Cheibub, José Antonio, 'Presidentialism and Democratic Performance', in Reynolds, Andrew, *The Architecture of Democracy: Constitutional Design, Conflict Management, and Democracy*, Oxford: Oxford University Press, 2002, pp. 104–140; Perez-Linan, Anabel and Mainwaring, Scott, 'Democratic Breakdown and Survival in Latin America, 1945–2005', in Brinks, Daniel; Leiras, Marcelo; and Mainwaring, Scott (eds), *Reflections on Uneven Democracies: The Legacy of Guillermo O'Donnell*, Baltimore, MD: Johns Hopkins University Press, 2014, p. 31.

55. Brownlee, Jason, 'Portents of Pluralism: How Hybrid Regimes Affect Democratic Transitions', *American Journal of Political Science*, Vol. 53, No. 3, 2009, pp. 515–532.

56. Przeworski, Adam, *Democracy and the Market: Political and Economic Reforms in Eastern Europe and Latin America*, Cambridge: Cambridge University Press, 1991.

57. O'Donnell, Guillermo; Schmitter Philippe C., and Whitehead, Laurence, *Transitions from Authoritarian Rule: Southern Europe, Vol. 1*, Baltimore, MD: Johns Hopkins University Press, 1986.

58. Lippmann, Walter, 'The Indispensable Opposition', *Atlantic Monthly*, Vol. 164, 1939, pp. 186–190.

59. Emphasis added.

60. James Madison, Federalist No. 10, 'The Same Subject Continued: The Union as a Safeguard Against Domestic Faction and Insurrection,' 23 November 1787, http://thomas.loc.gov/home/histdox/fed_10.html

61. Bellin, Eva Rana, 'Drivers of Democracy: Lessons from Tunisia', Crown Center Middle East Brief, No. 25, 2013; Stepan, Alfred., 'Tunisia's Transition and the Twin Tolerations', *Journal of Democracy*, Vol. 23, No. 2, 2012, pp. 89–103. See also Lust, Ellen and Khatib, Lina, '"The Transformation of Arab Activism"', POMED Policy Brief Series, May 2014.

62. Stepan, 'Tunisia's Transition and the Twin Tolerations', p. 93.

63. Bratton, Michael and Van de Walle, Nicholas, *Democratic Experiments in Africa: Regime Transitions in Comparative Perspective*, Cambridge: Cambridge University Press, 1997; Lust-Okar, Ellen, *Structuring Conflict in the Arab World: Incumbents, Opponents, and Institutions*, Cambridge: Cambridge University Press, 2005; Brownlee, Jason, 'Portents of Pluralism: How Hybrid Regimes Affect Democratic Transitions', *American Journal of Political Science*, Vol. 53, No. 3, 2009, pp. 515–532.

64. Lust, Ellen and Waldner, David, 'Parties in Transitional Democracies: Authoritarian Legacies and Post-Authoritarian Challenges', Technical Report, University of Gothenburg and University of Virginia, 2015.

65. Brownlee, Masoud and Reynolds, *The Arab Spring*, p. 190.

66. Ibid.

67. Ibid., p. 207.

68. Stepan, Alfred and Linz, Juan J., 'Democratization Theory and the "Arab Spring"', *Journal of Democracy*, Vol. 24, No. 2, 2013, pp. 15–30.

69. Brumberg, Daniel, 'Egypt on Precipice? Moving Beyond Crisis', *Al Monitor*, 26 June 2013, http://www.al-monitor.com/pulse/originals/2013/06/egypt-june-30-muslim-brotherhood-opposition-legitimacy.html

70. Hagopian, Frances, 'Parties and Voters in Emerging Democracies', in Boix, Carles and Stokes, Susan (eds), *The Oxford Handbook of Comparative Politics*, Oxford: Oxford University Press, 2007, pp. 583–84.

71. O'Donnell, Schmitter and Whitehead, *Transitions from Authoritarian Rule*.

72. Pepinsky, Thomas B., 'Political Islam and the Limits of the Indonesian Model', *Taiwan Journal of Democracy*, Vol. 10, No. 1, 2014, pp. 105–121.

73. Riedl, Rachel Beatty, *Authoritarian Origins of Democratic Party Systems in Africa*, Cambridge: Cambridge University Press, 2014, p. 15; Voltmer, Katrin, *Mass Media and Political Communication in New Democracies*, Abingdon: Routledge, 2006, p. 10; and LeBas, Adrienne, *From Protest to Parties: Party-building and Democratisation in Africa*, Oxford: Oxford University Press, 2011, p. 256.

74. Tsai, Lily L., 'Solidary Groups, Informal Accountability, and Local Public Goods Provision in Rural China', *American Political Science Review*, Vol. 101, No. 2, 2007, p. 355.

75. See Wickham, Carrie Rosefsky, *Mobilizing Islam: Religion, Activism, and Political Change in Egypt*, New York: Columbia University Press, 2003; and Wickham, Carrie Rosefsky, 'Interests, Ideas, and Islamist Outreach in Egypt', in Wiktorowicz, Quintan (ed.), *Islamic Activism: A Social Movement Theory Approach*, Bloomington, IN: Indiana University Press, 2004.

76. Wickham, 'Interests, Ideas, and Islamist Outreach in Egypt', p. 233.

77. Posusney, Marsha Pripstein, 1997, *Labor and the State in Egypt: Workers, Unions, and Economic Restructuring*, New York: Columbia University Press, 1997; Bianchi, Robert, 'The Corporatization of the Egyptian Labor Movement', *Middle East Journal*, Vol. 40, No. 3, 1986, pp. 429–444; Shehata, Samer Said, *Shop Floor Culture and Politics in Egypt*, Albany, NY: SUNY Press, 2009.

78. McCarthy, John D. and Zald, Mayer N., 'Resource Mobilization and Social Movements: A Partial Theory', *American Journal of Sociology*, 1977, pp. 1212–1241; Wiktorowicz, Quintan (ed.), *Islamic Activism: A Social Movement Theory Approach*, Bloomington, IN: Indiana University Press, 2004.

79. Angrist, Michele Penner, *Party Building in the Modern Middle East*, Seattle,

WA:University of Washington Press, 2011, p. 16; Lust, Ellen and Waldner, David, 'Parties in Transitional Democracies: Authoritarian Legacies and Post-Authoritarian Challenges', Technical Report, University of Gothenburg and University of Virginia, 2015.

80. Malinowski, Tom, 'The New Tunisian Model of Governance', Bureau of Democracy, Human Rights, and Labor, United States Department of State, 2 September 2015, http://www.state.gov/j/drl/rls/rm/2015/246584.htm. See also: http://jamaity. org/association/la-ligue-tunisienne-des-droits-de-lhomme/

81. Posusney, *Labor and the State in Egypt;* Bellin, Eva Rana, *Stalled Democracy: Capital, Labor, and the Paradox of State-sponsored Development*, Ithaca, NY: Cornell University Press, 2002, p. 106.

82. Beinin, Joel and Vairel, Frédéric, *Social Movements, Mobilisation, and Contestation in the Middle East and North Africa*, Stanford, CA: Stanford University Press, 2013; Toensing, Chris, 'Tunisian Labor Leaders Reflect Upon Revolt', *Middle East Report*, Vol. 25, 2011, http://www.merip.org/mer/mer258/tunisian-labor-leaders-reflect-upon-revolt-0

83. Hefny, Mostafa Hani, 'The Material Politics of Revolution and Counter-Revolution: Labor and Democratization in Egypt: 2011–2013', Columbia University, 2014, p. 31. For the importance of labour as a driver of democratic transitions, see Keck, Margaret E., *The Workers' Party and Democratization in Brazil*, New Haven, CT: Yale University Press, 1995.

84. 'Study on Civil Society Organizations in Tunisia', Foundation for the Future, Tunis, January 2013, p. 7. See also Ifāda's website: http://www.ifeda.org.tn/ar/

85. 31See: 'Ibrāhīm al-Hinaydī: al-shaʿb asqaṭ niẓāman fāsidan fī 30 yūnū wa dustūr 2014 ḥaẓā bil-shaʿbiya' ('Ibrahim Hinaydi: the people have overthrown a corrupt regime on 30 June and the constitution of 2014 enjoys popularity'), Egyptian State Information Service, 5 November 2014, http://www.sis.gov.eg/Ar/Templates/ Articles/tmpArticles.aspx?CatID=5395#.Vdn47NNViko. See also: 'Egypt's human rights record comes under scrutiny in UPR,' *Aswat Masriya* (Cairo), 31 January 2015, http://en.aswatmasriya.com/news/view.aspx?id=07b7b081-eb0f-4065-9f82-d6f47df367ea

86. Howard, Marc Morjé, *The Weakness of Civil Society in Post-Communist Europe*, Cambridge: Cambridge University Press, 2003.

87. Brownlee, Masoud,and Reynolds, *The Arab Spring*, p. 205.

88. Ibid.

89. Ross, Michael L., 'Does Oil Hinder Democracy?', *World Politics*, Vol. 53, No. 3, 2001, pp. 325–361; Lust-Okar, Ellen, 'Elections Under Authoritarianism: Preliminary Lessons from Jordan', *Democratization*, Vol. 13, No. 3, 2006, pp. 456–71; Schwedler, Jillian, *Faith in Moderation: Islamist Parties in Jordan and Yemen*, Cambridge: Cambridge University Press, 2006.

90. Forbis, Jeremy Scott, 'Organized Civil Society: A Cross National Evaluation of

the Socio-political Effects of Non-governmental Organization Density on Governmental Corruption, State Terror, and Anti-government Demonstrations', PhD Thesis, Ohio State University, 2008.

91. Mauritius' unrealistically low score (even lower than China or North Korea) highlights the likelihood of measurement error in the underlying source of the data, the Yearbook of International Organizations (published by the Union of International Associations). See Forbis's work for details.

92. Source: ʿAdad al-jawāmiʿ wa al-masājid al-muṣādiq ʿalā tarsīmihā ḍimn qāʾimat al-maʿālim alatī tanfiq ʿalayhā al-dawla, Tunisia Ministry of Religious Affairs, 2009. Document available from author. Thanks to Duncan Pickard for assistance in acquiring this information.

93. Source: Egyptian Ministry of Religious Endowments (Wizārat al-Awqāf), reported in Egypt in Figures 2011 (Miṣr fi Arqām), available at: http://www.sis. gov.eg/newvr/egyptinfigures/.

94. Putnam, Robert D., Bowling Alone: The Collapse and Revival of American Community, Simon and Schuster, 2000; and Putnam, Robert D.; Leonardi, Robert; and Y Nanetti, Raffaella, Making Democracy Work: Civic Traditions in Modern Italy, Princeton, NJ: Princeton University Press, 1994.

95. Cohen, Jean L. and Arato, Andrew, Civil Society and Political Theory, Boston, MA: MIT Press, 1994, p. 18.

96. Brownlee, Masoud and Reynolds, The Arab Spring, p. 204.

97. Lipset, Seymour Martin, 'Some Social Requisites of Democracy: Economic Development and Political Legitimacy', American Political Science Review, Vol. 53, No. 1, 1959, p. 84; Rueschemeyer, Dietrich; Stephens, Evelyne Huber; and Stephens, John D., Capitalist Development and Democracy, Cambridge: Cambridge University Press, 1992, p. 6; and Hechter, Michael C., 'From Class to Culture', American Journal of Sociology, Vol. 110, No. 2, 2004, pp. 400–445.

98. Lerner, Daniel, The Passing of Traditional Society: Modernizing the Middle East, New York: Free Press, 1958; Liska, Allen E., 'Modeling the Relationships Between Macro Forms of Social Control', Annual Review of Sociology, 1997, pp. 39–61; and Geertz, Clifford, 'The Rotating Credit Association: A 'Middle Rung' in Development', Economic Development and Cultural Change, Vol. 10, No. 3, 1962, pp. 241–263.

99. A binned scatterplot provides 'a non-parametric way of visualising the relationship between two variables,' by grouping 'the x-axis variable into equal-sized bins, [and] comput[ing] the mean of the x-axis and y-axis variables within each bin.' See Michael Stepner, 'BINSCATTER: Module to generate binned scatterplots', Stata package, available from http://fmwww.bc.edu/RePEc/bocode/b. Per capita GDP drawn from the World Bank's World Development Indicators. Forbis, 'Organized Civil Society'.

100. 2014 urbanisation and industrialisation figures drawn from the CIA World

Factbook entries for Tunisia and Egypt. Per capita GDP (US$) drawn from World Bank estimates for 2013: http://data.worldbank.org/indicator/NY.GDP.PCAP.CD

101. Goldberg, Ellis, 'The Foundations of State-Labor Relations in Contemporary Egypt', *Comparative Politics*, 1992, pp. 147–161; Utvik, Bjorn Olav, 'Filling the Vacant Throne of Nasser: The Economic Discourse of Egypt's Islamist Opposition', *Arab Studies Quarterly*, Vol. 17, No. 4, 1995, p. 29.

102. Bellin, *Stalled Democracy*.

103. Clark, William Roberts, Golder, Matt; and Golder, Sona Nadenichek, *Principles of Comparative Politics*, Washington, D.C.: CQ Press, 2012. See also Grubbs, Larry, *Secular Missionaries: Americans and African Development in the 1960s*, Amherst, MA: University of Massachusetts Press, 2009. For a review of modernisation theory and its critics.

104. Coleman, James S. and Halisi, C. R. D., 'American Political Science and Tropical Africa: Universalism vs. Relativism', *African Studies Review*, 1983, pp. 25–62. See also Keshavarzian, Arang, *Bazaar and State in Iran: The Politics of the Tehran Marketplace*, Cambridge: Cambridge University Press, 2007, pp. 47–50.

105. Inglehart, Ronald and Welzel, Christian, 'Changing Mass Priorities: The Link Between Modernisation and Democracy', *Perspectives on Politics*, Vol. 8, No. 2, 2010, pp. 551–567.

106. Waterbury, John. 'Democracy Without Democrats? The Potential for Political Liberalization in the Middle East', in Salamé, Ghassan, *Democracy Without Democrats?: Renewal of Politics in the Muslim World*, London: I. B. Tauris, 1994, pp. 23–47.

107. Przeworski, Adam and Limongi, Fernando, 'Modernisation: Theories and Facts', *World Politics*, Vol. 49, No. 2, 1997, pp. 155–183.

8. INTERNATIONAL ASSISTANCE TO ARAB SPRING TRANSITIONS

1. From 2011 to 2017, I was Senior Adviser on Constitution Building at International IDEA (based first out of Cairo and then out of Tunis), and in that capacity, I was involved in many of the transitions that took place in the Arab region, including in Tunisia, Libya, Egypt and Yemen. Many of the observations that I make in this chapter are based on my discussions with senior policy makers and constitutional drafters. The observation that this particular footnote relates to is also based on my discussions with a senior international official who had also been following transitions in the Arab region since the year 2000. Senior UN official, Interview with the author, February 2014.

2. For more on this last issue, see Landau, David, 'The Reality of Social Rights Enforcement', *Harvard International Law Journal*, Vol. 53, No. 1, 2012.

3. For more on the impact that procedural design can have on the outcome of a constitutional reform process, see Al-Ali, Zaid, 'Five Years of Arab Constitutional

Reform: Balancing Process Requirements with the Demands of Fragile Democratic Traditions', in Alkebsi, Abdelwahhab; Sparre, Charlotta; and Brown, Nathan J. (eds), *Reconstructing the Middle East*, Abingdon: Routledge, 2016.

4. This is in stark contrast to transitions that took place in other parts of the world (e.g. South Africa, Kenya, etc.) where they were anticipated well in advance, and restrictions on speech were loose enough to permit for progressive forces to formulate their positions and develop their (negotiation and drafting) skills so as to allow a more orderly transition.

5. An unofficial translation of Libya's interim constitution is available here: http://www.security-legislation.ly/node/32001. The Arabic original is available here: http://www.constitutionnet.org/ar/files/interim_constitution-3_aug_2011_arabic_signed.pdf. For a contemporaneous analysis of the interim constitution, see Al-Ali, Zaid, 'Libya's Draft Interim Constitution: An Analysis', Constitutionnet, 5 September 2011, http://www.constitutionnet.org/news/libyas-draft-interim-constitution-analysis

6. See S/RES/2009 (2011).

7. See paragraph 12 of S/RES/2009 (2011).

8. See S/2011/727 (2011).

9. For an account of Ian Martin's experiences as Special Representative see Martin, Ian, 'The United Nations' Role in the First Year of the Transition', in Cole, Peter and McQuinn, Brian (eds) *The Libyan Revolution and its Aftermath*, London: Hurst, 2015; Mitri, Tarek, 'Insight into the UN in Libya: Interview with Dr. Tarek Mitri, Head of the United Nations Support Mission in Libya (UNSMIL)', Issam Fares Institute for Public Policy and International Affairs, American University of Beirut, October 2012; see also Bartu, Peter, 'Libya's Political Transition: The Challenges of Mediation', International Peace Institute, December 2014.

10. Libya was traditionally subdivided into three provinces: western Tripolitana province (the most populous by far), eastern Cyrenaica province (the second most populous) and southern Fezzan province (the least populous by far).

11. See, for example, The Carter Center, 'General National Congress Elections in Libya: Final Report', 7 July 2012, https://www.cartercenter.org/resources/pdfs/news/peace_publications/election_reports/libya-070712-final-rpt.pdf. The Secretary General of the United Nations wrote in a report to the Security Council that 'amid the constraints imposed by a compressed electoral timetable, a volatile security environment and lack of previous experience in electoral administration, the elections were a remarkable achievement'; see S/2012/675.

12. See Mezran, Karim; Lamen, Fadel; and Knecht, Eric, 'Post-revolutionary Politics in Libya: Inside the General National Congress', Atlantic Council, 2013, http://www.atlanticcouncil.org/publications/issue-briefs/post-revolutionary-politics-in-libya-inside-the-general-national-congress.

13. See Bartu, Peter, 'Libya's Political Transition: The Challenges of Mediation',

International Peace Institute, December 2014, https://www.ipinst.org/wp-content/uploads/publications/ipi_e_pub_mediation_libya.pdf.

14. Amongst other problems, the government took close to no action to integrate irregular militias into the armed forces. A series of initiatives were launched and abandoned, often within months, allowing security concerns and challenges to fester over a period of years, eventually spiralling totally out of control. See Sayigh, Yezid, 'Crumbling States: Security Sector Reform in Libya and Yemen', Carnegie Middle East Center, June 2015, http://carnegie-mec.org/2015/06/18/crumbling-states-security-sector-reform-in-libya-and-yemen-pub-60422

15. See 'Seeking Security: Public Opinion Survey in Libya', National Democratic Institute and JMW Consulting, November 2013 (which notes that in May 2013, 37 per cent of Libyans described the GNC's performance as either poor or very poor, and that that figure had increased to 60 per cent in September 2013); see also Mezran, Karim and Pack, Jason 'Libya Stability at Risk', *Foreign Policy*, 2 May 2013, http://foreignpolicy.com/2013/05/02/libyan-stability-at-risk/; Shennib, Ghaith, 'Libyan PM dismisses army officer's plot to "rescue" country', Reuters, 14 February 2014, http://uk.reuters.com/article/libya-crisis-idINDEE-A1D0GW20140214; 'Libya: Wide popular opposition to the GNC's decision to extend its mandate', Mostapha al-Jaree', al-Maghreb, 28 December 2013. See also ICRC, 'Libya: Struggle to survive as services collapse', International Committee of the Red Cross, 9 December 2015, https://www.icrc.org/en/document/libya-struggle-survive-services-collapse

16. The Carter Center, 'The 2014 Constitutional Drafting Assembly Elections in Libya', June 2014, https://www.cartercenter.org/resources/pdfs/news/peace_publications/election_reports/libya-06112014-final-rpt.pdf.

17. See Constitutional Amendment No. (1) of 2012–13, March 2012.

18. An unofficial translation of the first draft is available here: http://www.constitutionnet.org/vl/item/libya-initial-draft-constitution-2014-english.

19. The October 2015 draft is available (in Arabic) here: http://www.constitutionnet.org/ar/vl/item/Lybia-Draft-Constitution-2015.

20. An official copy of the April 2016 draft is available here: http://www.constitutionnet.org/ar/vl/item/Libya-draft-constitution-19-april-2016-ar. For an unofficial English-language translation see: http://www.constitutionnet.org/vl/item/draft-libyan-constitution-april-2016-non-official-english-translation.

21. Since the dispute emerged, the two bodies have been trying to wrestle control over a number of vital services and resources from each other, including control over the Central Bank and oil export terminals.

22. For more, see Eljarh, Mohamed, 'Can the United Nations Save the Day in Libya?', *Foreign Policy*, 4 July 2014, http://foreignpolicy.com/2014/07/04/can-the-united-nations-save-the-day-in-libya/

23. There was further confusion when some members of the GNC and of the HoR signed an announcement of general principles on 6 December 2015 which called for the restoration of the monarchy's constitution, the establishment of a committee that would be responsible for amending that text, and for the formation of a government of national unity without the involvement of the United Nations. In November 2015, allegations were made that Mr León had spent much of his time as Special Representative coordinating with the UAE (which had a strong interest in the outcome of the negotiations) and negotiating with the Emirati government for a lucrative position as director of its diplomatic academy.

24. Most recently, in August 2016, the HoR rejected the national unity government that had been formed pursuant to the political agreement. It is unclear, at the time of writing, what options exist to move the process forward at this stage.

25. In particular, a breakdown in Yemen's state authority could threaten access to the Gulf of Aden and therefore to the Suez Canal, a major artery for international shipping. See for example 'Egypt will interfere militarily if Yemen's Bab al-Mandab strait is blocked: Suez Canal head', Ahram Online, 4 February 2015, http://english.ahram.org.eg/News/122219.aspx; Hussein, Walaa, 'Houthis' advance threatens Red Sea countries', al-Monitor, 1 December 2014, http://www.al-monitor.com/pulse/en/originals/2014/11/egypt-houthis-yemen-red-sea-initiative-bab-al-mandeb.html

26. Benomar was tortured and made to endure other forms of inhuman treatment during his period of detention. See Benomar, Jamal, 'Memories of Morocco', *New Internationalist*, Issue 163, September 1986.

27. Senior western official, Interview with the author, Sanaa, May 2014.

28. See Lackner, Helen, 'Yemen's Peaceful Transition from Saleh's Autocratic Rule: Could it Have Succeeded?', International IDEA, 2016, http://www.idea.int/sites/default/files/publications/yemens-peaceful-transition-from-autocracy.pdf

29. Ayesh, Abda, 'Vocal Rejection of the Decision to Divide Yemen into Regions', *Al-Jazeera*, 15 February 2014; *Mansoura News*, 'The Houthis: Federalism divides Yemen into wealthy and poor areas', 11 February 2014.

30. Based on my own personal observations during 2014.

31. The draft constitution is available in Arabic here: http://www.constitutionnet.org/ar/vl/item/lymn-mswd-dstwr-lymn-ljdyd-lm-2015.

32. At times, particularly at the start of its mandate, the CDC met for only 10–15 hours a week. Some members worked outside of the CDC's regular meetings, but most did not.

33. Amongst other things, the CDC did not include any official representatives of the powerful Houthi movement. One CDC member was ideologically in agreement with the Houthi movement but had not formally adhered to the movement and did not present himself in the CDC's discussions as a Houthi.

34. See 'Yemen: The revolutionary committee issues a constitutional declaration to

organize the rules of governance during the interim period', Saba Net, 6 February 2015; an unofficial translation of the constitutional declaration is available here: www.constitutionnet.org/vl/item/yemen-revolutionary-committee-issues-consti-tutional-declaration-organize-foundations.

35. At the time of writing, the conflict has not ended, and the status of the transition, and of the constitutional draft remains unclear.

36. For example, Morocco routinely prevents western human rights organisations from working in its national territory. In September 2015, it demanded that Human Rights Watch suspend its activities in the country. See Human Rights Watch, 'Statement regarding Human Rights Watch in Morocco', 2 November 2015, https://www.hrw.org/news/2015/11/06/statement-regarding-human-rights-watch-activities-morocco

37. Former UN official, Interview with the author, January 2016.

38. Paolo Lembo, Interview with the author, January 2016. The incident is described, somewhat incompletely, here: Giurovich, Dina and Keenan, Jeremy, 'The UNDP, the World Bank and Biodiversity in the Algerian Sahara', in Keenan, Jeremy (ed.), *The Sahara: Past, President and Future*, Abingdon: Routledge, 2007, p. 339.

39. For example, the United Nations Assistance Mission for Iraq was established in 2003.

40. A number of initiatives that were designed to strengthen judicial independence, in particular by reducing the scope for political interference in the judicial process, were blocked by the Iraqi government from 2005 to 2014.

41. This approach was followed in Yemen, where the constitutional drafting committee worked closely with experts from the United Nations and (to a lesser extent) International IDEA which provided information on comparative examples to the drafters.

42. These can include an author's educational background (e.g. if the author of a particular study has graduated from German educational institutions, the likelihood that her study will draw from German examples is necessarily heightened) and the author's ideological preferences (e.g. if an expert is politically conservative, she is unlikely to draw up on examples from most Latin American constitutions, many of which offer generous socio-economic rights to citizens).

43. In one Arab country, an international organisation that was providing background materials to a constitution drafting committee insisted on including in the folders of materials that were being prepared all basic laws from the region, including the basic laws of Saudi Arabia and Qatar, both totalitarian regimes.

44. In Egypt's 2012 and 2013 constitution drafting processes, the drafting assemblies did not engage with any international organisations specifically to prevent any foreign influence over their process.

45. S/RES/2009 (2001).

46. S/RES/2040 (2012).

47. See Martin, Ian, 'The United Nations' Role in the First Year of the Transition', in Cole, Peter and McQuinn, Brian (eds) *The Libyan Revolution and its Aftermath*, London: Hurst, 2015. (In his assessment of UNSMIL's work in Libya, Mr Martin does not come close to suggesting that SCR2040 had any impact on UNSMIL's work).

48. S/RES/1546 (2004).

49. See Haysom, Nicholas; Al-Ali, Zaid; and Law, Michele, 'History of the Iraqi constitution-making process', December 2005, http://zaidalali.com/resources/academic-articles/.

50. Ayman Ayoub, Interview with the author, Cairo, November 2014.

51. Paolo Lembo, Interview with the author, January 2016.

52. This was particularly true in Tunisia, Yemen and Libya. Based on my own personal observations from 2011 to 2015.

53. A number of international organisations provided substantive support to the Tunisian drafters and did so publicly. See, for example, Al-Ali, Zaid and Stacey, Richard (eds), 'Consolidating the Arab Spring: Constitutional Transition in Egypt and Tunisia', International IDEA and the Center for Constitutional Transitions, 2013, http://www.constitutionaltransitions.org/launch-consolidating-arab-spring/

54. This conclusion conforms with positions that I have taken on this issue elsewhere; see, for example, Al-Ali, Zaid and Dann, Philipp, 'The Internationalized Pouvoir Constituant: Constitution-making under external influence in Iraq, Sudan and East Timor', Max Planck UNYB 10, 2006, https://papers.ssrn.com/sol3/papers.cfm?abstract_id=1799308

55. See Al-Ali, Zaid, 'Constitutional Drafting and External Influence', in Ginsburg, Tom and Dixon, Rosalind (eds), *Comparative Constitutional Law*, Cheltenham: Edward Elgar Publishing, 2011, p. 91.

56. I am the author of the only contemporaneous analysis that I am aware of. See Al-Ali, Zaid, 'Libya's Draft Interim Constitution: An Analysis', Constitutionnet, 5 September 2011, http://www.constitutionnet.org/news/libyas-draft-interim-constitution-analysis.

57. See for example S/2011/727, paragraph 55; S/2012/129 paragraph 42; and SCR/2013/516, paragraph 36.

58. See Article 2(7), Chapter I of the United Nation's Charter. For a more in depth discussion of this issue, see Dann, Philipp, *The Law of Development Cooperation: A Comparative Analysis of the World Bank, the EU and Germany*, Cambridge: Cambridge University Press, 2013, p. 256.

59. See Al-Ali, Zaid, 'Constitutional Drafting and External Influence', pp. 90–91. That is obvious when one considers the situation of countries surrounding Iraq, Yemen and Libya.

60. Ibid.

61. Interviews with the author, January 2016.
62. In early 2005, the United Nations Assistance Mission in Iraq's Office of Constitutional Support carried out a review of comparable transition processes to determine which countries that had been in situations similar to Iraq had successfully negotiated their constitutions within a few months, as was required under Iraq's transition roadmap. It concluded that there were no successful precedents and that the likelihood that Iraq would be an exception to that trend was essentially nil. In addition, close to the end of the process, the Office of Constitutional Support commissioned a detailed analysis of the then draft constitution, which concluded that if the draft were to be applied, Iraq would be in 'grave danger', suggesting that the country could witness a new conflict. The United Nations chose not to publicise those conclusions. For the sake of transparency and completeness, I should note that I was a legal officer at the Office of Constitutional Support at the time.

9. CONFRONTING THE DICTATORIAL PAST IN TUNISIA TOWARDS A POLITICAL UNDERSTANDING OF TRANSITIONAL JUSTICE

1. See Nino, Carlos Santiago, *Radical Evil on Trial*, New Haven, CT: Yale University Press, 1999.
2. Teitel, Ruti, *Transitional Justice*, Oxford: Oxford University Press, 2000.
3. See Gready, Paul and Robbins, Simon, 'From Transitional to Transformative Justice: A New Agenda for Practice', *The International Journal of Transitional Justice*, Vol. 8, 2014, pp. 339–361. On liberal statebuilding more generally, see Paris, Roland, *At War's End: Building Peace After Civil Conflict*, Cambridge: Cambridge University Press, 2004.
4. Arthur, Paige, 'How Transitions Reshaped Human Rights', *Human Rights Quarterly*, Vol. 31, No. 2, 2009, pp. 321–367.
5. See Lederach, John-Paul, *Building Peace: Sustainable Reconciliation in Divided Societies*, Washington, DC: United States Institute of Peace, 1997; Richmond, Olivier and Franks, Jason, *Liberal Peace Transitions: Between Peacebuilding and Statebuilding*, Edinburgh: Edinburgh University Press, 2009; United Nations Security Council Report of the Secretary-General, 'The Rule of Law and Transitional Justice in Conflict and Post-conflict Societies', United Nations, 24 August 2004 (S/2004/616), http://www.unrol.org/doc.aspx?d=3096
6. de Greiff, Pablo, 'Transitional Justice, Security, and Development', *Security and Justice Thematic Papers*, Washington: World Bank Development Report, 2011.
7. Fukuyama, Francis, 'The End of History, Five Years Later', *History and Theory* Vol. 34, No. 2, 1999, pp. 27–43.
8. See for instance the 'Justice in Times of Transition' conference organised in Tunis by the ICTJ in May 2011, available online: http://www.ictj.org/publication/addressing-past-building-future-justice-time-transition-conference-report

9. See Khlifi, Omar, *L'assassinat de Salah Ben Youssef*, Tunis: MC-Editions, 2005.

10. Henry, Clement, 'Tunisia's "Sweet Little" Regime', in Rotberg, Robert I., *Worst of the Worst: Dealing with Repressive Rogue Nations*, Washington DC: Brookings Institution Press, 2007, p. 310.

11. Kaplan, Robert, 'One Small Revolution', *The New York Times*, 22 January 2011, http://www.nytimes.com/2011/01/23/opinion/23kaplan.html?pagewanted=all

12. See Brynen, Rex; Moore, Pete W.; Salloukh, Bassel; Zahar, Marie-Joëlle, *Beyond the Arab Spring: Authoritarianism and Democratisation in the Arab World*. Boulder, CO: Lynne Rienner, 2012, p. 18.

13. Boulby, Marion, 'The Islamic Challenge: Tunisia Since Independence', *Third World Quarterly*, Vol. 10, No. 2, 1988, p. 595.

14. The 'Tunisian Perspectives' movement, also known as El Amal Ettounsi ['the Tunisian worker'] is an opposition movement of the far left, which was very powerful in the 1960s and 1970s. It was severely repressed and many of its members were arrested, condemned, and forced to exile after 1965. While the members of the movement did support Bourguiba's policy in terms of modern reforms, defending rights of women, and defending a free Palestinian state, they accused him of leading an imperialistic foreign policy and were closer to a form of Maoism. See Camau, Michel and Geisser, Vincent, *Habib Bourguiba: La trace et l'héritage*, Paris: Karthala, 2004; Bouguerra, Abdeljalil, *De l'histoire de la gauche tunisienne: le mouvement Perspectives, 1963–1975*, Tunis: Cérès, 1993.

15. On 26 January 1978, or 'Black Thursday', a general strike called for by the UGTT turned into a bloodbath, with more than fifty killed. See: Chouika, Larbi and Gobe, Eric, *Histoire de la Tunisie depuis l'indépendance*, Paris: La Découverte, 2015, p. 110.

16. Riots broke out across the country following a rise in the price of cereals and bread on 27 December 1983. The Government imposed a state of emergency on 3 January 1984, but the riots left more than seventy dead.

17. The principle of life presidency was decided upon by the party at the Congress of Monastir. It was later integrated into the Constitution on 18 March 1975.

18. See Amnesty International, 'Tunisia: Continuing Abuses in the Name of Security', 2009.

19. Alexander, Christopher, 'Back from the Democratic Brink: Authoritarianism and Civil Society in Tunisia', *Middle East Report*, Vol. 205, 1997, pp. 34–38.

20. Many ministers of the post-revolution era are former political prisoners. This is the case of prime ministers Hamadi Jebali, and Ali Larayedh, who both spent fifteen years in prison, as well as Samir Dilou, minister of human rights and transitional justice, who served ten.

21. See Human Rights Watch, 'Tunisia: Military Courts that Sentenced Islamist Leaders Violated Basic Fair-Trial Norms', 1 October 1992, https://www.hrw.org/report/1992/10/01/tunisia-military-courts-sentenced-islamist-leaders-violated-basic-fair-trial-norms

22. See the report on persecutions by Human Rights Watch, 'A Larger Prison: Repression of Former Political Prisoners in Tunisia', 24 March 2010, https://www.hrw.org/report/2010/03/24/larger-prison/larger-prison

23. Kourda, Sami, *Le 'complot' Barraket Essahel: Chronique d'un calvaire*, Tunis: Sud Editions, 2014

24. In 2003, during an official visit, French President Jacques Chirac declared that 'the first of all human rights is the right to eat, to receive health care, and to have a home. From this perspective, Tunisia is doing better than most countries', Puchot, Pierre, *La révolution confisquée: enquête sur la transition démocratique en Tunisie*, Arles: Actes Sud, 2012, p. 1. In a volume edited by Robert Rotberg, Tunisia was ranked as a 'rogue state', along with North Korea, Zimbabwe and Uzbekistan. In the Freedom House Failed State Index, Tunisia received the lowest grade in terms of civil and political rights. See Rotberg, Robert I., *Worst of the Worst: Dealing with Repressive Rogue Nations*, Washington DC: Brookings Institution Press, 2007.

25. See International Crisis Group, 'Reform and Security Strategy in Tunisia', North Africa Report Vol. 161, 2015.

26. See Amnesty International, 'Tunisia: Continuing Abuses in the Name of Security', 2009, http://amnistia.pt/dmdocuments/Tunisia_abuses_in_the_name_of_security.pdf.

27. International Crisis Group, 'Popular Protest in North Africa and the Middle East (IV): Tunisia's Way', North Africa Report, Vol. 106, 2011, https://www.crisisgroup.org/middle-east-north-africa/north-africa/egypt/popular-protest-north-africa-and-middle-east-i-egypt-victorious, p. 10

28. 'White Paper' of the Ministry of Regional Development, 2011.

29. On the limitations of Tunisia's approach to tourism, see Puchot, *La révolution confisquée*, pp. 235–258.

30. Irregularities in the recruitment process to the Gafsa Phosphate Company, the main employer of the region, caused major turmoil in the region, from January to June 2008. The regime's response was brutal, killing four, wounding dozens and arresting hundreds of protesters. The movement was contained and very few media reported on it. In 2012, victims of the 2008 uprising were officially recognised as 'martyrs of the revolution'.

31. This corresponds to the day Mohamed Bouazizi set himself on fire, sparking a revolt across the country and the entire region.

32. Discussion with the President of the Commission, Tunis, November 2012.

33. On the functional adequacies between transitional justice and anti-corruption policies, see Andrieu, Kora, 'Dealing with a New Grievance: Should Corruption be Part of the Transitional Justice Agenda Too?' *Journal of Human Rights*, Vol. 11, No. 4, 2012. According to some experts, corruption is 'the act by which "insiders" profit at the expense of "outsiders"'. See Evans, Brian, 'The Cost of Corruption', *Tearfund*, 1999.

34. A 'Judicial Pole' was created by the Ministry of Justice in 2012, with judges specifically designated to deal with cases of corruption.

35. See *Al Huffington Post Maghreb*, 'La loi d'amnistie en question', 24 July 2013, http://www.huffpostmaghreb.com/2013/07/24/recrutement-fonction-publ_n_3643731.html. More than 4,500 victims were recruited in public administrations, according to the International Center for Transitional Justice.

36. See International Crisis Group, 'Tunisia: Transitional Justice and the Fight Against Corruption', *Middle East and North Africa Report* Vol. 168, 2016.

37. Ibid.

38. See Human Rights Watch, 'Tunisie: Les blessés de la révolution ont besoin de soins urgents', 28 May 2012.

39. Numbers provided by the Tunisian Ministry of Human Rights and Transitional Justice, Tunis, November 2013.

40. Mohsen Marzouk, the Secretary General of Nidaa Tounes called for the creation of an antiterrorist 'citizen watchdog' to assist the Ministry of Interior in dismantling terrorist activities. At the same time, many intellectuals have openly blamed Ennahda for the Bardo and Sousse terrorist attacks. More than eighty places of worship were closed.

41. Institute for Integrated Transitions (IFIT), 'Inside the Transition Bubble: International Expert Assistance in Tunisia', April 2013, p. 4.

42. Article 148.b of the 2014 Constitution sets that the state is to guarantee and implement transitional justice.

43. The Kasbah 1 movement took place between 23 January and 28 January 2011. Protesters asked for the resignation from the interim government of all ministers related to the former RCD party. One month later, the Kasbah 2 movement led to the resignation of Prime Minister Ghannouchi himself.

44. The use of military justice for prosecuting gross human rights violations is not recommended by the international community, due to fears of the judges' lack of independence, and issues of impartiality that can lead to impunity or dissimulations. See the 'Principles for the Struggle Against Impunity' (art. 29), 'Principles for the Administration of Justice by Military Tribunals', as well as the recommendations of the Committee against Torture for Chile.

45. See Human Rights Watch, 'Le procès de Ben Ali et des autres responsables accusés du meurtre des manifestants', 11 June 2012, http://www.hrw.org/fr/news/2012/06/11/tunisie-le-proc-s-de-ben-ali-et-des-autres-responsables-accus-s-du-meurtre-de-manifestants

46. See Human Rights Watch, 'Hope on Justice for Past Abuses', 22 May 2014, https://www.hrw.org/news/2014/05/22/tunisia-hope-justice-past-abuses

47. See Human Rights Watch, 'Tunisia: Honor Judges Request to See Case File', 15 January 2013, http://www.hrw.org/news/2012/01/16/tunisia-honor-judges-request-see-case-files

48. See Human Rights Watch, 'Tunisia: Law Falls Short on Judicial Independence. Increase Autonomy of Judges' Oversight Body', 2 June 2015, https://www.hrw.org/news/2015/06/02/tunisia-law-falls-short-judicial-independence.

49. See Crisis Group Middle East/North Africa Report No. 123, 'Tunisia: Combating Impunity, Restoring Security', 9 May 2012.

50. International Crisis Group, 'Reform and Security Strategy in Tunisia', 2015.

51. The draft law granting impunity to security forces—although not adopted at the time of writing—is a powerful example of this danger. See Amna Guellali, 'Après les attentats du Bardo, rhétorique anti droits humains en Tunisie', Human Rights Watch, 26 March 2015.

52. Those were named *munâchidîn*, or 'those who implored', referring to a 2010 petition signed by many Tunisian figures begging for Ben Ali to run again for President in 2014.

53. Blaise, Lilia, 'La loi d'immunisation de la révolution votée à l'Assemblée', Nawaat, 28 June 2013, http://nawaat.org/portail/2013/06/28/la-loi-dimmunisation-de-la-revolution-ou-la-difficulte-de-sortir-du-processus-revolutionnaire/

54. First elections of the Ben Ali era, considered as relatively open and to which Ennahda participated, before the repression of the 1990s.

55. Some 2 million Tunisians are believed to have been members of the RCD.

56. Following two political assassinations, the 2013 political crisis gave rise to a more consensual approach and paved the way to negotiations between Ennahda and their main opponent Nidaa Tounes, a political party comprising many former regime representatives who could have been targeted by the immunisation law. The draft law was abandoned during that same period.

57. In Libya, a 'Political Isolation Law' was adopted on 5 May 2013. It forced several major political figures associated with the former regime to retire from politics, even when they had supported the 2011 revolution to overthrow Muammar Gaddafi. The law is considered as having contributed to the destabilisation of the country and as a key factor in the conflict that started in 2014.

58. The case of Iraq is a landmark for the dangers of unfair, radical, vetting processes. See Sissons, Miranda and Al-Saiedi, Abdulrazzaq, 'A Bitter Legacy: Lessons from Debaathification in Iraq', *International Center for Transitional Justice*, 4 March 2013, http://www.ictj.org/sites/default/files/ICTJ-Report-Iraq-De-Baathification-2013-ENG.pdf

59. See Essebsi, Béji Caid, 'Nous prendrons des mesures antiterroristes sévères', Agence Tunis Afrique Presse, 26 June 2015.

60. The Truth and Dignity Commission was created to mediate cases related to corruption and economic crimes at the request of an accused person, a victim, or the government itself. Contrary to the amnesty law, the 'reconciliation agreement' in the TDC framework includes a statement of apology from the person responsible, to be made public, and reparations for the victim or the government. The

amnesty law operates in secrecy. See International Center for Transitional Justice, 'Tunisia's Proposed Reconciliation Law Would Grant Amnesty for Corruption, Fail to Grow the Economy', 21 July 2016, https://www.ictj.org/news/Tunisia-amnesty-economic-development

61. A mobilisation campaign called 'Manich Msamah' ('I do not forgive') was launched in several governorates, arguing that amnesty to corrupt officials would be a signal of impunity, and displaying 'Wanted' pictures of the alleged former regime figures in the streets of Tunis. Several demonstrations are still regularly organised when the People's Representative Assembly (ARP) discusses the law.

62. On the relation between State and religion in Tunisia and the complex positioning of the Islamists, see Allani, Alaya, 'The Islamists in Tunisia Between Confrontation and Participation: 1980–2008', *The Journal of North African Studies*, Vol. 14, No. 2, 2009.

63. Since then, Egypt and Mali have created similar institutions. The Libyan Government of National Accord also includes a minister for national reconciliation.

64. Rim El Gantri, 'Tunisia in Transition', ICTJ Briefing, September 2015.

65. The Special Rapporteur on the promotion of truth, justice, reparations and guarantees of non-repetition argued against this inclusion of socio-economic crimes. For him, it represents a problematic over-extension of the TDC's mandate while putting it at risk of being all the more politically targeted by those who may see their interests threatened by its work.

66. These include the repression of Salah Ben Youssef's supporters, leftist and Islamists activists throughout the 1960s to 1990s, victims of the January 1978 and January 1984 riots, those arrested under the anti-terrorist law of 2003, participants of the 2008 Gafsa mining movement, as well as victims of the 2010–2011 revolution and 2012 protest in Siliana.

67. These include the governorates of Kasserine and Jendouba, but also smaller areas such as the cities of Aïn Draham and Sidi Makhlouf and even neighborhoods of the greater Tunis. See Andrieu, Kora; Robins, Simon and Ferchichi, Wahid, 'La zone victime et les réparations collectives en Tunisie: si riches et pourtant si pauvres', Kawakibi Democratic Transition Center and Impunity Watch, 2015.

68. See Ben Hamadi, Monia, 'Au cœur de l'IVD: 60 ans d'histoire à reconstituer', *Inkyfada*, 17 November 2016.

69. International Crisis Group, 'Tunisia: Transitional Justice and the Fight Against Corruption', 2016.

70. Naccache, Gilbert, 'Pour la mémoire et contre l'oubli, Gilbert Naccache raconte sa première audition à l'IVD', *Tuniscope* (tuniscope.com), 18 December 2015.

71. The Institute for Integrated Transitions wrote a complete, and critical, analysis of international assistance to the democratisation process in Tunisia, claiming there was a lack of adaptation to the local context that weakened its impact. See Institute

for Integrated Transitions (IFIT), 'Inside the Transition Bubble: International Expert Assistance in Tunisia', April 2013, http://www.ifit-transitions.org/publications/inside-the-transition-bubble-international-expert-assistance-in-tunisia/inside-the-transition-bubble-en-full

72. On the links between transitional justice and memorial narratives, see Laplante, Lisa, 'The Peruvian Truth Commission's Historical Memory Project: Empowering Truth-Tellers to Confront Truth-Deniers', *Journal of Human Rights*, Vol. 6, No. 4, 2008, pp. 433–452. Other contexts such as the Balkans are interesting regarding the possible 'war of memories' that transitional justice mechanisms can reveal. See Subotic, Jelena, *Hijacked Justice: Dealing with the Past in the Balkans*. Ithaca, NY: Cornell University Press, 2009; Pavlakovic, Vjeran, 'Croatia, the International Criminal Tribunal for the former Yugoslavia, and General Gotovina as a Political Symbol', *Europe-Asia Studies*, Vol. 62, No. 10, 2010, pp. 1707–1740.

73. Teitel, Ruti, *Transitional Justice*, Oxford: Oxford University Press, 2000.

74. See de Greiff, Pablo, 'Theorising Transitional Justice', in Williams, Melissa; Nagy, Rosemary; and Elster, John (eds), *Transitional Justice Vol. 1*, New York: New York University Press, 2012.

75. Teitel, *Transitional Justice*, p. 6.

76. de Greiff, Pablo, 'Theorising Transitional Justice', p. 14.

77. Ibid.

78. During the 10th Congress of Ennahda in Hammamet in May 2016, its leader Rached Ghannouchi announced that the party would separate its religious from its political activities, thereby becoming 'Muslim democrats' rather than Islamists. See Wolf, Anne, *Political Islam in Tunisia. The History of Ennahda*, London: Hurst, 2017.

79. The revival of the historical figure of Abdelaziz Thaalbi—a conservative, Pan-Arabist leader who founded the national movement in 1920 and was excluded by Bourguiba in 1934—is revealing of this tendency. Thaalbi is presented as a common ancestor of both the Destourians and the Islamists, which gives their alliance a memorial legitimacy.

80. Contrary to popular beliefs, the Islamists were not behind the 2010–2011 revolution. When the protests started, Ennahda had been almost entirely crushed by the regime, and very few of its supporters were still active and in the country.

81. See the report of the United Nations Special Rapporteur for the Promotion of Truth, Justice, Reparations and Guarantees of Non-Repetition Pablo de Greiff, 'Addendum: Mission to Tunisia', *Human Rights Council*, 2013, A/HRC/24/42/Add.1.

82. This type of argument is frequent in transitional periods. It was also used to oppose the policy of affirmative action in South Africa, or the granting of reparations to Jews after World War II.

83. Ibid.

84. Ibid.

85. See, Amnesty International, 'Tunisia: Ensure Justice for Tunisian Torture Victim', 7 October 2013, http://www.amnesty.org/fr/for-media/press-releases/ensure-justice-tunisian-torture-victim-exhumed-after-22-year-campaign-2013/

86. Miller, Zinaida, 'Effects of Invisibility: In Search of the "Economic" in Transitional Justice', *International Journal of Transitional Justice*, Vol. 2, 2008, p. 267.

10. WITH OR WITHOUT YOU? TRANSITIONAL JUSTICE AND POLITICAL TRANSITIONS IN MOROCCO AND TUNISIA

1. The International Center for Transitional Justice was established in New York in 2001 by Alex Boraine, former vice-president of the South African Truth and Reconciliation Commission; Paul van Zyl, Executive Secretary of the TRC; and Priscilla Hayner, a leading expert in the field. It counts now more than thirty permanent workers and has offices in Uganda, Colombia, Ivory Coast, Belgium, Lebanon and Tunisia. Its creation was funded by various philanthropic organisations: The Ford Foundation, the John D. and Catherine T. McArthur Foundation, the Carnegie Corporation of New York, the Rockefeller Brothers Fund and the Andrus Family Fund. For a history of the ICTJ, see Dezalay, Sara, 'Des droits de l'homme au marché du développement: Note de recherche sur le champ faible de la gestion de conflits armés', *Actes de la recherche en sciences sociales*, Vol. 4, No. 174, 2008, pp. 68–79.

2. Theidon, Kimberley, 'Editorial note', *The International Journal of Transitional Justice*, Vol. 3, No. 3, 2009, p. 295–300.

3. Elster, Jon, *Sour Grapes: Studies in the Subversion of Rationality*, Cambridge: Cambridge University Press, 1985, p. 43.

4. Lefranc, Sandrine, *Politiques du pardon*, Paris: PUF, 2002, p. 331.

5. Lefranc, Sandrine, 'La violence d'État et le pardon politique', *Raisons politiques*, Vol. 1, 1998, p. 17. On Tunisia see: International Crisis Group, 'Tunisia: Combatting Impunity, Restoring Security', Middle East/North Africa Report, No. 123, 9 May 2012, p. 26.

6. 'Criminal courts, by themselves, may not be suited to revealing the broadest spectrum of crimes that took place during a period of repression, in part because they may convict only on proof beyond a 'reasonable doubt', Report of the International Commission of Inquiry on Darfur to the United Nations Secretary-General, pursuant to Security Council Resolution 1564 of 18 September 2004, 25 January 2005, p. 156, para 617. Regarding this substitution, see Lefranc, Sandrine, 'La professionnalisation d'un militantisme réformateur du droit: l'invention de la justice transitionnelle', *Droit et société*, Vol. 73, No. 3, 2009, p. 572.

7. In September 2012, a cartoon advertising transitional justice in Tunisia appeared on television and social media: http://www.youtube.com/watch?v=yo5uhMZokl0 (in Arabic).

8. Nassar, Habib, 'Transitional Justice in the Wake of the Arab Uprisings: Between Complexity and Standardisation' in Fisher, Kirsten J. and Stewart, Robert (eds), *Transitional Justice and the Arab Spring*, Abingdon: Routledge, 2014, p. 69.

9. See for example, Fisher, Kirsten J. and Stewart, Robert, 'After the Arab Spring: a new wave of transitional justice?' in Fisher, Kirsten J. and Stewart, Robert (eds.), *Transitional Justice and the Arab Spring*, Abingdon: Routledge, 2014, p. 1–13; Lekha Sriram, Chandra, 'Introduction. Transitional Justice in the MENA Region' and 'Transitional Justice in Comparative Perspective. Lessons for the Middle East', in Lekha Sriram, Chandra (ed.), *Transitional Justice in the Middle East and North Africa*, Oxford: Oxford University Press, 2016, pp. 1–12 and pp. 15–35.

10. Lamont, Christopher K., 'The Scope and Boundaries of Transitional Justice in the Arab Spring', in Lekha Sriram, Chandra (ed.), *Transitional Justice in the Middle East in North Africa*, op. cit., p. 85.

11. Lefranc, Sandrine, Vairel, Frédéric, 'The Emergence of Transitional Justice as a Professional International Practice', in Israël, Liora, and Mouralis, Guillaume (eds.), *Dealing with Wars and Dictatorships*, The Hague: Asser Press, 2014, pp. 235–252.

12. As the International Institute for Democracy and Electoral Assistance (IDEA) handbook: Bloomfield, David; Barnes, Teresa; and Huyse, Luc (eds.), *Reconciliation after a Violent Conflict: A Handbook*, Stockholm: IDEA, 2003 (to which several experts collaborated); see also Kritz, Neil J. (ed.), *Transitional Justice: How Emerging Democracies Reckon with Former Regimes*, Washington: United States Institute for Peace (three volumes), 1995, and Hayner, Priscilla B., 'Fifteen Truth Commissions. 1974 to 1994: A Comparative Study', *Human Rights Quarterly*, Vol. 16, No. 4, 1994, pp. 597–655.

13. International Center for Transitional Justice, Annual Report 2004–2005, 'ICTJ Mission and Statement', https://www.ictj.org/sites/default/files/ICTJ_ Annual Report_2004–5.pdf; see Bickford, Louis, 'Transitional Justice', *The Encyclopedia of Genocide and Crimes Against Humanity*, Vol. 3, New York: Macmillan Reference USA, 2004, pp. 1045–1047.

14. Lefranc Sandrine, 'La justice transitionnelle, une justice pour les temps nouveaux?' in Gobe, Eric (ed.), *Des justices en transition dans le monde arabe? Contributions à une réflexion sur les rapports entre justice et politique*, Rabat: Centre Jacques-Berque, 2016, pp. 211–234.

15. The cost of perpetrators' trials is another difficulty since state resources are limited and people consider they should be allocated to victims' compensation or country reconstruction.

16. Bickford, Louis, 'Transitional Justice'.

17. Ibid.

18. See the report by Tozy, Mohamed, *Forum national sur la réparation. Rapport général*, 2005.

19. Mendeloff, David, 'Truth-Seeking, Truth-Telling and Post-Conflict Peacebuilding:

Curb the Enthusiasm?', *International Studies Review*, Vol. 6, No. 3, September 2004, pp. 355–380.

20. Du Toit, André, 'La commission Vérité et Réconciliation sud-africaine. Histoire locale et responsabilité face au monde', *Politique africaine*, No. 92, 2003, p. 107. This is what President Beji Caid Essebsi explains bluntly, three months after his election: 'Transitional justice cannot sentence everyone, but it helped warm the hearts of victims of the *ancien regime*', *Paris Match*, March 2015.

21. International Center for Transitional Justice, Annual Report 2008, 'A World in Transition', https://www.ictj.org/sites/default/files/ICTJ_Annual_Report_2008. pdf

22. 'Les séances d'auditions publiques: document de référence', www.ier.ma, site unavailable, last accessed 12 December 2004.

23. Human Rights Watch, 'Morocco's Truth Commission. Honoring Past Victims during an Uncertain Present', 27 November 2005, https://www.hrw.org/sites/default/files/reports/morocco1105wcover.pdf

24. FIDH, Mouvement Mondial des Droits Humains, *Les commissions de vérité* et de *réconciliation: l'expérience marocaine*, No. 396, 2004, https://www.fidh.org/IMG/pdf/Ma396f.pdf; Opgenhaffen, Veerle and Freeman, Mark, *Transitional Justice in Morocco: a Progress Report*, International Center for Transitional Justice, 2005, https://www.ictj.org/ publication/transitional-justice-morocco-progress-report.

25. International Center for Transitional Justice Annual Report 2001/2002, https://www.ictj.org/sites/default/files/ICTJ_Annual_Report_2001–2002.pdf

26. International Center for Transitional Justice, 'Transitional Justice in Morocco: A Progress Report', 2005, http://www.ictj.org/sites/default/files/ICTJ-Morocco-Progress-Report-2005-English.pdf. For example, Statement by European Union, 23 July 2007, http://www.consilium.europa.eu/ueDocs/cms_Data/docs/pressData/en/er/95454.pdf

27. http://www.cndh.org.ma/an/thematic-reports/follow-report-implementation-equity-and-reconciliation-commission-recommendations

28. http://www.ivd.tn/fr/?page_id=428

29. Nassar, Habib, 'Transitional Justice in the Wake of the Arab Uprisings: Between Complexity and Standardisation' in Fisher, Kirsten J. and Stewart, Robert (eds), *Transitional Justice and the Arab Spring*, Abingdon: Routledge, 2014, p. 66.

30. Twentieth recommendation of the Consultative Council for Human Rights, 6 November 2003.

31. Vairel, Frédéric, *Politique et mouvements sociaux au Maroc. La révolution désamorcée?*, Paris: Presses de Sciences Po, 2014. On 'insurgent paths to democracy', see Wood, Elizabeth Jean, 'An Insurgent Path to Democracy: Popular Mobilization, Economic Interests, and Regime Transition in El Salvador and South Africa', *Comparative Political Studies*, Vol. 34, No. 8, 2001, pp. 862–888.

32. One of the signs of this roaring success is the adoption of the TRC model in 'civil

society initiatives'—what Louis Bickford calls 'Unofficial Truth Projects', *Human Rights Quarterly*, Vol. 29, No. 4, 2007, pp. 994–1035.

33. Nevertheless, even the ICTJ provides a nuanced view of the experience in a recent assessment: International Center for Transitional Justice, 'Morocco still a model for justice in MENA, but questions remain', 2 August 2016, https://www.ictj.org/news/morocco-still-model-justice-mena-questions-remain

34. http://www.cndh.org.ma/ar/blgt-shfy/lmjls-lwtny-ystqbl-wfd-mn-lhyy-ltwnsy-llhqyq-wlkrm-ltlh-l-ltjrb-lmgrby-fy-mjl-ldl-lntqly

35. A former ERC, Chaouki Benyoub, is presented as 'the (great) Moroccan expert'. He participated in numerous workshops and conferences; travelling to Tunisia thirteen times between 2011 and 2015 (personal interview, 10 April 2015).

36. Vairel, Frédéric, 'Morocco: From Mobilizations to Reconciliation?', *Mediterranean Politics*, Vol. 13, No. 2, 2008, pp. 229–241.

37. See among a body of literature: Allal, Amin, 'Becoming revolutionary in Tunisia, 2007–2011', in Beinin, Joel and Vairel, Frédéric (eds), *Social Movements, Mobilisation, and Contestation in the Middle East and North Africa: Second Edition*, Palo Alto, CA: Stanford University Press, 2013, pp. 185–204 and Hmed, Choukri, 'Abeyance Networks, Contingency and Structures. History and Origins of the Tunisian Revolution', *Revue française de science politique*, Vol. 62, Nos. 5–6, 2012, pp. 797–820.

38. Proceedings of the conference: http://tjtunis.blogspot.co.uk/2011_04_12_archive.html

39. El Gantri, Rim (Head of Office for ICTJ's Tunisia Program) 'International Center for Transitional Justice Program Report: Tunisia', 6 March 2014, https://www.ictj.org/news/ictj-program-report-tunisia

40. See Boujnch, Héla, 'Bilan de la justice transitionnelle en Tunisie part II', http://nawaat.org/portail/2013/02/19/bilan-de-la-justice-transitionnelle-part-ii-la-situation-tunisienne/

41. Among them: 'Nadwa 'iqlîmîya hawla al-'adâla al-'intiqâlîa: min mubâdara madanîya ilâ qarâr sîyâsî' [Regional Workshop on TJ: from a Citizen Initiative to a Political Decision], *The Al Kawakibi Democracy Transition Center*, 13–14 December 2011.

42. Andrieu, Kora, 'Confronter le passé de la dictature en Tunisie: la loi de 'justice transitionnelle' en question', IRIS, May 2014, p. 22, http://www.iris-france.org/docs/kfm_docs/docs/obs-monde-arabe/tunisie-justice-transitionnelle-mai-2014.pdf

43. Human Rights Watch, 'Morocco's Truth Commission. Honoring Past Victims during an Uncertain Present', 27 November 2005, p. 21, https://www.hrw.org/sites/default/files/reports/morocco1105wcover.pdf

44. ERC Final Report, 2004.

45. International Crisis Group, 'The Tunisian Exception: Success and Limits of

Consensus', Middle East and North Africa Briefing No. 37, 5 June 2014, https://www.crisisgroup.org/middle-east-north-africa/north-africa/tunisia/ tunisian-exception-success-and-limits-consensus

46. UGTT press release (30 July 2013), 'al-hay'a al-idârîa al-istisnâ'ia tutâlibu bi hall al-hukûma wa tataqada bi mubâdara li-kâfat al-atrâf' ['The extraordinary administrative commission asks for government demission and an initiative with all the parties'].

47. Camau, Michel, 'Usages et représentations de l'alternance en situations critiques. Illustrations égyptiennes et tunisiennes', in Aldrin Philippe; Bargel, Lucie; Bué, Nicholas; and Pina, Christine (eds), *Politiques de l'alternance. Sociologie des changements (de) politiques*, Vulaine-sur-Seine: Éditions du Croquant, 2016, pp. 381–407.

48. 'Tunisie-Politique: Chammari démissionne de l'Instance Vérité et Dignité', http://www.kapitalis.com/politique/22946-tunisie-politique-chammari-demissionne-de-l-instance-verite-et-dignite.html

49. El Gantri, Rim, 'Tunisia in Transition. One year after the Creation of the Truth and Dignity Commission', International Center for Transitional Justice Briefing, September 2015, p. 4, https://www.ictj.org/publication/tunisia-transition-one-year-after-creation-truth-dignity-commission

50. Interviews with former ERC members, Rabat, February and April 2015.

51. Interview with a former ERC member, Rabat, February 2015.

52. Actors are using the past or marks of the past as a political resource. This was the case with the publication in December 2013 of the 'Black Book: The Propaganda System Under Ben Ali's Rule', which made use of the president's archives to discredit hostile journalists.

53. Article 3 states: 'Violation shall mean any gross or systematic infringement of any human right committed by the State's apparatuses or by groups or individuals who acted in State's name or under its protection, even if they do not have the capacity or authority to do so. Violation shall also cover any gross or systematic infringement of any human right committed by organized groups.'

54. Interview to *Al-Tûnsîa*, 11 June 2014 (in Arabic). See also the account of a meeting between Beji Caïd Essebsi and Samir Dilou (minister of human rights and transitional justice), 6 April 2015, 'Tunisie. Beji Caïd Essebsi, Samir Dilou et "la justice transactionnelle"', http://www.kapitalis.com/politique/national/9282-tunisie-beji-caid-essebsi-samir-dilou-et-lla-justice-transactionneller.html

55. International Crisis Group, 'Tunisia: Transitional Justice and the Fight Against Corruption', Middle East and North Africa Report; No. 168, 3 May 2016, p. 18, https://www.crisisgroup.org/middle-east-north-africa/north-africa/tunisia/tunisia-transitional-justice-and-fight-against-corruption. In May 2015, Sihem Bensedrine announces that the TDC was granted access to the President's archives five months prior.

56. Investiture speech, 'There is no future for Tunisia without national reconciliation', 31 December 2014.

57. Under the banner of 'national reconciliation', these themes are found again in his interview with a French tabloid (*Paris Match*, March 2015), 'We have to stop settling scores with the past', (...) we have to turn the page of judicial proceedings in order for rich Tunisian to invest in Tunisia again and be useful for their country, we need a transaction between the state and businessmen so they can repatriate their funds to invest in Tunisia.'

58. See Mohammed Samih Beji Okkez, 'Al-hay'a al-waqtîa li murâqaba dustûrîa mashârî' al-qawânîn tatîh al-fasl 61', http://bit.ly/2aW84By

59. International Crisis Group, 'Tunisia: Transitional Justice and the Fight Against Corruption'.

11. TRANSITIONAL JUSTICE IN POST-REVOLUTIONARY EGYPT

1. The death sentence was overturned by the Court of Cassation in November 2016 but Morsi was sentenced to life in prison in other cases.

2. This ruling became final after the Court of Cassation rejected a challenge brought by victims' families in March 2017.

3. United Nations Security Council Report of the Secretary-General, 'The Rule of Law and Transitional Justice in Conflict and Post-conflict Societies', United Nations, 24 August 2004 (S/2004/616), para. 8.

4. Barsalou, Judy, 'The Walls will not be Silent: A Cautionary Tale about Transitional Justice and Collective Memory in Egypt', in Sriram, Chandra Lekha (ed.), *Transitional Justice in the Middle East and North Africa*, London: Hurst, 2017, p. 199.

5. Sahar Aziz argues that transitional justice did not occur in Egypt following 2011, for three reasons: first, a political transition never materialised; second, a conservative judiciary played a key role in ensuring that no political transition could occur; third, the different opposition groups calling for transitional justice diverged in their expectations of what that entailed. See Aziz, Sahar, 'Theater or Transitional Justice: Reforming the Judiciary in Egypt' in Sriram, Chandra Lekha (ed.), *Transitional Justice in the Middle East and North Africa*, London: Hurst, 2017, p. 211.

6. International Center for Transitional Justice, 'Criminal Justice', https://www.ictj.org/our-work/transitional-justice-issues/criminal-justice

7. For a list of incidents in which security forces have killed protesters between February 2011 and October 2013, see Human Rights Watch, 'Egypt: No Acknowledgment of Justice for Mass Protester Killings', 10 December 2013, http://www.hrw.org/news/2013/12/10/egypt-no-acknowledgment-or-justice-mass-protester-killings

8. He had been arrested in April 2011 only, following popular pressure and a sit-in in Tahrir Square.

9. Mubarak had been found guilty by Cairo Criminal Court in May 2014 of embezzling public funds for the renovation of his private properties and convicted to three years in prison. In its retrial in May 2015, the Cairo Criminal Court confirmed the three-year sentence.

10. Al-Masry Al-Youm, 'Government begins wide scale reconciliation with investors, former officials', Egypt Independent, 8 December 2014, http://www.egyptindependent.com/news/govt-begins-wide-scale-reconciliations-investors-former-officials

11. Wilcke, Christophe, 'Justice for Sale', Egypt Independent, 30 January 2013, http://www.egyptindependent.com/opinion/justice-sale

12. Amnesty International, 'Egypt: Roadmap to Repression', 2014, https://www.amnesty.be/doc/IMG/pdf/2014-01-_roadmap_to_repression_english-copie.pdf

13. Chick, Kristen, 'Why Mubarak's trial may not bring Egypt full justice', Christian Science Monitor, 3 August 2011, http://www.csmonitor.com/World/Middle-East/2011/0803/Why-Mubarak-s-trial-may-not-bring-Egypt-full-justice-VIDEO

14. Tawab, Ziad Abdel, 'The Crisis of Transitional Justice after the Arab Spring: The Case of Egypt', November 2013, Cairo Institute for Human Rights Studies, http://www.cihrs.org/wp-content/uploads/2013/09/Transitional-Justice.pdf

15. International Bar Association's Human Rights Institute, 'Egypt: Separating Law and Politics: Challenges to the Independence of Judges and Prosecutors in Egypt', 2014, http://www.legalbrief.co.za/article.php?story=20140211121632347

16. Egyptian Initiative for Personal Rights, 'Egypt: Where Impunity is Entrenched and Accountability is Absent', 31 December 2014, http://eipr.org/en/ pressrelease/2014/12/31/2320

17. The judge was removed from the criminal court in October 2014 and transferred to a civil court.

18. Egyptian Initiative for Personal Rights, 'Egypt: Where Impunity is Entrenched and Accountability is Absent'.

19. Moustafa, Tamir, 'Law Versus the State: The Judicialization of Politics in Egypt', Law and Social Inquiry, Vol. 28, 2003, pp. 883–930 and Moustafa, Tamir, 'The Political Role of the Supreme Constitutional Court: Between Principles and Practice', in Nathalie Bernard-Maugiron (ed.), Judges and Political Reform in Egypt, Cairo: American University in Cairo Press, 2008.

20. El-Rifae, Yasmin 'Egypt's Courts', 18 January 2014, Mada Masr, http://www.madamasr.com/en/2014/01/18/feature/politics/egypts-courts/

21. al-Houdaiby, Ibrahim, 'Judging the Judges. The Present Crisis Facing the Egyptian Judiciary', Arab Reform Initiative, 2014, http://www.arab-reform.net/en/node/616

22. International Bar Association Human Rights Institute, 'Egypt: Separating Law and Politics'.

23. Brown, Nathan J., 'Why do Egyptian courts say the darndest things?', *The Washington Post*, 25 March 2014, http://www.washingtonpost.com/blogs/monkey-cage/wp/2014/03/25/why-do-egyptian-courts-say-the-darndest-things/

24. In September 2014, the Supreme Judicial Council decided to add a new criterion to the appointment procedure: parents of the applicants must be university graduates. More than 100 candidates appointed in June 2013 were retroactively excluded from the public prosecution because their parents lacked higher education.

25. Aziz, Sahar, 'Egypt's Judiciary, Coopted', *Sada*, 20 August 2014, http://carnegieendowment.org/sada/?fa=56426

26. Said, Atef, 'A New Judicial Moment in Egypt', *Jadaliyya*, 25 December 2012, http://www.jadaliyya.com/pages/index/9247/a-new-judicial-moment-in-egypt

27. Judges considered this agreement as a violation of Article 151 of the 2014 Constitution according to which no treaty may be concluded, which results in ceding any part of state territories. Aman, Ayah, 'Are Egypt's Courts carrying out their own Revolution?', *Al-Monitor*, 1 July 2016, http://www.al-monitor.com/pulse/ originals/2016/07/egypt-judiciary-ruling-independence-islands-soccer.html#ixzz4DE16F39T

28. Following these rulings of the State Council, a new law was adopted in April 2017 requesting each highest court to send the names of three candidates to the president, sixty days before the vacancy of the positions of presidents of these jurisdictions. Previously, appointment of the presidents of these highest courts was based on the customary principle of seniority. The amendments caused wide controversy among judges and were viewed by some as a punishment directed at the vice-president of the State Council who confirmed Egyptian sovereignty over Tiran and Sanafir islands, by depriving him of his coming State Council Chairmanship (Arab Association of Constitutional Law's Judiciary Working Group, Egypt's Amended Judicial Authority Laws, *International Journal of Constitutional Law*, Blog, 24 May 2017, http://www.iconnectblog.com/2017/05/egypts-amended-judicial-authority-laws).

29. International Center for Transitional Justice, 'Truth and Memory', https://www.ictj.org/our-work/transitional-justice-issues/truth-and-memory

30. Hanna, Michael Wahid, 'Egypt's Search for Truth', *The Cairo Review of Global Affairs*, 2011, https://www.thecairoreview.com/essays/egypts-search-for-truth/

31. Rageh, Rawya, 'Egypt revolt fact-finding report is a mystery', *Al Jazeera English*, 11 May 2013, http://www.aljazeera.com/indepth/features/2013/05/201351118859142229.html

32. The website is no longer online.

33. Al-Shorouk, 'al-shurûq tanfarid bi-nashr nusûs min taqrîr lajna taqassî ah-haqâ'iq fî qadâyâ qatl al-thuwwâr' ['Al Shorouk to exclusively publish documents of the fact-finding committee about the assassination of rebels'], 15 March 2013, http://

www.shorouknews.com/news/view.aspx?cdate=15032013&id=df66473d-5df5–
4967-a901-9d89f152c507; Hill, Ewan and Mansour, Muhammad, 'Egypt's army
took part in torture and killings during revolution, report shows', *The Guardian*,
10 April 2013, online: http://www.theguardian.com/world/2013/apr/10/
egypt-army-torture-killings-revolution

34. Human Rights Watch, 'Egypt: Publish Fact-Finding Committee Report. Ensure
Right to Truth for Victims of Police and Military Abuse', 24 January 2013, http://
www.hrw.org/news/2013/01/24/egypt-publish-fact-finding-committee-report

35. Ibid.

36. Website of the campaign: http://www.warakombeltaqrir.blogspot.fr/

37. For a critical analysis of the decree establishing this commission and its shortcomings, see Egyptian Initiative for Personal Rights, Once Again... the Truth. EIPR's
commentary on the presidential decree number 698/2013 creating 'a national
independent fact-finding commission to gather information and evidence for the
events that accompanied the 30 June 2013 revolution and its repercussion, http://
eipr.org/sites/default/files/pressreleases/pdf/eiprs_commentary_on_the_presi-
dential_decree_number_698_for_2013.pdf

38. Mada Masr, 'Fact-finding committee puts blame on Islamists for Rabea violence',
26 November 2014, http://www.madamasr.com/news/fact-finding-committee-
puts-blame-islamists-rabea-violence

39. Ibid.

40. Ibid.

41. Ibid.

42. Egyptian Initiative for Personal Rights, 'The Weeks of Killing: State Violence,
Communal Fighting and Sectarian Attacks in the Summer of 2013', 2014, http://
eipr.org/sites/default/files/reports/pdf/weeks_of_killing_en.pdf

43. Egyptian Initiative for Personal Rights, 'The Executive Summary of the Fact-
Finding Commission's Report: Falls Short Of Expectations', 4 December 2014,
http://eipr.org/en/pressrelease/2014/12/04/2293

44. Human Rights Watch, 'All According to Plan', 12 August 2014, https://www.hrw.
org/report/2014/08/12/all-according-plan/raba-massacre-and-mass-killings-pro-
testers-egypt

45. Two conflicting draft laws amending the Judicial Authority Law were prepared
under Morsi: one under the supervision of the minister of justice and the other
by the Judges Club. But due to divisions within the judiciary and the dissolution
of the People's Assembly, none of them passed. For a comparative analysis of the
reform projects prepared under Morsi, see International Bar Association's Human
Rights Institute, 'Egypt: Separating Law and Politics: Challenges to the
Independence of Judges and Prosecutors in Egypt', 2014, http://www.legalbrief.
co.za/article.php?story=20140211121632347

46. A Justice Conference took place in 1986 to discuss potential remedies to the challenges the judicial system was facing.

47. Yussef Auf, cited by Atallah, Lina, 'A state in shackles', *Mada Masr*, 31 December 2013, http://www.madamasr.com/sections/politics/state-shackles

48. Auf, Yussef, 'Prospects for Judicial Reform in Egypt', *Atlantic Council*, 21 October 2014, http://www.atlanticcouncil.org/blogs/egyptsource/prospects-for-judicial-reform-in-egypt

49. On 14 March 2015, the Supreme Judiciary Council referred forty-one judges to retirement on charges of engaging in politics. NGOs condemned this decision: 'We believe the real reason for the retirements is not the judges' involvement in politics, as stated in the case files and inquiries, but rather for opinions they expressed in opposition to the current governing administration, especially given the lack of specific standards for acts that require disciplinary sanctions for judges or the loss of a judgeship. The judiciary law gives the disciplinary board the absolute authority to determine whether legal action should be taken in such cases': Cairo Institute for Human Rights Studies, 'Rights Groups Condemn Forced Retirement of 41 Judges for Expressing their Opinion', 18 March 2015, http://www.cihrs.org/?p=14650&lang=en

50. In June 2016, President al-Sisi issued a decree forcing him into retirement. *Daily News Egypt*, 'Al-Sisi forces judge into retirement for engaging in political work', 6 June 2016, http://www.dailynewsegypt.com/2016/06/06/al-sisi-forces-judge-retirement-engaging-political-work/?mc_cid=07bdbf63b8&mc_eid=[UNIQID

51. Ashour, Omar and Mohyeldeen, Sherif, 'Security Sector Reform and Transitional Justice after the Arab-Majority Uprisings: The Case of Egypt', in Sriram, Chandra Lekha (ed.), *Transitional Justice in the Middle East and North Africa*, London: Hurst, 2017, pp. 235–51.

52. Sayigh, Yezid, 'Missed Opportunity: The Politics of Police Reform in Egypt and Tunisia', Carnegie Middle East Center, 17 March 2015, http://carnegie-mec.org/publications/?fa=59391

53. Al-Shorouk, 3 January 2014, http://www.shorouknews.com/news/view.aspx?cdate=03012014&id=054860f4-deb2-4812-a1c5-97cdb1ac112a

54. Al-Masry al-Youm, 17 December 2013, http://www.almasryalyoum.com/news/details/356672

55. Mada Masr, 'Minister Defends Protest Law to US Official', 25 August 2014, http://www.madamasr.com/news/minister-defends-protest-law-us-official

56. Youssef, Abdelhrahman, 'Egypt's Brotherhood, Sisi both put out feelers for reconciliation', *Al-Monitor*, 13 July 2016, http://www.al-monitor.com/pulse/originals/2016/07/egypt-brotherhood-reconciliation-sisi-divide-detainees.html#ixzz4EZcqHuZU

57. El-Sherif, Ashraf, 'The Muslim Brotherhood and the Future of Political Islam in Egypt', Carnegie Endowment for International Peace, October 2014, http://carnegieendowment.org/files/mb_future_egypt.pdf

58. Omar, Rowida, 'The Delay of Transitional Justice in Egypt', Middle East Institute, 12 February 2014, http://www.mei.edu/content/delay-transitional-justice-egypt

59. Turner, Catherine, 'Transitional Justice in Egypt: A Challenge and an Opportunity', The Tahrir Institute for Middle East Policy, 14 May 2016, http://timep.org/tjp-analysis/transitional-justice-in-egypt-a-challenge-and-an-opportunity/

60. Tawab, Ziad Abdel, 'The Crisis of Transitional Justice after the Arab Spring: The Case of Egypt'.

61. Auf, Yussef, 'Transitional Justice Elusive in Egypt', Sada, 6 December 2013, http://carnegieendowment.org/sada/2013/12/06/transitional-justice-elusive-in-egypt/gvi0

BIBLIOGRAPHY

Abdel Razek, Sherine, 'Military Inc.?' Al-Ahram Weekly, 1 January 2015, http://weekly.ahram.org.eg/News/10053.aspx

Abdel-Malek, Anouar, *Egypt—Military Society: The Army Regime, the Left, and Social Change Under Nasser*, New York: Random House, 1968.

Abdulla, Rasha, 'Egypt's Media in the Midst of Revolution', Carnegie Endowment for International Peace, July 2014, http://carnegieendowment.org/files/egypt_media_revolution.pdf

Abou-Khalil, Naji and Hargreaves, Laurence, 'Libyan Television and its Influence on the Security Sector', US Institute of Peace Special Report, No. 364, 2015, https://www.usip.org/sites/default/files/SR364-The-Role-of-Media-in-Shaping-Libya%E2%80%99s-Security-Sector-Narratives.pdf

Abul-Magd, Zeinab, 'The Generals' Secret: Egypt's Ambivalent Market', Sada, Carnegie Endowment for International Peace, 9 February 2012.

———, 'The Egyptian Republic of Retired Generals', *Foreign Policy*, Middle East Channel, 28 May 2012, http://foreignpolicy.com/2012/05/08/the-egyptian-republic-of-retired-generals/

Ackerman, Bruce, *We the People: Foundations*, Cambridge, MA: Harvard University Press, 1993.

Al-Ali, Zaid, 'Constitutional Drafting and External Influence', in Ginsburg, Tom and Dixon, Rosalind (eds), *Comparative Constitutional Law*, Cheltenham: Edward Elgar Publishing, 2011.

———, 'Libya's Draft Interim Constitution: An Analysis', Constitutionnet, 5 September 2011, http://www.constitutionnet.org/news/libyas-draft-interim-constitution-analysis

———, 'Five Years of Arab Constitutional Reform: Balancing Process Requirements with the Demands of Fragile Democratic Traditions', in Alkebsi, Abdelwahhab; Sparre, Charlotta; and Brown, Nathan J. (eds), *Reconstructing the Middle East*, Abingdon: Routledge, 2016.

Al-Ali, Zaid and Dann, Philipp, 'The Internationalized Pouvoir Constituant: Constitution-making under external influence in Iraq, Sudan and East Timor', Max PlanckUNYB 10, 2006, https://papers.ssrn.com/sol3/papers.cfm?abstract_id= 1799308

Al-Ali, Zaid et al., 'The Egyptian Constitutional Declaration Dated 17 June 2012: A Commentary.' IDEA, June 2012, http://www.constitutionnet.org/vl/item/commentary-egyptian-constitutional-declaration-dated-17-june-2012

Al-Ali, Zaid and Stacey, Richard (eds), 'Consolidating the Arab Spring: Constitutional Transition in Egypt and Tunisia', IDEA and the Center for Constitutional Transitions, 2013, http://www.constitutionaltransitions.org/launch-consolidating-arab-spring/

Al-Araby al-Jadeed, 'Misr: al-jaysh wa al-shurta laysu "yad wahida"' [Egypt: the army and the police are not 'one hand'], 23 November 2014, http://www.alaraby.co.uk/politics/6f231f24-6bda-4515-ac53-452ca8e80e04

al-Houdaiby, Ibrahim 'Judging the Judges. The Present Crisis Facing the Egyptian Judiciary', Arab Reform Initiative, 2014, http://www.arab-reform.net/en/node/616

Al Huffington Post Maghreb, 'La loi d'amnistie en question', 24 July 2013, http://www.huffpostmaghreb.com/2013/07/24/recrutement-fonction-publ_n_3643731.html

Al-Jazeera, 'In Egypt, Demonstrations, Death Mark Anniversary of 1973 War', 7 October 2013, http://america.aljazeera.com/articles/2013/10/6/egypt-warns-brotherhoodagainstanniversaryprotests.html

Al-Maseryoon, 'Saad Eddine Ibrahim yutalibu bitahwil al-mudaris wa al-musajid ila ma'taqalat lil-Ikhwan' [Saad Eddine Ibrahim demands the transforming of mosques into detention centers for the Brothers], 24 January 2014, http://bit.ly/1wz6giZ

Al-Shorouk, 'al-shurûq tanfarid binashar nusûs min taqrîr lajna taqsî ahaqâ'iq fi qadâi-yya qutil al-thuwâr' ['Al Shorouk to exclusively publish documents of the fact-finding committee about the assassination of rebels'], 15 March 2013, http://www.shorouknews.com/news/view.aspx?cdate=15032013&id=df66473d-5df5-4967-a901-9d89f152c507

Al-Youm, Al-Masry, 'Government begins wide scale reconciliation with investors, former officials', *Egypt Independent*, 8 December 2014, http://www.egyptinde-pendent.com/news/govt-begins-wide-scale-reconciliations-investors-former-officials

Alexander, Christopher, 'Back from the Democratic Brink: Authoritarianism and Civil Society in Tunisia', *Middle East Report* Vol. 205, 1997, pp. 34–38.

———, 'Tunisia: The Best Bet', in *The Islamist are Coming: Who They Really Are*, Washington: Woodrow Wilson University Press, 2012.

Alexander, Anne and Aoragh, Miriyam, 'Egypt's Unfinished Revolution: The Role of the Media Revisited', *International Journal of Communication*, Vol. 8, 2014, pp. 890–915.

BIBLIOGRAPHY

Allani, Alaya, 'The Islamists in Tunisia Between Confrontation and Participation: 1980–2008', *The Journal of North African Studies*, Vol. 14, No. 2, 2009, pp. 257–272.

Allison, Graham, *Essence of Decision: Explaining the Cuban Missile Crisis*, New York: Longman, 1971

Aly, Ramy, 'Rebuilding Egyptian Media for a Democratic Future', *Arab Media and Society*, 31 May 2011, http://www.arabmediasociety.com/articles/downloads/20110531104306_Aly.pdf

Aman, Ayah, 'Are Egypt's Courts carrying out their own Revolution?', *Al-Monitor*, 1 July 2016, http://www.al-monitor.com/pulse/originals/2016/07/egypt-judiciary-ruling-independence-islands-soccer.html#ixzz4DE16F39T

Amara, Tarek, 'Tunisia's Biggest Union Tells Islamist-Led Government to Quit', Reuters, 30 July 2013, http://www.reuters.com/article/2013/07/30/us-tunisia-protests-idUSBRE96T0WM20130730

Amnesty International, 'Tunisia: Continuing Abuses in the Name of Security', 2009, http://amnistia.pt/dmdocuments/Tunisia_abuses_in_the_name_of_security.pdf

———, 'Tunisia: Ensure Justice for Tunisian Torture Victim', 7 October 2013, http://www.amnesty.org/fr/for-media/press-releases/ensure-justice-tunisian-torture-victim-exhumed-after-22-year-campaign-2013-

———, 'Egypt: Roadmap to Repression', 2014, https://www.amnesty.be/doc/IMG/pdf/2014_-_01_-_roadmap_to_repression_english_-_copie.pdf

Andrieu, Kora, 'Dealing with a New Grievance: Should Corruption be Part of the Transitional Justice Agenda Too?' *Journal of Human Rights*, Vol. 11, No. 4, 2012, pp. 537–557.

———, 'Confronter le passé de la dictature en Tunisie: la loi de 'justice transitionnelle' en question', IRIS, May 2014, http://www.iris-france.org/docs/kfm_docs/docs/obs-monde-arabe/tunisie-justice-transitionnelle-mai-2014.pdf

Angrist, Michele Penner, *Party Building in the Modern Middle East*, Seattle, WA:University of Washington Press, 2011.

———, 'Understanding the Success of Mass Civic Protest in Tunisia', *The Middle East Journal*, Vol. 67, No. 4, 2013, pp. 547–564.

Arato, Andrew, *Civil Society, Constitution, and Legitimacy*, Lanham, MD: Rowman and Littlefield, 2000.

Arato, Andrew, *Constitution Making Under Occupation*, New York: Columbia University Press, 2009.

Arthur, Paige, 'How Transitions Reshaped Human Rights', *Human Rights Quarterly*, Vol. 31, No. 2, 2009, pp. 321–367.

Ashour, Omar, 'From Bad Cop to Good Cop? The Challenge of Security Sector Reform in Egypt', Brookings Doha Center–Stanford University Project on Arab Transitions, Paper Series No. 4, 2012, http://www.brookings.edu/research/papers/2012/11/19-security-sector-reform-ashour

——, 'Disarming Egypt's Militarized State', Project Syndicate, July 2013, http://www.project-syndicate.org/commentary/disarming-egypt-s-militarized-state-by-omar-ashour

——, 'Egypt: Return to a generals' republic?', BBC News, 21 August 2013, http://www.bbc.co.uk/news/world-middle-east-23780839

Ashour, Omar and Ünlücayaklı, Emre, 'Islamists, Soldiers and Conditional Democrats: Behaviors of Islamists and the Military in Algeria and Turkey', *Journal of Conflict Studies*, Vol. 26, No. 2, 2006, pp. 104–132.

Atallah, Lina, 'A state in shackles', Mada Masr, 31 December 2013, http://www.madamasr.com/sections/politics/state-shackles

Auf, Yussef, 'Transitional Justice Elusive in Egypt', Sada, 6 December 2013, http://carnegieendowment.org/sada/2013/12/06/transitional-justice-elusive-in-egypt/gvi0

——, 'Prospects for Judicial Reform in Egypt', *Atlantic Council*, 21 October 2014, online: http://www.atlanticcouncil.org/blogs/egyptsource/prospects-for-judicial-reform-in-egypt

Ayesh, Abda, 'Vocal Rejection of the Decision to Divide Yemen into Regions', *Al-Jazeera*, 15 February 2014.

Aziz, Sahar, 'Egypt's Judiciary, Coopted', Sada, 20 August 2014, http://carnegieendowment.org/sada/?fa=56426

Baltayib, Nur al-Din, 'Al-'Alam al-Tunisi fi Qalb al-Mu'arika' ["The Tunisian media in the heart of the battle"]', *Al-Akhbar*, 27 September 2014.

Bartu, Peter 'Libya's Political Transition: The Challenges of Mediation', International Peace Institute, December 2014, https://www.ipinst.org/wp-content/uploads/publications/ipi_e_pub_mediation_libya.pdf.

Batatu, Hanna, *Syria's Peasantry, the Descendants of its Lesser Rural Notables and their Politics*, Princeton, NJ: Princeton University Press, 1999.

BBC News, 'Egypt's Army Backs Sisi as a Presidential Candidate', 24 January 2014, http://www.bbc.co.uk/news/world-middle-east-25917452

Beinin, Joel and Vairel, Frédéric, *Social Movements, Mobilisation, and Contestation in the Middle East and North Africa*, Stanford, CA: Stanford University Press, 2013.

Bellin, Eva Rana, *Stalled Democracy: Capital, Labor, and the Paradox of State-sponsored Development*, Ithaca, NY: Cornell University Press, 2002.

——, 'Drivers of Democracy: Lessons from Tunisia', *Crown Center Middle East Brief*, No. 25, 2013.

Bendor, Jonathan and Hammond, Thomas, 'Rethinking Allison's Models', *American Political Science Review*, Vol. 86, No. 2, 1992, pp. 301–322.

Benomar, Jamal, 'Memories of Morocco', *New Internationalist*, Issue 163, September 1986.

Berger, Miriam, 'A Revolutionary Role or a Remnant of the Past? The Future of the Egyptian Journalist Syndicate after the January 25 Revolution', *Arab Media and*

Society, Vol. 18, 10 June 2013, http://www.arabmediasociety.com/articles/down-loads/20130612130820_Berger_Miriam.pdf

Bertelsmann Stiftung, 'BTI 2016—Egypt Country Report', No. 18, 2016.

Bianchi, Robert, 'The Corporatization of the Egyptian Labor Movement', *Middle East Journal*, Vol. 40, No. 3, 1986, pp. 429–444.

Bickford, Louis, 'Transitional Justice', *The Encyclopedia of Genocide and Crimes Against Humanity*, Vol. 3, New York: Macmillan Reference USA, 2004, pp. 1045–1047.

———, 'Unofficial Truth Projects', *Human Rights Quarterly*, Vol. 29, No. 4, 2007, pp. 994–1035.

Blaise, Lilia, 'La loi d'immunisation de la révolution votée à l'Assemblée', Nawaat, 28 June 2013, http://nawaat.org/portail/2013/06/28/la-loi-dimmunisation-de-la-revolution-ou-la-difficulte-de-sortir-du-processus-revolutionnaire/

Bloomfield, David; Barnes, Teresa; and Huyse, Luc (eds), *Reconciliation after a Violent Conflict: A Handbook*, Stockholm: IDEA, 2003.

Boix, Carles and Stokes, Susan C., 'Endogenous Democratisation', *World Politics*, Vol. 55, No. 4, 2003, pp. 517–549.

Bouguerra, Abdeljalil, *De l'histoire de la gauche tunisienne: le mouvement Perspectives, 1963–1975*, Tunis: Cérès, 1993.

Boulby, Marion, 'The Islamic Challenge: Tunisia Since Independence', *Third World Quarterly*, Vol. 10, No. 2, 1988, pp. 590–614.

Bratton, Michael and Van de Walle, Nicholas, *Democratic Experiments in Africa: Regime Transitions in Comparative Perspective*, Cambridge: Cambridge University Press, 1997.

Brooks, Risa, 'Abandoned at the Palace: Why the Tunisian Military Defected from the Ben Ali Regime in January 2011', *Journal of Strategic Studies*, Vol. 36, No. 2, 2003, pp. 205–220.

Browers, Michaelle L., *Political Ideology in the Arab World: Accommodation and Transformation*, Cambridge: Cambridge University Press, 2009.

Brown, James, 'The Military and Society: The Turkish Case', *Middle Eastern Studies*, Vol. 25, No. 3, 1989, pp. 387–404.

Brown, Nathan J., 'Reason, Interest, Rationality, and Passion in Constitution Drafting', *Perspectives on Politics*, Vol. 6, No. 4, 2008.

———, 'Egypt's Failed Transition', *Journal of Democracy*, Vol. 24, No. 4, 2013, pp. 45–58.

———, 'Why do Egyptian courts say the darndest things?', *The Washington Post*, 25 March 2014, http://www.washingtonpost.com/blogs/monkey-cage/wp/2014/03/25/why-do-egyptian-courts-say-the-darndest-things/

Brownlee, Jason, 'Portents of Pluralism: How Hybrid Regimes Affect Democratic Transitions', *American Journal of Political Science*, Vol. 53, No. 3, 2009, pp. 515–532.

———, *Democracy Prevention: The Politics of the US-Egyptian Alliance*, Cambridge: Cambridge University Press, 2012.

Brownlee, Jason; Masoud, Tarek; and Reynolds, Andrew, *The Arab Spring: Pathways of Repression and Reform*, Oxford: Oxford University Press, 2015.

Brumberg, Daniel, 'Transforming the Arab World's Protection-Racket Politics', *Journal of Democracy*, Vol. 24, No. 3, 2013, pp. 88–103.

———, 'Egypt on Precipice? Moving Beyond Crisis', *Al Monitor*, 26 June 2013, http://www.al-monitor.com/pulse/originals/2013/06/egypt-june-30-muslim-brotherhood-opposition-legitimacy.html

Brynen, Rex; Moore, Pete W.; Salloukh, Bassel; Zahar, Marie-Joëlle, *Beyond the Arab Spring: Authoritarianism and Democratisation in the Arab World*, Boulder, CO: Lynne Rienner, 2012.

Cairo Institute for Human Rights Studies, 'Rights Groups Condemn Forced Retirement of 41 Judges for Expressing their Opinion', 18 March 2015, http://www.cihrs.org/?p=14650&lang=en

Calhoun, Craig; Juergensmeyer, Mark; and Van Antwerpen, Jonathan (eds), *Rethinking Secularism*, New York: Oxford University Press, 2011

Camau, Michel and Geisser, Vincent, *Habib Bourguiba: La trace et l'héritage*, Paris: Karthala, 2004.

Camau, Michel, 'Usages et représentations de l'alternance en situations critiques. Illustrations égyptiennes et tunisiennes', in Aldrin Philippe; Bargel, Lucie; Bué, Nicholas; and Pina, Christine (eds), *Politiques de l'alternance. Sociologie des changements (de) politiques*, Vulaine-sur-Seine: Éditions du Croquant, 2016.

The Carter Center, 'General National Congress Elections in Libya: Final Report', 7 July 2012, https://www.cartercenter.org/resources/pdfs/news/peace_publications/election_reports/libya-070712-final-rpt.pdf.

———, 'The 2014 Constitutional Drafting Assembly Elections in Libya', June 2014, https://www.cartercenter.org/resources/pdfs/news/peace_publications/election_reports/libya-06112014-final-rpt.pdf.

Charrad, Mounira, *States and Women's Rights in the Making of Post-Colonial Tunisia, Algeria, and Morocco*, Berkeley, CA: University of California Press, 2001.

Cheibub, José Antonio, 'Presidentialism and Democratic Performance', in Reynolds, Andrew, *The Architecture of Democracy: Constitutional Design, Conflict Management, and Democracy*, Oxford: Oxford University Press, 2002, pp. 104–140.

Chick, Kristen, 'Why Mubarak's trial may not bring Egypt full justice', Christian Science Monitor, 3 August 2011, http://www.csmonitor.com/World/Middle-East/2011/0803/Why-Mubarak-s-trial-may-not-bring-Egypt-full-justice-VIDEO

Clark, William Roberts, Golder, Matt; and Golder, Sona Nadenichek, *Principles of Comparative Politics*, Washington, D.C.: CQ Press, 2012.

Clot, André, *L'Egypte des Mamluks 1250–1517: L'empire des esclaves*, Paris: Tempus, 2009, pp. 41 and 70.

Cohen, Jean L. and Arato, Andrew, *Civil Society and Political Theory*, Boston, MA: MIT Press, 1994.

Cole, Peter and McQuinn, Brian (eds), *The Libyan Revolution and its Aftermath*, London: Hurst, 2015.

Coleman, James S. and Halisi, C. R. D., 'American Political Science and Tropical Africa: Universalism vs. Relativism', *African Studies Review*, 1983, pp. 25–62.

Cook, Steven A., *Ruling but not Governing: The Military and Political Development in Egypt, Algeria, and Turkey*, Baltimore, MD: Johns Hopkins University Press, 2007.

———, 'Where the Turkish Military Fails, Egypt's Succeds', *Foreign Affairs*, 19 July 2016, https://www.foreignaffairs.com/articles/turkey/2016–07–19/where-turkish-military-fails-egypts-succeeds

Cronin, Stephanie, *Armies and State-Building in the Middle East: Politics, Nationalism and Military Reform*, London: I. B. Tauris, 2014.

Dahl, Robert, *Polyarchy: Participation and Opposition*, New Haven, CT: Yale University Press, 1971.

Daily News Egypt, 'Al-Sisi forces judge into retirement for engaging in political work', 6 June 2016, http://www.dailynewsegypt.com/2016/06/06/al-sisi-forces-judge-retirement-engaging-political-work/?mc_cid=07bdbf63b8&mc_eid=[UNIQID

Dann, Philipp, *The Law of Development Cooperation: A Comparative Analysis of the World Bank, the EU and Germany*, Cambridge: Cambridge University Press, 2013.

David, Steven R., *Third World Coups d'État and International Security*, Baltimore, MD: Johns Hopkins University Press, 1987.

de Greiff, Pablo, 'Transitional Justice, Security, and Development', *Security and Justice Thematic Papers*, Washington: World Bank Development Report, 2011.

———, 'Theorising Transitional Justice', in Williams, Melissa; Nagy, Rosemary; and Elster, John (eds), *Transitional Justice Vol. 1*. New York: New York University Press, 2012.

———, 'Addendum: Mission to Tunisia', *Human Rights Council*, 2013, A/HRC/24/42/Add.1.

Dezalay, Sara, 'Des droits de l'homme au marché du développement: Note de recherche sur le champ faible de la gestion de conflits armés', *Actes de la recherche en sciences sociales*, Vol. 4, No. 174, 2008, pp. 68–79.

Diamond, Larry, 'Liberation Technology', *Journal of Democracy*, Vol. 21, 2010, pp. 69–83.

Dobry, Michel, *Sociologie des crises politiques: La dynamique des mobilisations multi-sectorielles*, Paris: Presses de Sciences Po, 2009.

Droz-Vincent, Philippe, 'Authoritarianism, Revolutions, Armies and Arab Regime Transitions', *The International Spectator*, Vol. 46, No. 2, 2011, pp. 5–21.

Du Toit, André, 'La commission Vérité et Réconciliation sud-africaine. Histoire locale et responsabilité face au monde', *Politique africaine*, No. 92, 2003, pp. 97–116.

Dutton, Jane E., 'The Making of Organizational Opportunities', *Research in Organizational Behaviour*, No. 15, 1993, pp. 1995–226.

Egypt Media Forum, 'Striving for Excellence in the Egyptian Media', 1–3 October

2014, published by *Arab Media and Society*, 12 January 2015, http://www.arab-mediasociety.com/?article=853

Egyptian Initiative for Personal Rights, 'The Weeks of Killing: State Violence, Communal Fighting and Sectarian Attacks in the Summer of 2013', 2014, http://eipr.org/sites/default/files/reports/pdf/weeks_of_killing_en.pdf

——, 'The Executive Summary Of The Fact-Finding Commission's Report: Falls Short Of Expectations', 4 December 2014, http://eipr.org/en/pressrelease/2014/12/04/2293

——, 'Egypt: Where Impunity is Entrenched and Accountability is Absent', 31 December 2014, http://eipr.org/en/pressrelease/2014/12/31/2320

Eickelman, Dale and Anderson, Jon W. (eds), *New Media in the Muslim World: The Emerging Public Sphere*, Bloomington: Indiana University Press, 2003.

El Azhary Sonbol, Amira, *The New Mamluks: Egyptian Society and Modern Feudalism*, Ithaca, NY: Syracuse University Press, 2000.

El-Issawi, Fatima, 'Tunisian Media in Transition', Carnegie Endowment for International Peace, 10 July 2012, http://carnegieendowment.org/2012/07/10/tunisian-media-in-transition-pub-48817

El Gantri, Rim (Head of Office for ICTJ's Tunisia Program), 'International Center for Transitional Justice Program Report: Tunisia', 6 March 2014, https://www.ictj.org/news/ictj-program-report-tunisia

——, 'Tunisia in Transition: One year after the Creation of the Truth and Dignity Commission', International Center for Transitional Justice Briefing, September 2015, https://www.ictj.org/publication/tunisia-transition-one-year-after-creation-truth-dignity-commission

El-Issawi, Fatima, 'Transitional Libyan Media: Free at Last?', Carnegie Endowment for International Peace, 14 May 2013, http://carnegieendowment.org/2013/05/14/transitional-libyan-media-free-at-last-pub-51747

El-Issawi, Fatima and Cammaerts, Bart, 'Shifting Journalistic Rules in Democratic Transitions: Lessons from Egypt', *Journalism*, Vol. 17, No. 5, 2016 pp. 549–566.

El-Rifae, Yasmin 'Looking for Justice Amid Relentless Politics', 18 January 2014, http://www.madamasr.com/sections/politics/egypt%E2%80%99s-courts

El-Sherif, Ashraf, 'The Muslim Brotherhood and the Future of Political Islam in Egypt', Carnegie Endowment for International Peace, October 2014, http://carnegieendowment.org/files/mb_future_egypt.pdf

El-Shimy, Yasser Magdy, 'Fumbled Democracy: Why Egypt's Transition Floundered', Presentation, Midwestern Political Science Association, 2015.

Eljarh, Mohamed, 'Can the United Nations Save the Day in Libya?', *Foreign Policy*, 4 July 2014, http://foreignpolicy.com/2014/07/04/can-the-united-nations-save-the-day-in-libya/

Elkins, Zachary; Ginsburg, Tom; and Melton, James, *The Endurance of National Constitutions*, Cambridge: Cambridge University Press, 2009.

Elmashed, Mohamed, 'We completely agree: Egyptian media in the era of President el-Sisi', Committee to Protect Journalists, 2015, https://cpj.org/x/5fe4

Elster, Jon, *Sour Grapes: Studies in the Subversion of Rationality*, Cambridge: Cambridge University Press, 1985.

———, *Ulysses Unbound: Studies in Rationality, Precommitment, and Constraints*, Cambridge: Cambridge University Press, 2000.

——— (ed.), *Deliberative Democracy*, Cambridge: Cambridge University Press, 1998, pp. 117–118.

Elster, Jon and Slagstad, Rune (eds), *Constitutionalism and Democracy*, Cambridge: Cambridge University Press, 1988.

Elster, Jon; Offe, Claus; and Preuss, Ulrich K., *Institutional Design in Post-Communist Societies: Rebuilding the Ship at Sea*, Cambridge: Cambridge University Press, 1998.

Esposito, John L.; Sonn, Tamara; and Voll, John O., *Islam and Democracy After the Arab Spring*, Oxford: Oxford University Press, 2015.

Farid, Doaa, 'Egyptian Army's Economic Empire: Unidentified Market Share Yet High Impact', *Daily News Egypt*, 7 November 2015.

Feaver, Peter D., 'The Civil-Military Problematique: Huntington, Janowitz, and the Question of Civil Control', *Armed Forces and Society*, Vol. 23, No. 2, 1996, p. 154.

FIDH, Mouvement Mondial des Droits Humains, *Les commissions de vérité et de réconciliation: l'expérience marocaine*, No. 396, 2004, https://www.fidh.org/fr/regions/maghreb-moyen-orient/maroc/Les-Commissions-de-verite-et-de

Filiu, Jean-Pierre, *The Arab Revolution: Ten Lessons from the Democratic Uprising*, London: Hurst, 2011.

Fletcher Forum Staff, 'An Interview with Bernardino León, EU Special Representative for the Southern Mediterranean,' The Fletcher Forum for World Affairs, 18 September 2014, http://www.fletcherforum.org/2013/09/18/leon/

Forbis, Jeremy Scott, 'Organized Civil Society: A Cross National Evaluation of the Socio-political Effects of Non-governmental Organization Density on Governmental Corruption, State Terror, and Anti-government Demonstrations', PhD Thesis, Ohio State University, 2008.

Ford Rojas, John-Paul, 'Muammar Gaddafi in his own words', *The Telegraph*, 20 October 2011.

Freelon, Deen; Lynch, Marc; and Aday, Sean, 'Online Fragmentation in Wartime: A Longitudinal Analysis of Tweets About Syria, 2011–13', *Annals of the American Academy of Political and Social Sciences*, Vol. 659, 2014, pp. 166–79.

Fukuyama, Francis, 'The End of History, Five Years Later', *History and Theory*, Vol. 34, No. 2, 1999, pp. 27–43.

Geertz, Clifford, 'The Rotating Credit Association: A "Middle Rung" in Development', *Economic Development and Cultural Change*, Vol. 10, No. 3, 1962, pp. 241–263.

Gelvin, James L., *The Arab Uprisings: What Everyone Needs to Know*, Oxford: Oxford University Press, 2015.

Ghannouchi, Rached, 'Tunisia's Perilous Path to Freedom', *The Wall Street Journal*, 15 January 2015, https://www.wsj.com/articles/rached-ghannouchi-tunisias-perilous-path-to-freedom-1421353952.

Ginsburg, Tom; Elkins, Zachary; and Blount, Justin, "Does the Process of Constitution-Making Matter?", *Annual Review of Law and Social Science*, Vol. 5, 2009, pp. 201–223.

Giurovich, Dina and Keenan, Jeremy, 'The UNDP, the World Bank and Biodiversity in the Algerian Sahara', in Keenan, Jeremy (ed.), *The Sahara: Past, President and Future*, Abingdon: Routledge, 2007.

Goldberg, Ellis, 'The Foundations of State-Labor Relations in Contemporary Egypt', *Comparative Politics*, 1992, pp. 147–161.

———, 'Mubarakism Without Mubarak: Why Egypt's Military Will Not Embrace Democracy', *Foreign Affairs*, 11 February 2011.

Gready, Paul and Robbins, Simon, 'From Transitional to Transformative Justice: A New Agenda for Practice', *The International Journal of Transitional Justice*, Vol. 8, No. 3 2014, pp. 339–361.

Grewal, Sharan, 'Why Tunisia Didn't Follow Egypt's Path', *The Monkey Cage*, 4 February 2015, http://www.washingtonpost.com/blogs/monkey-cage/wp/2015/02/04/why-egypt-didnt-follow-tunisias-path/

Grubbs, Larry, *Secular Missionaries: Americans and African Development in the 1960s*, Amherst, MA: University of Massachusetts Press, 2009.

Gunay, Niyazi, 'Implementing the "February 28" Recommendations: A Scorecard', Research Notes No. 10, Washington Institute for Near East Policy, 2001.

Hafez, Kai (ed.), *Arab Media: Power and Weakness*, London: Bloomsbury Academic, 2008.

Hart, Vivien, 'Democratic Constitution Making', United States Institute of Peace Special Report 107, July 2003, https://www.usip.org/publications/2003/07/democratic-constitution-making.

Hagopian, Frances, 'Parties and Voters in Emerging Democracies', in Boix, Carles and Stokes, Susan (eds), *The Oxford Handbook of Comparative Politics*, Oxford: Oxford University Press, 2007.

Hale, William, *Turkish Politics and the Military*, New York: Routledge, 1994.

Hamzawy, Amr, 'Isnaf al-Arab hasab al-'Alam Fashi ["Types of Arab Neo-Fascist Media"]', *Al-Masry al-Youm*, 19 July 2014; Egyptian journalist interviewed in Washington, DC, November 2014.

Hanna, Michael Wahid, 'Egypt's Search for Truth', *The Cairo Review of Global Affairs*, 2011, https://www.thecairoreview.com/essays/egypts-search-for-truth/

Harb, Imad, 'The Egyptian Military in Politics: Disengagement or Accommodation?', *The Middle East Journal*, 2003, pp. 269–290.

Harding, Henry, 'ANALYSIS: Egypt's Military-Economic Empire', *Middle East Eye*, 26 March 2016.

Harris, George S., 'The Role of the Military in Turkish Politics, Part I', *Middle East Journal*, Vol. 19, No. 1, 1965, pp. 54–66.

Haugbolle, Rikke H. and Cavatorta, Francesco, '"Vive la grande famille des médias tunisiens": Media reform, authoritarian resilience and societal responses in Tunisia', *Journal of North African Studies*, Vol. 17, No 1, 2012, pp. 97–112.

Hauslohner, Abigail, 'Egypt's Military Expands Its Control of the Country's Economy', *Washington Post*, 16 March 2014.

Hayner, Priscilla B., 'Fifteen Truth Commissions. 1974 to 1994: A Comparative Study', *Human Rights Quarterly*, Vol. 16, No. 4, 1994, pp. 597–655.

Haysom, Nicholas; Al-Ali, Zaid; and Law, Michele, 'History of the Iraqi constitution-making process', December 2005, http://zaidalali.com/resources/academic-articles/.

Hechter, Michael C., 'From Class to Culture', *American Journal of Sociology*, Vol. 110, No. 2, 2004, pp. 400–445.

Hefny, Mostafa Hani, 'The Material Politics of Revolution and Counter-Revolution: Labor and Democratization in Egypt: 2011–2013', Columbia University, 2014.

Henry, Clement, 'Tunisia's "Sweet Little" Regime', in Rotberg, Robert I., *Worst of the Worst: Dealing with Repressive Rogue Nations*, Washington DC: Brookings Institution Press, 2007.

Hill, Ewan and Mansour, Muhammad, 'Egypt's army took part in torture and killings during revolution, report shows', *The Guardian*, 10 April 2013, online: http://www.theguardian.com/world/2013/apr/10/egypt-army-torture-killings-revolution

Hmed, Choukri, 'Abeyance Networks, Contingency and Structures. History and Origins of the Tunisian Revolution', *Revue française de science politique*, Vol. 62, Nos. 5–6, 2012, pp. 797–820.

Horowitz, Donald L., *Constitutional Change and Democracy in Indonesia*, Cambridge: Cambridge University Press, 2013.

Hourani, Albert, *Arabic Thought in the Liberal Age*, Oxford: Oxford University Press, 1962.

———, *Arabic Thought in the Liberal Age, 1798–1939*, Cambridge: Cambridge University Press, 1983.

Howard, Philip and Hussain, Muzammil, 'The Role of Digital Media', *Journal of Democracy*, Vol. 22, 2011, pp. 35–48.

Howard, Marc Morjé, *The Weakness of Civil Society in Post-Communist Europe*, Cambridge: Cambridge University Press, 2003.

Howeydi, Fahmy, 'Al-La'ab fi al-'Alam ["Playing with the Media"]', *Al-Shorouk*, 20 August 2014.

Human Rights Watch, 'Tunisia: Military Courts that Sentenced Islamist Leaders Violated Basic Fair-Trial Norms', 1 October 1992, https://www.hrw.org/report/1992/10/01/tunisia-military-courts-sentenced-islamist-leaders-violated-basic-fair-trial-norms

BIBLIOGRAPHY

——, 'Morocco's Truth Commission. Honoring Past Victims during an Uncertain Present', 27 November 2005, https://www.hrw.org/sites/default/files/reports/morocco1105wcover.pdf

——, 'A Larger Prison: Repression of Former Political Prisoners in Tunisia', 24 March 2010, https://www.hrw.org/report/2010/03/24/larger-prison/larger-prison

——, 'Tunisie: Le procès de Ben Ali et des autres responsables accusés du meurtre des manifestants', 11 June 2012, https://www.hrw.org/fr/news/2012/06/11/tunisie-le-proces-de-ben-ali-et-des-autres-responsables-accuses-du-meurtre-de

——, 'Tunisie: Les blessés de la révolution ont besoin de soins urgents', 28 May 2012, http://www.hrw.org/fr/news/2012/05/28/tunisie-les-bless-s-du-soul-vement-ont-un-besoin-urgent-de-soins

——, 'Tunisia: Honor Judges Request to See Case File', 15 January 2013, http://www.hrw.org/news/2012/01/16/tunisia-honor-judges-request-see-case-files

——, 'Egypt: Publish Fact-Finding Committee Report. Ensure Right to Truth for Victims of Police and Military Abuse', 24 January 2013, http://www.hrw.org/news/2013/01/24/egypt-publish-fact-finding-committee-report

——, 'Egypt: Many Protestors Shot in Head or Chest', 28 July 2013, http://www.hrw.org/news/2013/07/28/egypt-many-protesters-shot-head-or-chest

——, 'Egypt: No Acknowledgment of Justice for Mass Protestor Killings', 10 December 2013, http://www.hrw.org/news/2013/12/10/egypt-no-acknowledgment-or-justice-mass-protester-killings

——, 'Hope on Justice for Past Abuses', 22 May 2014, https://www.hrw.org/news/2014/05/22/tunisia-hope-justice-past-abuses

——, 'All According to Plan', 12 August 2014, https://www.hrw.org/report/2014/08/12/all-according-plan/raba-massacre-and-mass-killings-protesters-egypt

——, 'Egypt: Rash Deaths in Custody', HRW Reports, 21 January 2015, http://www.hrw.org/news/2015/01/21/egypt-rash-deaths-custody

——, 'Tunisia: Law Falls Short on Judicial Independence. Increase Autonomy of Judges' Oversight Body', 2 June 2015, https://www.hrw.org/news/2015/06/02/tunisia-law-falls-short-judicial-independence

——, 'Statement regarding Human Rights Watch in Morocco', 2 November 2015, https://www.hrw.org/news/2015/11/06/statement-regarding-human-rights-watch-activities-morocco

Huntington, Samuel P., *The Third Wave: Democratisation in the Late Twentieth Century*, Norman, OK: University of Oklahoma Press, 1993.

——, *The Soldier and the State: The Theory and Politics of Civil-Military Relations*, Cambridge, MA: Harvard Belknap, 2002.

ICRC, 'Libya: Struggle to survive as services collapse', International Committee of the Red Cross, 9 December 2015, https://www.icrc.org/en/document/libya-struggle-survive-services-collapse

BIBLIOGRAPHY

Ikram, Khalid, *The Egyptian Economy, 1952–2000: Performance Policies and Issues*, Abingdon, Routledge: 2007.

Inglehart, Ronald and Welzel, Christian, 'Changing Mass Priorities: The Link Between Modernisation and Democracy', *Perspectives on Politics*, Vol. 8, No. 2, 2010, pp. 551–567.

Institute for Integrated Transitions (IFIT), 'Inside the Transition Bubble: International Expert Assistance in Tunisia', April 2013, p. 4, http://www.ifit-transitions.org/publications/inside-the-transition-bubble-international-expert-assistance-in-tunisia/inside-the-transition-bubble-en-full

International Bar Association's Human Rights Institute, 'Egypt: Separating Law and Politics: Challenges to the Independence of Judges and Prosecutors in Egypt', 2014, http://www.legalbrief.co.za/article.php?story=20140211121632347

International Center for Transitional Justice, Annual Report 2001/2002, https://www.ictj.org/sites/default/files/ICTJ_Annual_Report_2001–2002.pdf

——, Annual Report 2004–2005, 'ICTJ Mission and Statement', https://www.ictj.org/sites/default/files/ICTJ_AnnualReport_2004–5.pdf

——, 'Transitional Justice in Morocco: A Progress Report', 2005, http://www.ictj.org/sites/default/files/ICTJ-Morocco-Progress-Report-2005-English.pdf

——, Annual Report 2008, 'A World in Transition', https://www.ictj.org/sites/default/files/ICTJ_Annual_Report_2008.pdf

——, 'Truth and Memory', https://www.ictj.org/our-work/transitional-justice-issues/truth-and-memory

——, 'Tunisia's Proposed Reconciliation Law Would Grant Amnesty for Corruption, Fail to Grow the Economy', 21 July 2016, https://www.ictj.org/news/Tunisia-amnesty-economic-development

——, 'Morocco still a model for justice in MENA, but questions remain', 2 August 2016, https://www.ictj.org/news/morocco-still-model-justice-mena-questions-remain

International Crisis Group, 'Popular Protest in North Africa and the Middle East (IV): Tunisia's Way', North Africa Report Vol. 106, 2011, https://www.crisisgroup.org/middle-east-north-africa/north-africa/egypt/popular-protest-north-africa-and-middle-east-i-egypt-victorious

——, 'Tunisia: Combatting Impunity, Restoring Security', Middle East/North Africa Report, No. 123, 9 May 2012, https://www.crisisgroup.org/middle-east-north-africa/north-africa/tunisia/tunisia-combatting-impunity-restoring-security

——, 'The Tunisian Exception: Success and Limits of Consensus', Middle East and North Africa Briefing No. 37, 5 June 2014, https://www.crisisgroup.org/middle-east-north-africa/north-africa/tunisia/tunisian-exception-success-and-limits-consensus

——, 'Tunisia: Transitional Justice and the Fight Against Corruption', Middle East and North Africa Report, No. 168, 3 May 2016, https://www.crisisgroup.org/

middle-east-north-africa/north-africa/tunisia/tunisia-transitional-justice-and-fight-against-corruption

Isaac, Jeffrey C., 'Modernisation and Politics', *Perspectives on Politics*, Vol. 13, No. 1, 2015, pp. 1–6.

Jamal, Amaney A., *Barriers to Democracy: The Other Side of Social Capital in Palestine and the Arab World*, Princeton, NJ: Princeton University Press, 2007.

Jenkins, J. Craig and Kposowa, Augustine J., 'Explaining Military Coups d'État: Black Africa, 1957–1984', *American Sociological Review*, 1990, pp. 861–875.

Joyce, Robert, 'Live Blog: NCA Member Mohamed Brahmi Assassinated', Tunisia Live, 25 July 2013, http://www.tunisia-live.net/2013/07/25/nca-member-mohamed-brahmi-assassinated

Kalyvas, Stathis N., *The Rise of Christian Democracy in Europe*, Ithaca, NY: Cornell University Press, 1996.

Kamel, Ahmed, 'Saad Eddine Ibrahim yutalibu bitahwil al-mudaris wa al-musajid ila ma'taqalat "mu'aqata"' [Saad Eddine Ibrahim demands the transfer of schools and mosques to 'temporary' prisons], *Al-Watan*, 24 January 2014, http://www.elwatan-news.com/news/details/403381

Kandil, Hazem, *Soldiers, Spies and Statesmen: Egypt's Road to Revolt*, London: Verso, 2012.

Kaplan, Robert, 'One Small Revolution', *The New York Times*, 22 January 2011, http://www.nytimes.com/2011/01/23/opinion/23kaplan.html?pagewanted=all

Karl, Terry Lynn., 'Dilemmas of Democratisation in Latin America', *Comparative Politics*, Vol. 23, No. 1, 1990, pp. 1–21.

Keck, Margaret E., *The Workers' Party and Democratization in Brazil*, New Haven, CT: Yale University Press, 1995.

Kepel, Gilles, *Jihad: The Trail of Political Islam*, Cambridge, MA: Harvard University Press, 2002.

Keshavarzian, Arang, *Bazaar and State in Iran: The Politics of the Tehran Marketplace*, Cambridge: Cambridge University Press, 2007.

Khan, Zafrullah and Joseph, Brian, 'Pakistan After Musharraf: The Media Take Center Stage', *Journal of Democracy* Vol. 19, Issue 4, 2008.

Khlifi, Omar, *L'assassinat de Salah Ben Youssef*, Tunis: MC-Editions, 2005.

Kholaif, Dalia, 'The Egyptian Army's Economic Juggernaut', Al-Jazeera, 5 August 2013.

King, Daniel and LoGerfo, Jim, 'Thailand: Toward Democratic Stability', *Journal of Democracy*, Vol. 7, No. 1, 1996, pp. 102–117.

Kirkpatrick, David, 'Prominent Egyptian Liberal Says He Sought West's Support for Uprising', *The New York Times*, 4 July 2013 https://mobile.nytimes.com/2013/07/05/world/middleeast/elbaradei-seeks-to-justify-ouster-of-egypts-president.html

———, 'Egypt Military Enlists Religion to Quell Ranks,' *The New York Times*,

25 August 2013, http://www.nytimes.com/2013/08/26/world/middleeast/egypt.
html

——, 'Ousted general in Egypt is back, as Islamists' foe', *The New York Times*,
30 October 2013, http://www.nytimes.com/2013/10/30/world/middleeast/
ousted-general-in-egypt-is-back-as-islamists-foe.html

Kopstein, Jeffrey, '1989 as a Lens for the Communist Past and Post-Communist
Future', *Contemporary European History*, Vol. 18, No. 3, 2009, pp. 289–302.

Kornhauser, William, *The Politics of Mass Society*, Abingdon: Routledge, 2013.

Kourda, Sami, *Le 'complot' Barraket Essahel: Chronique d'un calvaire*, Tunis: Sud
Editions, 2014.

Krasner, Stephen, 'State Power and the Structure of International Trade', *World
Politics*, Vol. 28, No. 3, April 1976, pp. 317–347.

Kritz, Neil J. (ed.), *Transitional Justice: How Emerging Democracies Reckon with
Former Regimes*, Washington: United States Institute for Peace (three volumes),
1995.

Künkler, Mirjam and Stepan, Alfred (eds), *Democracy and Islam in Indonesia*, New
York: Columbia University Press, 2013.

Kuran, Timur, *Public Truth, Private Lies*, Cambridge, MA: Harvard University Press,
1995.

Kuru, Ahmet. T., 'Passive and Assertive Secularism: Historical Conditions, Ideological
Struggles, and State Policies Toward Religion', *World Politics*, Vol. 59, No. 4, 2007,
pp. 568–594.

——, *Secularism and State Policies Toward Religion: The United States, France and
Turkey*, Cambridge: Cambridge University Press, 2009.

Kurzman, Charles, 'Not Ready for Democracy? Theoretical and Historical Objections
to the Concept of Prerequisites', *Sociological Analysis*, Vol. 1, 1998, pp. 1–12.

Krishan, Mohamed, 'al-'Alam al-Tunisi wa Huma al-Intikhabat ["The Tunisian Media
and Election Fever"]', *Al-Quds al-Arabi*, 21 October 2014.

Lackner, Helen, 'Yemen's Peaceful Transition from Saleh's Autocratic Rule: Could it
Have Succeeded?', International IDEA, 2016, http://www.idea.int/sites/default/
files/publications/yemens-peaceful-transition-from-autocracy.pdf

Landau, David, 'The Reality of Social Rights Enforcement', *Harvard International
Law Journal*, Vol. 53, No. 1, 2012.

Laplante, Lisa, 'The Peruvian Truth Commission's Historical Memory Project:
Empowering Truth-Tellers to Confront Truth-Deniers', *Journal of Human Rights*,
Vol. 6, No. 4, 2008, pp. 433–452.

LeBas, Adrienne, *From Protest to Parties: Party-building and Democratisation in Africa*,
Oxford: Oxford University Press, 2011.

Lederach, John-Paul, *Building Peace: Sustainable Reconciliation in Divided Societies*,
Washington, DC: United States Institute of Peace, 1997.

Lefranc, Sandrine, 'La violence d'État et le pardon politique', *Raisons politiques*, Vol. 1,
1998, pp. 7–27.

————, *Politiques du pardon*, Paris: PUF, 2002.

————, 'La professionnalisation d'un militantisme réformateur du droit: l'invention de la justice transitionnelle', *Droit et société*, Vol. 73, 2009, pp. 561–589.

————, 'La justice transitionnelle, une justice pour les temps nouveaux?' in Gobe, Eric (ed.), *Des justices en transition dans le monde arabe? Contributions à une réflexion sur les rapports entre justice et politique*, Rabat: Centre Jacques-Berque, 2016, pp. 211–234.

Lerner, Daniel, *The Passing of Traditional Society: Modernizing the Middle East*, New York: Free Press, 1958.

Lerner, Daniel and Robinson, Richard D., 'Swords into Ploughshares: The Turkish Army as a Modernizing Force', *World Politics* Vol. 13, No. 1, 1960, pp. 19–44.

Lijphart, Arend, *Patterns of Democracy: Government Forms and Performance in Thirty-Six Countries*, New Haven, CT: Yale University Press, 1999.

Linz, Juan J., *Totalitarianism and Authoritarian Regimes*, Boulder, CO: Lynne Rienner Publishers, 2006.

Linz, Juan J. and Stepan, Alfred, *Problems of Democratic Transition and Consolidation: Southern Europe, South America, and Post-Communist Europe*, Baltimore, MD: Johns Hopkins University Press, 1996.

Lippmann, Walter, 'The Indispensable Opposition', *Atlantic Monthly*, Vol. 164, 1939, pp. 186–190.

Lipset, Seymour Martin, 'Some Social Requisites of Democracy: Economic Development and Political Legitimacy', *American Political Science Review*, Vol. 53, No. 1, 1959, pp. 69–105.

Liska, Allen E., 'Modeling the Relationships Between Macro Forms of Social Control', *Annual Review of Sociology*, 1997, pp. 39–61.

Longo, Pietro and Meringolo, Azzurra (eds), *The Tunisian Media: Between Polarization and Compromise*, Rome: Reset Doc, 2015.

Lust, Ellen and Waldner, David, 'Parties in Transitional Democracies: Authoritarian Legacies and Post-Authoritarian Challenges', Technical Report, University of Gothenburg and University of Virginia, 2015.

Lust, Ellen and Khatib, Lina, 'The Transformation of Arab Activism', POMED Policy Brief Series, May 2014.

Lust-Okar, Ellen, *Structuring Conflict in the Arab World: Incumbents, Opponents, and Institutions*, Cambridge: Cambridge University Press, 2005.

————, 'Elections Under Authoritarianism: Preliminary Lessons from Jordan', *Democratization*, Vol. 13, No. 3, 2006, pp. 456–71.

Lynch, Marc, *Voices of a New Arab Public: Iraq, Al-Jazeera, and Middle East Politics Today*, New York: Columbia University Press, 2006.

————, 'After Egypt: The Promise and Limits of Social Media', *Perspectives on Politics*, Vol. 9, No. 2, 2011, pp. 301–310.

————, *The Arab Uprising: The Unfinished Revolutions of the New Middle East*, New York: Public Affairs, 2012.

Lynch, Marc (ed.), *The Arab Uprisings Explained: New Contentious Politics in the Middle East*, New York: Columbia University Press, 2014.

Lynch, Marc; Freelon, Deen; and Aday, Sean, 'Syria in the Arab Spring', *Research and Politics*, Vol. 1, No. 3, 2014, DOI: 10.1177/2053168014549091

———, 'Syria's Socially Mediated Civil War', United States Intitute of Peace, Peaceworks No. 91, 2014.

———, *Blogs and Bullets V: How Social Media Undermined Egypt's Transition*, Washington, DC: Peacetech Lab, 2016.

Madison, James, '10: The Same Subject Continued: The Union as a Safeguard Against Domestic Faction and Insurrection', *The Federalist*, Vol. 10, 1787.

Malinowski, Tom, 'Jefferson in Benghazi', *The New Republic*, 9 June 2011, https://newrepublic.com/article/89645/benghazi-libya-rebels.

———, 'The New Tunisian Model of Governance', Bureau of Democracy, Human Rights, and Labor, United States Department of State, 2 September 2015, http://www.state.gov/j/drl/rls/rm/2015/246584.htm.

Marinov, Nikolay and Goemans, Hein, 'Coups and Democracy', *British Journal of Political Science*, Vol. 44, No. 4, 2014, pp. 799–825.

Marks, Monica, 'Complementary Status for Tunisian Women', *Foreign Policy*, 20 August 2012, http://foreignpolicy.com/2012/08/20/complementary-status-for-tunisian-women/

———, 'Convince, Coerce, or Compromise? Ennahda's Approach to Tunisia's Constitution', Brookings Doha Center paper, 2014, https://www.brookings.edu/research/convince-coerce-or-compromise-ennahdas-approach-to-tunisias-constitution/

Marshall, Shana, and Stacher, Joshua, 'Egypt's Generals and Transnational Capital', *Middle East Report*, No. 262, 2012.

Martin, Ian, 'The United Nations' Role in the First Year of the Transition', in Cole, Peter and McQuinn, Brian (eds) *The Libyan Revolution and its Aftermath*, London: Hurst, 2015.

Marzouki, Moncef, 'Winning Freedom', *Index on Censorship*, Vol. 18, No. 1, 1989, pp. 23–25.

Marzouki, Nadia, 'Dancing by the Cliff: Constitution Writing in Post-Revolutionary Tunisia; 2011–2014', in Bali, Asli and Lerner, Hanna (eds), *Constitution Writing, Religion and Democracy*, Cambridge: Cambridge University Press, 2017.

Maslin, Jared, 'Pro-regime journalists are shaping public opinion in Egypt', *Columbia Journalism Review*, 22 January 2015, http://www.cjr.org/b-roll/egypt_sisi_mona_iraqi.php.

Masoud, Tarek, 'Has the Door Closed on Arab Democracy?', *Journal of Democracy*, Volume 26, No. 1, 2015.

McCarthy, John D. and Zald, Mayer N., 'Resource Mobilization and Social Movements: A Partial Theory', *American Journal of Sociology*, 1977, pp. 1212–1241.

McDermott, Anthony, *Egypt from Nasser to Mubarak: A Flawed Revolution, Vol. 3*, Abingdon: Routledge, 2012.

Mendeloff, David, 'Truth-Seeking, Truth-Telling and Post-Conflict Peacebuilding: Curb the Enthusiasm?', *International Studies Review*, Vol. 6, No. 3, September 2004, pp. 355–380.

Mezran, Karim; Lamen, Fadel; and Knecht, Eric, 'Post-revolutionary Politics in Libya: Inside the General National Congress', Atlantic Council, 2013, http://www.atlanticcouncil.org/publications/issue-briefs/post-revolutionary-politics-in-libya-inside-the-general-national-congress.

Mezran, Karim and Pack, Jason, 'Libya Stability at Risk', *Foreign Policy*, 2 May 2013, http://foreignpolicy.com/2013/05/02/libyan-stability-at-risk/

The Military Balance, Annual, London: International Institute of Strategic Studies, 2011.

Miller, Zinaida, 'Effects of Invisibility: In Search of the "Economic" in Transitional Justice', *International Journal of Transitional Justice*, Vol. 2, 2008, p. 267.

Milton, Andrew K., 'Bound but Not Gagged: Media Reform in Democratic Transitions', *Comparative Political Studies*, Vol. 34, 2001, pp. 493–526.

Mitri, Tarek, 'Insight into the UN in Libya: Interview with Dr. Tarek Mitri, Head of the United Nations Support Mission in Libya (UNSMIL)', Issam Fares Institute for Public Policy and International Affairs, American University of Beirut, October 2012.

Moustafa, Tamir, 'Law Versus the State: The Judicialization of Politics in Egypt,' *Law and Social Inquiry*, Vol. 28, 2003, pp. 883–930.

Moustafa, Tamir, 'The Political Role of the Supreme Constitutional Court: Between Principles and Practice', in Nathalie Bernard-Maugiron (ed.), *Judges and Political Reform in Egypt*, Cairo: American University in Cairo Press, 2008.

Nassar, Habib 'Transitional Justice in the Wake of the Arab Uprisings: Between Complexity and Standardisation' in Fisher, Kirsten J. and Stewart, Robert (eds), *Transitional Justice and the Arab Spring*, Abingdon: Routledge, 2014.

Nassif, Hicham Bou, 'Generals and Autocrats: How Coup-Proofing Predetermined the Military Elite's Behavior in the Arab Spring', *Political Science Quarterly*, Vol. 130, No. 2, 2015, pp. 245–275.

———, 'A Military Besieged: The Armed Forces, the Police, and the Party in Bin 'Ali's Tunisia, 1987–2011', *International Journal of Middle East Studies*, Vol. 47, No. 1, 2015, pp. 65–87.

Nino, Carlos Santiago, *Radical Evil on Trial*, New Haven, CT: Yale University Press, 1999.

O'Callaghan, Derek; Prucha, Nico; Greene, Derek; Conway, Maura; Carthy, Joe and Cunningham, Pádraig, 'Online Social Media in the Syria Conflict: Encompassing the Extremes and the In-Betweens', August, 2014, https://arxiv.org/abs/1401.7535.

O'Donnell, Guillermo; Schmitter Philippe C., and Whitehead, Laurence, *Transitions from Authoritarian Rule: Southern Europe, Vol. 1*, Baltimore, MD: Johns Hopkins University Press, 1986.

Omar, Rowida, 'The Delay of Transitional Justice in Egypt', Middle East Institute, 12 February 2014, http://www.mei.edu/content/delay-transitional-justice-egypt

Opgenhaffen, Veerle and Freeman, Mark, *Transitional Justice in Morocco: a Progress Report*, International Center for Transitional Justice, 2005, https://www.ictj.org/publication/transitional-justice-morocco-progress-report

Ottaway, Marina, 'Al-Sisi's Egypt: The Military Moves on the Economy', Middle East Program Occasional Paper Series, Woodrow Wilson International Center for Scholars, 4–5, 2015.

Owen, Roger, *The Rise and Fall of Arab Presidencies for Life*, Cambridge, MA: Harvard University Press, 2012.

Parvaz, Dorothy, 'Nasr City: What Remains after a Massacre', Al-Jazeera, 27 July 2013, http://www.aljazeera.com/indepth/features/2013/07/2013727182042553247.html

Paris, Roland, *At War's End: Building Peace After Civil Conflict*, Cambridge: Cambridge University Press, 2004.

Pavlakovic, Vjeran, 'Croatia, the International Criminal Tribunal for the former Yugoslavia, and General Gotovina as a Political Symbol', *Europe-Asia Studies*, Vol. 62, No. 10, 2010, pp. 1707–1740.

Pepinsky, Thomas B., 'Political Islam and the Limits of the Indonesian Model', *Taiwan Journal of Democracy*, Vol. 10, No. 1, 2014, pp. 105–121.

Perez-Linan, Anabel and Mainwaring, Scott, 'Democratic Breakdown and Survival in Latin America, 1945–2005', in Brinks, Daniel; Leiras, Marcelo; and Mainwaring, Scott (eds), *Reflections on Uneven Democracies: The Legacy of Guillermo O'Donnell*, Baltimore, MD: Johns Hopkins University Press, 2014.

Peterson, Mark A., 'Egypt's Media Ecology in a Time of Revolution', *Arab Media and Society*, 2011, http://www.arabmediasociety.com/?article=770.

Plattner, Marc F., 'Media and Democracy: The Long View', *Journal of Democracy*, Vol. 23, 2012, pp. 62–73.

Pollack, Kenneth Michael, *Arabs at War: Military Effectiveness, 1948–1991*, Lincoln, NE: University of Nebraska Press, 2002.

Posusney, Marsha Pripstein, 1997, *Labor and the State in Egypt: Workers, Unions, and Economic Restructuring*, New York: Columbia University Press, 1997.

Powell, Jonathan M. and Thyne, Clayton L., 'Global Instances of Coups from 1950 to 2010: A New Dataset', *Journal of Peace Research*, Vol. 48, No. 2, 2011, pp. 249–259.

Power, Timothy, 'Theorizing a Moving Target: O'Donnell's Changing Views of Postauthoritarian Regimes', University of Oxford, unpublished working paper, 19 March 2012, http://kellogg.nd.edu/odonnell/papers/power.pdf

Przeworski, Adam, *Democracy and the Market: Political and Economic Reforms in Eastern Europe and Latin America*, Cambridge: Cambridge University Press, 1991.

Przeworski, Adam and Limongi, Fernando, 'Modernisation: Theories and Facts', *World Politics*, Vol. 49, No. 2, 1997, pp. 155–183.

Puchot, Pierre, *La révolution confisquée: enquête sur la transition démocratique en Tunisie*, Arles: Actes Sud, 2012.

Putnam, Robert D., *Bowling Alone: The Collapse and Revival of American Community*, New York: Simon and Schuster, 2000.

———, Leonardi, Robert; and Y Nanetti, Raffaella, *Making Democracy Work: Civic Traditions in Modern Italy*, Princeton, NJ: Princeton University Press, 1994.

Qallash, Yahya, 'Al-'Alam al-Masri ba'd 25 January wa 30 June ["The Egyptian Media After 25 January and 30 June"]', *Al-Ahram*, 19 October 2014.

Quinliven, James T., 'Coup Proofing: Its Practice and Consequences in the Middle East', *International Security*, Vol. 24, No. 2, 1999, pp. 131–165.

Rageh, Rawya, 'Egypt revolt fact-finding report is a mystery', *Al Jazeera English*, 11 May 2013, http://www.aljazeera.com/indepth/features/2013/05/2013511 859142229.html

Randal, Jonathan, *The Tragedy of Lebanon*, New York: Just Books, 2012.

Richmond, Olivier and Franks, Jason, *Liberal Peace Transitions: Between Peacebuilding and Statebuilding*, Edinburgh: Edinburgh University Press, 2009.

Riedl, Rachel Beatty, *Authoritarian Origins of Democratic Party Systems in Africa*, Cambridge: Cambridge University Press, 2014.

Ross, Michael L., 'Does Oil Hinder Democracy?', *World Politics*, Vol. 53, No. 3, 2001, pp. 325–361.

Rubin, Humberto, 'One Step Away from Democracy', *Journal of Democracy*, Vol. 1, No. 4, 1990, pp. 59–61.

Rueschemeyer, Dietrich; Stephens, Evelyne Huber; and Stephens, John D., *Capitalist Development and Democracy*, Cambridge: Cambridge University Press, 1992.

Rugh, William, *Arab Mass Media*, New York: Praeger, 2004.

Rustow, Dankwart A., 'Transitions to democracy: Toward a dynamic model', *Comparative Politics*, 1970, pp. 337–363.

Rutherford, Bruce, *Egypt After Mubarak: Liberalism, Islam, and Democracy in the Arab World*, Princeton, NJ: Princeton University Press, 2013.

Said, Atef, 'A New Judicial Moment in Egypt', Jadaliyya, 25 December 2012, http://www.jadaliyya.com/pages/index/9247/a-new-judicial-moment-in-egypt

Sakallıoğlu, Ümit Cizre, 'The Anatomy of the Turkish Military's Political Autonomy', *Comparative Politics*, Vol. 29, No. 2, 1977, pp. 151–166.

Sakr, Naomi, *Arab Television Today*, New York: I. B. Tauris, 2007.

———, *Transformations in Egyptian Journalism*. London: I. B. Tauris, 2013.

Salamé, Ghassan (ed.), *Democracy Without Democrats? The Renewal of Politics in the Muslim World*, London: I. B. Tauris, 1994.

Sayigh, Yezid, 'Above the State: The Officers' Republic in Egypt', Carnegie Endowment for International Peace, August 2012, http://carnegieendowment.org/files/offic-ers_republic1.pdf

———, 'Missed Opportunity: The Politics of Police Reform in Egypt and Tunisia', Carnegie Middle East Center, 17 March 2015, http://carnegie-mec.org/publications/?fa=59391

———, 'Crumbling States: Security Sector Reform in Libya and Yemen', Carnegie Middle East Center, June 2015, http://carnegie-mec.org/2015/06/18/crumbling-states-security-sector-reform-in-libya-and-yemen-pub-60422

Schwedler, Jillian, *Faith in Moderation: Islamist Parties in Jordan and Yemen*, Cambridge: Cambridge University Press, 2006.

Sharp, Jeremy, 'Egypt: Background and U.S. Relations', Congressional Research Service, 24 March 2017, http://fas.org/sgp/crs/mideast/RL33003.pdf

Shehata, Samer Said, *Shop Floor Culture and Politics in Egypt*, Albany, NY: SUNY Press, 2009.

Shennib, Ghaith, 'Libyan PM dismisses army officer's plot to "rescue" country', Reuters, 14 February 2014, http://uk.reuters.com/article/libya-crisis-idINDE EA1D0GW20140214

Singh, Naunihal, *Seizing Power: The Strategic Logic of Military Coups*, Baltimore, MD: Johns Hopkins University Press, 2014.

Sissons, Miranda and Al-Saiedi, Abdulrazzaq, 'A Bitter Legacy: Lessons from Debaathification in Iraq', *International Center for Transitional Justice*, 4 March 2013, http://www.ictj.org/sites/default/files/ICTJ-Report-Iraq-De-Baathification-2013-ENG.pdf

Soliman, Samer, *The Autumn of Dictatorship: Fiscal Crisis and Political Change in Egypt Under Mubarak*, Stanford, CA: Stanford University Press, 2011.

St John, Ronald Bruce, *Libya: Continuity and Change*, Abingdon: Routledge, Second Edition, 2015.

Springborg, Robert D., 'Egypt's Future: Yet Another Turkish Model?', *The International Spectator*, Vol. 49, No. 1, 2014, pp. 1–6.

Stepan, Alfred, *Rethinking Military Politics: Brazil and the Southern Cone*, Princeton, NJ: Princeton University Press, 1998.

———, *Arguing Comparative Politics*, Oxford: Oxford University Press, 2000.

———, 'Religion, Democracy and the "Twin Tolerations"', *The Journal of Democracy*, Vol. 11, 2000.

———, 'Tunisia's Transition and the Twin Tolerations', *Journal of Democracy*, Vol. 23, No. 2, 2012, pp. 89–103.

———, 'Rituals of Respect: Sufis and Secularists in Senegal in Comparative Perspective' *Comparative Politics*, Vol. 44, No. 4, July 2012, pp. 379–401.

Stepan, Alfred and Skach, Cindy, 'Constitutional Frameworks and Democratic Consolidation: Parliamentarianism versus Presidentialism', *World Politics*, Vol. 46, No. 1, 1993, pp. 1–22.

Stepan, Alfred; Linz, Juan J. and Yadav, Yogendra, *Crafting State Nations: India and Other Multinational Democracies*, Baltimore, MA: Johns Hopkins University Press, 2011.

Stepan, Alfred and Linz, Juan J., 'Democratization Theory and the "Arab Spring"', *Journal of Democracy*, Vol. 24, No. 2, 2013, pp. 15–30.

Stepan, Alfred and Taylor, Charles (eds), *The Boundaries of Toleration*, New York: Columbia University Press, 2014.

Subotic, Jelena, *Hijacked Justice: Dealing with the Past in the Balkans*, Ithaca, NY: Cornell University Press, 2009.

Tawab, Ziad Abdel, 'The Crisis of Transitional Justice after the Arab Spring: The Case of Egypt', November 2013, Cairo Institute for Human Rights Studies, http://www. cihrs.org/wp-content/uploads/2013/09/Transitional-Justice.pdf

Taylor, Paul, 'West Warned Egypt's Sisi to the End: Don't Do It', Reuters, 14 August 2013, http://uk.reuters.com/article/2013/08/14/uk-egypt-protests-west-idUK BRE97D16E20130814

Teitel, Ruti, *Transitional Justice*, Oxford: Oxford University Press, 2000.

Toensing, Chris, 'Tunisian Labor Leaders Reflect Upon Revolt', *Middle East Report*, Vol. 25, 2011, http://www.merip.org/mer/mer258/tunisian-labor-leaders-reflect-upon-revolt-0

Tozy, Mohamed, *Forum national sur la réparation. Rapport général*, 2005.

Trinkunas, Harold A., 'Ensuring Democratic Civilian Control of the Armed Forces in Asia', East-West Center Occasional Papers, 1999.

Tsai, Lily L., 'Solidary Groups, Informal Accountability, and Local Public Goods Provision in Rural China', *American Political Science Review*, Vol. 101, No. 2, 2007.

Tucker. Robert C., *The Marx-Engels Reader*, New York: W. W. Norton, 1978.

Tudor, Maya, 'Renewed Hope in Pakistan?', *Journal of Democracy*, Vol. 25, No. 2, 2014, pp. 105–118.

Turner, Catherine, 'Transitional Justice in Egypt: A Challenge and an Opportunity', The Tahrir Institute for Middle East Policy, 14 May 2016, http://timep.org/tjp-analysis/transitional-justice-in-egypt-a-challenge-and-an-opportunity/

United Nations Security Council Report of the Secretary-General, 'The Rule of Law and Transitional Justice in Conflict and Post-conflict Societies', United Nations, 24 August 2004 (S/2004/616), para. 8, http://www.unrol.org/doc.aspx?d=3096

Utvik, Bjorn Olav, 'Filling the Vacant Throne of Nasser: The Economic Discourse of Egypt's Islamist Opposition', *Arab Studies Quarterly*, Vol. 17, No. 4, 1995, p. 29.

Vairel, Frédéric, 'Morocco: From Mobilisations to Reconciliation?', *Mediterranean Politics*, Vol. 13, No. 2, 2008, pp. 229–241.

———, *Politique et mouvements sociaux au Maroc. La révolution désamorcée?*, Paris: Presses de Sciences Po, 2014.

Voltmer, Katrin, *Mass Media and Political Communication in New Democracies*, Abingdon: Routledge, 2006.

———, *The Media in Transitional Democracies*, New York: Polity Press, 2013.

Ware, L. B, 'The Role of the Tunisian Military in the Post-Bourguiba Era', *Middle East Journal*, Vol. 39, No. 1, 1985, pp. 27–47.

Waterbury, John. 'Democracy Without Democrats? The Potential for Political Liberalization in the Middle East', in Salamé, Ghassan, *Democracy Without Democrats?: Renewal of Politics in the Muslim World*, London: I. B. Tauris, 1994, pp. 23–47.

Webb, Edward, *The Media in Tunisia and Egypt*, New York: Palgrave Pivots, 2014.

Wickberg, Sofia, 'Overview of Corruption and Anti-Corruption in Egypt', Transparency International, No. 4, 2015.

Wickham, Carrie Rosefsky, *Mobilizing Islam: Religion, Activism, and Political Change in Egypt*, New York: Columbia University Press, 2003.

———, 'Interests, Ideas, and Islamist Outreach in Egypt', in Wiktorowicz, Quintan (ed.), *Islamic Activism: A Social Movement Theory Approach*, Bloomington, IN: Indiana University Press, 2004.

———, *The Muslim Brotherhood: Evolution of an Islamist Organization*, Princeton, NJ: Princeton University Press, 2013.

Widner, Jennifer, 'Constitution Writing in Post-conflict Settings: An Overview *William and Mary Law Review*, 49, 2008, http://scholarship.law.wm.edu/wmlr/vol49/iss4.

Wiktorowicz, Quintan (ed.), *Islamic Activism: A Social Movement Theory Approach*, Bloomington, IN: Indiana University Press, 2004.

Wilcke, Christophe, 'Justice for Sale', *Egypt Independent*, 30 January 2013, http://www.egyptindependent.com/opinion/justice-sale

Wollenberg, Anja and Pack, Jason, 'Rebels With a Pen: Observations on the Newly Emergent Media Landscape in Libya', *Journal of North African Studies*, Vol. 18, No. 3, 2013, pp. 191–210.

Wood, Elizabeth Jean, 'An Insurgent Path to Democracy: Popular Mobilization, Economic Interests, and Regime Transition in El Salvador and South Africa', *Comparative Political Studies*, Vol. 34, No. 8, 2001, pp. 862–888.

World Bank, World Development Indicators 2012.

Younes, Najwa, 'Six of Tunisia's Ten Leading Television Networks Under Political Ownership', Tunisia Live, 13 July 2016, http://www.tunisia-live.net/2016/07/13/six-of-tunisias-ten-leading-television-networks-under-political-ownership/

Youssef, Abdelhrahman, 'Egypt's Brotherhood, Sisi both put out feelers for reconciliation', Al-Monitor, 13 July 2016, http://www.al-monitor.com/pulse/originals/2016/07/egypt-brotherhood-reconciliation-sisi-divide-detainees.html#ixzz4EZcqHuZU

Zakaria, Fareed, 'Why democracy took root in Tunisia and not Egypt,' *Washington Post*, 30 October 2014, https://www.washingtonpost.com/opinions/fareed-zakaria-why-democracy-took-root-in-tunisia-and-not-egypt/2014/10/30/c5205adc-606a-11e4-9f3a-7e28799e0549_story.html

Zolberg, Aristide R., 'Moments of Madness', *Politics and Society*, Vol. 2, Issue 2, 1972, p. 183–207.

INDEX

'Abbasi, Hussayn , 123
Abbasid Caliphate (750–1517), 80, 81
Abdellatif, Ibtihel, 211
abortion, 14
Abu Ghazala, Mohamed Abd el-Halim, 50, 63
Ackerman, Bruce, 32
Acre, siege of (1291), 82
Addressing the Past, Building the Future conference (2011), 207
Adenauer, Konrad, 12
el-Adly, Habib, 49
Afghanistan, 176
Aherdane, Mahjoubi, 213
Ahram Online, 18
Aïn Jalout, battle of (1260), 81
Algeria, 4, 5–6, 14, 85–8
  Civil War (1991–7), 14, 83, 86–8, 90, 169–70
  constitution, 151
  coup d'état (1965), 82
  coup d'état (1992), 5–6, 14, 19, 54, 86, 90, 91
  dominant institution model, 47
  FLN (Front de libération nationale), 85–6
  FIS (Front Islamique du Salut), 85, 87

GIA (Groupe Islamique Armé), 86, 87
HCE (Haut Comité d'État), 86
Mamluks, 5, 75, 78, 81, 82, 83, 85–8
military, 5, 14, 47, 48
Moroccan Sand War (1963), 82
MSP (Mouvement de la société pour la paix), 87
parliamentary elections (1991), 5, 14
presidential election (1995), 86
al-Qaeda in the Islamic Maghreb (AQIM), 87
riots (1988), 85
and United Nations, 155, 158
War of Independence (1954–62), 79–80, 83
al-Ali, Zaid, 6, 141–64
Allende, Salvador, 12
el-Amal Ettounsi, 267
Amer, Mohamed Abdel Hakim, 50, 82
Amnesty International, 170, 203
Amor, Abdelfattah, 173
Andrieu, Kora, 6, 165–97
Angola, 121
Angrist, Michelle Penner, 116
Ansar al-Sharia, 174
Ansar Beit Maqdis, 90
apostasy, 23–4

April 6 Movement, 239
Arab Institute for Human Rights, 207
Arab Kingdom of Syria (1918–20), 79
Arab League, 65, 79
Arab Renaissance, 77, 78, 79
Arab Revolt (1916–18), 79
al-Arabiya, 98, 108
Arato, Andrew, 33–4, 36, 39
Arthur, Paige, 166
Ashour, Omar, 74, 78
al-Askari, Bakr Sidqi, 46
al-Assad, Bashar, 8, 47, 51, 55, 85, 90, 91
al-Assad, Hafez, 82, 85
Association of South East Asian Nations (ASEAN), 11
Atatürk, Mustafa Kemal, 13, 24, 67, 79
Australia, 121
authoritarianism
   breakdown, 2, 3, 31–2
   coalitions against, 12, 14, 18, 124
   and coups, 54, 62
   definition of, 42
   knocking on the barracks door, 18
   and media, 94
   and militaries, 54, 62, 74
   and pluralism, 64
   resurgence, 2, 4, 36, 90, 94, 111
   and status quo, 59
el-Ayed, Samir, 239
Ayyubid dynasty (1171–1250), 81, 82
Azerbaijan, 121
al-Azhar University, 14
Aziz, Sahar, 226, 278
Azziman, Omar, 213

Baath party, 84
al-Baghdadi, Abu Bakr, 90
Bahaa-Eldin, Ziad, 232
Bahrain, 30, 35, 98, 108
al-Bakr, Ahmad Hassan, 84

Ban Ki Moon, 145
al-Banna, Hassan, 245
el-Baradei, Mohamed, 55, 65, 232
Baraket Essahel affair (1991), 170, 180
Batatu, Hanna, 82
Battle of Aïn Jalout (1260), 81, 82
Battle of Kayseri (1418), 82
Battle of Mansoura (1250), 81, 82
Baybars, Sultan of Egypt and Syria, 81
Belaïd, Chokri, 21, 89, 107, 176, 210, 270
Belkheir, Larbi, 86
Bellin, Eva, 128, 137
Ben Achour, Yadh, 19, 182
Ben Achour Commission, 19, 21, 182–3
Ben Ali, Zine el-Abidine
   Baraket Essahel affair (1991), 170, 180
   coalitions against, 13, 16–17, 124, 238
   constituency for coercion, 14, 16
   Convention against Torture (1985), 169, 180
   corruption, 170, 171, 173–4, 216
   coup d'état (1987), 84, 120, 168
   Ennahda ban (1991), 15, 27, 169
   general election (1989), 15
   and human rights, 169–80, 189
   and judiciary, 181
   liberalisation, 169
   and media, 106–7
   and military, 75, 120
   presidential election (2009), 183
   RCD (Rassemblement Constitutionnel Démocratique), 25, 169, 171, 177, 182–3, 211, 270
   Saudi Arabia, exile in (2011–), 179
   and terrorism, 170
   and torture, 169, 170, 180
   and transitional justice, 169–80,

182–3, 211, 213, 214, 215, 216, 270

trial and sentencing (2011–12), 179–80

uprising (2011), 19, 78, 88, 122, 124, 128, 132, 143, 167, 205, 207

Ben Jaafar, Mustapha, 16, 22, 185, 211

Ben Youssef, Salah, 80, 83, 168, 169, 185, 189, 271

Bendjedid, Chadli, 85–6, 88

Benomar, Jamal, 149–50, 162–3, 263

Bensedrine, Sihem, 189–90, 205, 211, 214–15

Benzekri, Driss, 204, 205, 213, 214

Bernard-Maugiron, Nathalie, 7

Berrada, Abderrahim, 206

al-Biltagi, Muḥammad, 124

Bizerte crisis (1961), 83–4, 168

Blank Coup (1997), 68

Blount, Justin, 35

Boix, Carles, 111

Bonn International Center for Conversion, 120

Boraine, Alex, 273

Bou Nassif, Hicham, 120

Bouazizi, Mohamed, 193, 268

Bouderbala, Taoufik, 172, 176

Boudiaf, Mohamed, 86

Bouguerra, Lilia Brik, 212

Boumediene, Houari, 82, 85, 87

Bourguiba, Habib, 14, 15, 21, 177–8, 183, 195–6, 214

and el-Amal Ettounsi, 267

and Ben Youssef, 80, 83, 189, 271

Bizerte crisis (1961), 83–4, 168

constitution (1959), 24

coup d'état (1987), 84, 120, 168

Destour party, 168, 178

and economy, 138, 169

and military, 75

Personal Status Code, 14, 168

president for life proclamation (1975), 169

and private sector, 138

secularism, 13, 24

and Thaalbi, 272

and transitional justice, 183, 185, 189, 195–6, 215

Bouteflika, Abdelaziz, 87

Brahmi, Mohamed, 21, 89, 122, 176, 210, 270

Bratton, Michael, 119, 128, 251

Brazil, 18, 20, 166

bread riots (1977), 64

British Broadcasting Corporation (BBC), 96

Browers, Michaelle, 40

Brown, Nathan, 5, 29–59, 226

Brownlee, Jason, 128, 129, 130

Brumaire coup (1799), 18

Brumberg, Daniel, 130

Burns, William, 55

Cairo police riot (1986), 83

Cairo and the People, 105

Caisse de Dépôt et de Gestion, 203

'Call from Tunis' (2003), 16

Canada, 166

Cardoso, Fernando Henrique, 20

Carter Center, 159

Carthage Palace, 215

CCDH (Conseil Consultatif des Droits de l'Homme), 204, 206, 209, 213

censorship, 96

Central Security Forces, 49, 53, 63, 64

al-Chaab, 212

Chad, 35

Chambi mountains, 90

Chammari, Khemais, 212

Champions of Jerusalem, 90

Chebbi, Lazhar Karoui, 207

Chile, 12–13, 14, 18, 76, 200, 203
Chirac, Jacques, 268
Christian Democracy, 10, 12
Churchill, Winston, 15
civil society, 3, 8, 10, 114
    Egypt, 6, 19, 62, 130–39
    Indonesia, 13
    knocking on the barracks door, 18,
        113, 114, 116, 122, 123–5, 239
    Tunisia, 6, 16, 19, 22, 130–39,
        186–7, 189, 238
*Civil Society, Constitution, and Legiti-
    macy* (Arato), 33–4
Clark, William Roberts, 139
Clot, André, 81
CNN, 101
coalitions, 12–19, 40, 124, 238
Coleman, James, 139
'Collectif du 18 Octobre pour les
    Droits et les Libertés' (2005), 16
Colombia, 201
compulsion in religion, 15, 17
Congo, 35
Consensus Committee, 22–3
consensus, 15, 34, 36, 37, 40
constituency for coercion, 14, 16
Constitutional Court, Tunisia, 24
constitutionalism, 5, 29–43
    in Algeria, 151
    Arato on, 33–4, 36, 39
    and control, 36–42
    in Egypt, 30, 37, 39, 48, 51–3, 57,
        58, 62, 66, 67, 88, 95, 151, 222,
        232, 239
    'façade' constitutions, 41
    and history, 41–2
    in Iraq, 34, 35, 158, 163
    in Jordan, 151
    in Latin America, 37, 41, 264
    in Libya, 30, 37, 57, 141–9, 151
    and 'moments of madness', 37–8

in Morocco, 30, 35, 41, 42, 96, 151
old constitutionalism, 30–31
in Poland, 37
and rationality, 37–9
in Soviet Union, 41
in Spain, 37
in Syria, 57, 151
in Tunisia, 2, 13, 21, 23–4, 30, 37,
    40, 89, 106, 151, 177, 188
in Turkey, 34, 68, 70, 71, 72
in United States, 127–8
in Yemen, 37, 40, 57, 149–55
Consultative Council on Human
    Rights (CCDH), 204, 206, 209, 213
Convention against Torture (1985),
    169, 180
Cook, Steven, 5, 61–76, 78
Coptic Christians, 54, 105, 222
corrective movements, 82
corruption
    Egypt, 48, 50, 51, 52, 222
    Tunisia, 107, 170, 171, 173–4, 188,
        197, 215, 271
    Turkey, 72
    Yemen, 152, 153, 154
coups, 54, 112–25, 129
    as corrective movements, 82
    and empirical pluralism, 113–14,
        125–30
    eradicators versus dialogists, 54, 55
    knocking on the barracks door, 18,
        113, 114, 116, 122, 123–5, 239
    and political centrality of military,
        119–21, 129
    proofing against, 47, 64
    and size of military, 116–19
Covenant of Social Peace, 13
CPR (Congrès pour la République),
    16–17, 21, 185, 211, 212
Crusade, Seventh (1248–54), 81, 82
Cyprus, 82

Cyrenaica, Libya, 146

Dahl, Robert, 9
Darrag, Amr, 55
David, Steven, 123
De Gaulle, Charles, 13, 83
de-Baathification, 184
Democracy Reporting International, 159
'democracy with democrats', 11, 12, 13, 27
Democracy without Democrats, 4, 11
Democratic Forum, 13
democratisation theory, 12
Denmark, 10
Derb Moulay Cherif sit-in (2000), 207
Destour party, 168, 178, 192
development, 137–8
Diagne, Bashir Souleymane, 17
dialogists, 54, 55
Dilou, Samir, 186, 267
divorce, 14, 168
Dobry, Michel, 3
dominant institution model, 5, 47, 48
double jeopardy, 179–80
Droz-Vincent, Philippe, 116, 119

Eastern European transitions, 31, 40, 59, 113, 176
Ebert, Friedrich, 12
Economist, 11
Egypt, 4, 5, 6, 8, 17–19, 25, 45–59, 61–7, 111–40, 219–34
    Ansar Beit Maqdis, 90
    April 6 Movement, 239
    associations, 132, 136
    Ayyubid dynasty (1171–1250), 81
    British occupation (1882–1922), 48, 79, 117
    bread riots (1977), 64
    business-political class, 63

Cairo police riot (1986), 83
Central Security Forces, 49, 53, 63, 64
civil society, 6, 19, 62, 130–39
constitution, 30, 37, 39, 48, 51–3, 58, 62, 66, 67, 88, 95, 151, 222, 232, 239
Coptic Christians, 54, 105, 222
Corrective Revolution (1971), 82
corruption, 48, 50, 51, 52, 222
coup d'état (1952), 40, 46, 48, 54, 56, 62, 80, 117
coup d'état (2013), 2, 5, 21–2, 45, 46, 50, 52–8, 66, 89, 100, 105–6, 112, 122, 123
development, 6, 137–8, 259
dominant institution model, 5, 47
empirical pluralism, lack of, 125, 128–30
fact-finding commissions, 227–31
Free Officers, 40, 46, 48, 54, 56, 62, 80, 117
Freedom and Justice Party (FJP), 53, 55, 66, 67, 125, 233
Freedom House score, 129, 134, 238
French occupation (1798–1801), 77, 78
General Intelligence Service, 64, 66
Global Militarization Index (GMI) score, 121
Hizb al-Nour, 3
human rights, 49, 55, 219–34
hybrid democracy, 18
industrialisation, 6, 138, 259
inheritance issue, 50, 62–3, 85
Islamism, 18, 46, 48, 49, 56, 89, 95, 105, 124–5, 128, 130, 135, 137, 229–31
Israel, relations with, 48, 49, 51, 63, 83
Jihadism, 57
judiciary, 225–7, 231, 281, 282

Kifaya movement, 124
knocking on the barracks door, 18,
    122, 123, 124, 125, 239
Law on Illicit Gains (1975), 222
Mamluks, 6, 75, 78, 81, 82, 85,
    88–90
Maspero protests (2011), 54, 105,
    222
media, 93, 95, 96, 97, 98–9, 101–6
military, see Egyptian Armed Forces
Ministry of Defence, 62, 66, 76
Ministry of Interior, 49, 57, 63–4,
    66, 99, 228, 232
Morsi presidency (2012–13), see
    under Morsi, Mohamed
mosque density, 135–6
Mubarak presidency (1981–2011),
    see under Mubarak, Hosni
Muslim Brotherhood, see Muslim
    Brotherhood
Nahda, 78
al-Nahda Square protests (2013), 55,
    89, 230, 244–5
Nasser presidency (1956–70), 49,
    80, 82, 84, 137–8
National Defense Council, 53
National Democratic Party, 50, 65,
    222, 228, 232
Nour Party, 3, 125
October crackdown (2013), 54
parliamentary elections (2010), 50
parliamentary elections (2011–12),
    40, 46, 58, 65–6, 125
police, 49, 53, 57, 63, 83, 227–9
Port Said stadium massacre (2012),
    88
praetorian state, 119
presidential election (2012), 18, 25,
    52, 65, 66, 89, 99, 105
presidential election (2014), 50–51,
    89–90

Presidential Palace protests (2012),
    224
prisons, 57
Rabaa al-Adawiyya Square protests
    (2013), 54, 55, 89, 106, 211, 223,
    229–31, 244
Sadat presidency (1970–81), 49,
    50, 82
Salafism, 3
Saudi Arabia border deal (2016),
    227
secularism, 18, 124, 125, 135, 137,
    221, 225
Selmi Document (2011), 66
Sharia, 24
Sinai insurgency (2011–), 2, 8, 90,
    91
al-Sisi presidency (2014–), 2, 8, 51,
    66–7, 89–90
Six-Day War (1967), 63, 64
State Security Investigations, 49,
    50, 63
Suez Canal, 263
Tahrir Square protests (2011), 1, 52,
    63, 79, 132
Takfirism, 57
Tamarod, 21–2, 89, 105, 240
terrorism, 224
torture, 57, 58, 229
transitional justice, 219–34
Revolution (1919), 48, 79
Revolution (2011), see Egyptian
    Revolution
Supreme Constitutional Council, 89
Supreme Council of the Armed
    Forces, 46, 50–59, 64–7, 88–90,
    105, 222
Supreme Council of the Police, 49
trade unions, 132
Ultras, 88
Unilateral Declaration of Indepen-
    dence (1922), 79

United States, relations with, 47, 49, 52, 55, 124

urbanisation, 6, 138, 259

Yemen Arab Republic (1962–90), 80

Egyptian Armed Forces, 2, 5, 18–22, 37, 39, 40, 45–59, 62–7, 74–6, 88–90, 112–25

coup d'état (2013), 2, 5, 21–2, 45, 46, 50, 52–8, 66, 89, 100, 105–6, 112, 122, 123

fact-finding commission on, 228–9

Maspero protests (2011), 54, 105, 222

al-Nahda Square protests (2013), 55, 89, 230, 244–5

October crackdown (2013), 54

Port Said stadium massacre (2012), 88

presidential election (2014), 50–51, 89–90

Rabaa al-Adawiyya Square protests (2013), 54, 55, 89, 106, 211, 223, 229–31, 244

and transitional justice, 222–3, 234, 243

United States aid, 47

uprising (2011), 45, 49–52, 62–6, 74, 88, 228–9

Egyptian Initiative for Personal Rights (EIPR), 230

Egyptian Revolution (2011), 1, 5, 79

and coalitions, 40, 124–5, 238

and fact-finding commissions, 227–9

and Mamluks, 88

and media, 93, 97, 104

and military, 45, 49–53, 56–8, 61, 62–6, 111

and transitional justice, 219–23

Eissa, Ibrahim, 105

Elkins, Zachary, 35

Elster, Jon, 38, 200

empirical pluralism, 113–14, 125–30

Ennahda, 14–18, 39

ban on (1991), 15, 27, 169–70

and Belaïd assassination (2013), 21, 270

and Ben Achour Commission, 19–20

and Brahmi assassination (2013), 21, 270

'Call from Tunis' (2003), 16

and coalitions, 5, 14–18, 26–7, 184, 185, 238

'Collectif du 18 Octobre pour les Droits et les Libertés' (2005), 16

and compulsion in religion, 17

and Constituent National Assembly, 16, 22, 120, 122, 123, 125, 196

and constitution (2014), 2, 22

general election (1989), 15

Ghannouchi's leadership, 209

and al-Jazeera, 98

and media, 98, 99, 107

presidential election (2014), 25, 26, 89

and proportional representation (PR), 19–20, 128

and security sector reform, 182

and Sharia, 24, 241

and terrorism, 21, 169, 182, 210, 269

and transitional justice, 169–70, 175, 184, 185–6, 189, 192, 209, 211, 212

Troika government (2011–14), 21, 22, 89, 211, 212

and 'two sheikhs' compromise, 5, 26–7

Enough movement, 124

Equity and Reconciliation Commission (ERC), 7, 199–218

eradicators, 54, 55
Erbakan, Necmettin, 68
Erdogan, Recep Tayyip, 69, 71
Ergenekon conspiracy, 69, 70, 72
Essebsi, Beji Caid, 21, 25, 26, 175, 177–8, 184, 209, 211, 214–15, 218
Ettakatol, 16–17, 21, 185, 211, 212
European Union, 10, 55, 62, 69, 203, 206
Evangelical Lutheranism, 10
Ezz, Ahmed, 50

façade constitutions, 41
Facebook, 93, 101
fact-finding commissions, 227–31
Fairmont Group, 238
Fawzy, Mohamed, 50
feminism, 17, 23, 213, 239
FIDH (Fédération internationale des ligues des droits de l'homme), 203, 206
Filiu, Jean-Pierre, 5–6, 13, 75, 77–91
Finland, 10
first-past-the-post system, 19, 128
FIS (Front Islamique du Salut), 85, 87
FLN (Front de libération nationale), 85–6
Forbis, Jeremy Scott, 133–4, 136, 137, 138, 259
France
    Algerian War (1954–62), 79–80, 83
    Bizerte crisis (1961), 83–4, 168
    Brumaire coup (1799), 18
    'Call from Tunis' (2003), 16
    Catholicism, 13
    'Collectif du 18 Octobre pour les Droits et les Libertés' (2005), 16
    Crusade, Seventh (1248–54), 81, 82
    Egyptian campaign (1798–1801), 77, 78
    and Ghannouchi, 17

Law Concerning the Separation of Churches and the State (1905), 10, 24
    Revolution (1789–99), 59
    secularism, 10, 11, 12, 13, 24
    Mandate for Syria and Lebanon (1923–46), 79
    Tunisia protectorate (1881–1956), 13, 79, 185
Free Officers
    Egypt, 40, 46, 48, 54, 56, 62, 80, 117
    Libya, 84
free trade, 36
Freedom and Justice Party (FJP), 53, 55, 66, 67, 125, 233
Freedom House, 11, 129, 134, 135, 236, 238, 268
Freelon, Deen, 101
Freeman, Mark, 176
Fukuyama, Francis, 166

Gaddafi, Muammar, 8, 47, 51, 55, 62, 73, 74, 84, 108
Gafsa, Tunisia, 171, 188, 194, 268, 271
Gandhi, Mohandas, 11
Geertz, Clifford, 205
Gelvin, James, 116
General Intelligence Service, Egypt, 64, 66
General National Congress, Libya, 144, 146–9, 263
Germany
    Ben Youssef assassination (1961), 168
    Christian Democratic Union, 12
    Nuremberg trials (1945–6), 166, 180
Gezi Park protests (2013), 71
al-Ghaiyi, Muhammad, 245
Ghana, 201
Ghannouchi, Rached, 15–17, 19, 25, 26, 169, 177, 209, 239, 269

Ghezaiel, Ben Abbès, 86
GIA (Groupe Islamique Armé), 86, 87
Ginsburg, Tom, 35
Global Militarization Index (GMI), 121
Golder, Matt, 139
Golder, Sona Nadenichek, 139
Government of National Accord, Libya, 73
Great Depression (1929–39), 71
Greece, 54
Green Book (Gaddafi), 84
de Greiff, Pablo, 165, 191–2, 195
gross domestic product (GDP), 120, 137–8
guardian model, 47
Guardian, The, 228
Guellali, Amna, 24
Guenaizia, Abdelmalek, 86
Guignard, Xavier, 8
Gülen, Fethullah, 70
Gulf Cooperation Council (GCC), 149, 150
Gulf War (1990–91), 85

Habermas, Jürgen, 36
Haftar, Khalifa, 73
Halisi, Clyde Ray Daniels, 139
Hamas, 224
Hamdi, Ibrahim, 82
Hammad, Gamal, 56
Hamzawy, Amr, 106
Hanibal TV, 106
hard-liners, 54
Hart, Vivien, 32
Hassan II, King of Morocco, 213
Hayner, Priscilla, 273
HCE (Haut Comité d'État), 86
Hefny, Mostafa, 132
Hezbollah, 224
High Commission to Supervise Elections, Tunisia, 183

High Institute for Judicial Independence, Tunisia, 181
historical cycles, 78–80
al-Hiwar TV, 107
Hizb al-Nour, 3, 125
Hizb ut-Tahrir, 184
Horowitz, Donald, 13, 34
Hourani, Albert, 13, 77
House of Representatives, Libya, 148, 263
Houthis, 8, 149, 151, 153, 154, 155
Howard, Marc Morjé, 132
human rights
    in Egypt, 49, 55, 220–34
    and constitutionalism, 35
    in Indonesia, 13
    in Morocco, 204, 206–7, 209, 213, 264
    and transitional justice, 165, 166, 167
    in Tunisia, 17, 22, 23–4, 131, 166–97, 205, 207, 211, 212, 216, 240, 268
    in Yemen, 153
Human Rights Watch, 24, 159, 180, 203, 216, 229, 230–31
Huntington, Samuel, 75, 112
Hussayn, Magdi Ahmad, 125
Hussein, King of Jordan, 85
Hussein, Sharif of Mecca, 79
Hussein, Mahmud, 245
hybrid democracy, 18

Ibn Abd al-Wahhab, 78
Iceland, 10
IDEA, 159, 260, 264
Idris, King of Libya, 84
Ifada, 132
ijmā', 15
immunisation of the revolution, 183–4
inclusiveness, 36, 39

India, 11–12, 13, 21
Indonesia, 11, 12, 13, 14, 15, 17, 20, 24
industrialisation, 6, 138, 171, 259
Inglehart, Ronald, 139
inheritance issue, 50
international assistance, 141–64
International Atomic Energy Agency, 65
International Bar Association Human Rights Institute (IBAHRI), 225
International Center for Transitional Justice (ICTJ), 199, 202, 203–4, 205, 206, 207–8, 216, 266
International Crisis Group, 170
International Federation for Human Rights (FIDH), 203, 206
International Institute of Strategic Studies, 117–19
Iran, 85, 169, 224
Iraq, 25
  Baath party, 84, 184
  constitution, 34, 35, 158, 163
  coups d'état, 46, 80, 84
  de-Baathification, 184
  Gulf War (1990–91), 85
  Islamic State (IS), 1–2, 90
  and Mamluks, 84–5
  media, 95
  military, 48
  Saddam presidency (1979–2003), 51, 84–5
  and United Nations, 85, 150, 155, 157–8, 266
  United States-led War (2003–11), 48, 88, 176, 184
  uprisings (1991), 85
Islamic State (IS), 1–2, 90
Islamism, 8
  in Algeria, 85–7, 169–70
  in Egypt, 18, 46, 48, 49, 56, 89, 95, 105, 124–5, 128, 130, 135, 137, 229–31
  in Jordan, 85
  and media, 95, 98, 99, 105, 107, 108, 109
  in Morocco, 207
  and Nahda, 77, 78, 79
  in Syria, 108
  in Tunisia, 2, 5, 13–27, 99, 107, 112, 116, 120–40, 169–70, 174–5, 182, 192–4, 196
  in Turkey, 68–73
Israel, 48, 49, 51, 63, 64, 80, 82, 83

Jadid, Salah, 82
jamlaka, 85
Jaunzems, Eva, 8
al-Jazeera, 52, 94, 95, 96, 97, 98, 101, 108
Jebali, Hamadi, 267
el-Jem, Tunisia, 171
Jendoubi, Mouldi, 240
Jenkins, J. Craig, 119
Jihadism, 1, 2, 8, 14, 57, 86–7, 89–91
Johan Skytte Prize, 9
Jolys, Marie-Zénaïde, 8
Jomaa, Mehdi, 23
Jordan, 30, 41, 83, 85, 96, 107, 133, 151
Jribi, Maya, 122
judicial independence, 41
Justice and Development Party (AKP), 47, 68–73

Kafi, Ali, 86
Kallel, Abdallah, 180
Kalyvas, Stathis, 10
Kandil, Hazem, 117
Karl, Terry Lynn, 123
Kasbah demonstrations (2011), 177, 182, 269
Kasserine, Tunisia, 171, 179, 188
al-Kawakibi Democracy Transition Center, 208

Kayseri, battle of (1418), 82
Le Kef, Tunisia, 178
Kemalism, 13, 24, 67–8, 70, 73, 75
el-Ketatny, Saad, 55
al-Khatib Abdelkrim, 213
Kifâya movement, 124
Kingdom of Nejd and Hijaz (1926–
    32), 79
knocking on the barracks door, 18, 113,
    114, 116, 122, 123–5, 127, 239
Kopstein, Jeffrey, 112–13
Koran, 15, 17
Kposowa, Augustine, 119
Krasner, Stephen, 36
Krichi, Khaled, 211
Kurds, 71
Kurzman, Charles, 114
Kuwait, 83, 85, 108
Kuwait Foundation for the Advance-
    ment of Science (KFAS), 8
Kyrgyzstan, 121

laïcité, 10, 12, 13, 14, 24
Lamari, Mohammed, 86
Larayedh, Ali, 107, 240, 267
Latin America, 12, 37, 41
    Brazil, 18, 20, 166
    Chile, 12–13, 14, 18, 76, 200, 203
    Colombia, 201
    constitutions, 37, 41, 264
    coups, 54
    knocking on the barracks door, 123
    Paraguay, 201
    Peru, 204
    El Salvador, 200, 203
    transitional justice, 166, 200, 201,
        204, 207
    Uruguay, 19
Law Concerning the Separation of
    Churches and the State (1905), 10,
    24

Law on Establishing and Organising
    Transitional Justice (2013–14),
    178–9, 183, 186–7, 193, 204–5,
    208, 210, 211, 216
Law on Illicit Gains (1975), 222
Lebanon, 79, 83
legal continuity, 34, 36
León, Bernardino, 55, 148–9, 263
less-politicised model, 47
liberal age (1798–1939), 77
Libya, 4, 5, 6, 7, 143–9
    Civil War (2011–), 2, 55, 57, 62,
        73–4, 95, 96, 98, 101, 108, 143
    constitution, 30, 37, 57, 141–9, 151
    Constitution Drafting Assembly,
        147–8
    coup d'état (1969), 74, 80, 84
    electoral law (2012), 145–6, 147
    Gaddafi's governance (1969–2011),
        8, 47, 51, 55, 62, 73, 74, 84, 108,
        143
    General National Congress, 144,
        146–9, 263
    Government of National Accord, 73
    House of Representatives, 148, 263
    international assistance, 142, 143–9
    Jamahiriyya, 73, 84
    and Mamluks, 84
    media, 93, 95, 96, 98, 101, 108
    military, 5, 47, 48, 55, 57, 73
    militias, 73–4, 262
    National Forces Alliance, 147
    National Transitional Council,
        143–6, 161
    NATO intervention (2011), 55
    Political Isolation Law (2013), 184,
        270
    Revolutionary Command Council,
        84
    tribal-sectarian model, 47, 48, 74
    and United Nations, 73, 145–9, 155,
        157–62, 261, 263

uprising (2011), 2, 5, 7, 55, 61, 62, 93, 143
Lijphart, Arend, 9
Limongi, Fernando, 140
Linz, Juan, 9–10, 20, 21, 112, 124, 130
Lippmann, Walter, 127, 128
Lipset, Seymour Martin, 111
local coordination committees (tansiqi-yyat), 3
Louis IX, King of France, 81
Lutheranism, 10
Lynch, Marc, 6, 93–109

Mabahith Amn al-Dawla, *see* State Security Investigations
Madison, James, 127–8
Mady, Abu al-Ila, 55
Mahfoudh, Mohamed Fadhel, 240
Mainwairing, Scott, 256
majoritarianism, 34, 36, 128, 147
Makhlouf, Zouhair, 212
Makhlouf, Najwa, 254
Mamluk Sultanate (1250–1516), 5–6, 75, 81, 82
Mandela, Nelson, 125
Mansour, Adly, 89, 229–31, 232
Mansoura, battle of (1250), 81
Marks, Monica, 239, 240
Martin, Ian, 145
Marx, Karl, 140, 239
Marzouki, Moncef, 16, 17, 107, 183, 185, 211
Masoud, Tarek, 6, 111–40, 238
Maspero protests (2011), 54, 105, 222
Mauritius, 134, 259
al-Mayadeen, 108
McDermott, Anthony, 117
Mecca, 79
media, 6, 93–109
Mediene, Mohammed, 86
Medina, 79

militaries, 5, 45–59, 61–76
    Algeria, 5, 14, 47, 48
    Balance assessments, 117–19
    dominant institution model, 5, 47, 48
    Egypt, *see* Egyptian Armed Forces
    enclaves, 82
    Global Militarization Index (GMI), 121
    guardian model, 47
    Iraq, 48
    knocking on the barracks door, 18, 113, 114, 116, 122, 123–5, 239
    less-politicised model, 47
    Libya, 5, 47, 55, 57, 73–4
    Morocco, 210
    political centrality, 119–21, 129
    security mantra, 82
    size of, 116–19
    Sudan, 48
    superiority complexes, 56–7
    Syria, 5, 47, 57, 75
    tribal-sectarian model, 47, 48, 74
    Tunisia, 18, 47, 58–9, 75, 112–25, 179–80
    Turkey, 47, 67–73, 74, 75–6
    United States, 75
    Yemen, 5, 57, 75
Ministry of Defence, Egypt, 62, 66, 76
Ministry of Finance, Tunisia, 173
Ministry of Human Rights and Transitional Justice, Tunisia, 176, 186, 193
Ministry of Information, Tunisia, 106
Ministry of Interior
    Egypt, 49, 57, 63–4, 66, 99, 228, 232
    Morocco, 210, 218
    Tunisia, 58–9, 120, 122, 130, 132, 170, 182
Ministry of Justice, Tunisia, 181, 193
Ministry of Regional Development, Tunisia, 171

Ministry of Religious Affairs, Tunisia, 135

Misratan militia, 73

modernisation, 75, 79, 114, 116, 137–40

Mohammed VI, King of Morocco, 201, 204, 209, 213, 214

moments of madness, 37–8

Monastir, Tunisia, 169, 171

Mongol Empire (1206–1368), 81, 82

Morocco, 4
    Algerian Sand War (1963), 82
    Benomar's imprisonment (1976–84), 150, 263
    constitution, 30, 35, 41, 42, 96, 151
    Consultative Council on Human Rights, 204, 206, 209, 213
    coups d'état, 83
    Derb Moulay Cherif sit-in (2000), 207
    Equity and Reconciliation Commission, 7, 199–218
    feminism, 213
    human rights, 204, 206–7, 209, 213, 264
    Islamism, 207
    media, 96, 107
    military, 210
    Ministry of Interior, 210, 218
    National Council for Human Rights, 204, 206, 209
    reparations, 203
    transitional justice, 166, 199–218
    Truth and Justice Forum, 207

Morsi, Mohamed, 51, 53, 54, 56, 89, 99, 105–6, 219, 220
    coup d'état (2013), 2, 5, 21–2, 45, 46, 50, 52–8, 66, 89, 100, 105–6, 112, 122, 123
    fact-finding commissions, 228–9
    and judiciary, 225, 231, 281

presidential election (2012), 18, 25, 52, 65, 66, 89, 99, 105

Presidential Palace protests (2012), 224

and Tamarod, 21–2, 89, 105, 240

trials (2013–16), 219, 220, 221, 223–5

mosque density, 135–6

Mosul, Iraq, 90

Moussa, Ahmed, 105

Moussa, Amr, 65

MSP (Mouvement de la société pour la paix), 87

MTI (Movement of the Islamist Tendency), 169

Mubarak, Alaa, 50

Mubarak, Gamal, 50, 51, 62–3, 85

Mubarak, Hosni, 49, 51, 62–6, 89
    coalitions against, 124
    human rights abuses, 49, 55, 219, 220, 221–3
    inheritance issue, 50, 62–3, 85
    and judiciary, 225, 226
    and media, 104
    and military, 49, 50, 51, 52, 62–6, 88
    trials (2011–15), 219, 221, 279
    uprising (2011), 18, 46, 51, 52, 62, 78, 88, 89, 117, 219–23

Mubarak, Susan, 51

Muhammad, Prophet of Islam, 79, 81, 83

munâchidîn, 270

Munsir, Adnan , 122

Muslim Brotherhood
    and el-Baradei, 55, 65
    constitution (2012), 53
    coup d'état (1952), 48
    coup d'état (2013), 2, 5, 21–2, 45, 46, 50, 52–8, 66, 89, 100, 105–6, 112, 122, 123
    Freedom and Justice Party (FJP), 53, 55, 66, 67, 125, 233

and al-Jazeera, 98
and Mamluks, 88
and media, 98, 99, 105
Morsi presidency (2012–13), 2,
    5, 18, 21, 50, 51, 53, 56, 65, 99,
    105–6
al-Nahda Square protests (2013), 55,
    89, 230, 244–5
parliamentary elections (2011–12),
    40, 46, 58, 65–6, 125
presidential election (2012), 25, 52,
    65, 66, 89, 99, 105
prosecution of, 7, 67, 124, 220,
    223–5, 232, 233
Rabaa al-Adawiyya Square protests
    (2013), 54, 55, 89, 106, 211, 223,
    229–31, 244
and repression, 88
and secularists, 18, 124
and Tamarod, 21–2, 89, 105, 240

Nablus, Palestine, 82
Nahda, 77, 78, 79, 80, 83
al-Nahda Square protests (2013), 55,
    89, 230, 244–5
Napoleon I, Emperor of the French,
    239
Nasser, Gamal Abdel, 49, 50, 82, 84,
    137–8
National Confiscation Commission,
    Tunisia, 173–4
National Constituent Assembly, Tuni-
    sia, 15, 16, 19, 20–24, 123
    Committee of Martyrs and Wound-
        ed, 176, 193
    constitution (2014), 2, 21, 23–4, 30,
        37, 40, 89, 106, 151, 177, 188
    elections (2011), 19, 20, 21, 88, 120,
        125, 131, 173, 181, 185, 196
    and judiciary, 181
    Provisional Organisation of Public
        Authorities (2011), 185–6, 208

and reparations, 176
and Truth and Dignity Commission,
    185, 187, 189, 205, 211–12, 215
National Council for Human Rights,
    Morocco, 204
National Defense Council, Egypt, 53
National Democratic Party, Egypt, 50,
    65, 222, 228, 232
National Dialogue Conference, Yemen,
    150–55
National Forces Alliance, Libya, 147
National Forum on Reparations, Mo-
    rocco, 203
National Human Rights Institution,
    Tunisia, 176
National Security Council, Turkey, 68
National Transitional Council, Libya,
    143–6, 161
nationalism, 78–9, 80
Nationalist Movement Party, 71–2
native knowledge, 205
Nehru, Jawaharlal, 11
Nejd and Hijaz, Kingdom of (1926–
    32), 79
neopatrimonialism, 128
new constitutionalism, 5, 30–43
New York Times, 54, 101
newspapers, 6, 94, 97, 98, 99, 101, 104,
    105, 108
Nezzar, Khaled, 86
Nidaa Tounes, 21, 25–7, 89, 107, 183,
    185, 192, 209, 211, 269, 270
no punishment without a law, 200
Nobel Prize, 9, 55
non-governmental organisations
    (NGOs), 47, 134, 159, 203, 208,
    212
North Atlantic Treaty Organization
    (NATO), 55
Norway, 10
Nour Party, 3, 125

Nour, Tarek, 105
nulla poena sine lege, 200
Nuremberg trials (1945–6), 166, 180

O'Donnell, Guillermo, 3, 54, 127, 128
al-Obaydi, Abd al-Salam, 107
Okasha, Tawfik, 105
Oman, 83
Omar Ashour, 5
Omar, Rowida, 233
OMDH (Organisation marocaine des droits humains), 213
ONTV, 104
Organic Law on Establishing and Organising Transitional Justice (2013–14), 178–9, 183, 186–7, 193, 204–5, 208, 210, 211, 216
Ottoman Empire (1299–1923), 78, 79, 81

pacted transitions, 12
Palestine, 80, 82, 83, 267
Pan-Arabism, 168
Papua New Guinea, 121
Paraguay, 201
passion, 37, 38–9
PDP (Progressive Democratic Party), 122
People's Democratic Party, 71
People's Democratic Republic of Yemen (1967–90), 80
Perez-Linan, Anibal, 256
Périer, Miriam, 8
Perspectives movement, 169
Peru, 204
de Peyer, Jon, 8
phosphate mining, 171–2, 268, 271
piggybacking, 131
Pinochet, Augusto, 12–13
plebiscites, 13, 31, 40, 82, 85, 90
pluralism, 15, 64, 111, 113–14, 125–30

plurality of democracies, 34
Poland, 37, 176
political crises, 3
political fluidity, 3
polygamy, 14, 168
Popular Front, 27, 211
Port Said stadium massacre (2012), 88
Powell, Jonathan, 117–18
praetorian state, 119
Problems of Democratic Transition and Consolidation (Stepan and Linz), 9–10, 112, 124, 130
proportional representation (PR), 19–20, 128
Provisional Organisation of Public Authorities (2011), 185–6, 208
Przeworski, Adam, 38, 42, 113, 127, 140
public interest (*maslaha*), 79
publicity, 34, 36

al-Qaeda
   in the Arabian Peninsula (AQAP), 90, 149
   in the Islamic Maghreb (AQIM), 87
Qandīl, ʿAbd al-Ḥalīm, 125
Qatar, 98, 133, 175, 194, 264
Qutuz, Sultan of Egypt and Syria, 81
Quwat al-Amn al-Markazi, *see* Central Security Forces

Rabaa al-Adawiyya Square protests (2013), 54, 55, 89, 106, 211, 223, 244
Radio Mosaique, 106
radio, 6, 93, 96, 98, 106–7
al-Rajhi, Farhat, 120, 181–2, 190
Randal, Jonathan, 248
Raqqa, Syria, 90
rationality, 37–9
Rawls, John, 29, 34, 39
al-Rayyan, Jamal, 106

RCD (Rassemblement Constitutionnel Démocratique), 25, 169, 171, 177, 182–3, 211, 270
rebuilding the ship at sea, 39
Reconciliation in the Economic and Financial Sectors law (2015), 215–16
Redeyef, Tunisia, 194
referenda, 31, 70–72, 85, 88, 89, 144
reflexivity, 34
reparations, 174–6, 186, 187, 188, 193–5, 203
Republican Party of Tunisia, 122
'Revisiting Democratic Transition Theory', 4
Revolutionary Command Council, 84
revolutionary justice, 177
revolutionary moments, 2–3
Reynolds, Andrew, 128, 129, 130
right to truth, 166, 186
rogue states, 268
Roosevelt, Franklin, 70–71
Ross, Michael, 133
Rotberg, Robert, 268
Rustow, Dankwart, 127, 128

Sadat, Anwar, 49, 50, 82
Saddam Hussein, 51, 84–5
Saladin, Sultan of Egypt and Syria, 81
Salafism, 3, 174
Salamé, Ghassan, 4, 11
Saleh, Ali Abdallah, 8, 80, 82, 85, 90, 149, 150, 153
El Salvador, 200, 203
Sanafir Island, 227, 280
satellite television, 52, 93, 94, 95, 96, 97–8, 108
Saud family, 78, 79, 83
Saudi Arabia, 79, 80, 98, 179, 227, 264, 280
Sayegh, Yezid, 232
Sbeitla, Tunisia, 171

Schmitter, Philippe, 3, 54, 127, 128
Sciences Po, 4, 8
sectarian-tribal model, 47, 48, 74
secularism
    Egypt, 18, 124, 125, 135, 137, 221, 225
    France, 10, 11, 12, 13
    Tunisia, 5, 13, 14, 16–17, 20–27, 112, 116, 124, 125, 130, 135–7, 195–6
    Turkey, 13, 24, 68
    United States, 10, 11, 12
security sector reform, 57–9
self-secularization, 10
Selmi Document (2011), 66
Senegal, 11, 12, 13, 15, 17
September 11 attacks (2001), 49, 170
Seventh Crusade (1248–54), 81, 82
Sfax, Tunisia, 178
Shafiq, Ahmed, 65, 89, 227–8
Shams FM, 106
Sharia, 15, 24, 154, 168, 241
el-Sherif, Ashraf, 233
el-Shimy, Yasser, 119
al-Shorouk, 228
shûrâ, 15, 241
Sidi Bouzid, Tunisia, 171, 188
Sierra Leone, 200, 203
Siliana protests (2012), 271
Sinai insurgency (2011–), 2, 8, 90, 91
Singh, Naunihal, 116, 118
al-Sisi, Abdel Fattah, 2, 8, 45, 51, 54, 56, 66–7, 89–90, 106
Six-Day War (1967), 63, 64
Skach, Cindy, 256
slavery, 13, 80
Sledgehammer investigation (2010), 69, 70, 72
small constitution, *see* Provisional Organisation of Public Authorities
social media, 6, 94, 95, 96, 97, 99–104

soft-liners, 54

Solomon Islands, 35

Sonbol, Amira El-Azhary, 81

Sousse, Tunisia, 169, 171, 184, 269

South Africa, 32, 125, 166, 176, 200, 202, 203, 273

South America, *see under* Latin America

South Korea, 18

Southern Movement, 151, 153

Soviet Union (1922–91), 37, 41, 132

Spain, 18, 20, 21, 37, 166

Specialised Judicial Chambers, 178, 179, 188, 205

Sri Lanka, 121

St Vincent and the Grenadines, 134

State Security Investigations, 49, 50, 63

Stepan, Alfred, 4, 9–27, 112, 113, 124, 127, 128, 130, 256

Stokes, Susan, 111

Sudan, 48

Suez Canal, 263

Sufism, 17

Suharto, 13

superiority complexes, 56–7

Supreme Constitutional Council, 89

Supreme Council of the Armed Forces (SCAF), 46, 50–59, 64–7, 88–90, 105, 222–3, 234, 243

Supreme Council of the Police, 49

Supreme Judicial Council, Tunisia, 181

Sweden, 10

Syria, 4, 5, 6

 Ayyubid dynasty (1171–1260), 81

 Arab Kingdom (1918–20), 79

 Arab League, foundation of (1945), 79

 Baath party, 84

 Civil War (1979–82), 83

 Civil War (2011–), 8, 25, 55, 90, 91, 94, 96, 98, 100, 101, 108

 constitution, 57, 151

 coup d'état (1949), 80

 coup d'état (1970), 82

 French Mandate (1923–46), 79

 Islamic State (IS), 1–2, 90

 jamlaka, 85

 Lebanon, occupation of (1976–2005), 83

 local coordination committees (*tansiqiyyat*), 3–4

 Mamluks, 6, 75, 78, 81, 82, 83, 85, 90

 media, 93, 94, 96, 98, 100–104, 108

 military, 5, 47, 48, 57, 75

 torture, 90

 tribal-sectarian model, 47, 48

 uprising (2011), 90, 108

al-Tahrir, 105

Tahrir Institute for Middle East Policy, 233

Tahrir Square protests (2011), 1, 52, 63, 79, 132

Takfirism, 57

Tamarod, 21–2, 89, 105, 240

Tantawy, Mohamed Hussein, 54, 55, 88, 89

Teitel, Ruti, 166, 191

television, 52, 54, 93–8, 101, 104, 106–8, 172, 186

terrorism, 49, 169, 170, 174, 176, 182, 184, 224, 269

Thaalbi, Abdelaziz, 272

Thala, Tunisia, 179

three historical cycles, 78–80

Thyne, Clayton, 117–18

Tiran Island, 227, 280

Tobruk, Libya, 148

el-Tohamy, Mohamed Farid, 54

torture, 200

 Egypt, 57, 58, 229

Syria, 90

Tunisia, 14, 169, 170, 180, 182, 188, 189, 215

Trabelsi, Leila, 170

trade unions, 21, 22, 23, 89, 123, 130, 132, 171, 210

transitional justice, 6–7, 165–97, 199–218, 219–34

tribal-sectarian model, 47, 48, 74

Trifi, Mokhtar, 240

Tripolitana, Libya, 146

Troika government (2011–14), 21, 22, 89, 211, 212

Truth and Dignity Commission, Tunisia, 7, 180, 182, 184–93, 199–218, 271

Truth and Justice Forum, Morocco, 207

Truth and Reconciliation Commissions (TRCs), 199–218, 273

Tunisia, 2, 4–5, 6, 7, 9–27, 111–40, 165–97, 199
  abortion, 14
  Addressing the Past, Building the Future conference (2011), 207
  el-Amal Ettounsi, 267
  amnesties, 174–5, 215, 271
  Ansar al-Sharia, 174
  apostasy, 23–4
  associations, 132, 136
  Bar Association, 22, 216
  Baraket Essahel affair (1991), 170, 180
  Belaïd assassination (2013), 21, 89, 107, 176, 210, 270
  Ben Achour Commission (2011), 19, 21, 182–3
  Ben Ali presidency (1987–2011), see under Ben Ali, Zine el-Abidine
  Ben Youssef assassination (1961), 168

Bizerte crisis (1961), 83–4, 168

Bourguiba presidency (1957–87), see under Bourguiba, Habib

Brahmi assassination (2013), 21, 89, 122, 176, 210, 270

'Call from Tunis' (2003), 16

al-Chaab, 212

Chambi mountains, 90

civil society, 6, 16, 19, 22, 130–39, 186–7, 189, 238

'Collectif du 18 Octobre pour les Droits et les Libertés' (2005), 16

Consensus Committee, 22–3

constituency for coercion, 14, 16

Constituent National Assembly, see National Constituent Assembly

constitution (1861), 13

constitution (1959), 24

constitution (2014), 2, 21, 23–4, 30, 37, 40, 89, 106, 151, 177, 188

Constitutional Court, 24

corruption, 107, 170, 171, 173–4, 188, 197, 215, 271

coup d'état (1987), 84, 120, 168, 176

coup d'état attempt (1963), 169

Covenant of Social Peace (1857), 13

CPR (Congrès pour la République), 16–17, 21, 185, 211, 212

crisis (2013–14), 18, 20, 107

Destour party, 168, 178, 192

development, 6, 137–8, 259

divorce, 14, 168

Economist Country of the Year (2014), 11

empirical pluralism, 125, 128–30, 255–6

Ennahda, see Ennahda

Ettakatol, 16–17, 21, 185, 211, 212

Establishing and Organising Transitional Justice law (2013–14), 178–9, 183, 186–7, 193, 204–5, 208, 210, 211, 216

exports, 171
feminism, 17, 23, 239
Freedom House score, 11, 129, 134, 135, 236, 238, 268
French protectorate (1881–1956), 13, 79
general election (1989), 15
Global Militarization Index (GMI) score, 121
High Commission to Supervise Elections, 183
High Institute for Judicial Independence, 181
human rights, 17, 22, 23–4, 131, 166–97, 205, 207, 211, 212, 216, 240, 268
immunisation of the revolution, 183–4
Independence (1956), 13, 40, 168
industrialisation, 6, 138, 171, 259
Islamic State (IS), 2
Islamism, 2, 5, 13–27, 99, 107, 112, 116, 120–40, 169–70, 174–5, 182, 192–4, 196
Kasbah demonstrations (2011), 177, 182, 269
al-Kawakibi Democracy Transition Center, 208
knocking on the barracks door, 18, 116
League of Human Rights, 17, 22, 131, 207, 211, 212, 216, 240
less-politicised model, 47
and Mamluks, 6, 75, 78, 83–4, 88–9, 90, 91
Manich Msamah, 271
media, 93, 95, 96, 97, 98–9, 100, 106–7
military, 18, 47, 58–9, 75, 112–25, 179–80
mining region uprising (2008), 194, 271

Ministry of Finance, 173
Ministry of Human Rights and Transitional Justice, 176, 186, 193
Ministry of Information, 106
Ministry of Interior, 58–9, 120, 122, 130, 132, 170, 182
Ministry of Justice, 181, 193
Ministry of Religious Affairs, 135
mosque density, 135–6
MTI (Movement of the Islamist Tendency), 169
Nahda, 78
National Confiscation Commission, 173–4
National Constituent Assembly, see National Constituent Assembly
National Human Rights Institution, 176
National Independent Coordination for Transitional Justice, 208
Nidaa Tounes, 21, 25–7, 89, 107, 183, 185, 192, 209, 211, 269, 270
non-governmental organisations (NGOs), 208, 212
parliamentary elections (2014), 23, 25, 26, 89, 112, 192, 208
PDP (Progressive Democratic Party), 122
Personal Status Code, 14, 168
Perspectives movement, 169
phosphate mining, 171–2, 268, 271
political police, 170, 182
polygamy, 14, 168
Popular Front, 27, 211
presidential election (2014), 25, 107, 112, 183, 192, 208
proportional representation (PR), 19–20, 128
Provisional Organisation of Public Authorities (2011), 185–6, 208
RCD (Rassemblement Constitu-

tionnel Démocratique), 25, 169, 171, 177, 182–3, 211, 270

Reconciliation in the Economic and Financial Sectors law (2015), 215–16

reparations, 174–6, 186, 187, 188, 193–5

Republican Party, 122

Revolution (2011), *see* Tunisian Revolution

secularism, 5, 13, 14, 16–17, 20–27, 112, 116, 124, 125, 130, 135–7, 195–6

security sector reform, 181–2

Sharia, 15, 24, 168, 241

slavery, abolition of (1846), 13

small constitution, *see* Provisional Organisation of Public Authorities

Specialised Judicial Chambers, 178, 179, 188, 205

Supreme Judicial Council, 181

Tamarod, 240

terrorism, 21, 169, 170, 174, 176, 182, 184, 210, 269

torture, 14, 169, 170, 180, 182, 188, 189, 215

tourism, 171

trade unions, 21, 22, 23, 89, 123, 130, 132, 171

transitional justice, 166–97, 199–218

trials of former regime, 178–80

Troika government (2011–14), 21, 22, 23, 175, 177–8, 182, 185

Truth and Dignity Commission, 7, 180, 182, 184–93, 199–218, 271

two sheikhs compromise, 5, 26–7

UGTT (Union Générale Tunisienne du Travail), 21, 22, 89, 123, 132, 210, 211, 216, 254

unemployment, 172

and United Nations, 159

urbanisation, 6, 138, 259

UTICA (Union tunisienne de l'industrie, du commerce et de l'artisanat), 23, 211, 240

women's rights, 14, 15, 16, 17, 20, 23, 168, 239

Zeitouna Mosque University, 13–14, 168

Tunisia Center for Transitional Justice, 208

Tunisian Center for Human Rights and Transitional Justice, 208

Tunisian Horizons, 122

Tunisian League of Human Rights, 17, 22, 131, 207, 211, 212, 216, 240

Tunisian Network for Transitional Justice, 208

Tunisian Perspectives, 267

Tunisian Revolution (2010–11), 78, 88, 111, 143
  Bouazizi's self-immolation, 193, 268
  and coalitions, 5, 124, 238
  and inequality, 171–2
  and media, 93, 97
  and Ministry of Interior, 122
  and trade unions, 132
  and transitional justice, 7, 167, 175–7, 179, 188, 193–5, 205, 207

Turkey, 4, 5, 61, 67–73
  constitution, 34, 68, 70, 71, 72
  coups d'état, 67, 68, 69, 72
  Ergenekon conspiracy, 69, 70, 72
  and European Union, 62, 69
  Gezi Park protests (2013), 71
  guardian model, 47
  Gülenists, 70
  Islamism, 68–73
  Justice and Development Party (AKP), 47, 68–73
  Kemalism, 13, 24, 67–8, 70, 73, 75

military, 47, 67–73, 74, 75–6
Nationalist Movement Party, 71–2
National Security Council, 68
People's Democratic Party, 71
referenda, 70, 71, 72
secularism, 13, 24, 68
Sledgehammer investigation (2010), 69, 70, 72
28 February Process, 68
Welfare Party, 68
twin tolerations, 10, 12
Twitter, 93, 95, 97, 101–4
two sheikhs compromise, 5, 26–7
two-election test, 2, 112

UGTT (Union Générale Tunisienne du Travail), 21, 22, 89, 123, 132, 210, 211, 216, 254
United Arab Emirates, 80
United Kingdom
    Aden (1874–1967), 80
    Arab Revolt (1916–18), 79
    Egypt, occupation of (1882–1922), 48, 79, 117
    first-past-the-post system, 19, 128
    Ghannouchi's exile (1991–2011), 15, 17
    Trucial States (1820–1971), 80
United Nations, 6, 143, 145–50, 155, 157–63
    and Algeria, 155, 158
    Convention against Torture (1985), 169
    and human rights, 206, 207
    and Iraq, 85, 150, 155, 157–8, 266
    and Libya, 73, 145–9, 155, 157–62, 261, 263
    and transitional justice, 165, 166, 191–2, 195, 203, 206, 207
    and Tunisia, 159
    and United Arab Emirates, 80

and Yemen, 149–50, 155, 158, 159, 160, 163, 264
United States
    Afghanistan War (2001–14), 176
    Chilean coup d'état (1973), 12
    constitution, 127–8
    Egypt, relations with, 47, 49, 52, 55, 124
    Gülen's exile (1999–), 70
    Gulf War (1990–91), 85
    Iraq War (2003–11), 48, 88, 176, 184
    military, 75
    New Deal (1933–36), 70–71
    secularism, 10, 11, 12
    September 11 attacks (2001), 49, 170
    War on Terror, 49, 170
urbanisation, 6, 138, 259
Uruguay, 19
UTICA (Union tunisienne de l'industrie, du commerce et de l'artisanat), 23, 211, 240

Vairel, Frédéric, 7
Van de Walle, Nicholas, 119, 128, 251
Van Zyl, Paul, 273
veil of ignorance, 29, 34, 39
Venice Commission, 159
Voice of America (VOA), 96

Wahhabism, 78, 79, 83
Wahid, Abdurrahman, 13, 17
War on Terror, 49, 170
warlords, 83, 248
al-Wasat Party, 55
Welfare Party, 68
Welzel, Christian, 139
al-Wesal, 108
Whitefield, Stephen, 239
Whitehead, Laurence, 3, 127, 128
Wickham, Carrie Rosefsky, 18, 131, 238

INDEX

Widner, Jennifer, 35
Wilcke, Christoph, 222
women's rights
  Morocco, 213
  Tunisia, 14, 15, 16, 17, 20, 23, 168,
    239
World Bank, 132, 138, 160
World Values Surveys, 133, 135

Yearbook of International Organiza-
  tions, 259
Yemen, 2, 4, 5, 6, 8, 25, 90–91, 149–55
  Aden, British (1874–1967), 80
  Arab Republic (1962–90), 80, 82
  Bab al-Mandab strait, 263
  Civil War (1994), 83
  Civil War (2015–), 2, 96, 155
  constitution, 37, 40, 57, 149–55
  Constitutional Drafting Commis-
    sion, 151–5, 263
  coup d'état (1974), 82
  and Gulf Cooperation Council, 149,
    150
  Hamdi assassination (1977) 82
  Houthis, 8, 149, 151, 153, 154, 155,
    263
  international assistance, 142,
    149–55

Mamluks, 6, 75, 78, 81, 82, 85, 90
media, 95, 96, 100
military, 5, 48, 57, 75
National Dialogue Conference,
  150–55
People's Democratic Republic
  (1967–90), 80, 82
al-Qaeda in the Arabian Peninsula
  (AQAP), 90, 149
Saleh presidency (1978–2012), 8,
  80, 82, 85, 90, 149, 150
Saudi intervention (2015–), 155
Sharia, 154
Southern Movement, 151, 153
tribal-sectarian model, 48
unification (1990), 80
and United Nations, 149–50, 155,
  158, 159, 160, 163, 264
uprising (2011), 2, 149
Youssef, Bassem, 106

Zaytouna TV, 107
Zeitouna Mosque University, Tunis,
  13–14, 168
Zeituna, 106
Zeroual, Liamine, 86, 87
Zintani militia, 73
Zolberg, Aristide, 37